Poe Evermore

ALSO BY DAVID HUCKVALE
AND FROM MCFARLAND

Hammer Films' Psychological Thrillers, 1950–1972 (2014)

*The Occult Arts of Music: An Esoteric Survey
from Pythagoras to Pop Culture* (2013)

*James Bernard, Composer to Count Dracula:
A Critical Biography* (2006; paperback 2012)

*Ancient Egypt in the Popular Imagination:
Building a Fantasy in Film, Literature, Music and Art* (2012)

*Visconti and the German Dream:
Romanticism, Wagner and the Nazi Catastrophe in Film* (2012)

*Touchstones of Gothic Horror: A Film Genealogy
of Eleven Motifs and Images* (2010)

Hammer Film Scores and the Musical Avant-Garde (2008)

Poe Evermore

The Legacy in Film, Music and Television

DAVID HUCKVALE

McFarland & Company, Inc., Publishers
Jefferson, North Carolina

LIBRARY OF CONGRESS CATALOGUING-IN-PUBLICATION DATA

Huckvale, David.
Poe evermore : the legacy in film, music and television / David Huckvale.
          p.   cm.
Includes bibliographical references and index.

ISBN 978-0-7864-9441-5 (softcover : acid free paper) ∞
ISBN 978-1-4766-1721-3 (ebook)

1. Poe, Edgar Allan, 1809–1849—Criticism and interpretation. 2. Poe, Edgar Allan, 1809–1849—Influence.   I. Title.
PS2638.H83 2014   818'.309—dc23   2014035920

BRITISH LIBRARY CATALOGUING DATA ARE AVAILABLE

© 2014 David Huckvale. All rights reserved

No part of this book may be reproduced or transmitted in any form or by any means, electronic or mechanical, including photocopying or recording, or by any information storage and retrieval system, without permission in writing from the publisher.

On the cover: poster art from *House of Usher*, 1960 aka *The Fall of the House of Usher* (Photofest)

Printed in the United States of America

*McFarland & Company, Inc., Publishers
Box 611, Jefferson, North Carolina 28640
www.mcfarlandpub.com*

To Ian Spiby

Contents

Preface　1

Introduction　3

The Angel of the Odd　17

Annabel Lee　21

The Assignation　23

The Balloon Hoax　29

The Bells　33

Berenice　36

The Black Cat　38

The Cask of Amontillado　44

The City in the Sea　48

The Colloquy of Monos and Una *and*
The Conversation of Eiros and Charmion　52

A Descent into the Maelström　55

The Devil in the Belfry　57

The Domain of Arnheim, or The Landscape Garden　61

The Duc De L'Omelette　64

Eleonora　66

Eureka　69

The Facts in the Case of M. Valdemar　74

The Fall of the House of Usher　76

The Gold-Bug　92

The Haunted Palace　93

Ligeia   95
Maelzel's Chess-Player   101
The Man Who Was Used Up   102
The Masque of the Red Death   104
Mellonta Tauta   110
Metzengerstein   111
Morella   112
The Murders in the Rue Morgue   115
The Mystery of Marie Rogêt   118
The Narrative of Arthur Gordon Pym of Nantucket   120
Never Bet the Devil Your Head   126
The Oblong Box   128
The Oval Portrait   129
Philosophy of Furniture   131
The Pit and the Pendulum   134
A Predicament   144
The Premature Burial   146
The Purloined Letter   152
The Raven   153
Some Words with a Mummy   160
The Sphinx   162
The System of Dr. Tarr and Professor Fether   164
A Tale of the Ragged Mountains   169
The Tell-Tale Heart   171
"Thou Art the Man"   176
Three Sundays in a Week   178
The Unparalleled Adventure of One Hans Pfaall   179
William Wilson   182

Epilogue   187
Notes   189
Bibliography   200
Index   203

Preface

This book is primarily a response to the ways in which Edgar Allan Poe's work has inspired aspects of twentieth-century culture. It also necessarily concerns itself with some of the major influences upon Poe's work and the work itself, in order to illuminate that main objective further. Alphabetically arranged, it is not intended as an exhaustive guide to everything Poe wrote. My aim is to discuss the cultural impact of the most significant tales, essays and poems: on other writers, in art and music and ultimately in film and television.

Poe, the great American synesthete, would surely have approved of this approach. As he himself expressed it: "The Poetic Sentiment, of course, may develop itself in various modes—in Painting, in Sculpture, in Architecture, in the Dance—very especially in Music—and very peculiarly, and with a wide field, in the composition of the Landscape Garden."[1] In film we see all these elements combined with the iconography of the unconscious. For painting, we may substitute photography; for sculpture, the living form; for architecture, the film set; for dance, the movement of the camera; for the landscape garden, the widescreen panorama.

Poe claimed that music was supreme. "It is in Music, perhaps, that the soul most nearly attains the great end for which, when inspired by the Poetic Sentiment, it struggles."[2] Richard Wagner would have agreed with him, even though he never turned his back on the concept of music-drama, which anticipated the cinema in so many ways. Ralph Vaughan Williams, who scored several films himself, added, "film contains potentialities for the combination of all the arts such as Wagner never dreamt of."[3]

Film is a medium Poe would doubtless have found fascinating in theory, if sometimes disappointing in practice; but for Poe the medium mattered less than the mood it creates and the poetic sentiment it expresses. It is therefore highly appropriate that his work should have inspired responses from so many creative artists in their various differing but often united fields.

From childhood's hour I have not been
As others were—I have not seen
As others saw—I could not bring
My passions from a common spring.
—from Poe's poem "Alone"

"Poe constantly and inevitably produced magic where his greatest contemporaries produced only beauty."
—George Bernard Shaw, "Edgar Allan Poe,"
The Nation (London), January 16, 1909

"No man, I repeat, has told, with greater magic the exceptions of human life and nature."
—Charles Baudelaire [trans. H. Curwen],
Edgar Allan Poe: His Life and Works,
London 1873

Introduction

The first author I came to love was Edgar Allan Poe. I enjoyed his prose style long before I worked out what it meant. "Meaning" in Poe came to me later, but I responded immediately and *musically* to his style. Sometimes, of course, Poe doesn't mean anything. The "wan and misty-winged *Ashtophet* of idolatrous Egypt" mentioned in "Ligeia"[1] is a poetic construct. No such god ever existed. Poe invented it, exploiting the sound of his coinage for its mood-manufacturing power. The same applies to his narrator's comparison of Ligeia's eyes to "the gazelle eyes of the tribe of the valley of Nourjahad."[2] Poe was an expert in what he called "Mystification," and even wrote a story about it. His world is one of moods and images, of emotions and ideas. Psychological action is often favored over dramatic action. The perspective of a single character is preferred to the portrayal of characters interacting with each other, or, at least, the presentation of their point of view.

Many artists have illustrated him: Odilon Redon and Edouard Manet, Arthur Rackham, Aubrey Beardsley and Harry Clarke, Alfred Kubin and Alberto Martini—even the German-born American graphic designer Wilfried Sätty. I collected them all and passed many a mesmerized afternoon in contemplation of their respective visions, but I have to admit that no mere image could ever replace the *sound* of Poe. As his biographer Kenneth Silverman explains, Poe was "the first writer in English, or perhaps in any modern literature, to consistently apply to prose fiction some of the techniques of poetry."[3]

My introduction to Poe was from the movies. Ever since receiving a copy of Denis Gifford's *A Pictorial History of Horror Movies* for my fifteenth birthday, in which I found fascinating stills of Roger Corman's film adaptations, I had eagerly scanned the television listings for late-night screenings of horror movies that were hard to find in the days before videos and DVDs. Back in those distant 1970s, one relied on television. As an alternative to the Wednesday-afternoon military drill of the Combined Cadet Force, which I, as something of a latent Roderick Usher myself, managed to avoid, my rather old-fashioned British school insisted I re-decorate the living room of two disabled pensioners. While drinking milky tea in their crowded sitting room, and leafing through their copy of the *Radio Times* (a luxury we never had at home), I read, with a quickening of the heart, that *The Tomb of Ligeia* (dir. Roger Corman, 1964) was to be shown that very evening. To me, at that time, it would not have been an overstatement to have described my excitement in terms of one of Poe's own phrases from the story that inspired this best of Corman's Poe adaptations: "I felt that my vision grew dim, that my reason wandered; and it was only by a violent effort that I at length succeeded in nerving myself to the task which duty thus once more had pointed out."[4] The memory of that moment is still vivid: the table, the plate of biscuits, the chair (so much more comfortable than a military drill), the racing on the television, and (such is the transformative power of art and the imagination, which flourishes in the most unlikely places) my head full of Poe.

Subsequently, I grew familiar with the other Corman-Poe films in which Vincent Price wore a snow-white wig in *House of Usher* (1960), a Spanish ruff in *Pit and the Pendulum* (1961), an Arab fancy-dress costume in *The Masque of the Red Death* (1964), a puce silk dressing gown in the "Morella" section of *Tales of Terror* (1962), and whose face melted into what Poe describes as "detestable putrescence" at the end of that film's adaptation of "The Facts in the Case of M. Valdemar." I soon discovered, however, that Corman's enjoyably claustrophobic films, with their garish color and atmospheric settings, were not at all the same thing as the thickly embroidered, allusive prose of Poe. It is because of Poe's emphasis on literary *style* that film versions of his tales translate so awkwardly to the screen. Poe's material is too condensed to provide more than a mere basis for a ninety-minute melodrama; there is too much of the soliloquy in them to generate dramatic action, and consequently, new material must frequently be added to it. In some tales there is hardly any action at all. "The Domain of Arnheim" and "Landor's Cottage" are two very good examples. In "Landor's Cottage," there is not even a principal character and no plot at all, merely a description "of Mr. Landor's residence—as I found it," to quote Poe's final sentence. No one has ever filmed it; it would make a wonderful, though very uncommercial film. Some films based on Poe, marvelous though they are, often have little more in common with the tale than the title. The Universal horror movie *The Black Cat* (dir. Edgar G. Ulmer, 1934) is a case in point, having nothing to do with Poe's story apart from several shots of the eponymous animal being caressed by Karloff or running through threatening shadows. At least the black comedy of Corman's *The Raven* (1963) offered Vincent Price's beautiful recitation of lines from that poem at the beginning; the rest of the film similarly had nothing to do with the Bard of Baltimore. Films of Poe often require original subplots or, indeed, entirely original plots to lead up to the particular effect or event on which Poe relies for his climaxes: an instrument of torture, a murder, or a re-animated corpse. Sometimes, several tales are combined. Much more successful are those versions that approach Poe in the way he himself approached prose—in a poetic, stylized, *psychological* manner, which is unconcerned about commercial considerations such as traditional narrative, naturalism or length.

I bought recordings of the tales on LPs, read, again, by the elegant and highly mannered Price (both qualities, along with his American nationality, making him preeminent among the interpreters of Poe). In the 1970s, Bill Mitchell, another American, living in England at the time, recorded a quartet of tales which he intoned in a resonantly transatlantic bass, which even Orson Welles was said to imitate. His renditions were accompanied by sound effects and effective minimalist music, apparently created by plucking the strings of a piano or by a resonant zither. Later, Christopher Lee recorded several more stories in his characteristically clipped, rather disdainful tones; and through repeated listenings of all three interpretations I gradually learned whole passages of Poe by heart—learned them without paying much attention to the meaning of those cherished phrases, but sometimes that was Poe's approach as well. After all, did Poe know who the tribe of Nourjahad (mentioned so floridly in "Ligeia") actually were? I certainly didn't bother to find out, because that was surely beside the point. (It was, I later learned, Frances Sheridan, mother of the playwright, who invented the name in her Oriental tale *The History of Nourjahad,* posthumously published in 1769.) In his insightful essay on Poe, D.H. Lawrence called "the gazelle eyes of the tribe of Nourjahad" "blarney."[5]

I would listen to Poe's linguistic symphonies, anticipating the rhythms of his ripe vocabulary, his multiple adjectives, his somber and self-conscious syntax, which indeed had a life beyond the meaning it was all apparently meant to convey; though, to reiterate, Poe did not always have "meaning" uppermost in his mind. As he himself explained in a famous letter to James Russell Lowell: "I am profoundly excited by music.... Music is the perfection of the soul, or idea, of Poetry. The *vagueness* of exaltation aroused by a sweet air (which should be strictly indefinite and never too strongly suggestive) is precisely what we should aim at in poetry."[6] It is therefore appropriate that Poe should have admired Tennyson most of all, for Tennyson shared a similarly musical approach to poetic composition. Tennyson returned the compliment, calling him "the most original American genius" and, when asked to compose an epitaph for a Poe memorial in Baltimore, declined, and expressed the opinion that "so strange and so fine a genius, and so sad a life" could not be condensed into a single line.[7]

Listening to my regularly repeated recordings, with their scratches and glitches, certain phrases took on a purely musical life of their own, quite independent of the tales from which they came. I often found myself using them as mantra when I was walking to school, waiting for a bus or having a bath:

> I cannot for my soul remember how, when or even precisely where I first became acquainted with the lady Ligeia.
> Lo! 'tis a gala night
> Within the lonesome latter years.
> I purchased and put in some repair an abbey, which I shall not name, in one of the wildest and least frequented portions of fair England.
> "Yes, let us be gone."
> "The vaults are insufferably damp. They are encrusted with nitre."
> That the result would be death, and a death of more than customary bitterness, I knew too well the character of my judges to doubt.
> And have I not told you that what you mistake for madness is but over-acuteness of the senses?

and, most memorable of all:

> Ligeia, the beloved, the august, the beautiful, the entombed!

How long I could go on, stringing these dark pearls onto the long string of my memory. I wound them around me and was always running them through my mind like a monk worrying his rosaries. (My *pièce de résistance* was to declaim the whole of "The Conqueror Worm" either to myself and the wind, on deserted platforms waiting for a train, or to the general astonishment of whatever captive audience I could find.) These phrases held a particular resonance for me, and gave me a curiously comforting sense of reassurance. Poe's poetic world seemed so much more interesting and familiar to me than the world of buses and trains, the daily grind of school, the burdensome toil of my prosaic, though simultaneously anxious existence. I wondered at how the majority endured the crushing boredom of life without the salvation of an imagination. I found sanctuary in Poe's images of death and love, of remote places and even remoter states of mind. I identified with the general air of morbid introversion exuded by his tales, his descriptions of lavish luxury, and the terrors of the men who dwelt amid such opulence, with only ghosts from their now renounced communion with the world for company; or, of course, the unfortunate women whom they so often buried alive or murdered in the end.

Poe had originally only fascinated my ear, but as soon as I had penetrated his style, he spoke to me in other ways. The point of reading is surely self-recognition. I identified with Poe's overly-refined and decadent connoisseurs, who suffered from a morbid acuteness of the senses, who murder what offends them and sometimes end up being killed themselves. I understood his perverse criminals, who act out their crimes for no other reason than the fact that they know it is wrong to commit them. Characters motivated by revenge formed for me a kind of alter-ego. Poe's poetic chisel gradually chipped away the outer layers of my personality. I too had murdered, metaphorically speaking: One Friday afternoon at junior school I had quietly torn off the corner of a classmate's painting for the very good reason (not at all perverse!) that it offended me. Encouraged to exchange our paintings in the spirit of sociability, I, even at only eight years old, was reluctant to endure what I found unattractive. Public humiliation followed when the teacher discovered what I had done; but, like the murderer in "The Tell-Tale Heart" who has nothing against the old man he eventually murders, I held nothing against the boy who had painted the picture. It was merely his art that offended me, just as the eye of the old man offended Poe's neurasthenic narrator.

Later, I dreamed of living in an abbey like the widower of Ligeia: a somber retreat, furnished theatrically with ottomans and golden candelabra of Eastern figure, a bridal couch of solid ebony and a sarcophagus of black granite. Or if not an abbey, I would quite happily have settled for a Venetian palazzo, like the one in "The Assignation," filled with huge carvings of untutored Egypt, and hung with rich draperies which trembled to the vibrations of low, melancholy music. Even better, I dreamed of a Proud Tower from which I might look "gigantically down" as Death does in Poe's poem "The City in the Sea."

I next discovered the music of composers who shared my fascination with Poe. Whereas I had first listened to Poe as a kind of music, I now listened to music inspired by Poe as a kind of poetry. Rachmaninoff (*The Bells*), Debussy (*The Fall of the House of Usher*), Myaskovsky (*Silence*) and lesser names such as André Caplet, Florent Schmitt and Josef Holbrooke were all inspired by Poe. Then there were the film scores that accompanied Poe films. As I read more, listened to more music and acquainted myself with Poe's analysis of his own method of composition, I began to realize just how modern Poe was. Edward Lockspeiser's biography of Debussy informed me that Poe's influence on twentieth-century music was immense. Via his influence on Auguste Villiers de L'Isle-Adam, he reached out to the Italian modernist composer, Luigi Dallopiccola (1904–1975), whose opera *Il Prigionero* was based on Villiers' story "La torture par l'espérance" ("Torture by Hope"). Via his influence on Henry James, Poe could claim a hand in Benjamin Britten's operatic adaptation of James' famous ghost story, *The Turn of the Screw*.[8] Via his influence on Maurice Maeterlinck, he contributed to the symbolist *frissons* of Debussy's opera *Pélleas et Mèlisande*.

Having noticed that Poe was part of the "people we like" on the cover of The Beatles' *Sgt. Pepper* album—surely the ultimate accolade from the world of popular culture—I also began to realize Poe's immense influence on two of the twentieth century's most resilient genres of science fiction and detective fiction, for without Poe there would have been no Jules Verne, no *2001—A Space Odyssey*—who knows, perhaps no moon landing in 1969, for Poe anticipated them all. Without Poe's Auguste Dupin there would have been no Sherlock Holmes or Hercule Poirot—and therefore, no Philip Marlowe, Columbo, Kojak, Ironside, or Starsky and Hutch, let alone *CSI: Crime Scene Investigation*.

As I grew older, I grappled with the satirical, comical and hoaxing aspects of Poe's work. I had failed to engage with those stories when younger, but now they became increasingly intriguing. The process was similar to my youthful preference of Byron's Romantic "Romaut," *Childe Harold's Pilgrimage*, over the comic profundity of *Don Juan*; maturity helped me to take a more balanced approach to both. The possibility that everything Poe wrote was in some way a hoax or a satire—a point of view exhaustively argued by G. R. Thompson in *Poe's Fiction: Romantic Irony in the Gothic*—was also intriguing.

Poe's satires have generally proved less inspiring to filmmakers and musicians, but they form almost half of Poe's output of tales. Among them are "How to Write a Blackwood Article," "The Angel of the Odd," "Never Bet the Devil Your Head," "Some Words with a Mummy" and "The Devil in the Belfry." There is also the possibility that apparently serious tales like "Ligeia," "The Fall of the House of Usher" and "Metzengerstein" were intended as satires of the Gothic tradition, just as "The Assignation" might have been a satire of the Byronic legend. Could it be that those elaborately sumptuous phrases with which I consoled myself all those years ago weren't meant to be taken seriously? Would Poe have laughed at me and my taste—my Gothic decadence? Had he been laughing all along at everyone who had taken him "seriously"? Were the overwrought extremes of "Ligeia" and "The Fall of the House of Usher," of "The Assignation" and "Metzengerstein" elaborately disguised spoofs? Or were they simultaneously straight and satirical? These questions are much disputed. As one reviewer of Thompson's book put it,

> The thesis of this unabashedly thesis book is that Edgar Allan Poe belongs to the tradition of German Romantic Irony. Poe, according to Mr. Thompson, is a super-conscious super-rational super ironist who never meant any of the things that, for some hundred years, scholars, critics, and general readers thought he was saying. All these years the real Poe has been lurking contemptuously behind his masks "mocking irony," "ironic mockery," "hoaxlike parody," "satiric parody," "satiric irony," "hoaxing irony," "hoaxing satire," "satiric hoax."[9]

Thompson eloquently points out that the Gothic and comic tales alternated so regularly during Poe's career that they were really two sides of the same satiric coin:

> Poe's first published story, "Metzengerstein," is ostensibly a Gothic tale; but it was one of five that Poe sent to the *Philadelphia Saturday Courier* in 1831, four of which ("The Duc de L'Omelette," "A Tale of Jerusalem," "Loss of Breath," and "Bon-Bon") are comic and satiric. These comic tales, published after "Metzengerstein" early in 1832, were followed in the next three years by four ostensibly Gothic stories ("MS. Found in a Bottle," "The Assignation," "Berenice," and "Morella"). Then came three comic and satiric tales ("Lionizing," "Hans Pfaall," and "King Pest") in the middle of 1835, followed by the ostensibly Gothic tale "Shadow." Then two more comic and satiric tales ("Four Beasts in One" in 1836 and "Mystification" in 1837) were followed by two more Gothic tales ("Silence" in 1837 and "Ligeia" in 1838). From the winter of 1838–39 to the winter of 1839–40, we find four satiric tales ("How to Write a Blackwood Article," "A Predicament," "The Devil in the Belfry," and "The Man That Was Used Up") followed by three Gothic tales ("The Fall of the House of Usher," "William Wilson," and "The Conversation of Eiros and Charmion"), followed in turn

by the comic "Why the Little Frenchman Wears His Hand in a Sling." This loose pattern of alternation continues to the end of Poe's career, even suggesting conscious self-parody; the Dupin stories (1841 to 1845) are burlesqued in the comic detective story "Thou Art the Man" (1844); the suspended animation of "M. Valdemar" (1845) is made comic in Count Allamistakeo's resurrection in "Some Words with a Mummy" in the same year; the living burials of Madeline Usher and of Berenice are travestied in "The Premature Burial" (1844); the Gothic décor of "The Masque of the Red Death" (1842) and the revenge theme in "The Cask of Amontillado" (1846) became part of an absurd, though savage, fairy tale in "Hop-Frog" (1849).[10]

Even though Kenneth Silverman cannot agree with "this general line of interpretation,"[11] he observes that Poe was able "to treat the same material at one time seriously and at another satirically."[12] Whatever side of the argument one chooses, there is no denying that the Gothic tales in particular also anticipated certain strands of modern psychoanalysis; but it was Poe's technique, despite the baroque complexities of his style, that seemed modern to me. I suggested to myself that his writings were *constructed,* rather that composed—constructed from a long-established reservoir of effects, situations and characters. (For example, "A Tale of the Ragged Mountains" contains the line "Upon a dim warm, misty day, towards the close of November," while "The Fall of the House of Usher" famously begins in a similar manner and mood: "During the whole of a dull, dark, and soundless day in the autumn of the year." Similarly, the serious "Ligeia" begins, "I cannot for my soul remember how, when or even precisely where I first became acquainted with the lady Ligeia," whereas the comic tale "The Man That Was Used Up" begins, "I cannot just now remember when or where I first made the acquaintance of that truly fine-looking fellow, Brevet Brigadier-General John A.B.C. Smith." Indeed, the many other parallels one could draw between Poe's comic and apparently "serious" tales suggests a continuity that supports Thompson's theory.

Poe's "learning," displayed in the obscure epigrams that often introduced the tales, was effective but not always accurate, nor always evidence of Poe's familiarity with the sources from which he quoted. Was Lowell right when he wrote

> There comes Poe, with his Raven, like Barnaby Rudge,
> Three fifths of him genius and two fifths sheer fudge,
> Who talks like a book of iambs and pentameters,
> In a way to make people of common sense damn metres,
> Who has written some things quite the best of their kind,
> But the heart somehow seems all squeezed out by the mind.[13]

Poe half-confessed this fudging quality (under the cover of satire, of course) in his piece "How to Write a Blackwood Article": *"PIQUANT EXPRESSIONS. The Venerable Chinese novel Ju-Kiao-Li"* Good! By introducing these few words with dexterity you will evince your intimate acquaintance with the language and literature of the Chinese.... Properly introduced, [such words] will show not only your knowledge of the language, but your general reading and wit."[14] But might the "fudge" in Poe be deliberate, the excesses of literary style, which were disapproved of by the likes of Henry James and T.S. Eliot, deliberate too—a secret jest at the expense of those not in on the joke, a hidden satire of popular Gothic-Romantic taste? Is Poe continually indulging in what he called "Diddling?"— conning the public, mystifying them, baffling them, pretending to be offering them the opposite of what appears on the surface to be either serious or comic? Poe wrote the article

"Diddling—Considered as One of the Exact Sciences," perhaps to suggest that he was holding a key to the reader with which to unlock the enigma of his oeuvre. Significantly, it was published posthumously. "Diddling, rightly considered," he wrote, "is a compound, of which the ingredients are minuteness, interest, perseverance, ingenuity, audacity, *nonchalance,* originality, impertinence, and *grin*."[15] Isn't that an accurate definition too of Poe's approach to fiction in general?

Whether this is the case or not, it is certainly true that everything Poe wrote is held together by this famous (infamous?) style. Indeed, one could argue that everything he wrote is primarily an exercise *in* style. As D.H. Lawrence pointed out, "All Poe's style ... has this mechanical quality, as his poetry has a mechanised rhythm. He never sees anything in terms of life, almost always in terms of matter, jewels, marble, etc.—or in terms of force, scientific. And his cadences are all managed mechanically. This is what is called 'having a style.'"[16] Poe, according to Lawrence, is "inordinately mechanically sensitive to sounds and effects, associations of sounds, associations of rhythm, for example—mechanical, facile, having no root in any passion."[17] This is what makes both Poe and Richard Wagner nineteenth-century prophets of our own age, an age in which we assemble style industrially, but unfortunately, unlike them, tend to leave content to look after itself.

If Poe's works were assembled on a production line out of components, the same could be said of Wagner's music-dramas, which are assembled from component leitmotifs. The Prelude of *Das Rheingold* is perhaps the most extreme example in all music of style triumphing over content. Thomas Mann denied that it was music at all. "It was not. It was an acoustic idea: the idea of the beginning of all things. It was the self-willed dilettante's exploitation of music to express a mythological idea."[18] Poe similarly used the music of poetry to express ideas and moods rather than narratives and the interaction of characters.

Wagner and Poe were masters of theatrical effect. This aspect has also drawn the venom of critics. Lawrence derided Poe's descriptions of the interior decoration of the abbey in "Ligeia" as an example of "the bad taste of sensationalism." If Wagner was "a dilettante raised to the level of genius," as Thomas Mann argued, Poe might similarly be termed a "charlatan raised to the level of genius,"[19] for Philip Van Doren Stern indeed described Poe as "charlatan, plagiarist, pathological liar, whimpering child, egomaniac, braggart, and irresponsible drunkard [who] tapped the rich reservoir of the subconscious mind to set free the terrible images which had seldom been allowed to stalk the printed page."[20] Indeed, Mann explicitly drew the comparison between Poe and Wagner, referring to Baudelaire's admiration for both:

> These two, Wagner and Poe, are Baudelaire's gods—a singular juxtaposition to the German ear! It puts Wagner's art all at once in a new light; it suggests associations with which our patriotic commentators have not familiarized us. It opens up a whole world of colour and fancy, lovesick for death and beauty, the Western world of high and late romanticism; a pessimistic world, adept in strange intoxicants and refinements of the senses, fantastically addicted to all sorts of æsthetical speculations and combinations; in Hoffmannian, Kreislerian dreams of the correspondence and inner relation between colours, sounds, and odours, of the mystical transformations of the mingled sense.[21]

Poe anticipated Wagner's concept of Gesamtkunstwerk, arguing in his essay "The Poetic Principle," "[T]here can be little doubt that in the union of Poetry with Music in its popular sense, we shall find the widest field for the Poetic development."[22] Symbolist writers, so greatly inspired by Baudelaire's translations of Poe, often argued that Baudelaire's

French improved on Poe's American English. George Moore eloquently disagreed,[23] but the success of Baudelaire's translations ironically suggests a comparison with the nineteenth-century's fascination with the bibelot, its consumerist predilection for the copy and the reproduction, which the symbolists and decadents so despised. Symbolist painting is essentially literary, for symbolism is primarily concerned with the veiled expression of *ideas*—their *suggestion* rather than statement. It is appropriate that Poe should have inspired artists such as the symbolist Odilon Redon and the surrealist René Magritte, whose *Domain of Arnheim* is a direct reference to Poe's tale of the same name. (Surrealism was, after all, merely an extension of the dream-world of the symbolists. Indeed, a painting by the symbolist artist William Degouves de Nuncques, *La Maison Aveugle* [*The Blind House*, 1894], foreshadowed Magritte's *Empire of Lights* with its contradictory lighting scheme: a dark sky and garden but a glowing orange facade of brickwork. It was apparently inspired by a reading of Poe's "The Fall of the House of Usher."[24]) Later, in the twentieth century, Salvador Dalí said of his own works: "My whole ambition in the pictorial domain is to materialize the image of concrete irrationality with the most imperialist fury of precision."[25] Poe, more than any other writer, perfectly impaled the moths and butterflies of his dreams on the pin of his poetic prose.

Among the fundamental aims of symbolist artists was the reproduction on canvas of the moods we find in Poe's work: its atmospheres of Gothic gloom, its iconography of the ideal object of desire (which Poe had analyzed so brilliantly in "Ligeia") and its anatomy of psychological states (such as morbid anxiety or fear), as opposed to the mere representation of the everyday. One of the reasons why Baudelaire was so drawn to Poe was the American's disdain for America:

> From the midst of a society, insatiable in its materialistic appetites, Poe launched into a dream world. Smothered as he was by the American atmosphere, he wrote as epigraph to Eureka: "I offer this book to those that have put their faith in dreams as the only realities!" He was therefore an admirable protest in himself; he both was one and made one after his own manner, in his own way. The author who, in his Colloquy of Monos and Una, releases floods of scorn and disgust over democracy, progress and so-called civilization, that author is the very same one who, to win over the credulous, to enchant the gaping idleness of his compatriots, proclaimed, with the utmost energy, the sovereignty of man, and spun the most ingeniously elaborate hoaxes of the kind most flattering to the pride of modern man. Seen in that light, Poe appears to me like a helot who wants to shame his own master. In short, to state my view beyond any peradventure, Poe was always great, not only in his noble conceptions, but also as a hoaxer.[26]

Baudelaire was an enemy of the modern bourgeoisie, just as the bourgeois was "an enemy of roses and of perfumes, and a maniac for utensils."[27] As Richard Gilman explains, the symbolist and decadent movements which flourished in the wake of Baudelaire (and therefore Poe), had a string of characteristics: "the cult of Satanism; neurasthenia and sexual perversity; boredom combined with exquisite refinement; nostalgia for the corrupt; fascination with the splendors and despairs of ancient cultures; hatred of the 'natural' as the enemy of human invention and transcendence, 'progress' as an anathema; taste as a means of survival: it all went to compose a paradigm of 'decadence' and has come down to us in that large outline."[28]

But Baudelaire also specified another aspect of Poe, which made him even more appealing to symbolist poets:

[Poe] divided the world of mind into pure intellect, taste and moral sense, and he applied his criticism according to which of the three divisions the object of his analysis belonged to. Above all, he was sensitive to the degree of perfection in the structure, and to formal correction. He would take literary works to pieces like a defective mechanism (defective, that is, in relation to its avowed aims), noting carefully the faults in manufacture.[29]

The high priest of symbolist verse, Stéphane Mallarmé (1842–1898), claimed to have taught himself English to enable him to appreciate Poe in his original language, and it was Poe's almost scientifically rigorous analysis and application of poetic technique as demonstrated in "The Philosophy of Composition" which fascinated him. D.H. Lawrence later agreed that Poe "is rather a scientist than an artist."[30] Poe's use of symbolic imagery (the house of Usher, the teeth of Berenice, the pit and the pendulum, the haunted palace, etc.) pointed the way towards the self-conscious search for a symbolist style that *suggested* rather than described. As Robert Greer Cohen explains, "For Mallarmé, Poe was a princely poet because his daemonic genius, which chanted romantic themes like 'the death of a beautiful woman' (and could occasionally refine into the tingling pre-symbolist atmosphere of *The Fall of the House of Usher*), was coupled with extreme critical lucidity, as expressed in *The Poetic Principle*."[31] Edmund Wilson pointed out, "The French have always reasoned about literature far more than the English have; they always want to know what they are doing and why they are doing it: their literary criticism has acted as a constant interpreter and guide to the rest of their literature. And it was in France that Poe's literary theory, to which no one seems to have paid much attention elsewhere, was first studied and elucidated."[32]

In an 1891 interview with Jules Huret, Mallarmé famously argued, "To *name* an object is to suppress three-quarters of the enjoyment of the poem, which derives from the pleasure of step-by-step discovery; to *suggest*, that is the dream. It is the perfect use of this mystery that constitutes the symbol: to evoke an object little by little, so as to bring out of it a state of the soul through a series of unravelings."[33] Anticipating Mallarmé, Poe wrote, "I *know* that indefiniteness is an element of the true music [of poetry]—I mean of the true musical expression ... a suggestive indefiniteness of vague and therefore of spiritual *effect*."[34]

As a tribute to Poe's influence on him, Mallarmé composed his 1876 poem "Le tombeau d'Edgar Poe" for the unveiling of the Poe Memorial in Baltimore:

> Tel qu'en Lui-même enfin l'éternité le change,
> Le Poète suscite avec un glaive nu
> Son siècle épouvanté de n'avoir pas connu
> Que la mort triomphait dans cette voix étrange!
>
> Eux, comme un vil sursaut d'hydre oyant jadis l'ange
> Donner un sens plus pur aux mots de la tribu,
> Proclamèrent très haut le sortilège bu
> Dans le flot sans honneur de quelque noir mélange.
>
> Du sol et de la nue hostiles, ô grief!
> Si notre idée avec ne sculpte un bas-relief
> Dont la tombe de Poe éblouissante s'orne
> Calme bloc ici-bas chu d'un désastre obscur
> Que ce granit du moins montre à jamais sa borne
> Aux noirs vols du Blasphème épars dans le futur.

The Tomb of Edgar Poe

As to Himself at last eternity changes him
The Poet reawakens with a naked sword
His century appalled at never having heard
That in this voice triumphant death had sung its hymn.

They, like a writhing hydra, hearing seraphim
Bestow a purer sense on the language of the horde,
Loudly proclaimed that the magic potion had been poured
From the dregs of some dishonoured mixture of foul slime.

From the war between earth and heaven, what grief!
If understanding cannot sculpt a bas-relief
To ornament the dazzling tomb of Poe:

Calm block here fallen from obscure disaster,
Let this granite at least mark the boundaries evermore
To the dark flights of Blasphemy hurled to the future.

Jules Huret interviewed Maurice Maeterlinck the following year, and Maeterlinck similarly confessed, "Edgar Allan Poe has exercised over me, together with the rest of my generation, a great, lasting and profound influence. I owe to him the birth in myself of a sense of mystery, and a passionate interest in the life beyond."[35] One might usefully compare the situation of the narrator in "The Pit and the Pendulum" with that of the characters in Maeterlinck's play *Les Aveugles*. The protagonist of Poe's story is plunged into "the blackness of eternal night."[36] Similarly, all the characters of *Les Aveugles* are blind and have no idea where they are. Anticipating Samuel Beckett's *Waiting for Godot*, these blind people are waiting for someone. "Is he coming yet?" one of them asks. "We want to know where we are!" another complains. "It must be time to go back to the asylum," a third admits.[37] Hungry and thirsty, they can hear nothing other than each other's questions. Poe's evocation of darkness and the terror of darkness is thus turned into a philosophical metaphor by Maeterlinck. But according to his interview with Huret, Maeterlinck's favorite Poe tale was "The Fall of the House of Usher," and it is intriguing that when Debussy was setting Maeterlinck's *Pelléas et Mélisande* to music, he had Poe's story in mind. Three years earlier, in 1890, he had begun work on his never-to-be completed opera based on "The Fall of the House of Usher," and his fascination and identification with it never left him. Edward Lockspeiser observes, "In his letter to Chausson of 6th September 1893, the month the opera was begun, he goes so far as to quote the very words used by Baudelaire in his translation of *Usher* to describe his state of mind."[38]

Maeterlinck's *Pélleas et Mélisande* has much in common with Poe. Mélisande is a child-wife like Annabel Lee. Her fragile nature echoes the similarly wan Madeline Usher, whom Poe describes as suffering from "a gradual wasting away of the person," accompanied by "frequent although transient affections of a partially cataleptical character."[39] Pélleas and Mélisande being brother and sister—and in love with each other—also reflects the similarly incestuous relationship between Roderick and Madeline Usher. The action of *Pélleas* (such as it is in this deliberately static drama) takes place in a moldering castle akin to the melancholy House of Usher. Maeterlinck's castle is also built over ancient ancestral vaults. The smell of the tombs "infects the castle." Another character, Golaud, explains, "The King will not believe that it comes from here. It would be well to wall up the cavern that contains this stagnant water. It is time, moreover, that these vaults should be examined. Have you noticed the crevices in the walls and in the pillars of the vaults?"

"Yes," Pélleas replies, "there is a smell of death creeping up around us..."[40] Like the House of Usher, the *Pélleas* castle is a metaphor of spiritual decay. Maeterlinck's play also features a cave by the sea. "Is it the sound of the cave that frightens you?" asks Pélleas of Mélisande. "It is the sound of night, the sound of silence."[41] Both works end in death, but Maeterlinck gives Mélisande a much more understated demise than Poe gave Madeline. Mélisande simply drifts away; Arkël observes, "She has gone away without a word..."[42] Madeline, by contrast, appears in her blood-stained shroud, strangles her brother, and the House of Usher collapses around them.

Villiers de L'Isle Adam reveled in Poe-esque excess in his symbolist drama *Axël,* which was again set in a castle amid deeply wooded mountains. A vast treasure is discovered (symbolic of the treasures of the imagination), which bursts upon the protagonists much as the avalanche of gems cascades over Arianne in Maeterlinck's version of the Bluebeard story *Arianne et Barbe-Bleu.* In *Axël,* Villiers describes "a scintillating torrent of gems, a rustling rain of diamonds and, a moment later, slithering gems of all colours, bathed in lights, a myriad of brilliants with lighted facets, more ponderous diamond necklaces, countless flaming jewels, pearls.—This torrential rustling stream of lights suddenly floods SARA'S shoulders, hair and garments. The precious stones and pearls dart around her on all sides, tinkle on the marble tombs, and rebound in sheaves of dazzling sparks upon the white statues with the crackling of a blazing fire."[43] In *Arianne et Barbe-Bleu* "Cataracts of enormous diamonds of the first water pour into the hall; myriads of sparks, flashes, flecks of fire, and prismatic rays mingle, are extinguished, blaze forth again and multiply, outspreading as they fall. ARIANNE, startled, gives a dazed cry. She stoops, picks up a diadem, a necklace, and handfuls of the glistening splendour, and therewith she decks at random her hair, her arms, her throat, her hands."[44] These gems are part of her wedding gift from Bluebeard, but they derive from Poe's fascination with opulent imagery—the props and metaphors of his imaginary world. In "Ligeia" the narrator decorates the abbey to which he retires after the death of his beloved wife, with "more than regal magnificence." He furnishes it with "gorgeous and fantastic draperies" and "carpets of tufted gold."[45] In "The Assignation," Poe's Byronic hero inhabits a palazzo that has been designed "to dazzle and astound." "I see you are astonished at my apartment," he says to the unnamed narrator who has visited him, "—at my statues—my pictures—my originality of conception in architecture and upholstery! absolutely drunk, eh, with my magnificence?"[46] Even in his descriptions of the natural world, Poe uses extravagant, synesthetic imagery. In "The Domain of Arnheim," he describes "purple mountains, whose bases are laved by a gleaming river throughout the full extent of their circuit. Meantime the whole Paradise of Arnheim bursts upon the view. There is a gush of entrancing melody, there is an oppressive sense of strange sweet odor,—there is a dream-like intermingling to the eye of tall slender Eastern trees—bosky shrubberies—flocks of golden and crimson birds—lily-fringed lakes—meadows of violets, poppies, hyacinths and tube-roses—long intertangled lines of silver streamlets."[47]

In this respect, Poe was summoning the cinema. Though he had inspired film adaptations since the days of silent cinema, he became ubiquitous in the technicolor world of 1960s horror films, for, like Prince Prospero in "The Masque of the Red Death," Poe "had a fine eye for colors and effects."[48] The irony here is that Poe, whose fame has been so mangled and magnified by the movies, was an avowed enemy of technological progress and mass culture. He would have been very surprised, and perhaps uncomfortable to find himself making a personal appearance in the segment of the Amicus portmanteau film *Torture Garden* (dir. Freddie Francis, 1967), called "The Man Who Collected Poe," in which Jack Palance and Peter Cushing play competitive Poe obsessives. Cushing's character is appropriately called Lancelot Canning, after the author mentioned by Poe in "The Fall of the House of Usher," whose "Mad Trist" is read to Roderick by the narrator towards the end of the tale. Sir Lancelot possesses the ultimate relic: the reanimated corpse of Poe himself, the syllables of whose name James Bernard's accompanying score intones with his usual resonance. This idea had already been explored by Walter de la Mare in his 1932 story "The Revenant," in which the ghost of Poe attends a lecture about him by a certain Professor Monk. The professor is superficially respectful to Poe's work but implicitly critical of it and of Poe's life. Poe's ghost accuses him afterwards, in a dreary ante-chamber, of defamation:

> I awaited in vain the faintest intimation that our poet was perhaps the first of his kind to foresee the triumphs and the tyranny of modern science; that he was no mere groping novice in astronomy, physics and the science of the mind. Creature of darkness his imagination may have been; but was there no light in his *mind*? If you could meet him face to face, professor, at this moment, here, now—I ask you, I entreat you to confide in me, would you deny him the light of his Reason? You might even try to forgive his extravagances, his miseries.[49]

De la Mare had, like another of his formative influences, Arthur Machen, been something of a Poe obsessive himself in his youth. Machen praised Poe as being "infinitely more wonderful and more admirable than his best lovers suppose,"[50] and it was from Machen that de la Mare learned the technique of making the supernatural appear out of the prosaic, as in "The Revenant." However, in de la Mare's early attempt at a novel, *The Master,* Poe's influence is more to the fore. It concerns the encounter of an aesthetic decadent hero called Robin with the mysterious Master of the title. This magus lives in a barge on the Thames; the anteroom is decorated and furnished entirely in black, a motif de la Mare obviously derived from Poe's "The Masque of the Red Death." Beyond the anteroom is a picture gallery containing the Master's blue canvas of "Nothing," which nonetheless contains many staring eyes when looked at more closely.[51]

All these *fin-de-siècle* Poe fanatics laid the ground for Cushing's Lancelot Canning—not that there weren't cinematic precedents too. Bela Lugosi had played a similar type in *The Raven* (dir. Lew Landers, 1935), this time with a chip on his shoulder and an ego to match. Lugosi's Dr. Richard Vollin is a brilliant surgeon but also an untrustworthy outsider. He recites Poe's poem to visitors who sit in the shadow of a splendid stuffed specimen of that bird, and has constructed a torture chamber in his cellar, with realizations of Poe's instruments of torture from "The Pit and the Pendulum." These prove to be most efficacious when he is foiled in his attempt to marry: The father of the unwilling girl is strapped to Vollin's torture slab and subjected to Poe's ponderous pendulum.

It was this kind of sociopathic obsessive whom Thornton Wilder satirized in his 1973 novel *Theophilus North*. Here we encounter one Elbert Hughes, who belongs to that "wearisome category of human beings known as 'sensitive.'"[52] A Bostonion (of course), he wears "a black velveteen jacket and a flowing black tie," along with a "tentative mustache."[53] He has difficulty sleeping, suffers from "depletion," and is also a great admirer of Poe ("The Fall of the House of Usher" in particular). The hearty Theophilus North tries to persuade

Hughes not to read any more Poe. "He's not right for you," he insists, "all those crypts and vaults."[54] But Poe was right for so many others. Indeed, Theophilus North is fully aware of the value of Poe ephemera, which he relates in a paragraph that would fit in well to the screenplay of *Torture Garden*'s "The Man Who Loved Poe":

> I knew that any first edition of a work by Edgar Allan Poe was among the greatest prizes in all American book-collecting and that any letter from his pen was eagerly sought. Poe had paid an extensive visit to Providence, only thirty miles away; but there was no record of his having visited Newport. If I could discover a bundle of Poe's letters—what a lively interest for me and, later, what an addition to my capital savings![55]

Alas, he finds no Poe letters, but does receive a copy of Poe's "Ulalume" written out in copperplate script by Hughes, whom his doctor later describes as "not all there. He's a genius; he's a little bit crazy. He thinks he's Edgar Allan Poe."[56]

Another fictional character who thinks he is Poe can be found in Andrew Sinclair's 1979 novel *The Facts in the Case of E.A. Poe*. This Poe obsessive, Ernest Albert Pons, has taken to psychoanalysis to help him with his problem. He searches the telephone directory for a doctor called Dupin, the name of Poe's famous detective in "The Murders in the Rue Morgue," and sets out on a voyage of self-discovery. (Pons of course shares Poe's initials.) As therapy, Dr. Dupin encourages his patient to research Poe's life story and in the process perhaps learn more about himself. This Pons does, and in writing it up, he continually peppers his prose with Poeisms. Having charted Poe's troubled existence, he confronts his own traumatic experiences in a Nazi concentration camp, his love for his mother, and Poe's influence not only on his own life but also on twentieth century culture and society. He also juxtaposes Poe's "The Premature Burial" with the fate of the elderly in modern American society. "Is it not—oh! is it *not* a pitiful sight?" says the narrator of Poe's tale, during a vision of the awakening dead. "Is it not—O, God! is it *not* a very pitiful sight?" Sinclair suggests that the abandoned elderly have been virtually buried alive: "It was a very pitiful sight that Pons saw in Poe Park—the surviving old men in felt hats playing checkers, the remaining old ladies nodding and noddling at their chat—the hospital as their terminal on the square, to which they would soon be carted from their waiting-rooms in the high tenement apartments about—a deserted bandstand playing no heavenly music nor even a fiddling tune—and an undertaker's sign, declaring: THE FAMILY SHOULD GET TOGETHER TO DECIDE HOW YOU ARE BURIED." But worse was the premature burial of Hitler's victims—"the despairing cries of the murdered six million: 'Is it not—O, God! is it *not* a very pitiable sight?"[57]

As he puts it in his closing "editorial note," "I believe that through his obsession that he was Poe, Ernest Albert Pons stumbled on an original way of translating the psyche of an age to a very different one, and of recreating a dead man's personality through his increasing awareness of his own."[58]

The novel reveals another obsessive: Sinclair himself, who crams as much information as possible—both critical and biographical—within the structure of his half-fictional, half-biographical framework. Poe does seem to attract obsessives—after all, his stories often concern them. The monomaniac Egæus in "Berenice" is capable of being "absorbed, for the better part of a summer's day, in a quaint shadow falling aslant upon the tapestry or upon the floor." He can lose himself for an entire night in watching the perfume of a flower. He repeats "monotonously, some common word, until the sound, by dint of frequent repetition, ceased to convey any idea whatsoever to the mind." He loses "all sense of motion or physical existence, by means of absolute bodily quiescence long and obstinately persevered in."[59] His ultimate obsession is with the teeth of his beloved, which he removes from her corpse. Roderick Usher is obsessed by his own madness; the murderer of "The Tell-Tale Heart" is morbidly offended and goaded to murder by his obsession with an old man's eye; the artist in "The Oval Portrait" grows "wild with the ardor of his work, and turned his eyes from his canvas rarely."[60] Even the narrator of "The Pit and the Pendulum" argues, "He who has never swooned, is not he who finds strange palaces and wildly familiar faces in with coals that glow; is not he who ponders over the perfume of some novel flower; is not he whose brain grows bewildered with the meaning of some musical cadence which has never before arrested his attention."[61]

This book is, similarly, the result of my own obsession with Poe, but it is also the result of a fascination with what inspired him and how he has inspired others. Admiration should never blind one to the faults of those we admire, however, and Poe had many. His plagiarism, for example, may have been unconscious, though it is hard to believe so when comparing, for example, his own "The Tell-Tale Heart" with a line by the English novelist Edward Bulwer-Lytton—a writer whom Poe much admired. Bulwer-Lytton's novel *Night and Morning*, first published in 1841, predates Poe's tale of 1843. In it, he describes the eye of one Mr Birnie, the sinister accomplice of a coin forger. On page 232 of the "Stevenage Edition" of *Night and Morning*, the damning evidence is there for all who care to look:

> [I]t was not a bright eye: on the contrary, it was dull, and, to the unobservant, lifeless, of a pale blue, with a dim film over it—the eye of a vulture.

Poe virtually lifted this intact for his own description of the old man's eye in "The Tell-Tale Heart":

> I think it was his eye! Yes, it was this! He had the eye of a vulture—a pale blue eye, with a film over it.

This is merely one of the more spectacular of Poe's "borrowings"—a fault of which one can also accuse Wagner, Poe's teutonic doppelgänger. Wagner's "theft" of Liszt's musical ideas is well-known, but it makes him no less of a genius and does nothing to affect the immensity of his influence. The same can be said of Poe, whose work and legacy will truly live for evermore.

The Angel of the Odd

I had thrown myself over a precipice, and should inevitably have been dashed to pieces but for my good fortune in grasping the end of a long guide-rope, which depended from a passing balloon.[1]

This "extravaganza" from 1844 begins with a description of the narrator's over-indulgence—both alcoholic and literary. His brain accordingly befuddled by wine and reading, his attention is drawn to a bizarre accident reported in a newspaper: A man, "playing 'puff the dart,' which is played with a long needle inserted in some worsted, and blown at a target through a tin tube ... placed the needle at the wrong end of the tube and drawing his breath strongly to puff the dart forward with force, drew the needle into his throat."[2]

No sooner has he read this than a curious voice, with a comic Dutch-German accent, introduces himself as "The Angel of the Odd." The creature's body is made from a wine-pipe, or rum-puncheon, his legs of two kegs and two long bottles for arms. Its head is "a Hessian canteen which resembles a large snuff-box with a hole in the middle of the lid."[3] A funnel serves as his cap. Presumably induced by the narrator's alcoholic over-indulgence, this creature then explains that he is responsible for the accident reported in the newspaper—and others equally bizarre. Soon, the narrator is to discover the Angel's powers for himself. He forgets to renew his fire insurance, taking a nap instead, and then wakes up to find his house in flames. A ladder is raised to his window by a concerned crowd that has gathered outside. As he steps onto the first rung, a huge hog decides to scratch itself against the ladder and throws the narrator to the ground, whereupon he fractures his arm. His hair singed by the conflagration, he is forced to wear a wig, and when his fiancée discovers this impediment, she jilts him. After another failure to win a bride (she accuses him of ignoring her, whereas in fact a particle of dirt had temporarily blinded him) he decides to commit suicide. He strips off his clothing and plunges into a river, when a crow suddenly flies off with his breeches. The narrator leaps out of the river in pursuit of the crow, and suddenly finds that he has run over the edge of a cliff. Fortunately—but very *oddly* indeed—he manages to grab hold of a rope dangling from a passing hot-air balloon, from the car of which he can distinguish the Angel of the Odd leaning over and shouting at him. The Angel drops a bottle of Kirschenwasser over the side of the car, which hits the narrator's head. The Angel asks if he now believes in his powers, but the narrator refuses, and so the Angel cuts the rope and the narrator tumbles to earth, crashing through the roof of his house.

This truly bizarre comedy, with its succession of unlikely perils, near-misses and slapstick stunts, has the mood of a Harold Lloyd or Buster Keaton film. One only has to think of Lloyd hanging from the hands of a clock high over a city street in *Safety Last* (dir. Fred C. Newmeyer & Sam Taylor, 1923) to have an equivalent of Poe's narrator hanging from a balloon rope. Keaton had his own "ladder gag" in *Cops* (dir. Edward F. Cline & Buster Keaton, 1922) in which a ladder, pivoted over a fence, becomes a crazy seesaw, pulled up and down by two groups of cops trying to shake off Keaton, who balances in the middle. Laurel and Hardy also had fun with a ladder gag in a film whose title echoes Poe's ladder-scratching hog: In *Hog Wild* (dir. James Parrott, 1930), Ollie climbs a ladder that has been

The voluble, egocentric and opinionated Edgar in *StrAngel* (dir. Georg-Sebastian Dreßler, Daniel von Braun, 2013).

made tall enough to reach the roof of a house by resting on Stan's car. Ollie climbs the ladder, but Stan accidentally starts the car, propelling Ollie away with him on a madcap journey through the suburbs of Los Angeles.

The Angel of the Odd might well be said to be the Spirit of Slapstick. But comedy pratfalls are very close to genuine horrors; the fine dividing line between the two was elegantly exploited by Robert Fuest's two "Dr. Phibes" films, starring Vincent Price as a hideously mutilated organist, hell-bent on revenge and immortality. The camp, art deco knowingness of *The Abominable Dr. Phibes* (1971) and *Dr. Phibes Rises Again* (1972) are, like so much of Poe's output, exercises in *style* (and they are consequently among the most *stylish* of horror films); their narrative *raison d'etre* is an excuse for a series of very grisly but equally bizarre murders. In the first film, Phibes kills the doctors responsible for the death of his wife, using the ten plagues of Egypt as the basis for their methods of dispatch. One is stung to death; another is attacked by bats; a psychiatrist has his head crushed by a frog mask; the fourth victim has his blood drained from his body; a fifth doctor is frozen to death; another doctor, who is an amateur pilot, crashes his plane when rats are let loose in the cockpit; a brass unicorn head impales the seventh doctor, and a nurse is eaten alive by a plague of locusts. The ninth plague, "the death of the first born," is enacted when Phibes kidnaps the leading doctor's son. The final plague of darkness concerns Phibes himself, who embalms his own body, joining his wife in death.

Similarly grotesque demises await the victims of the second film, over which Poe's Angel of the Odd also presides, and Phibes takes as much relish as the Angel in the weirdness of the horrors for which he is responsible. Poe describes the Angel as a creature of "impudence, cruelty, and affectation,"[4] which concisely sums up Phibes as well. His affectation, cruelty and impudence are everywhere apparent: In the first film he watches the pilot crash his plane while Vulnavia plays her violin. In the second film she does the same (though another actress plays her) while a victim is being stung to death by scorpions. Phibes, dressed as a sheik, languidly lifts a pineapple from the array of exotic fruit on display before him. His victim screams in agony. "Give me excess of it," says Phibes, wickedly paraphrasing Shakespeare. *Dr. Phibes Rises Again* also borrows from Wilkie Collins' equally odd story "The Terribly Strange Bed," in which the canopy of a four-poster bed is attached to a screw. This crushes its unfortunate occupants, much as Dr. Phibes' concertina effect, similarly operated by a screw, squashes his victim from head to foot as he sleeps. As Collins himself was greatly influenced by Poe, this is a satisfying circularity.

"The Angel of the Odd" also provided the title of the first instrumental number of Eric Woolfson's Edgar Allan Poe musical, first performed in 2003. (As we shall see, Poe inspired Woolfson's collaboration with Alan Parsons in the 1970s.) This short, enigmatic piece has nothing of the comic tone of Poe's story, taking a more serious approach to oddness, with a soulful guitar solo against brooding string chords suggesting something more Gothic in keeping with the rest of the show; but rather more in tune with its inspiration is a German, twenty-minute animation based on the story, directed by Daniel von Braun and Georg-Sebastian Dreßler in 2013. In this adaptation, called *StrAngel—The Angel of the Odd,* Edgar, an insufferably logical and consequently heartless bachelor, is of the opinion that "stupid things only happen to stupid people." The film demonstrates how wrong he is, and also points out the error of his ways rather in the manner of Dickens' moral education of Scrooge in *A Christmas Carol.*

Poe's story also provided the title of an 2013 art exhibition at the Musée d'Orsay in

Paris, devoted to examples of what it termed "Dark Romanticism" (including Carlos Schwabe, Goya, Fuseli, Max Ernst and others). The exhibition curator, Felix Krämer, explained:

> From the 1880s, seeing the vanity and ambiguity behind the belief in progress, many artists picked up this legacy of Dark Romanticism, turning towards the occult, reviving myths and exploiting the new ideas about dreams, in order to bring Man face to face with his fears and contradictions: the savagery and depravity hidden in every human being, the risk of mass degeneration, the harrowing strangeness of daily life revealed in the horror stories of Poe and Barbey d'Aurévilly. And so, right in the middle of the second industrial revolution, hordes of witches, sniggering skeletons, shapeless devils, lecherous Satans and deadly enchantresses suddenly appeared, expressing a defiant, carnivalesque disillusionment with the present.[5]

Such an appropriation of Poe's title nicely brings out the ambiguity of the word "odd": It can be both comic and horrific at once. "Oddness" is unnerving, disturbing, bizarre and even horrific ... but, as Anthony Hinds, the producer of Hammer Films' greatest successes, understood very well, "There's a great danger with horror films that people will start laughing." Though Hinds confessed "We thought we'd put a stop to that,"[6] Poe remained more ambivalent.

The Angel of the Odd is also related to Poe's Imp of the Perverse, which he discussed in the essay-story of that name in 1845. Whereas the Angel perverts reason and probability by creating bizarre accidents, the Imp encourages us to go against reason by performing acts which in all probability will prove ultimately self-destructive. Whether these acts are against others or ourselves, they are performed merely "for the reason that we should *not*."[7] Poe cites vertigo as an example of this: "because our reason violently deters us from the brink, *therefore* do we the most impetuously approach it."[8] As in "The Black Cat," perversity incites us not only to murder, but also to confess to it. The narrator of "The Black Cat" explains that he killed his pet cat "*because* I knew that it had loved me and *because* I felt it had given me no reason of offence;—hung it *because* I knew that in so doing I was committing a sin—a deadly sin that would so jeopardize my immortal soul as to place it—if such a thing were possible—even beyond the reach of the infinite mercy of the Most Merciful and Most Terrible God."[9] There is nothing here of sadism as Geoffrey Gorer defined it in his insightful study *The Life and Ideas of the Marquis de Sade*. Gorer defines sadism there as "the pleasure felt from the observed modifications on the external world produced by the will of the observer.... It will be seen that this definition is extremely wide and covers an enormous range of human activity from the creation of works of art to the blowing up of bridges, from making little girls happy by giving them sweets to making them cry by slapping them."[10] The aspect of *pleasure* is essential in this Sadeian analysis of cruelty. Poe's hero in "The Black Cat" takes no pleasure in his act. The motivation is self-destructive.

Oscar Wilde knew this impulse all too well, summarizing it in the well-known line "Each man kills the thing he loves" from "The Ballad of Reading Goal." In Wilde's novel *The Picture of Dorian Gray*, a former lover of Dorian, Alan Campbell, insists "Nobody ever commits a crime without doing something stupid."[11] Perhaps he had been reading "The Imp of the Perverse," the narrator of which is unable to resist the impulse to betray his otherwise perfect, undetectable murder of a woman. (A similar perversity overwhelms the madman in "The Black Cat," who raps needlessly against the wall behind which he has entombed his murdered wife.) Wilde was fully aware of his own tendency to the allure of perversity, which Poe had identified before him: "I was so typical a child of my age," he wrote in *De Profundis,* "that in my perversity, and for that perversity's sake, I turned the good things of my life to evil, and the evil things of my life to good."[12]

Heroes of literary decadence similarly cannot help themselves from doing what they know will bring them harm. Hans Castorp, in Thomas Mann's *The Magic Mountain,* lingers in the sanatorium he originally intended to visit for only a few days, fascinated by disease and sickness. Gustav von Aschenbach in Mann's "Death in Venice" returns to the city knowing that he is likely to contract cholera—he returns half-wanting to die, seduced by the beauty of the boy Tadzio, unable to resist what he knows will destroy him. Friedrich Nietzsche even regarded Christianity as a manifestation of this perverse and decadent impulse: "[It] has at its basis the *rancune* of the sick, the instinct directed *against* the healthy, *against* health. Everything well-constituted, proud, high-spirited, beauty above all, is hurtful to its ears and eyes."[13] Poe, however, was the first to articulate this irrational psychology, which Freud later discussed as a death-drive "beyond the pleasure principle," a drive which was eventually labelled Thanatos:

> [W]e took as our starting point a sharp distinction between the ego-instincts (= death-instincts) and the sexual instincts (= life-instincts). We were prepared indeed to reckon even the alleged self-preservative instincts of the ego among death-instincts, a position which we have since corrected and withdrawn from. Our standpoint was a dualistic one from the beginning, and is so to-day more sharply than before, since we no longer call the contrasting tendencies egoistic and sexual instincts, but life-instincts and death-instincts.[14]

The Angel of the Odd and the Imp of the Perverse are opposite sides of the medal Poe awarded to the irrational impulses of the unconscious.

Annabel Lee

It was many and many a year ago,
In a kingdom by the sea,
That a maiden there lived whom you may know
By the name of ANNABEL LEE[1]

From grotesque slapstick, we move to Poe's short, lyrical love poem, which was actually Poe's last, dating from 1849. There is considerable doubt about which of Poe's various female friends inspired it. He describes Annabel Lee as "a child," which might suggest that he was thinking of his own wife Virginia, whom he married when she was only 13. His biographer Kenneth Silverman believes that Annabel Lee "represents all the women he loved and lost."[2] Poe famously remarked, apropos of "The Raven," that the death of a beautiful woman "is, unquestionably, the most poetical topic in the world,"[3] but whereas the hero of "The Raven" is separated from his beloved Lenore forever and will clasp her "nevermore," the lover of Annabel Lee is reunited with her after death:

> And neither the angels in heaven above,
> Nor the demons down under the sea,
> Can ever dissever my soul from the soul
> Of the beautiful ANNABEL LEE.[4]

The internal rhymes of the third line are characteristic of Poe's highly musical approach to poetry and prose, the final line containing each of the five vowel sounds.

The poem was set to music by the British composer Josef Holbrooke (1878–1958), who was almost as obsessed by Poe as was Peter Cushing's Lancelot Canning in *Torture Garden*. Unfortunately, his acerbic personality and outrageous egocentricity succeeded in alienating nearly everyone who might have helped him, with the exception of that other egomaniac Sir Thomas Beecham and the much more genial Sir Granville Bantock, whose own music Holbrooke's somewhat resembles. The work of both composers was neglected until relatively recently. Holbrooke, like Bantock, was prolific, and wrote over thirty works based on Poe, which he termed his "Poeana," though not all these pieces have a specifically programmatic connection with the titles he appended to the music itself. Indeed, he regularly changed the titles of pieces, sometimes several times, which makes one doubt that they were always inspired by any literary text at all. The music itself, conceived in late–Romantic style, is full of sound and fury but unfortunately often signifies rather less than one might hope for. Interest in Holbrooke's vast output has revived in recent years. One of his early champions, George Lowe, attempted to explain the fascination the composer had for Poe in his study *Josef Holbrooke and His Work,* published in 1920. The following passage from it is particularly interesting as it reveals the inherent distrust of Poe's work in the Anglo-Saxon cultural arena of the time:

> There is one poet ... with which the name of Holbrooke must always be associated, and that is the American poet, Edgar Allan Poe. We feel that, in some sub-conscious manner, these two creative minds of different ages meet on the same spiritual plane in a manner that is both inevitable and wonderful. The work of the one artist seems to complete that of the other so as to form a subtle link between literature and music. Other conjoined names, such as those of Schumann and Heine, Hugo Wolf and Mörike, Debussy and Maeterlinck, also rise to mind as typical examples of other supreme alliances between the sister arts.
>
> To some critics, the poetry of Poe appears little more than the morbid exhalation of a contorted brain. They entirely overlook the fertile imagination that underlies it and the wonderful phraseology that falls so musically upon the ear. Few poets indeed have had a greater gift of creating atmosphere or a more subtle sense of word values. The situations that Poe creates are often terrible and at times ghastly, but, behind them all, it is hard not to feel the warmth of the Promethean fires. At the root of all his poetry there is a sincerity and depth of feeling that cannot be ignored. The pictures that he evokes are so vivid that we are arrested by their glare and held spellbound by their weird fascination. Only a poet of exceptional qualities possesses this power of subjugating our human senses.[5]

With regard to Holbrooke's setting of "Annabel Lee," which Holbrooke dedicated to his wife, Lowe has this to say:

> The strange spirit and phraseology of this poem has been most wonderfully caught by the composer. His fine gift of being able to spread a poetic atmosphere through the whole fabric of his music has never been more fully realised than here. Being of absolute originality, the song is apt to puzzle those who hear it for the first time. It is a supreme achievement, however, and Holbrooke has projected his ideas in strange, beautiful music that is half weird and half solemn, but that is always permeated with the true spirit of romance. The song is written for a baritone voice with orchestra, and in this orchestra no flutes, trumpets, or trombones are employed, though there are parts for cor anglais, bass clarinet, harps and double bassoon.[6]

The setting begins with *misterioso, pianissimo,* syncopated strings. When Poe makes reference to "The angels, not half so happy in heaven," Holbrooke introduces a descending three-note ostinato to suggest eternity. The mood broadens with longer phrases for "But our love it was stronger by far than the love / Of those who were older than we," and ostinato triplets return to suggest eternity once more, for "the demons down under the sea, Can ever dissever my soul from the soul / Of the beautiful Annabel Lee. "The sustained syncopated rhythms of the opening then return to bring this fluid setting to a *pianissimo* close.

"Annabel Lee" has inspired very many other musical settings, being, along with "Eldorado," "Israfel," "To One in Paradise" and "A Dream Within a Dream" the most popular of Poe's short lyrics to be chosen by nineteenth-century composers. Among the Americans, John Philip Sousa (1854–1932) and George Templeton Strong (1856–1948) both composed "Annabel Lee" settings, while in Britain, Michael William Balfe (1808–1870), who immortalized Tennyson's "Come into the Garden, Maud," followed suit. And in 1901, Sir Arthur Somervell (1863–1937), who also set Tennyson, Rossetti and Housman, provided his own gently rocking, traditionally 6/8 accompaniment for the poem, which he entitled "A Kingdom by the Sea."

In more recent times, "Annabel Lee" has been recorded by Frankie Laine, Jim Reeves and Joan Baez. The poem has also been beautifully recited by Marianne Faithfull with an ethereal synthesized accompaniment on the Hal Wilner produced 1997 album *Closed on Account of Rabies,* which features settings by various artists of Poe texts. It also received a prog-rock treatment in Eric Woolfson's 2009 Poe musical, where it took the form of a duet ("Let the Sun Shine on Me") between Edgar and his first love, Elmira. As we shall see, "Annabel Lee" also informs aspects of D.W. Griffith's film *The Avenging Conscience* (1914), Ken Russell's *The Fall of the Louse of Usher* (2002), and James McTeigue's *The Raven* (2012).

The Assignation

It is with a confused recollection that I bring to mind the circumstances of that meeting. Yet I remember—ah! how should I forget?—the deep midnight, the Bridge of Sighs, the beauty of woman, and the Genius of Romance that stalked up and down the narrow canal.[1]

Dating from 1834, "The Assignation" is in some respects a trial run for aspects of "Ligeia," published four years later. Set in Venice, it concerns a suicide pact between the Marchesa Aphrodite and a mysterious, fabulously wealthy Byronic hero, who like the unnamed narrator of "Ligeia" lives amid an extravagant decor of excess: "The eye wandered from object to object, and rested upon none—neither the *grotesques* of the Greek painters, nor the sculptures of the best Italian days, nor the huge carvings of untutored Egypt."[2] Indeed, this tale foreshadows the opulent confusion of the Vittoriale, the crowded home of the decadent Italian poet Gabrielle D'Annunzio. As described by his biographer Anthony Rhodes, the Vittoriale is "a monument to the decadent age of *fin de siècle,* with the cushions, velvets, damasks, brocades and the scents of des Esseintes in the incense burners. It bristles with flags, daggers, medals, rifles, proclamations, machine-guns and other implements of war; and yet a crucifix by Giotto will hang next to an aeroplane propeller."[3]

The lines that follow the initial description of the stranger's palazzo exploit the synesthetic imagery in which Poe so often indulged and which subsequently appealed so much to Charles Baudelaire when he discovered a kindred spirit in the American writer:

> Rich draperies in every part of the room trembled to the vibration of low, melancholy music, whose origin was not to be discovered. The senses were oppressed by mingled and conflicting perfumes, reeking up from strange convolute censers, together with multitudinous flaring and flickering tongues of emerald and violent fire.[4]

The sense of recognition Baudelaire experienced on first reading Poe was overwhelming:

> In 1846 or 1847 I came across a few fragments of Edgar Poe; I experienced a singular mental shock; since it was not until after his death that his works were issued in a single collected edition, I took the trouble to scrape an acquaintance with certain Americans living in Paris in order to borrow from them files of the journals that Poe had edited. And it was then that I discovered, believe me or not as you choose, poems and stories of which the idea had occurred to me earlier but only in a vague, confused, and chaotic form, but which Poe had been able to combine and bring to perfection. Such was the origin of my enthusiasm and the pains I took.[5]

Baudelaire's fascination was no doubt centered on Poe's interest in synesthetic imagery. Just as Baudelaire claims that "Les parfums, les couleurs et les sons se répondent" ("The perfumes, the colors and the sounds respond") in his 1857 poem "Correspondences," so too does Poe exploit synesthetic impressions in this and many of his other tales; and Baudelaire's championship of Poe's particular genius was to have an interesting effect on French culture, inspiring the Symbolist generation and composers such as Claude Debussy. The synesthetic ideal is ultimately a transcendental one, the sum of the whole being greater than the individual parts; and it is indeed possible to interpret the extravagant juxtaposition of objects and styles in the stranger's room as a metaphor of timelessness itself—that state beyond death, which the stranger eventually enters, along with his beloved at the end of the tale. The stranger explains that the effect of such a "medley of architectural embellishments" is "is incongruous to the timid alone. Proprieties of place, and especially of time, are the bugbears which terrify mankind from the contemplation of the magnificent."[6] The "magnificent" here is that world beyond time, where everything exists timelessly alongside everything else. The decor of the room is therefore symbolic of the after life. Historical reality was never anywhere near as important to Poe as the use of artifacts and decor to articulate the higher reality of the soul. Right at the start of the tale, he places the aesthetic effect of alliteration over architectural fact, referring to the "Palladian palaces" of Venice. (In fact, apart from designs for the rooms in the Ducal Palace, Palladio did not design any palazzos in Venice, his activity in the city being otherwise restricted to a handful of nonetheless very important churches, such as the Redentore and the church for San Giorgio Maggiore.)

However, some critics have argued that Poe was also being ironic in this tale, basing it upon the affair Lord Byron enjoyed with Countess Teresa Gamba Guiccioli during his residence in Venice.[7] She was only nineteen when they first met in 1819. Her husband, Count Alessandro Guiccioli, had been married twice before, first to a woman who had made him immensely rich and whom he was suspected of having murdered. His second wife bore him six children before he finally married her. After she died, he married Teresa. An older man, a beautiful young bride and a handsome lover in the form of Byron certainly matches the love triangle in "The Assignation," and the sexual imagery embedded in the story exploits the scandalous nature of Byron's liaison, of which Byron himself left an account in a letter to his publisher, John Murray:

> Tonight, as Countess Guiccioli observed me poring over "Don Juan," she stumbled by mere chance on the 137th stanza of the first canto, and asked me what it meant. I told her, "Nothing—but 'your husband is coming.'" As I said this in Italian, with some emphasis, she started up in a fright, and said, *"Oh my God, is* he *coming?"* thinking it was *her own*, who either was or ought to have been at the theatre. You may suppose we laughed when she found out the mistake. You will be amused, as I was—it happened not three hours ago.[8]

Poe suggests that the stranger in his story is an Englishman like Byron, and he also refers to a portrait of the Marchesa in which her left hand points to a "curiously fashioned vase." This might imply a vaginal symbolism, especially in the light of the phallic symbolism in the subsequent quotation from George Chapman's 1641 tragedy *Bussy D'Ambois*:

> He is up
> There like a Roman statue! He will stand
> Till Death hath made him marble![9]

The phrases "He is up" and "He will stand" certainly seem to have possible sexual meaning here. When the stranger finally drinks his poison, Poe suggests further sexual implications: the idea of a Liebestod, indeed, in use of the words "erecting" and "ejaculated":

> At length, erecting his frame, he looked upwards, and ejaculated the lines of Henry King, the Bishop of Chichester:
>
> > "Stay for me there! I will not fail
> > To meet thee in that hollow vale."[10]

These lines form the epigram of the story and emphasize its central point that the illicit lovers are united beyond space and time in an existence beyond death. The opening scene, in which the stranger plucks the Marchesa's child from the gloomy waters of the canal, also points to this dénouement. By rescuing the child from death, the stranger seems to be demonstrating to the Marchesa that their "assignation" in death will similarly rescue her from the death-in-life she suffers in her earthly marriage to Montoni, and raise her up to a more meaningful spiritual life. "Thou hast conquered," she says to her lover—implying that his metaphorical demonstration has been understood: "one hour after sunrise—we shall meet—so let it be!"[11]

But there is a complicating factor in the tale's symbolism, which is the considerable allusion to statues in the text. Poe's narrator describes the Marchesa as being more like a statue than a woman, with her "classical head" and "snowy-white and gauze-like drapery," the folds of which resembles "heavy marble."[12] He refers to "the pallor of the marble countenance, the swelling marble bosom, the very purity of the marble feet" and suggests that she is a statue that has "started into life!"[13] The stranger is described as being "like a deity" with a forehead "all light and ivory" with "classically regular" features reminiscent of the marble statue of Emperor Commodus. The conversation between the narrator and the stranger is often taken up with a discussion of statues. Canova is mentioned, along with Michelangelo's couplet—

> Non ha l'ottimo artista alcun concetto
> Che un marmo solo in se non circunscriva.[14]

[The best of artists does not have a concept, that the marble block does not circumscribe.]

Such a preoccupation with statuary suggests that these characters are not really alive. Only in death will they really begin to live. And that connects the story to the vampire literature which Byron had already begun to promote in poems such as "The Giaour" (1813) and the unfinished tale he began at the same time that Mary Shelley conceived of *Frankenstein*. In life, the Marchesa and the stranger are like statues, but in death, like the undead, they will live so much more intensely! That the stranger is dedicated to such a course is implied in the line that describes him, as being "so essentially apart from all other human beings."[15] Of course, "The Assignation" is not a literal vampire tale, it merely suggests the romantic allure of the immortal, more vital existence of the vampire; and this implication, coupled with the decadent Venetian setting, went on to spawn vampire progeny in Augusto Caminito and Mario Caiano's 1988 film *Vampires in Venice,* starring Klaus Kinski, along with the 2010 *Doctor Who* episode "The Vampires of Venice" (dir. Jonny Campbell), and the scenes set in that city described in *The Vampire Armand,* the sixth in Anne Rice's Vampire Chronicles series. Rice's novel tells the story of an icon painter who is apprenticed to one Marius, an undead Venetian artist of the renaissance with whom he has a sexual relationship that eventually leads him into being initiated into vampirism. In addition, a 1977 episode from the BBC series *Supernatural* entitled "The Ghost of Venice" presented the city (via studio sets) as a place of timelessness—a place haunted by the ghost of an actor's wife. In Rosemary Timperley's prose adaptation of Robert Muller's teleplay, the actor (played by Robert Hardy) describes the city as "a timeless city, the name of which I forget—which is curious, since the city's contours are more real to me than any episode or relationship from my own life. In my mind's eye, then, the city has the *feeling* of Venice where my wife, myself and my company of players celebrated our greatest triumphs." He describes it as a "city of haunted squares, dingy alleys and moonstruck bridges, renaissance arches, dark vaults, and subterranean passages, of crumbling masonry" and as a "forever-dying city."[16]

Each of these examples presents Venice as a decadent, opulent and demonic arena in the manner of Poe, in which the common restraints of time are challenged. Venice becomes a symbol of damned immortality. Caminito's ravishing imagery, unfortunately not matched by the dramatic qualities of the film, is distinctly in the manner of Poe. Kinski, "a man apart," stands in a gondola that drifts down misty canals. He advances on unsuspecting pigeons in a deserted, equally misty and lamplit St. Mark's Square. Fireworks, carnival revelers in elaborate costumes and masks, whose smiles vanish when Nosferatu passes by, dark passageways resonant with Kinski's footsteps—all derive from a Gothic tradition Poe helped to elaborate in a particularly aesthetic manner in "The Assignation."

So too does the decadent atmosphere of Thomas Mann's "Death in Venice" (1912), in which he describes a gondola in distinctly Gothic terms:

> Is there anyone but must repress a secret thrill, on arriving in Venice for the first time—or returning thither after long absence—and stepping into a Venetian gondola? That singular conveyance, come down unchanged from ballad times, black as nothing else on earth except a coffin—what pictures it calls up of lawless, silent adventures in the plashing night; or even more, what visions of death itself, the bier and solemn rites and last soundless voyage! And has anyone remarked that the seat in such a bark, the armchair lacquered in coffin-black and dully black-upholstered, is the softest, most luxurious, most relaxing seat in the world?[17]

Visconti picked up on all this in his 1971 film version. Mann had Mahler in mind when writing his novella, and Visconti picked up on this too, but behind it all was the ghost of Richard Wagner, who composed the richly somber third act of *Tristan und Isolde* in Venice. Tony Palmer's 1983 Wagner biopic, starring Richard Burton, made much of Mann's funereal imagery, introducing the film with a flash-forward of the final scenes of the gondolas bearing Wagner's coffin down the Grand Canal, accompanied, appropriately, by Siegfried's Funeral March from *Götterdämmerung*. Though a historical fact, the imagery here becomes almost mythic—certainly decadent and decidedly Gothic. D'Annunzio had aided this mystification of Wagner's funeral in his novel *The Flame* (1900), in which the hero, Stelio Effrena, is actually one of Wagner's pallbearers:

> The passage from the boat to the shore was very short, but those few steps felt like a long, long journey. The water was rattling against the posts of the landing-stage, the howling was bursting out of the canal as though from the inner regions of a cavern, the bells of St. Mark's were ringing vespers, but the confused noise lost all immediate reality and seemed to be infinitely profound and distant, like a lamentation from the Ocean.
>
> They carried the Hero's weight on their arms, they carried the half-dead body of the One who had spread the power of his oceanic soul across the word, the dying flesh of the Revealing One who had transformed into infinite song the essences of the Universe for the religion of men.[18]

Palmer's film may well have inspired Caminito's *Vampires in Venice*, as it too shows Wagner in a gondola—"a man alone"—and Wagner is also seen wandering down dark, misty alleyways. At other times, he walks before the massive windows of his regal palazzo, much as does the vampire hunter played by Christopher Plummer in Caminito's film. Andrew Cruikshank's narration emphasizes the Poe-like introversion of Wagner's Venetian mood along with his equally Poe-like need for sumptuous luxury:

> When he got there, he found it gloomy. The gloom about him reinforced the gloom within him.... He sank deeper and deeper into himself until he could stand it no longer and demanded the biggest apartment that could be found. Hang the expense! Space was what he needed!

All this imagery can be traced back to the imagery of "The Assignation."

However, Poe's story did not appear from nowhere. It picks up on the Venetian setting of E.T.A. Hoffmann's 1814 story "Das verlorene Spiegelbild" ("The Lost Reflection") from *Die Abendteuer der Sylvester-Nacht* (*The Adventures of New Year's Eve*), in which the protagonist has his reflection stolen, much as a vampire, who has no reflection of his own, steals the reflections of its victims. (The story later formed part of Offenbach's 1851 opera *Les Contes d'Hoffmann*, which one hundred years after its première was filmed by Michael Powell and Emeric Pressburger. The highly stylized Venetian section of this film features an ethereal gondola which seems to fly rather than float, while carrying the exotic Ludmilla Tchérina as Giulietta towards her assignation with magic and death.)

Ann Radcliffe had begun the popular association of Venice with Gothic fantasy in her famous novel *The Mysteries of Udolpho* (1794). Indeed, the name of her villain is Montoni, which Poe echoes in the name of the Marchesa's husband, Mentoni, in "The Assignation." Radcliffe paints a melancholy image of the city: "the rising moon, which threw a shadowy light upon the terraces, and illuminated the porticos and magnificent arcades that crowned them." As in *Vampires in Venice*, the heroine, Emily St. Aubert, observes from her gondola "groups of masks ... dancing on the moonlight terraces, and seemed almost to realize the romance of fairy-land."[19]

Byron, a great admirer of Radcliffe, cemented the melancholy resonance of the city in the fourth canto of his *Childe Harold's Pilgrimage* in 1818:

> I stood in Venice, on the Bridge of Sighs,
> A palace and a prison on each hand:
> I saw from out the wave her structures rise
> As from the stroke of the enchanter's wand:
> A thousand years their cloudy wings expand
> Around me, and a dying Glory smiles
> O'er the far times, when many a subject land
> Looked to the wingéd Lion's marble piles,
> Where Venice sate in state, throned on her hundred isles!

Poe builds his own Venetian edifice upon these foundations, and dwells with similar Byronic gloom upon the Bridge of Sighs. It is there that he first encounters the Marchesa Aphrodite. In a kind of paraphrase of Byron, he writes: "Yet I remember!—ah! how should I forget?—the deep midnight, the Bridge of Sighs, the beauty of woman, and the Genius of Romance that stalked up and down the narrow canal."[20]

Though Poe's dreary Venice went on to form a template for many a later Gothic entertainment, "The Assignation," despite its synesthetic elements, did not inspire Debussy or Florent Schmitt, who were among France's most musical enthusiasts of Poe enthusiasts. Instead, it informed the decadent and violent atmosphere of Erich Wolfgang Korngold's early (1916) opera *Violanta,* which is also set in Venice. Composed when Korngold was only eighteen years old, it tells how the title character avenges her sister's suicide. Unable to endure her cruel husband's tyranny, Violanta's sister drowned herself. Violanta now persuades her own husband to murder the tyrant. She entices him to her home, but before the murder can take place, she realizes she is desperately in love with him. She throws herself in the path of her husband's dagger and dies in his arms, singing of the spiritual purity which she has now attained.

As Korngold's biographer Jessica Duchen points out, renaissance tales were very popular in Germany at this time. Korngold's librettist, Hans Müller, may also have been inspired by Titian's *Portrait of a Young Woman* (*Violanta*), which hangs in the Vienna Kunsthistorisches Museum. But behind these influences lies, even if only on an unconscious level, "The Assignation" and its Byronic agenda. The opulence of the Venetian setting, which the opera shares with Poe's tale, is matched by Korngold's sumptuous orchestration. This includes parts for bells, harps, choirs and tuned percussion—the combined effect of which anticipates the equally colorful film scores Korngold composed for Warner Bros. during his time in Hollywood. And Hollywood would later make much of Poe.

The Balloon Hoax

We have crossed the Atlantic—fairly and easily crossed it in a balloon! God be praised! Who shall say that any thing is impossible hereafter?[1]

Poe's journalistic hoax first appeared on April 13, 1844, in a New York newspaper called *The Sun.* This fictional account of a trans–Atlantic voyage in a hot-air balloon was

Opposite: "A prison and a palace on each hand"—engraving by J.C. Armytage of the Bridge of Sighs in Venice by J.M.W. Turner.

so convincing that many people thought it was a genuine account. It therefore anticipated that even more sensational science fiction hoax perpetrated by Orson Welles and his Mercury Theatre of the Air when, with the help of composer Bernard Herrmann, an adaptation of H.G. Wells' *The War of the Worlds,* in the style of an extended news bulletin, was broadcast on Halloween 1938. The date of the broadcast failed to alert many listeners to the jest, and mass panic ensued as thousands of people fled their homes in terror at an apparently imminent Martian invasion. Wells' theme of total war was already in the air thanks to Hitler's disastrous foreign policy, which would erupt into the Second World War the following year, adding extra verisimilitude to the affair. Like Welles, with his simulation of radio journalism, Poe exploited an aspect of the Zeitgeist that was on everyone's lips at the time. He also adopted the style of contemporary newspapers, using a variety of fonts, "magnificent capitals,"[2] and liberal punctuation, to advertise this apparently genuine event:

ASTOUNDING NEWS! BY EXPRESS VIA NORFOLK: THE ATLANTIC CROSSED IN THREE DAYS! SIGNAL TRIUMPH OF MR. MONCK MASON'S FLYING MACHINE!!! Arrival at Sullivan's Island, near Charlestown, S.C., of Mr. Mason, Mr. Robert Holland, Mr. Henson, Mr. Harrison Ainsworth, and four others, in the STEERING BALLOON "VICTORIA," AFTER A PASSAGE OF SEVENTY-FIVE HOURS FROM LAND TO LAND. FULL PARTICULARS OF THE VOYAGE!!![3]

The popular writer of historical romance fiction, William Harrison Ainsworth (1805–1882) had published his serial based on the real-life eighteenth-century criminal Jack Sheppard over the winter of 1839–1840. Indeed, Poe mentions Jack Sheppard in his text. Poe obviously felt that he needed a literary celebrity on board (much as celebrities "endorse" events and products today), but Poe was careful to select a writer he didn't much respect, just in case the writer took exception to being a part of the affair. William Samuel Henson (1805–1888) was an aviation engineer who set up the Aerial Steam Transportation Company in 1842. (He also invented the modern T-shaped safety razor.) The Irishman, Thomas Monck Mason (1803–1889), was not only a genuine balloonist but also a composer, flautist and writer who, in the company of Robert Hollond (1808–1977) and the professional balloonist Charles Green (1785–1870), had indeed made an epic 500-mile balloon trip in 1836. It took eighteen hours and was commemorated in Monck's book *Account of the Late Aeronautical Expedition from London to Weilburg* published the same year. Poe changed the spelling of Hollond's name but otherwise made sure to include an appropriate and believable cast for his "jeu d'esprit," as he called it. A painting by John Hollins commemorates these men and their associates. Entitled *A Consultation prior to the Aerial Voyage to Weilburgh,* it now hangs in London's National Portrait Gallery, and shows Monck, Hollond, Green, William Milbourne James (the Lord Chief Justice), a lawyer called William Prideaux and the artist himself, all consulting a chart, with the balloon awaiting the aeronauts in the background.

It is important to realize how newsworthy these men were in their own time to understand the success of Poe's hoax. It consists of two parts: a description of the balloon, and a "Journal" of the voyage itself. In his description of the balloon, Poe might be said to justify D.H. Lawrence's observation that Poe was more of a scientist than an artist, for the text is a catalogue of technical information, concerning weights, materials, shapes, and mechanical processes; but such lists are merely a scientific version of his proto-decadent descriptions of furnishings and décor, proving Lawrence's point that Poe "never sees anything in terms of life, almost always in terms of matter, jewels, marble, etc.—or in terms of force, scientific."[4]

To muddy the waters further, Poe also includes fictional characters along with the genuine names, but he was careful to provide correct information with regard to the real people. He discusses Green's advocacy of coal gas over hydrogen, which is "not only much less costly, but is easily procured and managed."[5] (Green's first balloon flight using coal gas took place in 1821.) The *Journal* describes how the crew dropped a bottle in the sea which contained a slip of parchment giving "a brief account of the principle of the invention."[6] This echo of Poe's first successful tale, "MS. Found in a Bottle," might have given the game away to those who had followed Poe's career, but there weren't many people who had. The balloonists originally only intended to cross the English Channel from Paris; an accident and a change in the wind inspired Ainsworth to suggest they attempt an Atlantic crossing. Poe even includes a supposed footnote by Ainsworth, who describes the ocean waves as "dumb gigantic fiends struggling in impotent agony."[7] Given Poe's uncomplimentary review of Ainsworth's fiction, Poe might have had in mind that the words he put into Ainsworth's mouth and the adventurous situation in which he placed him were more interesting than Ainsworth's novels. Of Ainsworth's novel *Crichton*, Poe wrote:

> Upon a perusal of the novel so belauded, we found it a somewhat ingenious admixture of pedantry, bombast, and rigmarole. No man ever read *Crichton* through twice. From beginning to end it is one continued abortive effort at effect. The writer keeps us in a perpetual state of preparation for something magnificent; but the something magnificent never arrives.

Poe went on to damn Ainsworth's *Jack Sheppard* with faint praise:

> Corrupt and vulgar it undoubtedly is, but it is by no means so flat (if we understand the critic's idea of the term) as the *Crichton* to which it is considered so terribly inferior. By "flat" we presume "uninteresting" is intended. To us, at least, no novel was less interesting than *Crichton*.[8]

Jules Verne (1828–1905) was rather more complimentary about Poe, whose influence upon his own science fiction he fully acknowledged. He was not entirely uncritical, however. As his grandson, Jean Jules-Verne, remembered, "Verne was struck by the bizarreness of Poe's stories but criticized their lack of verisimilitude."[9] In an 1864 essay, Verne argued, "The characters in Poe are just about feasible: they are eminently human, yet endowed with a highly nervous, supercharged sensibility.... They are the most fearsome analysts: starting from the merest trifle, they reach absolute truth."[10] Curiously, Verne regarded Poe as another apostle of materialism, which couldn't have been further from the truth: "but I imagine," he added, "that it is not so much the fault of his temperament as the influence of the purely practical and industrial society of the United States; he wrote, thought and dreamed as an American, as a positivist."[11] There is no doubt that Poe would not have recognized himself in this description, being, as he was, an outspoken critic of "progress" and technology. He was also far from an atheist, unorthodox though his views on God certainly were (see the entry for "Eureka"). As Jean Jules-Verne adds, "though deistic to the core, thanks to his upbringing, [Verne also] limited divine intervention in his stories to the moments when human strength, will and ingenuity could go no further. In the main, however, Verne's fiction is a glorification of human energy."[12] And, it is hardly necessary to point out, none of his heroes are "unhealthy and nervous,"[13] as he characterizes so many

Poster for *Five Weeks in a Balloon* (dir. Irwin Allen, 1962).

of Poe's. What Verne really found wanting in Poe was a secure grasp of scientific thinking, in place of mere scientific *posturing.* He believed that Poe's science fiction tales would have been more convincing "had he respected a few elementary laws of physics,"[14] and it was this element that Verne added to Poe's formula, while leaving behind all of Poe's ambivalence, irony and psychological enquiry.

Inspired by "The Balloon Hoax," Verne set himself the task of improving upon it, and in 1863, *Cinq semaines en ballon* (*Five Weeks in a Balloon*) was published. Whereas Poe had relied on what he knew about Hollond, Mason and Green, mixing it with imaginative speculation, Verne applied rather more rigorous scientific thinking to the problem, inventing a balloon that could tack with the wind in differing altitudes. His balloon uses a heated coil to change the temperature of hydrogen to achieve this. The novel was given a considerable publicity boost by Verne's photographer friend Nadar (Gaspard-Félix Tournachon, 1820–1910), who wanted to set up a Society for Aerial Locomotion. To attract money for the cause he arranged to float an immense balloon from the Champ-de-Mars in Paris. Like Poe's balloon, it carried celebrities who each paid a thousand francs for the privilege. Coincidentally, *Cinq semaines en ballon* appeared at the same time and further stimulated interest in Verne's picaresque adventure novel.

Consequently, we may claim Irwin Allen's 1962 adaptation of Verne's novel, starring Red Buttons, Sir Cedric Hardwicke and Peter Lorre, as another cinematic legacy of Poe, even though at one stage removed. Fabian, who plays Dr. Fergusson's young assistant Jacques, explains Verne's principle in clear-cut terms: "The air circulates through the pipes into this heating chamber. You turn up the heat, the gas expands, and up we go. We turn down the heat, and we drop like a busted balloon." A poster-paint Saturday matinee affair, it features a comedy chimp, Arabian Nights clichés, a pompous British aristocrat (played by Richard Haydn), a specially composed song for Fabian to sing to his own squeeze-box accompaniment, marauding natives, slave-traders, love interest, and aerial thrills. It also involves newspapermen (Buttons' distinctly annoying role). The whole expedition to make aviation history by flying to West Africa, is financed by a newspaper tycoon, adding another echo of Poe to the proceedings.

The Bells

How we shiver with affright
At the melancholy menace of their tone!
For every sound that floats
From the rust within their throats
Is a groan.[1]

One of Poe's most musical poems, "The Bells" has fittingly attracted the attention of many composers. There are well over thirty choral settings of these lines by composers both remembered and obscure. Among the better known are by the Norwegian national Romantic, Halfdan Kjerulf (1868), Michael William Balfe (1808–1870), the American writer on music and composer, Henry C. Lahee (1826–1912), the founder of the Philadelphia Mendelssohn Club, William Wallace Gilchrist (1846–1916), Arthur Foote (1853–

1937), and the 1960s American protest singer Phil Ochs (1946–1970). Balfe, like many others, used repeated ostinati patterns to suggest pealing bells in his piano accompaniment, while Lahee prefaced his part song for four voices with the instruction "With much variety in tone and attention to mark of expression," which might suggest an attempt at conveying the varying moods of the text, but in fact he sets only the second section, "Hear the mellow wedding bells." Foote, an associate of Edward MacDowell and champion of both Brahms and Wagner, also contributed a four-voice part-song, again setting the opening section of the poem.

Rather more obscure is the setting made by the British composer Alfred Plumpton (1848–1902), who toured Asia as an opera conductor before settling in Melbourne, Australia. His 1867 song setting of "The Bells" again imitates bell-peals by means of descending scalic passages in the piano accompaniment, though sets only the optimistic opening section of the poem. Lines from "The Bells" were also set by the Scottish composer, choir master, and founder of the Glasgow Orpheus Choir, Sir Hugh S. Roberton (1874–1952). His somewhat Mendelssohnian part-song for two sopranos and alto, "Hear the Sledges with the Bells" is marked "Crisp, vivacious," and its snowy imagery makes it suitable for Christmas performance. Intriguingly, it is dedicated "To William Wilson and his 'St. George' singers"—presumably no relation to the William Wilson of Poe's doppelgänger story. The piece was published by Curwen in 1919 and reissued by his son Kenneth, who ran Roberton Publications for fifty years from the rather Poe-esque environment of a windmill in the village of Wendover in Buckinghamshire, England. When I visited this windmill in the 1980s, the immense weight of all the printed editions which Mr. Roberton stored in the upper floors suggested a possible Poe scenario of being crushed literally by music.

A brief reference to the iron bells of Poe's fourth stanza crops up in the lyrics of Pink Floyd's "Time" from *The Dark Side of the Moon* (1973), but the most impressive impact of "The Bells" on popular music to date is Eric Woolfson's 2003 prog-rock response in the follow-up album to his earlier *Tales of Mystery and Imagination* with the Alan Parsons Project, later incorporated into his Poe musical. This rapid, motoric choral number effectively reflects the differing moods of the four stanzas, the insistent repetition of the melody nicely articulating, within the context and limitations of a five-and-a-half minute track, the mounting tension and apprehension of Poe's poem.

The most celebrated setting of the poem is Rachmaninoff's 1913 choral work *Kolokola* (*The Bells*), which set Konstantin Balmont's very free translation of Poe's poem. Since his youth in Novgorod, Rachmaninoff (1873–1943) had always been fascinated by the sound of cathedral bells, which he believed could express contrasting emotions, and the doom-laden theme of Poe's poem was tailor-made for a composer of such an introspective and melancholy disposition as his. Indeed, Rachmaninoff always claimed *The Bells* was, of all his works, the one he liked best. The four sections of the poem also usefully correspond to the four movements required of a traditional symphonic structure, and Rachmaninoff followed the example of Tchaikovsky's 6th "Pathétique" Symphony by making his last movement a slow, lugubrious one to match the dark imagery of Poe's lines: "Iron bells! What a world of solemn thought their melody compels!" But to create the contrasting optimistic and sleigh-bell imagery of the first section, and the "world of merriment their melody foretells," he employed celesta, woodwind and triangle.

The second movement is slower, reflecting the golden bells of marriage, with long lyrical lines for the soprano. The third section conveys the alarm of brazen bells, and Rachmaninoff responds to Poe's "clamor and the clangor of the bells" with a terrifying scherzo. The last movement is a rumination on death, but throughout the whole work, Rachmaninoff incorporates an echo of the famous Dies Irae plain-chant melody, which he also used, among other works, in the tone poem *The Isle of the Dead* and the *Symphonic Dances* as a leitmotif of Death itself.

Poe's obsession with Death and his theme of mournful and never-ending remembrance was very much in tune with Rachmaninoff's own tendency to introspection—even depression, which, coupled with a lively sense of humor, and a love of fast cars and speed boats matched Poe's somewhat manic-depressive temperament. Rachmaninoff also had practical experience of hypnotism, a subject that similarly fascinated Poe. After the première of his first symphony, which was a fiasco, Rachmaninoff suffered a nervous breakdown and felt that he was unable to compose again. On the advice of his family, he visited Dr. Nikolay Dahl, a specialist in this field, though as Geoffrey Norris points out, "It seems likely that actual hypnosis played a less important role in the treatment than the extended conversations which Dahl had with Rachmaninoff on a wide range of music topics, for Dahl himself was an accomplished amateur musician."[2] Rachmaninoff related that Dahl kept telling him that he would write a great concerto, and the therapy, whatever it was, worked, for Rachmaninoff soon began work on his famous Second Piano Concerto. It was a result every bit as spectacular as the achievement of Poe's mysterious "P," who hypnotizes Monsieur Valdemar at the moment of death itself, and who later relates the facts in the case of his friend.

In 1903, some years before Rachmaninoff's Poe setting, Josef Holbrooke had turned to the same poem. His approach to "The Bells" somewhat resembles Rachmaninoff's in his rich, lugubrious scoring. Like Rachmaninoff, Holbrooke uses tubular bells as well as percussion and celesta create various bell-like effects, and it is intriguing to listen to each version consecutively. (It is highly unlikely that Rachmaninov knew anything about Holbrooke's version when he composed his own.) Completed in 1903, and dedicated to Sir Edward Elgar, it was not performed until 1906 at the Birmingham Musical Festival. George Lowe devoted several pages to the work in his study of Holbrooke, pointing out the exotic effects, such as a section when "the various instruments drop out of action one by one in order to effect a beautifully graduated diminuendo till the tone is reduced to a *pppp* chord for strings alone with which the Prelude impressively closes."[3] He also gives a clear idea of the immensity of the forces required to perform the piece:

> The orchestra employed is a large one: strings (60), 3 flutes, 1 piccolo, 2 clarinets, 1 bass clarinet, 2 bassoons, 1 contra bassoon, 4 horns (8 if possible), 4 trumpets, 3 trombones, 1 contra bass tuba, 1 euphonium, 3 tympani, 1 big drum, 1 side drum, 1 tenor drum, 1 stier horn in B, large cymbals, small cymbals, 1 large gong, 1 small gong, 1 xylophone, tubular bells and 4 mushroom bells, 1 handbell in C, glockenspiel, triangle, tambourine, large jingles, small jingles, soprano concertina, 2 harps, 2 grand pianofortes, and celesta, and where the woodwind, strings, and euphonium can be increased, it is the wish of the composer that this should be done. The chorus desired is one from 300 to 500 voices.[4]

During performances, Holbrooke wanted the auditorium "to be in semi-darkness, the light, if possible, to be kept entirely from the audience and centered on the singers and orchestra."[5] Ernest Newman's explanatory notes, which were printed alongside the Breitkopf und Härtel edition of the score, pointed out with regard to the prelude alone, "The orchestral colour is again laid on in its strongest tints; the bells and gong are frequently used.... The climax is overwhelming."[6]

Berenice

He pointed to my garments; they were muddy and clotted with gore. I spoke not, and he took me gently by the hand: it was indented with the impress of human nails. He directed my attention to some object against the wall. I looked at it for some minutes: it was a spade.[1]

"How is it that from beauty I have derived a type of unloveliness?"[2] asks the hero of "Berenice" (1835). The answer is that, just as racism is a form of aestheticism gone wrong, love can degenerate into obsession. "Berenice" is a masterly analysis of both obsession and aestheticism. Egaeus is an archetypal aesthete born into an aesthetic family. The prototype of Joris-Karl Huysmans' Des Esseintes in *À Rebours,* he is a recluse, devoted to art and thought. The family mansion of Egaeus is also Poe's blueprint for Des Esseintes' home, Fontenay. It contains frescoes, tapestries, a gallery of antique paintings, unusual "chiselling of some buttresses in the armory" and a library filled with books that reflect the reputation of his family as a "race of visionaries."[3] Egaeus is actually born in the library of this ivory tower, and he spends his youth in it, a recluse navigating an interior world of the mind. He calls it his "palace of imagination."[4] He loiters away his boyhood and dissipates his youth in reverie. "The realities of the world affected me as visions, and as visions only, while the wild ideas of the land of dreams became, in turn, not the material of my everyday existence, but in very deed that existence utterly and solely in itself."[5]

Similarly, Des Esseintes is lost to the world beyond his aesthetic domain. His aim is to bury himself in a hermit's cell, far away from the world of everyday affairs and devote his life to aesthetic contemplation. He devotes extreme care to the color scheme of his environment. He arranges his library of ancient Roman classics against walls of blue and orange, and Huysmans discusses his literary tastes and prejudices in minute detail. Significantly, Des Esseintes has his edition of Poe's "Adventures of Arthur Gordon Pym," as he calls it, "bound in sea-green morocco" and printed on paper bearing a seagull watermark.[6] (Huysmans writes: "Poe possessed those close affinities of spirit that fulfilled the demands Des Esseintes had formulated in the course of his meditations."[7]) He arranges one of his rooms as a ship's cabin, with clockwork fish to swim past fake portholes, but voyages solely in the mind. He experiments with an organ of perfume, he delights in a tortoise whose shell is encrusted with jewels, he contemplates paintings and etchings, and on one occasion attempts an expedition to England but feels that he has sufficiently imagined what London will be like through the descriptions of Dickens, and deems the reality is irrelevant. He therefore returns home before leaving France. Just like Egaeus, the outside world, for Des Esseintes, is only a mere "vision." His reality is the world of his imagination.

Poe was the first author to describe the modern aesthete. Via Baudelaire's enthusiasm for and translation of his work, Egaeus became the model for all later manifestations of the type, from Baudelaire himself to Des Esseintes and ultimately, Oscar Wilde's Dorian Gray, whose aesthetic lifestyle inspired several film adaptations.

It is this decadent introversion that Huysmans transferred to the hero of his *À Rebours*. And we see it in Wilde's homage to that novel, for Dorian similarly studies the art of perfumes, distilling heavy-scented oils and "burning odorous gums from the East." He devotes himself to music, in "a long, latticed room with a vermillion-and-gold ceiling and walls of olive-green lacquer."[8] He is fascinated by embroideries and tapestries, and has a "special passion for ecclesiastical vestments."[9] Whereas Des Esseintes binds Poe's novel in sea-green morocco, Dorian procures nine editions of *À Rebours* (Wilde never mentions the book by title but this is obviously the book he means) and has them bound in different colors "so that they might suit his various moods."[10]

But Egaeus is more than an aesthete, he is also an obsessive. He terms himself a monomaniac, and we experience the kind of obsessional states experienced by Egaeus in Huysmans' detailed descriptions of paintings by Gustave Moreau and Odilon Redon. In 1883, Redon provided an unnerving charcoal and chalk response to "Berenice" featuring a pair of clenched teeth radiating light, which floats before a bookcase. The effect is certainly bizarre but to the more ironical temperament it might suggest an advertisement for denture cleaning fluid. Harry Clarke responded to Redon's image in his own 1919 illustration of the story, which features a positive flotilla of such teeth, floating across the black background. This dental diagonal divides the picture's two representation of Egaeus, who simultaneously stares out at the viewer from the bottom left hand corner and violates the body of Berenice in the top right hand corner.

Des Esseintes is equally obsessed by Poe. After reading Poe's stories, "whose mirages of hallucination and effects of terror Odilon Redon seemed to have transferred into a sister art, he would rub his eyes and gaze at a radiant figure that, amid these frenzied designs, rose calm and serene, a figure of *Melancholia,* seated before a round sun's disk, on rocks, in an attitude of depression and despondency."[11] Des Esseintes would "meditate for hours"[12] upon these images just as Egaeus muses "for long unwearied hours, with my attention riveted to some frivolous device on the margin or in the typography of a book," or becomes absorbed "for the better part of a summer's day, in the quaint shadow falling aslant upon the tapestry or upon the floor."[13] Egaeus can lose himself in the contemplation of a flame, the perfume of a flower, or repeat a word to himself until it loses its meaning. But he also has a more troubling obsession: the teeth of his beloved cousin Berenice. Even when she is not in the room with him, the memory of her teeth remains in his brain:

> The teeth!—the teeth!—they were here, and there, and everywhere, and visibly and palpably before me; long, narrow, and excessively white, with the pale lips writhing about them, as in the very moment of their first terrible development.[14]

Berenice falls ill and enters an epileptic state, and is prepared for burial. But, as is so often the case in Poe's tales, she is buried alive. Egaeus also enters a cataleptic state and forgets what he does next, which is to dig up the still living body and remove all her teeth, which he puts in a box for safe-keeping. His hand and clothing bears evidence of the struggle, but when he realizes what he has done, he is horrified. So too were the original readers of Poe's tale, which had the kind of impact upon them that a film like *The Silence of the Lambs* had on audiences in the 1990s. Like that film's anti-hero Hannibal Lecter (Anthony Hopkins), Egaeus is also prototype serial killer. Both characters are aesthetes, both are obsessional and both indulge in particularly gruesome forms of human mutilation. Admittedly, Egaeus is not a cannibal, like Lecter, and is filled with remorse, unlike Gray, whose implied homosexuality was, at the time, perhaps even more of a crime than murder; but Egaeus' remorse does not change what he actually does in the story. Whereas Lecter, in one of the film's famous lines, admits, "A census taker once tried to test me. I ate his liver with some fava beans and a nice Chianti," Egaeus emerges from his cousin's tomb with garments muddy and clotted with gore,"[15] and places the teeth in a little box for future contemplation, though in his horror over the atrocity it falls from his grasp and the teeth scatter all over the floor. He no doubt intended to contemplate these much as Hurd Hatfield's Dorian Gray contemplates his coin collection in Albert Lewin's 1945 film adaptation of Wilde's famous story. As Dorian carefully catalogues his collection, he discusses the corruption of his soul to Lowell Gilmore's Basil Hallward, whose portrait of him molders away in his nursery upstairs. Poe, however, does not tell us what happens to Egaeus after he discovers his cousin's teeth in the box. Though Dario Argento included the horrific imagery of "Berenice" in *Two Evil Eyes* (1990), and Geoffrey Ciani adapted the tale in his 2004 movie of dubious taste, a film such as *The Picture of Dorian Gray* actually comes closer to the spirit of Poe's poetic exploration of aesthetics, obsession and remorse.

The Black Cat

I am above the weakness of seeking to establish a sequence of cause and effect.[1]

"The Black Cat," from 1843, describes the psychological destruction and eventual criminal conviction of the narrator, a victim of alcoholism, perversity and, perhaps, the supernatural agency of a black cat. In fact, the story should be called "The Black Cats" as there are two animals, one the possible double of the other. The first is tortured and eventually killed by the narrator. The second causes his downfall. From the very beginning of the story, the narrator insists that he is not mad, and, indeed, the eloquence with which he relates his history seems to support this claim. While Poe incorporates the possibility of a supernatural explanation, and provides a traditional Christian context, his main aim is to offer a psychological interpretation of the events described.

The cat which the narrator originally loves is called Pluto, after the god of the underworld, and by giving the cat this name, Poe exploits the traditional association of black cats with witches. But Pluto, despite his name, is not the emissary of evil. It is drink that drives the narrator to attack the animal that was once his friend. Goaded by the cat's indifference to him one evening, he catches it and cuts one of its eyes from its socket. But can alcohol alone have been responsible for such an atrocity?

One of Poe's most resonant psychological observations is the impulse to which he would devote "The Imp of the Perverse" two years later: the impulse to do what we know to be wrong for no other reason than that we know we should not. In "The Black Cat," he observes, "Philosophy takes no account of this impulse," but the narrator (and Poe by implication) is convinced that it is "one of the primitive impulses of the human heart." It is the expression of "the unfathomable longing of the soul to *vex itself*."[2] As we have seen, such self-destructive tendencies anticipate Freud's death instinct, which lies beyond the Pleasure Principle. The death wish might even be said to be a psychological expression of the molecular tension caused by the binding of pure energy at the molecular level, and the impulse of energy to return to its original state. Whatever the justification for this theory (Freud was reacting to his own perplexity at the horrors of the first world war and desperately attempting to find a psychological motivation for such a catastrophe), it nonetheless attempts to address scientifically the impulse isolated intuitively by Poe in "The Black Cat," "The Tell-Tale Heart" and "The Imp of the Perverse." In Wagner's *Ring* Cycle, Wotan similarly rises to the tragic height of willing his own destruction.

Christianity, of course, would offer a more traditional moral explanation, arguing that Poe's narrator is the victim of Satanic pride, a demonic will to defy God, and Poe indeed includes this as a possible explanation. The narrator describes how he hangs his beloved pet, "hung it *because* I knew that it had loved me, and *because* I felt it had given me no reason of offence;—hung it *because* I knew that in so doing I was committing a sin—a deadly sin that would so jeopardize my immortal soul as to place it—if such a thing were possible—even beyond the reach of the infinite mercy of the Most Merciful and Most Terrible God."[3] But Poe does not leave it at that. The Christian framework is overwhelmed by the psychological one. When the narrator blinds the cat in a drunken rage, he metaphorically blinds his own psychological insight, but he does not blind his moral conscience, as is sometimes claimed, for he remains fully aware of the enormity of his crimes. He blushes, he burns, he shudders when he describes them, and if he were mad or morally incapable, he would surely feel no remorse. That he has not cut himself off from moral responsibility is made clear the following morning when, after a fire that destroys his house, the image of a hanged cat is "graven in *bas-relief* upon the white surface"[4] of a remaining wall. This phenomenon is explained scientifically, but the psychological implication (expressed in symbolically supernatural terms) is more to the point, indicating that the moral conscience of the narrator is haunting him. Poe does not discuss how the fire started, and we are left to decide if it was merely an accident, or if the narrator himself was responsible. Given the self-destructive tendencies of the man, it would seem likely that it was the latter.

When Pluto's double appears and befriends the narrator, the patch of white fur on the animal's breast eventually develops into the image of a gallows. Understandably, the narrator loathes this double, though there is no hard evidence that the new animal has anything to do with Pluto. The connection may well be made entirely in the narrator's mind, but doubles are traditionally harbingers of death (a trope Poe explores in more detail in "William Wilson"). Having killed Pluto, the narrator now murders his wife, who drives him to the deed by her patience and affection for him. He buries an axe in her brain and walls her up, but fails to realize he has also walled up the cat. When the police call to investigate the disappearance of his wife, the spirit of perversity again guides his actions. At the moment of his victory over the authorities, he gives himself away. He detains the officers of the law and comments on how excellently well-constructed the house is. He raps his cane on the brickwork behind which stands the body of his wife, and this summons the ghostly cry of the cat—the narrator's avenging conscience and the symbol of his own death wish. His final claim is that it was the cat—Pluto's double—who seduced him into murder, but the guilt is entirely his own, the motivation, despite the Christian context of the tale, entirely psychological.

This psychological interpretation of the events in the story was followed by director Dwain Esper in *Maniac* (1934). It is ironic that this film, now regarded as one of the worst ever made, is nonetheless one of the handful of movies that actually dramatizes the main events of Poe's famous tale. It is certainly a much more faithful adaptation of Poe's tale than Universal's *The Black Cat*, made the same year and starring Boris Karloff and Bela Lugosi, not to mention a second Universal version from 1941, with Lugosi and Basil Rathbone. With four screenwriters, whose combined comedy effort was "suggested" by Poe's story, it is predictable that this 1941 film and the story on which it was supposedly inspired have very little in common. Cats are, however, are always on the prowl in the creepy mansion owned by a wealthy elderly lady (played by Cecilia Loftus), whose relatives are all after her cash. As Broderick Crawford later jests, "Everything here is for the cats; that's why the place has gone to the dogs." The Black Cat of the title wanders around yowling, in an attempt to match Poe's much more frightening description, at the very end of his story, of "a howl—a wailing shriek, half of horror and half of triumph, such as might have arisen only out of hell, conjointly from the throats of the damned in their agony and of the demons that exult in the damnation." In fact, the cat's yowl in the film sounds as though it has been created by a voice artiste. It is also amusing to hear Lugosi, as an obvious red herring, call out, "Here, Kitty, Kitty," and Crawford even accuses Basil Rathbone's character of thinking he's Sherlock Holmes, which, of course, he was in other films. Perhaps the most striking image of the film is the moment when two candles on a mantlepiece and a roaring fire in the grate below suggest a cat's face with glowing eyes and open mouth, but the element that survived, admittedly only half intact from Poe's original, is when the real villain of the piece, played by Gladys Cooper, attempts to destroy the still living Anne Gwynne in the family crematorium (perhaps punningly pronounced Creamatorium" by the film's principle comedy lead Hugh Herbert). The Black Cat announces the fact, saves the girl and brings the picture to close.

A bizarre mixture of absurd melodrama and some graphically compelling images, *Maniac* blatantly parades that it has pseudo-psychoanalytic pretensions by intercutting the action with slabs of psychiatric text describing mania, dementia praecox, paranoia, etc., accompanied by the kind of palm court music that would be more appropriate for tea and cakes in a hotel foyer rather than this heady mix of murder, insanity, semi-nudity, and cat fights. There are indeed two cat fights—one between genuine felines, another between two women in a cellar, which is quite violent and, for the time, distinctly shocking. The story concerns Dr. Meirschultz (Horace B. Carpenter), who has developed a serum to bring the dead back to life. His unwilling assistant is Don Maxwell (William Woods), an ex-vaudeville artiste, whom Meirschultz has rescued from penury. Having revivified a black cat (suitably called Satan) and a female suicide victim, the good doctor suggests that his assistant kill *himself* so that he can replace his heart and bring him back to life too. Predictably, Maxwell declines this medical opportunity and shoots the doctor instead. He then uses his makeup skills to impersonate Meirschultz. It is now that Maxwell's delusions take hold of him, manifested by the superimposition of clutching hands and demonic figures, drawn from Benjamin Christensen's Swedish classic *Witchcraft Through the Ages* (1922). Plagiarism though this is, it is nonetheless rather effective.

As soon as Maxwell adopts his disguise, he is called upon to assist a Mrs. Buckley (played by one Phyllis Diller—though no relation to the comedienne of that name). Mrs. Buckley's husband believes himself to be the orang-outang in Poe's "The Murders in the Rue Morgue." To cure him of this delusion, Maxwell intends to inject a mere placebo of water into the unfortunate Buckley's veins. But he mixes up his hypodermics and injects him with the serum that brought the dead girl back to life. This enhances Buckley's delusions, and when the formerly revived suicide wanders by, Poe's "Rue Morgue" is compressed into a thirty-second abduction and ravishment.

When Mrs. Buckley subsequently discovers Meirschultz's dead body, Maxwell decides to wall it up in the cellar, following Poe's model. Previously, during a struggle with a black cat, one of the unfortunate creature's eyes had popped out. This too parallels what happens in Poe. The gruesome addition of Maxwell eating it like a grape has no basis in Poe. Unseen by our insane impersonator, the cat leaps through a gap in the uncompleted wall. The image of the dead doctor staring sightlessly through this gap is a compelling one, even in the context of the film's surrounding absurdity. In fact, the absurdity and crudity of the film as a whole actually enhances its attempt to depict mania. Mania *is* absurd and crude, after all. Eventually, the crime is discovered, and the police pull down the wall to reveal the black cat perching on the shoulders of the corpse.

Universal's two *Black Cat* films have only their titles in common with Poe's story, trading, as they do, on Poe's reputation rather than what he actually wrote. The visually striking 1934 version does, however, involve that central aspect of Poe's work: the death and resurrection of a beautiful woman, to which we will be returning with "Ligeia," "The Raven" and "Morella." Karloff's character, Hjalmar Poelzig, does not wall up his wife like Poe's narrator, but he does keep her corpse (and other women's corpses) in glass cases in his cellar. His opponent, played by Lugosi, is terrified of Poelzig's black cat, but that is about as far as this film's connection with Poe goes.

Roger Corman's adaptation, which forms the second of the three segments of *Tales of Terror* (1962), is a comic conflation of "The Black Cat" and "The Cask of Amontillado" in which Peter Lorre plays the alcoholic Montresor Herringbone opposite Vincent Price's effete wine connoisseur Fortunato Lucresi. Both stories share certain themes—alcohol and the walling of up of either a corpse or, as in the case of "The Cask of Amontillado," a living man—so it made perfect sense to unite the two. (The names Montresor, Fortunato and Lucresi are, however, all derived from "The Cask of Amontillado.") Black comedy also forms part of the scheme of things in Poe's "Amontillado" story, the dialogue being propelled along by means of dramatic irony and euphemism; but the theme of alcoholism, which is taken so seriously by Poe in "The Black Cat," is played for laughs by Corman and his cast, the wine-tasting duel at the center of the segment providing Price and Lorre with an opportunity to upstage each other in a delightfully knowing manner. Things become a little more macabre when Monstresor walls up both his wife and Fortunato, having learned that they indulged in a love affair behind his back, and this neatly personifies the union of the two Poe stories at work here. Later, a drink-induced nightmare causes Montresor to imagine that his wife and Fortunato have returned from the dead. They pull off Montresor's head and play ball with it in a strikingly distorted and vividly colored dream sequence. Faithfully following Poe's dénouement, two policeman call in the next scene, the cat wails, the wall is pulled down and the dreadful deed is discovered.

A 1966 film version directed by Harold Hoffman updated the story, but Poe's tales are usually too short to adapt comfortably to full-length feature films, which is why so many movie adaptations involve entirely original plots or at least original plot elements. Lucio Fulco, famous for his gore and splatter films, was no exception to this when he made his imaginative response to "The Black Cat" in his 1981 *Gatto Nero*, which maintains the main elements of the plot but amplifies the role of the cat into a positively demonic force.

This transforms the primarily psychological thrust of Poe's story into a more overtly supernatural experience. Fulco's black cat is truly a super-cat, with the power to open doors, hypnotize, and murder. Its owner, a reclusive former university professor (played by British horror film stalwart Patrick Magee), claims that his cat dominates him and has supernaturally responded to his suppressed hated of various people in the village where he lives; the cat then kills them for him. (This situation reverses the relationship of Dr. Caligari and the somnambulist Cesare in Robert Wiene's 1919 classic *The Cabinet of Dr. Caligari*.)

All in all this cat murders five people before the professor drugs it and hangs it, following Poe's formula. What happens next echoes the feline double that haunts Poe's narrator after he has committed the same atrocity. The professor's cat returns from the dead and involves the investigating police inspector (David Warbeck) in a near-fatal car accident. The cat then induces his owner to knock out an American photographer (Mimsy Farmer) who has discovered what's been going on. Thinking her dead, Miles walls her up; but the police arrive in time to hear the cat howl, pull down the wall and rescue the girl. The very corporeal ghost cat then leaps out of the cavity and advances with suitably malevolent tread on the professor, staring with green eyes and baring its fangs before we are shown the film's final image of a hanged cat etched onto the wall, just as Poe describes in his tale.

In 1990, Dario Argento and George A. Romero teamed for *Two Evil Eyes,* which conflated "The Black Cat" and Poe's "The Facts in the Case of M. Valdemar." The "Black Cat" segment follows Poe's tale reasonably faithfully, updating the action to late twentieth-century Pittsburgh. As we have seen, Poe adaptations frequently combine several stories under the banner of the main narrative, but by the time of *Two Evil Eyes,* this approach had become even more ironic and fragmented, somewhat in the manner of Andrew Sinclair's *The Facts in the Case of E.A. Poe*. Throughout that novel, Sinclair makes liberal use of quotations to convey how Pons' entire world is affected by his obsession. For example, Pons sees a sign "which merely advertised *The Black Pussycat*. The spirit of perverseness seized his soul, as it had Poe's hero who had hanged his ghastly pet. For it *is* one of the primitive sentiments which give direction to the character of man! As Pons pushed open the door of the *Pussycat,* he whispered to himself, 'Who has not, a hundred times, found himself committing a vile or a stupid action, for no other reason than because he knows he should *not*?'"[5] Similarly, Argento scatters references to other Poe stories throughout his telling of "The Black Cat." His protagonist (Harvey Kietel) is called Rod Usher. He is a forensic photographer, and we first encounter him recording a bizarre murder involving a pendulum blade that has cut a woman in two. A later crime involves the extraction of a murder victim's teeth—"all thirty-two of them"—echoing the grotesque conclusion of Poe's "Berenice" (though without any of that story's poetic concern with obsessional states of mind). A neighbor goes by the name of Mr. Pym, the namesake of the hero in Poe's only novel. But despite these interpolations and the contemporary setting, Argento trusts Poe's narrative while simultaneously losing no opportunity to make the horror of the events as bloody and graphic as possible. His only real narrative innovation appears in the dénouement, when we learn that the black cat has given birth while being walled up and that its offspring have eaten their way through the body of the walled-up girlfriend. Poe may have been a master of the grotesque but was never merely gratuitous, and this is the weakness of the film, for Argento's interest is primarily in bloody horror. Poe, even at his most horrific, was always primarily a psychologist, an aesthete.

The demonic associations of black cats is, of course, as old as folklore itself. The magistrate and witch-hunter Nicolas Remy, whose *Demonalatry* of 1595 became a standard work on the subject until more enlightened times, took a witch's ability to change her shape into a cat for granted:

> The witches of Dieuze, Vergaville, and Forbach, and nearly all who have hitherto been tried for this crime in the kingdom of Austria, and whose confession have come into my hands, have maintained that they changed themselves from men into cats as often as they wished to enter another man's house secretly at night. These statements are borne out and substantiated by the evidence of many who have reported that they have been attacked by witches in such shape; and the evidence has tallied in all respects with regard to the fact itself, the place, the persons, the time, and every circumstance and detail which could be required to establish complete proof. The case of Barbeline Rayel (Blanville, Jan. 1587) is quite recent. She confessed that she had transmuted herself into a cat, so that in that shape she might the more easily enter, and the more safely prowl about the house of Johannes Ludovicus: and that when she had done this, she found his two-year-old child and killed it by sprinkling over it a poison powder which she was carrying in her paw.[6]

Hammer films exploited this age-old association in *The Witches* (dir. Cyril Frankel, 1966), in which Gwen Ffrangcon-Davies' Nanny Rigg has her black cat familiar, Vesper. More intriguingly, Algernon Blackwood's 1908 short story "Ancient Sorceries" concerns an entire town of cat-people, who attempt to entice Vezin, the protagonist, to become one of them. A firm believer in reincarnation, Blackwood interprets Vezin's strange experiences as the result of "a very vivid revival of the memories of an earlier life, caused by coming into contact with the living forces still intense enough to hang about the place."[7] Blackwood's psychic investigator, Dr. John Silence, to whom Vezin tells his story, explains that Vezin's ancestors had lived in this town where scores of witches had been burned at the stake centuries before. The "cat-people" Vezin encounters are therefore echoes of this psychic memory, and Blackwood's description of them conveys exactly the sinister feline qualities of Poe's black cat and Fulco's well-trained animal. Blackwood describes the cool and calculating manner of cats as they watch their prey: "Positively, the town was muffled. Although the streets were paved with cobbles the people moved about silently, softly, with padded feet, like cats. Nothing made a noise. All was hushed, subdued, muted. The very voices were quiet, low-pitched like purring. [...]—an outward repose screening intense inner activity and purpose."[8] The daughter of the hotel proprietor, at whose establishment Vezin, stays is "a young girl, lithe and slim ... with sinuous grace, like a young panther."[9] Her mother seems like "an immense cat" with "some terrible dignity clothing her about that instantly recalled the girl's strange saying that she was a queen."[10]

Blackwood's story was combined with Poe's psychological approach in Val Lewton's *Cat People* (dir. Jacques Tourneur, 1942). In that film, the spirit, if not the plot and dramatic details of Poe's "The Black Cat" reached perhaps its most eloquent expression. Poe's narrator believes that his crimes were inspired by the cat, which we as readers know is merely the symbol of his own conscience. Alcohol, as Poe quite clearly points out, is the true devil in his story. He even calls it "the Fiend Intemperance."[11] The finale of the story rekindles the supernatural element, but without destroying the possible rational explanation of what has happened. Such ambiguity was masterfully exploited by Tourneur and Lewton in *Cat People*.

Simone Simon's Irene believes herself to be possessed by the spirit of her Serbian ancestors, who, legend has it, could turn themselves into cats. Simon's features are suitably kittenish for this to be a distinct possibility. She also wears a black fur coat, and is drawn to the similarly black-coated panther in the zoo. She likes to hear the sound of the lions roaring, which far from being frightening is "natural and soothing" to her. She also likes the dark, thinking it "friendly." But she is troubled by the legends of her Serbian village; its inhabitants were shape-shifting witches. Birds are terrified of her, as she discovers in a pet shop where her boyfriend, Oliver (Kent Smith), exchanges the cat he has bought for her, for a canary. The animals in the shop "seem to know who's not right," according to the pet shop owner. Irene and Oliver fall in love and are married, but a strange cat-like woman (Elizabeth Russell) calls Irene "sister" (in Serbian) during their wedding celebration. Though Oliver insists that Irene is the victim of a fairy tale, she nonetheless feels that there is "something evil" in her soul. She is terrified that she will turn into a cat if she consummates her marriage. A psychiatrist (Tom Conway) tries a rational approach to a cure, but Irene's jealousy of Oliver's work-colleague, Alice (Jane Randolph), sets the curse in motion. Tourneur is careful not to be too explicit in his imagery, and though a dream sequence of animated cats eloquently suggests that her problem is purely psychological, there are other moments in the celebrated sequences in which Alice is pursued by Irena, when we are never quite sure if Irene turns into a cat or not. A final encounter with the psychiatrist suggests more forcefully that she does, and this ambiguity fully reflects the ambiguous tone of Poe's tale, even though the story itself is quite different.

"The Black Cat" has had less influence on music, though it did inspire one of Hollywood's most notable early film scores for the 1934 Universal adaptation. Director Edgar G. Ulmer was keen to have his masterpiece accompanied by classical music, and his musical director Heinz Roemheld compiled a score from classical excerpts. This approach was not so different from the technique that was applied in the so-called "silent" era, but the almost continuous music score of *The Black Cat* is unusual in early sound film, which often exploited the new opportunity to use sound effects and dialogue *without* music. (Tod Browning's *Dracula,* released in 1931, is a good example of this approach, and, indeed, silence but for the scuttling of armadillos and howling wolves would have been very unnerving to an audience used to wall-to-wall music in silent films.) Consequently, in the first cue alone, Roemheld managed to conflate Liszt's B minor piano sonata, Tchaikovsky's *Romeo and Juliet* Overture, and a Liszt Hungarian Rhapsody.

"The Black Cat" has also been given a curiously gravelly recitation on the Poe album *Closed on Account of Rabies,* by the Californian avant garde musician Diamanda Galás. Effectively accompanied by an understated lute improvisation, her speaking voice fully lives up to the reputation of being capable of the most unnerving vocal terror when singing. For her operatic trilogy "Masque of the Red Death," she does just that, using Poe's title as a metaphor for AIDS—a gruesome pleasure yet to come.

The Cask of Amontillado

"I forget your arms."
"A huge human foot d'or, in a field azure; the foot crushes a serpent rampant whose fangs are imbedded in the heel."
"And the motto?"
"Nemo me impune lacessit."[1]

Poe scholars have suggested that this revenge story from 1846 had its origins in a literary spat between Poe and writer-politician Thomas Dunn English (1819–1902); they had fallen out over a minor scandal regarding some of Poe's letters, and had even come to blows over the affair. English had then written a novel called *1844—or The Power of S.F.*, a story of political intrigue. S.F. stands for the name of a secret organization called "Startled Falcons," which attempts to influence the outcome of a presidential election, and one of the characters in the novel, Marmaduke Hammerhead, is described as "a hack journalist with 'broad, low, receding, and deformed forehead,' author of the 'Black Crow.'"[2] "This was obviously intended as a caricature of Poe, whom English further defamed by making Hammerhead a drunkard. And to add insult to injury, in the end Hammerhead goes mad. This was too much for Poe who responded in kind with his classic revenge story of Montresor, who lures the bibulous and arrogant Fortunato to the catacombs of his palazzo where he promptly walls him up. Poe makes various references to English's novel in the text, the opening lines of which, as Kenneth Silverman suggests,[3] fully expresses Poe's sense of outrage over English's attack upon him: "The thousand injuries of Fortunato I had borne as best I could; but when he ventured upon insult, I vowed revenge."[4] However, the precise cause of the squabble between Fortunato and Montresor is not revealed.

Another source for the story may have been Edward Bulwer-Lytton's hugely successful 1834 novel *The Last Days of Pompeii,* which Poe mentioned in his review of the author's *Rienzi* in 1836. In Poe's opinion, *Rienzi* was "vastly superior,"[5] but this does not rule out the possibility of Poe having been impressed by the following scene from *Pompeii* in which the sorcerer Arbaces exacts revenge in a manner very similar to that of Montresor:

> The light trembled against a small door deep set in the wall, and guarded strongly by many plates and bindings of iron, that intersected the rough and dark wood. From his girdle Arbaces now drew a small ring, holding three or four short but strong keys. Oh, how beat the griping heart of Calenus, as he heard the rusty wards growl, as if resenting the admission to the treasures they guarded!
>
> "Enter, my friend," said Arbaces, "while I hold the lamp on high, that thou mayst glut thine eyes on the yellow heaps."
>
> The impatient Calenus did not wait to be twice invited; he hastened towards the aperture. Scarce had he crossed the threshold, when the strong hand of Arbaces plunged him forwards. "The word shall never be spoken!" said the Egyptian, with a loud exultant laugh, and closed the door upon the priest.
>
> Calenus had been precipitated down several steps, but not feeling at the moment the pain of his fall, he sprung up again to the door, and beating at it fiercely with his clenched fist, he cried aloud in what seemed more a beast's howl than a human voice, so keen was his agony and despair: "Oh, release me, release me, and I will ask no gold!"
>
> The words but imperfectly penetrated the massive door, and Arbaces again laughed. Then, stamping his foot violently, rejoined, perhaps to give vent to his long-stifled passions:
>
> "All the gold of Dalmatia," cried he, "will not buy thee a crust of bread. Starve, wretch! Thy dying groans will never wake even the echo of these vast halls; nor will the air ever reveal, as thou gnawest, in thy desperate famine, thy flesh from thy bones, that so perishes the man who threatened, and could have undone, Arbaces! Farewell!"
>
> "Oh, pity—mercy! Inhuman villain; was it for this..."
>
> The rest of the sentence was lost to the ear of Arbaces as he passed backward along the dim hall. A toad, plump and bloated, lay unmoving before his path; the rays of the lamp fell upon its unshaped hideousness and red upward eye. Arbaces turned aside that he might not harm it.

"Thou art loathsome and obscene," he muttered, "but thou canst not injure me; therefore thou art safe in my path."

The cries of Calenus, dulled and choked by the barrier that confined him, yet faintly reached the ear of the Egyptian. He paused and listened intently.

"This is unfortunate," thought he; "for I cannot sail till that voice is dumb for ever. My stores and treasures lie, not in yon dungeon it is true, but in the opposite wing. My slaves, as they move them, must not hear his voice. But what fear of that? In three days, if he still survive, his accents, by my father's beard, must be weak enough, then!—no, they could not pierce even through his tomb. By Isis, it is cold!—I long for a deep draught of the spiced Falernian."

With that the remorseless Egyptian drew his gown closer round him, and resought the upper air.[6]

Whereas Arbaces exploits his victim's greed, Montresor exploits Fortunato's pride in his own wine connoisseurship to lure him to his vaults. He explains that he has some doubts about the authenticity of a pipe of Amontillado he has recently acquired, but seeing that Fortunato is too busy to help him ascertain its authenticity, he had thought of asking one Luchesi about it.

"Luchesi cannot tell Amontillado from Sherry," Fortunato insists, a reply which at once informs us that Fortunato knows very little about wine, Amontillado being a form of sherry itself. That Montresor encounters him during the carnival season dressed in a fool's cap and bells only enhances our impression of Fortunato as a braggart who is all bluster. He is also a fool in another way, for he allows Montresor to manipulate his vanity as a means to lure him to his destruction. (It was this foolishness that Odilon Redon attempted to convey in his 1883 charcoal drawing of Fortunato. As Fred Leeman has observed, Redon draws the viewer's attention to Fortunato's "lack of willpower" by means of his "passive expression, slumped shoulder, and the tilted angle of his neck," but he concludes, "The story's moral implication of this fatal tumble into the depths of one's own weakness is completely absent from Redon's interpretation."[7])

There is considerably more dialogue in "The Cask of Amontillado" than in many of Poe's other stories, and it is the dialogue that conveys much of the story's irony: Fortunato has a bad cough, but insists that he will not die of a cough. "True—true," replies Montresor, having quite a different fate in mind for him. Montresor also drinks to Fortunato's long life, so that he may suffer all the more in his dungeon doom. Fortunato makes a strange gesticulation, which Montresor fails to understand. "You do not comprehend?" Fortunato inquires. "Then you are not of the brotherhood." By this he means the Masonic brotherhood, but Montresor produces a trowel, assuring Fortunato that he is indeed a mason. "You jest," Fortunato exclaims uneasily, unaware that Montresor is being quite literal, the trowel being the instrument of his revenge.[8]

Oscar Wilde may well have had the next detail of this story in mind when writing the scene between Dorian Gray and the chemist Alan Campbell in *The Picture of Dorian Gray*. In Wilde's novel, Dorian needs Campbell's help to dispose of the body of Basil Hallward, whom Dorian has just killed. He at first asks Campbell to help him out of friendship. (They have presumably been lovers in the past.) Campbell refuses. Dorian "entreats" him. Again, Campbell refuses. Dorian then gets what he wants by blackmailing him. Similarly, in "The Cask of Amontillado," Montresor gives Fortunato several opportunities to escape. When Fortunato starts to cough in the damp air of the catacombs, Montresor offers to return to the surface. Fortunato refuses. Montresor repeats the offer just as they are approaching the niche in which he plans to wall up his enemy alive. "Once more let me *implore* you to return. No? Then I must positively leave you. But I must first render you all the little attentions in my power."[9]

As we have seen with regard to "Berenice," Wilde was greatly impressed by the aesthetic example of Poe, and here we see something of Poe's ironic black comedy influencing Wilde's own dialogue. It is well-known that Wilde admired Poe, referring to him as a "Lord of Romance."[10] He was also keen to include Poe in his choice of "The Best Hundred Books" at the request of the *Pall Mall Gazette* in February 1886, and referred to the American writer as a "marvellous lord of rhythmic expression" who is worthy of elbowing out Southey.[11]

The dramatic dialogue of "The Cask of Amontillado" lends itself readily to dramatic rendition, and Roger Corman accordingly used some of Poe's lines in his comedy version of "The Black Cat" in *Tales of Terror*. A drinking duel between Peter Lorre's Montresor and Vincent Price's Fortunato gives both actors a thirstily grasped opportunity to upstage each other, Price's elegant connoisseur indulging in much pretentious lip-smacking and cheek-sucking. Lorre offers him a glass of Amontillado with the toast "To your long life," (an ironic line if ever there was one) and when Fortunato is being walled up, he utters, "An excellent jest. We'll have many a good laugh about it," almost as Poe wrote it. He also cries out "For the love of God" as in the text, to which Lorre authentically responds, "Yes, for the love of God." And it is here that the previously black comic tone is momentarily undercut by the grimness of the situation.

Ric White's 2006 film *Nightmares from the Mind of Poe* included a faithful dramatization of the story, placing it within the context of Poe's own life—hence its New England setting. It begins with Poe (played by White) explaining the origins of his tale in 1846:

> Madness. There is another subject I know well. I have always been extremely nervous to an unusual degree. I have gone through bouts of drinking, opium and depression with blackouts and temporary loss of sanity. Perhaps that is how I am able to tap into the deep recesses of the soul where man has rarely ventured to go, writing of strange and terrible images seldom allowed to stalk the printed page. Nightmares were often the place where I conjured up desires for things that I could not have in life. Perhaps that is why John Allan [Poe's unloved and unloving foster father] appears so often in them. He is easy to recognize. He is the one usually tormented, tortured and exposed of. He is Fortunato in "The Cask of Amontillado."

To celebrate the bicentenary of Poe's birth in 2009, Mario Cavalli added another short, atmospherically photographed film adaptation with Anton Blake and Patrick Monckton as Monstresor and Fortunato. Filmed as a period piece with a handheld camera throughout, and exploiting some effective use of double-exposure, this faithful dramatization similarly draws on Poe's dialogue with remarkably few alterations.

The story also inspired an orchestral overture by Josef Holbrooke. *Amontillado*, Op. 123, perhaps inadvisedly uses a full orchestra to convey the unnervingly intimate environment of the story, which might have been better served by a chamber ensemble, but it does attempt to describe the various moods of the tale, from a rousing carnival atmosphere at the beginning in contrast to the macabre conclusion.

"The Cask of Amontillado" also resonated in the world of progressive rock music, forming the basis of the fourth track of the Alan Parsons Project's 1975 album *Tales of Mystery and Imagination*. Beginning as a rather mournful ballad, with piano accompaniment, the "Cask of Amontillado" track contrasts the characters of Fortunato and

Montresor by having them sung by two different voices (John Miles and Terry Sylvester). Poe's words, however, are not used, Eric Woolfson and Alan Parsons' lyrics neatly summing up the story in four stanzas, accompanied by choir and orchestra alongside the usual rock ensemble.

Montresor gets away with his crime, relating his story fifty years after the event, and so is presumably an old man by that stage. The final lines are still as shocking as they were in 1846, especially the ironic—even blasphemous—concluding words, "*In pace requiescat*!"

The City in the Sea

While from a proud tower in the town
Death looks gigantically down.[1]

This striking Gothic poem from 1845 is a frightening evocation of Death's subaqueous domain. Poe frequently used sea imagery as a metaphor for eternity and the eerie stillness of Death's domain. *The Narrative of Arthur Gordon Pym* is his most sustained use of it, but it also pervades the individual poems. The tragic love story of "Annabel Lee," for example, takes place in "a kingdom by the sea." "Nor demons down under the sea / Can ever dissever my soul from the soul / Of Annabel Lee," who dwells "In the sepulchre there by the sea— / In her tomb by the sounding sea."[2] In "Dreamland" Poe describes a land "Out of SPACE out of TIME," in which there are "seas without a shore / Seas that restlessly aspire," "Lakes that endlessly outspread / Their lone waters—lone and dead— / Their still waters—still and chilly / With the snows of the lolling lily."[3] In "To F—" the memory of the beloved is "Like some enchanted far-off isle / In some tumultuous sea,"[4] while in "Eulalie" the poet describes his soul as "a stagnant tide."[5] "Silence" suggests that "There is a twofold *Silence*—sea and shore— / Body and soul,"[6] and in "The Lake. To—" Poe describes a man who contemplates suicide. He stares at "the terror of the lone lake" and remarks how "Death was in that poisonous wave."

> And in its gulf a fitting grave
> For him who thence could solace bring
> To his lone imagining—
> Whose solitary soul could make
> An Eden of that dim like.[7]

"The City in the Sea" may well have been inspired by Coleridge's "Kubla Khan," which is not surprising given the influence Coleridge had in general on Poe's imagination. Kenneth Silverman has pointed out Poe's flagrant plagiarism of Coleridge in his prefatory poem "Letter to Mr. --" of 1831:

> Even more surprisingly derivative is [Poe's] climactic formulation of the aim of poetry:
>> A poem, in my opinion, is opposed to a work of science by having, for its *immediate* object, pleasure, not truth...
>
> At the same time that he scorned those who claimed the opinions of others as their own, Edgar filched this definition verbatim from Coleridge's *Biographia Literaria*. There Coleridge defines poetry as a kind of composition
>> which is opposed to works of science, by proposing for its *immediate* object pleasure, not truth.[8]

Whereas Kubla Khan decrees the stately pleasure dome of Xanadu, Poe's vision has Death dwelling in a "proud tower" in the midst of his sinister city in the sea, the turrets of which "seem pendulous in air." Like Xanadu, which is situated where "Alph, the sacred river, ran / Through caverns measureless to man / Down to a sunless sea,"[9] Poe's city is situated beneath a "lurid sea." "No rays from the holy heaven come down / On the long night-time of that town."[10] Instead, an eerie light from the sea itself illuminates the turrets and towers. The pleasure dome of Kubla Khan is mirrored by Poe's lines "Up domes—up spires—up kingly halls."[11] Where Coleridge describes a "lifeless ocean,"[12] Poe informs us that "No ripples curl" upon the surface of Death's ocean, which is "a wilderness of glass" and is "hideously serene."[13] In "Silence—A Fable," Poe's other fabulous description of terrifying stillness, he describes how the lilies, which crowd in the river Zaïre, "signed one unto the other in the solemnity of their desolation."[14] Similarly, in "The City in the Sea," the senseless, timeless, emotionless existence of the dead is superbly expressed in succinct, short lines: "Resignedly beneath the sky / The melancholy waters lie." "There open fanes and gaping graves / Yawn level with the luminous waves." And over all, Death looks "gigantically down" from his "proud tower in the town."[15] The imagery of a proud tower may derive from the ninth canto in the second book of Spencer's *Faery Queen*:

> Nor that proud Tower of Troy, tho richly gilt,
> From which young Hector's Blood by cruel Greeks was spilt.[16]

It aptly went on to form the title of Barbara Tuchman's popular history of European civilization in the years leading up to the first world war. Indeed, Poe had pointed the way to that ghastly feast of death with the poem's imagery of "gaping graves" and its final Götterdämmerung:

> The waves have now a redder glow—
> The hours are breathing faint and low—
> And when, amid no earthy moans,
> Down, down that town shall settle hence,
> Hell, rising from a thousand thrones,
> Shall do it reverence.[17]

In her postscript to *The Proud Tower*, Tuchman again summons Poe's title and the oceanic imagery of the poem to add a mythic resonance to her description of the catastrophe of 1914:

> The four years that followed were, as Graham Wallas wrote, "four years of the most intense and heroic effort the human race has ever made." When the effort was over, illusions and enthusiasms possible up to 1914 slowly sank beneath a sea of massive disillusionment. For the price it had paid, humanity's major gain was a painful view of its own limitations.
> The proud tower built up through the great age of European civilization was an edifice of grandeur and passion, of riches and beauty and dark cellars.[18]

"The City in the Sea" also inspired the third movement of Josef Holbrooke's much less well-known Choral Dramatic Symphony, op. 48. Subtitled "Homage to E.A. Poe," the first movement is a setting of Poe's "The Haunted Palace," the second his "Hymn," and the finale, "The Valley of Unrest." Begun in 1902, the whole thing took Holbrooke another six years to complete, when he conducted himself at the Leeds Choral Union. In his study of Holbrooke, George Lowe is again keen to defend his hero from charges of unhealthy morbidity:

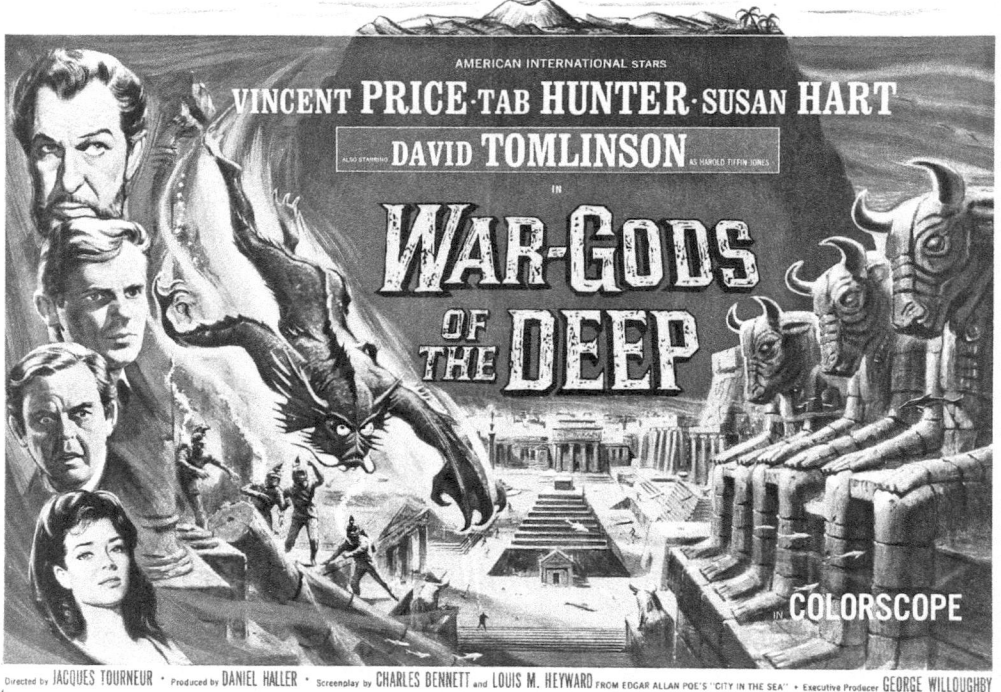

The visually misleading poster for a retitled version of *City in the Sea* (dir. Jacques Tourneur, 1965).

> The music, too, in spite of its occasional uncanny quality, is both healthy and sane. Its very boldness saves it from the reproach of being designated as morbid in fancy. Fantastic it may be, but fantasy is a legitimate generator of art. The orchestral painting excellently realises for us the subjects of the poems, and the many beauties of tonal effect that the composer achieves in this work show how quick his brain is to conceive the aesthetic effect of certain instrumental combinations. It is only on very rare occasions, in his music, that he lapses into mere noise or is guilty of writing ugly passages, though, as we have seen, he has not always been clear of that offence. How much more often, however, does Richard Strauss, the composer to whom Holbrooke has so often been compared, deserve censure in this respect![19]

Lowe nonetheless describes the poem as "a weird and dismal thing," before discussing the music:

> A short instrumental prelude introduces the vocal portion of the movement, and it contains a theme, moderate misterioso, which becomes of great importance later. This is given out by strings. The ensuing solo for bass voice is broad and vigorous in character, with a wave-like movement from the orchestra.... This movement is vastly superior vocally to either of the sections that preceded it, not only in the cleverness of its technique, but also in the beauty of its thematic material and in the variety of its harmonic colouring. Many parts of it rank with the composer's most inspired work, and many parts of it are also of extreme difficulty for the singers.[20]

There is also a rather disappointing film from 1965, the title of which casually removed Poe's definite article. *City in the Sea*, inevitably starring Vincent Price, was directed by the great Jacques Tourneur, who sadly despaired of this embarrassing late addition to his previous canon of excellence. The screenplay by Charles Bennett and Louis M. Heyward takes some of Poe's imagery but makes an entirely different story out of it in the manner of a Jules Verne adventure. This is understandable to a point, given Verne's indebtedness to Poe, but the film only does justice to the poem in those sections in which Price reads Poe's lines with a sonorous luster that not even Basil Rathbone could match in his well-known recording of the poem.

Alas, the rest of the film fails to live up to the promise of Price's recital, eloquently juxtaposed though it is with shots of a surging sea and a corpse washed ashore in a storm. It is also known as *War-Gods of the Deep*; it seems likely that Brian Hayles exploited his memory of this film when scripting the later *Warlords of Atlantis* (dir. Kevin Connor, 1978), the American title of which bears the almost identical title of *War-Lords of the Deep*. Both films feature similar events and ideas, including a nineteenth-century setting, gill-men, and a totalitarian system of government. In the case of *Warlords of Atlantis* it is the "superior" Atlanteans (in fact Martians who have crashlanded in the Atlantic Ocean) who control the underwater world. In *The City in the Sea*, Vincent Price's despotic smuggler captain is in charge. When he is asked if the underwater city in which he and his men have been trapped for over a century is Atlantis, he replies: "Atlantis? Perhaps; a name is as good as another."

Warlords of Atlantis begins on board a rather smart yacht. *City in the Sea* has a more traditionally Gothic exposition set in a gloomy cliffside Victorian house. In it, David Tomlinson (playing an artist called Harold), his annoying pet hen (trans-sexually named Herbert), and Tab Hunter (as the even more annoying Ben) discover a secret passage which leads to the captain's underwater world. The sailors in *Warlords* enter the world of Atlantis via a whirlpool; Harold and Ben enter the city in the sea by the same method. This all helps to explain how one of Harold's books and, perhaps more importantly, Susan Hart's Jill have gone missing; and we later learn that it was one of the underwater gill-men, whom the captain commands, who has stolen the book and abducted the girl. (The captain, having seen Harold's portrait of Jill in the stolen book, is astonished at her resemblance to his dead wife Beatrice, a full-size oil painting of whom he keeps in his study. Hence Jill's abduction.) The captain later explains how he and his men arrived in this terrible place: All smugglers, they escaped from excise men through the same route as Harold and Herbert. No one gets old beneath the waves, due to the special quality of the air down there, but they have become so acclimatized to the atmosphere that they can't make their way back to the surface because light would destroy them, like vampires. Unfortunately, a volcano threatens their survival. So they are all trapped. The gill-men once inhabited the City in the Sea but have become a degenerate race. As the captain puts it, "They believe that I am Death. Death looking gigantically down from my tower—and they're right—and I am!"

Poe's poem has another opportunity to shine when we learn that previous raids have given them an opportunity to steal a copy of the first British edition of Poe's work from 1847. Price obliges with a few more beautifully modulated lines, but despite their appropriateness to their new situation, the others decide that "the poem is a coincidence," which, from the point of view of the script, it is. Boris Karloff was also due to appear in this turgid affair, but was replaced by John Le Mesurier at the last moment. He plays a confused, elderly priest, who reveals an escape route for the protagonists but decides to face his end down below. There is also a sinister tolling bell, which announces executions, so perhaps Poe's "The Bells" also made its contribution to the script.

A conceivably more inept tribute to this poem is Debbie Harry's performance of the text, accompanied by the Jazz Passengers on the CD *Closed on Account of Rabies*. Saxophone and brass seem inappropriate for Poe's somber imagery, and attractive though Harry's voice is, this jazzy setting has little to offer as an illumination of one of Poe's most fascinating poems. The Swiss-German band The Ocean also adapted this text to open their 2006 album *Aeolian*, which requires an *aficionado* of heavy metal fully to appreciate, so here is a review of it by xXCannibalHate666Xx, from the Encyclopaedia Metallum:

> The Ocean have come up with a sludge album that can stand up to the massive Mastodon sweeping the metal world. This German 8 piece has released powerhouse CDs back to back that have absolutely crushed listeners. Aeolian being my favorite of the two, I have decided that it is high time they get a hail for their amazing work.
>
> The CD starts out with a battery of drums and solid bass and guitars synched to perfection. The vocal attacks on this CD are so brutal I would rather classify the vocals as Death Metal, but they fit the onslaught very well. The time signatures in some of the songs have a very Meshuggah feel to them, but while keeping the sludge feel to the whole CD. The guitars throughout the CD are very technical and at times just old school heavy as hell, skull-crushing chords. The bass is very clear in all the tracks so you get that Crowbar, Down, and Pantera feel that categorizes Sludge Metal.[21]

The Colloquy of Monos and Una *and* The Conversation of Eiros and Charmion

I breathed no longer, The pulses were still. The heart ceased to beat.[1]

Both "Colloquy" (1841) and its companion piece, "The Conversation of Eiros and Charmion" (1839) are examples of Poe's conflation of science fiction and metaphysics. In "Colloquy," the process of dying is explored not so much from a physiological point of view as from one that anticipated Einstein's theory of relativity. Poe attempts to describe timeless eternity here, having his main character, Monos, give an account of his death to the disembodied spirit of his beloved Una. Kenneth Silverman observes that the names of the two protagonists reflect Poe's concern with unity in this dialogue. Indeed, the piece reiterates Poe's belief that all things are one—an idea he elaborated further in his essay *Eureka* (1848). In "Colloquy," Poe is concerned with the "erasure of the boundary between existence and inexistence," and with the aim to express "a distinction without a difference."[2] Silverman interprets this from his biographical perspective as an expression of Poe's own need to believe that "you can never lose yourself or your home or the people you love."[3]

The ecological concerns of the story are also remarkably prescient, and predate the comparable ecological agenda of Wagner's *Ring* Cycle which, with its allegory of the exploitation of natural resources in the quest for power, is often regarded as the most significant nineteenth-century precursor to our own climate change anxieties. It is unlikely, though possible, that "The Colloquy" made its mark on Wagner's imagination at the time he wrote the text of *Das Rheingold* in 1852, but we are on firmer ground to remark on the fact that both artists were responding to the same concerns about industrialization and over-population. Poe is also mentioned in the diary of Wagner's wife Cosima as one of the authors with whom they were both familiar: On December 27, 1870, Cosima compared Poe (unfavorably) with E.T.A. Hoffmann: "I place Hoffmann distinctly above Edgar [Allan] Poe, although the latter has more art, because H. is a poet."[4] Unfair to Poe though this comment is (not to mention inaccurate), it does provide evidence that the Wagners were aware of the American writer (even if at a considerably later date than the conception of *Das Rheingold*). This, in itself, is a significant connection, given the joint interest Baudelaire had in Poe and Wagner, and the consequent impact of both Poe and Wagner on the French symbolist movement. The ecological element in Poe's "Colloquy" is expressed in Monos' doubts about "the propriety of the term 'improvement,' as applied to the progress of our civilization." He is of the opinion that humanity "should have taught our race to submit to natural laws, rather than attempt their control."[5]

As in Wagner's vision of a Golden Age before the dwarf Alberich created civilization out of natural resources, Monos laments the lost "holy, august and blissful days when blue rivers ran undammed, between hills unhewn, into far forest solitudes, primeval, odorous, and unexplored."[6] Intriguingly, in Patrice Chéreau's 1976 centennial production of the *Ring* cycle at Bayreuth, the river Rhine was dammed to drive a hydro-electric power station. Monos also rails at the nineteenth-century world of commerce and progress, which Poe similarly despised, criticizing its proto–McDonald's ethic as "wild attempts at an omniprevalent Democracy."[7] He criticizes "huge smoking cities" and "rectangular obscenities," and laments how "green leaves shrank before the hot breath of furnaces."[8] Such a state of affairs informed eco-science fiction films of the 1970s such as *Silent Running* (dir. Douglas Trumbull, 1972), in which the sole survivor of a space mission carrying the remains of Earth's flora goes quietly mad, having refused orders to abort the mission.

In the earlier piece, "The Conversation of Eiros and Charmion," Poe imagines the end of the world. A comet is discovered to be on a collision course with the Earth; the chemical consequences cause the Earth to burst into flames. Again, the cataclysm is described by the disembodied spirits of two of the catastrophe's victims, who meet after the deaths of their bodies on the other side of time. There was nothing particularly new about the idea of a comet destroying the Earth: Poe was exploiting the theories of the doomsday prophet William Miller (1782–1849), whose theories of the end of the world were very much in vogue in the 1830s. However, Poe's metaphysical context give the story a different perspective, and his troubling account of phenomena caused by the proximity of the comet to Earth anticipates the science fiction tropes of mutation and abnormality, which were later articulated by writers such as John Wyndham in *The Day of the Triffids* (1951) and *The Midwich Cuckoos* (1957) along with the films they inspired. Poe describes flowers that grow to unnatural dimensions: "our vegetation had perceptibly altered…. A wild luxuriance of foliage, utterly unknown before, burst upon every vegetable thing."[9] A comet also nearly destroys the world in Tove Jansson's 1946 children's classic *Comet in Moominland:*

> The comet was diving headlong to earth. It was exactly forty-two minutes and four seconds past eight. There was a rush of air as if a million rockets were being let off at once, and the

Kirsten Dunst as Justine in *Melancholia* (dir. Lars von Trier, 2011).

earth shook.... If it had come a tiny bit nearer to the earth I am quite sure that none of us would be here now. But it just gave a whisk of its tail and swept off to another solar system far away, and has never been seen since.¹⁰

    Hollywood has also flirted with destruction from above, most recently in *Armageddon* (dir. Michael Bay, 1998), in which Bruce Willis prevents an asteroid from colliding with Earth, and *Deep Impact* (dir. Mimi Leder, 1998), in which Man takes on a comet; but the closest Poe's "Conversation" has been to a cinematic adaptation is Lars von Trier's 2011 *Melancholia,* in which the Earth really is destroyed, though by another planet rather than a comet. Von Trier's approach is more psychological (and sociological) than descriptive, but he does show us the cataclysm. The finale, accompanied by the prelude to Wagner's *Tristan und Isolde,* certainly parallels Poe's final paragraph:

> For a moment there was a wild lurid light alone, visiting and penetrating all things, Then— let us bow down, Charmion, before the excessive majesty of the great God!—then, there came a shouting and pervading sound, as if from the mouth itself of HIM; while the whole incumbent mass of ether in which we existed, burst at once into a species of intense flame, for whose surpassing brilliancy and all-fervid heat even the angels in the high Heaven of pure knowledge have no name. Thus ended all.¹¹

    Although von Trier does not follow Poe's suggestion that the souls of his protagonists survive in another sphere, his film is much closer in mood to the poetic effect of Poe's

"Conversation," discussing, as it does, the melancholia of the situation (the planet which eventually collides with Earth is even called "Melancholia"), rather than the mere heroics it inspires.

A Descent into the Maelström

The edge of the whirl was represented by a broad belt of gleaming spray; but no particle of this slipped into the mouth of the terrific funnel, whose interior, as far as the eye could fathom it, was a smooth, shining, and jet-black wall of water, inclined to the horizon at an angle of some forty-five degrees, speeding dizzily round and round with a swaying and sweltering motion, and sending forth to the winds an appalling voice, half shriek, half roar, such as not even the mighty cataract of Niagara ever lifts up in its agony to Heaven.[1]

This terrifying account of a boat and its crew being sucked into a giant funnel of water inspired a short ballet in 1986, with characteristically repetitious arpeggios from the minimalist composer Philip Glass. Until then, "A Descent into the Maelström," first published in 1841, had been rather neglected by other media, though it inspired some notable illustrations by Rackham, Clarke and Sätty. Josef Holbrooke also wrote an orchestral piece based on the story in the early twentieth century, now, alas, lost forever. Other than these exceptions, the influence of "A Descent into the Maelström" has been lateral. Not only was Poe's imagery of the giant water funnel borrowed by *Warlords of Atlantis*, when Doug McClure, Peter Gilmore and crew are sucked down to the underwater kingdom of Atlantis, but Poe's Maelström also informed the spiraling Black Hole that sucks towards it a spaceship in Walt Disney's film of that name (dir. Gary Nelson, 1979). It even lurks behind the vortex imagery of the television series, *The Time Tunnel,* not to mention the "tunnel" effect of the opening titles of the BBC's *Doctor Who* series. It could even be said to have cast its spell over the spiral imagery of Alfred Hitchcock's *Vertigo* (1958).

The story is primarily Poe's anticipation of the disaster movie—a graphic account of an overwhelming catastrophe and of the narrator's ingenuity in escaping it by means of ratiocination. Off the coast of Norway, the giant Maelström sucks all who pass into its voracious maw—a black hole indeed (Poe makes great effect of the ebony walls of this watery monstrosity). By careful observation of the centrifugal events around him, the narrator is able to escape from his ordeal.

But there are other ways of interpreting this imagery. Poe begins his account with a quotation from the English philosopher and divine, Joseph Glanville (1636–1680): "The ways of God in Nature, as in Providence, are not as *our* ways; nor are the models that we frame in any way commensurate to the vastness, profundity, and unsearchableness of His works, *which have a depth in them greater than the well of Democritus.*" This is drawn from Glanville's *Against Confidence in Philosophy and Matters of Speculation* (1676), an essay that also makes its presence felt in "Ligeia." Poe altered (or merely misremembered) the original text, which should read: "The ways of God in *Nature* (as in *Providence*) are not as *ours* are: Nor are the models we frame any way commensurate to the vastness and profundity of his Works, which have a *Depth* in them greater than the *Well of Democritus.*"[2]

Descent into the Time Tunnel: the 1960s science fiction television series, created by Irwin Allen, starring James Darren and Robert Colbert.

Since Poe frames this story with a quotation about God and the *depth* of his work, one is tempted to suggest a more mystical meaning to the imagery of the vortex.

Philip Glass' rippling arpeggios not only provide an appropriate musical symbol for the circular motion of the spiraling waters, but might also be equated with a more esoteric interpretation. In the number named "Tranquility," the music of which rather belies its sub-section title, he combines an ascending bass line with a descending arpeggio top line, and this brings to mind the upward and downward spiral forms discussed by Jill Purce in her study of *The Mystic Spiral*. There, she discusses the vortex meditation technique taught to the poet W.B. Yeats by the occultist Samuel MacGregor Mathers:

> Two conical spirals are visualized, whirling in opposite directions, one going up through the body and the other coming down to meet it. The two worlds, still distinct, are mirror images: the soul of man, the *materia prima* (below) reflects the universal spirit (above). The goal of the meditation is the union or inner penetration of these two.[3]

By being drawn into and then lifted out of the vortex, Poe's seafaring Norwegian hero achieves an approximation of the penetration Purse describes here. Indeed, the sailor confesses to a meditative calm when he realizes he has been drawn into the vortex: "It may appear strange, but now, when we were in the very jaws of the gulf, I felt more composed than when we were only approaching it."[4] He goes even further by admitting that he felt at the time "how magnificent a thing it was to die in such a manner, and how foolish to think of so paltry a consideration as my own individual life, in view of so wonderful a manifestation of God's power. I do believe that I blushed with shame when this idea crossed my mind. After a little while I became possessed with the keenest curiosity about the whirl itself. I positively felt a *wish* to explore its depths, even at the sacrifice I was going to make."[5]

This story is therefore more than a bold example of ratiocination in perilous circumstances. Poe's use of Glanville at the outset of the tale implies a transcendental meaning. The ways of God are not our ways, and they have a profundity greater than the Well of Democritus. By descending part of the way into that Well, and then rising to the surface, the sailor, by his own admission, moves closer to God, and achieves the kind of interpenetration of vortexes described by Purce. Yeats referred to these vortexes as "gyres" and believed, as his biographer Richard Ellmann put it, "that he had discovered in this figure of interpenetrating gyres the archetypal pattern which is mirrored and remirrored by all life, by all movements of civilization or mind or nature. Man or movement is conceived of as moving from left to right and then from right to left; no sooner is the fullest expansion of the objective cone reached than the counter-movement towards the fullest expansion of the subjective cone begins, is conceived of as moving from left to right and then from right to left; no sooner is the fullest expansion of the objective cone reached than the counter-movement towards the fullest expansion of the subjective cone begins."[6] Yeats, whose dismissive opinion of Poe was that he was "vulgar," would have found good reason in "A Descent into the Maelström" to have been less critical.

The Devil in the Belfry

> *He was really the most finicky little personage that had ever been seen in Vondervotteimittiss. His countenance was of a dark snuff-color, and he had a long hooked nose, pea eyes, a wide mouth, and an excellent set of teeth, which latter he seemed anxious of displaying, as he was grinning from ear to ear.*[1]

"The Devil in the Belfry," first published in 1839, is set in a dull, dreary, conformist Dutch town call Vondervotteimittiss, where everything runs like clockwork. It is populated by respectably dull citizens, each of whom has mantel-pieces carved with timepieces and cabbages. The town council is formed of "very little, round, oily, intelligent men, with big saucer eyes and fat double chins."[2] They ensure that nothing changes, for, in the words of their three important resolutions, "it is wrong to alter the good old course of things," "There is nothing tolerable out of Vondervotteimittiss," and "We will stick by our clocks and our cabbages."[3]

But all this platitudinous predictability is soon to change with the appearance of a curious little man with a "grinning, an audacious and sinister kind of face," who leaps into the belfry of the town's prized seven-faced clock and causes it to chime thirteen. This is sympathetically echoed by all the clocks in the homes of the good citizens. Back in the belfry, the curious little man—who is the devil, of course—pulls the bell-rope with his teeth and scrapes at a fiddle on his lap (thus making everyone dance to the devil's tune).

Though Roger Corman's *Tales of Terror* and *The Raven* were hardly faithful adaptations, Corman nevertheless rescued Poe from his popular image as an exclusively morbid writer, for nothing could be further from the truth. As Edmund Wilson suggested, Poe's reputation as a writer of "horror" is really a misunderstanding. After all, Poe never used the word "Horror" to describe his tales, but rather defined them as tales of the "Grotesque," the "Arabesque," of "Mystery," and, perhaps most important of all, of "Imagination."

> The real significance of Poe's short stories does not lie in what they purport to relate. Many are confessedly dreams; and, as with dreams, though they seem absurd, their effect on our emotions is serious. And even those that pretend to the logic and the exactitude of actual narratives are, nevertheless, also dreams. [No one] understood better than Poe that the deepest psychological truth may be rendered through phantasmagoria. Even the realistic stories of Poe are, in fact, only phantasmagoria of a more circumstantial kind.... Poe's mentality was a rare synthesis.... He had elements in him that corresponded with the indefiniteness of music, and the exactitude of mathematics.[4]

This "indefiniteness," a word which Poe himself used to describe the poetic effect of "true music," resonated with Debussy, whose own approach to composition seems uncannily to have been anticipated by Poe's belief that "suggested indefiniteness" brings about "a definiteness of vague and therefore spiritual effect."[5] Debussy was also intrigued by Poe's schizophrenic literary persona, which was able to leap from writing an absurd little conceit such as "The Devil in the Belfry" to the sonorously Gothic gloom of "The Fall of the House of Usher." From their very inception, Debussy's plans for an opera based on "The Fall of the House of Usher" were coupled with a complimentary "satyr" play based on "The Devil in the Belfry." He worked on them simultaneously: "I go to sleep with them, and on waking find either the sombre melancholy of the one or the derisive laughter of the other."[6]

Debussy began to write his own libretto for both operas, but really only got as far as drafting a scenario for "The Devil in the Belfry," which nonetheless expanded upon Poe's original quite significantly. He added a bell-ringer and his son, and a town mayor and his daughter. After making the clock strike thirteen and having everyone dance to his violin, the devil leads the townspeople to a canal, which he jumps into, and it looks as though the good townspeople will all follow him. But "like a good conductor cutting off the end of a piece," he stops them with one shake of his bow.[7] We then move to a second scene set in an Italian village. Whereas Debussy intended the first part to be primarily orchestral, this second part was to be primarily choral. Robert Orledge paraphrases the action as follows:

The girl's fiancé, Jean, remains outside the devil's influence through his love for her, but she disowns him and laughs in his face. When the devil prevents him from approaching her, Jean climbs the belfry and prays aloud. As the bells ring out, it is the devil's turn to shudder. He lays his hands on the villagers and they fall down one by one: the light fades…. Then everything returns to normal, presumably as it was in the first tableau, for the "raging river" becomes a canal again. The bells ring midday as usual: the villagers check their watches and are greatly relieved when they can stop counting at twelve.[8]

Alas, the only thing to emerge from Debussy's long-considered project is a short piano piece derived from sketches for the opera. He planned many intriguing developments in the music, which are now lost for ever. Of particular note were his thoughts on how to use the choir. Criticizing Wagner's use of the choir for the townspeople of Nuremburg in *Die Meistersinger* ("They are an army solidly organised in the German manner, marching in rows"), he wanted to create "something more scattered and split up, something both more nimble and intangible, something apparently inorganic, and yet with underlying control—a real human crowd in which each voice is free and in which all the voices combined nevertheless produce the impression of an ensemble."[9] Having said that, *Le Diable dans le beffroi* would have been Debussy's *Meistersinger*, just as *La Chute de la maison Usher* would have been his *Tristan und Isolde*. (Wagner similarly thought of *Meistersinger* and *Tristan* as complementary, even quoting music from *Tristan* at a crucial moment in his comic opera.) Wagner loomed large in Debussy's aesthetic, an influence he absorbed and atomized to create his own very different musical style, which is nonetheless shot through almost perpetually with echoes of Wagner's work,[10] and it is quite possible to compare the middle-class, complaisant Dutch setting of *Le Diable dans le beffroi*, its riot caused by music, and its devil who breaks all the social rules, with *Die Meistersinger*'s bürgherlich, Nuremburg setting, its similar riot at the end of Act II caused by Beckmesser's serenade, and its hero, Walther von Stolzing, who breaks the musical rules of the Meistersingers guild.

It remains intriguing that Poe's apparently lightweight little tale should have fascinated Debussy so much, but if one looks beyond the grotesque humor of the piece (Poe's cod–Dutch dialect and dubious puns), the underlying meaning is clear: Bourgeois conformity is stultifying and deadly, and we all need the devil (which one may interpret as innovation, change, development) to keep us on our toes if life is to mean anything at all. (This is very much the program behind Wagner's *Meistersinger*, and the meeting of Wagner and Poe at the crossroads of Debussy's art is a replay of Baudelaire's earlier infatuation with the Meister of Bayreuth and the Bard of Baltimore.)

Astonishingly, Poe's story about the necessity of change and the dangers of bourgeois complacency also anticipated the ideas of Søren Kierkegaard, whose treatise *The Sickness Unto Death* first appeared in 1849. In the third chapter of that work, Kierkegaard writes:

> There are very few men who live even only passably in the category of spirit; yea, there are not many even who merely make an attempt at this life, and most of those who do so, shy away. They have not learned to fear, they have not learned what "must" means, regardless, infinitely regardless of what it may be that comes to pass. Therefore they cannot endure what even to them seems a contradiction, and which as reflected from the world around them appears much more glaring, that to be concerned for one's own soul and to want to be spirit is a waste of time, yes, an inexcusable waste of time, which ought if possible to be punishable by law, at all events is punished by contempt and ridicule as a sort of treason against men,

as a forward madness which crazily fills up time with nothing.... At the same time they are Christians, tranquilized by the parson with regard to their salvation.[11]

Kierkegaard continues:

> Devoid of imagination, as the Philistine always is, he lives in a certain trivial province of experience as to how things go, what is possible, what usually occurs. Thus the Philistine has lost his self and God. For in order to be aware of oneself and God, imagination must enable a man to soar higher than the misty precinct of the probable, it must wrench one out of this and, by making possible that which transcends the *quantum satis* of every experience, it must teach him to hope and fear, or to fear and hope. But imagination the Philistine does not possess, he does not want to have it, he abhors it. So here there is no help. And if sometimes reality helps by tenors which transcend the parrot-wisdom of trivial experience, then philistinism despairs—that is, it becomes manifest that it was in despair. It lacks the possibility of faith in order by God's help to be able to deliver itself from certain destruction.
>
> Fatalism and determinism, however, have enough imagination to despair of possibility, and have possibility enough to discover impossibility. Philistinism tranquilizes itself in the trivial, being equally in despair whether things go well or ill. Fatalism or determinism lacks the possibility of relaxing and soothing, of tempering necessity, and so it lacks possibility as assuagement. Philistinism lacks possibility as revival from spiritlessness. For philistinism thinks it is in control of possibility, it thinks that when it has decoyed this prodigious elasticity into the field of probability or into the mad-house it holds it a prisoner; it carries possibility around like a prisoner in the cage of the probable, shows it off, imagines itself to be the master, does not take note that precisely thereby it has taken itself captive to be the slave of spiritlessness and to be the most pitiful of all things. For with the audacity of despair that man soared aloft who ran wild in possibility; but crushed down by despair that man strains himself against existence to whom everything has become necessary. But philistinism spiritlessly celebrates its triumph.[12]

Via Kierkegaard, we might therefore connect the *meaning* if not the details of Poe's "The Devil in the Belfry" to Dennis Potter's once banned 1976 television drama *Brimstone and Treacle,* which is introduced by two superscriptions, one of which derives from the third problem of Kierkegaard's *Fear and Trembling* of 1843: "There resides infinitely more good in the demonic man than in the trivial man." The BBC recognized the brilliance of *Brimstone and Treacle* but it also realized that the sight of a handsome young devil raping a disabled girl was "likely to outrage viewers to a degree that its importance as a play does not support."[13] For the original television production, Michael Kitchen played the devil, Denholm Elliott was Mr. Bates and Patricia Lawrence played his wife. For the subsequent 1987 film version, Sting took over from Kitchen. Elliott remained; Mrs. Bates, now played by Joan Plowright, had her first name changed to Norma to emphasize (entirely unnecessarily) the surname's resemblance to the psychopath in Hitchcock's *Psycho*. As W. Stephen Gilbert puts it, "Richard Loncraine's direction pulled out all the stops, swathing the original sitcom-land setting in Hammer Films sensibility."[14]

Potter's play is still shocking, but only if one views the rape scene in isolation rather than as a demonstration of the Kierkegaard quotation. A devil appears from nowhere and ingratiates himself into the family of Pattie Bates, the disabled girl. He flatters her downtrodden mother and exposes the lukewarm, half-hearted, rather grumpy racist ideas of her father, who eventually concedes, having been shown the error of his ways, "I simply want the world to stop where it is, and go back a bit. There is no God," he moans, "and there are no miracles." But there are, even if "only" the miracles of art and imagination. The devil then quotes from Bishop Henry King's *Exequy,* which was not only a favorite text of Potter's but also, as we have seen, prefaces Poe's "The Assignation," and further suggests the presence of Poe's ghost behind this remarkable drama. After the rape, Pattie miraculously recovers (one might regard the process as an extreme form of shock therapy) and, in rapid flashback, we learn what happened: Shocked by discovering her father in bed with her best friend, Pattie ran from the friend's flat and was hit by a passing car. The devil, therefore, rather like Goethe's Mephistopheles in *Faust,* is "Part of that Power which would / Do evil constantly, and constantly does good."[15] Hence the Kirkegaarde quotation at the top of the play. The Bates family, like the inhabitants of Vondervotteimmitiss, are dead to themselves, locked in triviality, philistinism, hypocrisy and sickness unto death. Only the devil can bring them back to life.

Debussy understood this implicitly. Indeed, in a letter to André Messager, written when he was working on the libretto of *Le diable dans le beffroi,* he described the devil as "an ironical and cruel devil, much more of a devil than that sort of red-hot brimstoned clown which we illogically regard as traditional. I should also like to destroy the idea of the devil as the spirit of evil! He is more simply the spirit of contradiction and it is he perhaps who whispers to those who do not think like everybody else?"[16] The use of the word "brimstoned" again suggests Potter's ironic use of the phrase "Brimstone and Treacle." The devil whispers to non-conformists everywhere.

The Domain of Arnheim, or The Landscape Garden

No definition had spoken of the landscape-gardener as of the poet; it seemed to my friend that the creation of the landscape-garden offered to the proper Muse the most magnificent of opportunities.[1]

Poe regarded "The Domain of Arnheim" as one of his best writings, and one which "expresses *much of my soul*."[2] But being a relatively abstract aesthetic disquisition on beauty and the imagination, it has never been one of his most popular tales. Neither has it inspired a specific film adaptation. Though unsurprising, this is nonetheless disappointing, as film would serve its highly descriptive, indeed transcendental passages very well.

"The Domain of Arnheim" has no traditional narrative structure; it is more of an essay than a story, concerning a man called Ellison who uses his fortune to create an ideal landscape park. Poe may have had in mind the English millionaire William Beckford (1760–1844), whose immense Gothic Fonthill Abbey Poe mentions in the piece. The purpose of Ellison's domain is to create nothing less than paradise on earth, and paradise, like the story itself, is without plot or character, without even emotion, for all these suggest conflict of some sort. In Arnheim, all is perfect and therefore *void* of humans, though it is not inaccessible to humanity. Ellison makes sure of that by locating his Domain within reach of civilization.

According to Poe, "The original beauty [of nature] is never so great as that which may be introduced," but Ellison aims to combine nature and artifice to create "a nature which is not God, nor an emanation from God, but which still is nature in the sense of the handiwork of the angels that hover between man and God."[3] In effect, much of his approach is not so much landscaping as a Herculean task of tidying up:

> Not a dead branch—not a withered leaf—not a stray pebble—not a patch of the brown earth was anywhere visible. The crystal water welled up against the clean granite, or the unblemished moss, with a sharpness of outline that delighted while it bewildered the eye.[4]

There are also, as we shall see, elements of architectural artifice at work here. The distinctly surrealist perfection Poe describes, capturing the vivid unreality of a dream, made the title of the tale highly suitable for Magritte's disturbing mountain landscape of the same name from 1962. The German meaning of "Arnheim" is "Domain of the Eagles," and Magritte obliges by suggesting that an eagle is indeed emerging from the rocky summit of a mountain range, their slopes forming its wings. In the foreground, a nest shelters a clutch of eggs, presumably laid by this gigantic stone bird. Their meaning becomes clearer when we understand that Magritte interpreted Poe's story, and its association with his painting, as an allegory of the powers of the imagination, the eggs representing its offspring, so to speak: perception, understanding and aesthetic appreciation, but also anxieties and terrors. (The painting is deliberately disturbing in this respect.) The message is that the imagination is all that matters, for (in a Hegelian sense, derived from Kant) it is the mind that creates the world, rather than the other way round. Whatever reality is, we can only know it through our mental interpretation of it. It is what is going on in our minds rather than the phenomena to which we are responding, whatever they are, that is of most interest to us. The value of all landscape lies primarily in what we bring to it. The point of landscape is, as Poe puts it, "the display of imagination in the endless combining of forms of novel beauty." He points out that though the individual parts of nature are incomparable, natural landscapes are unable to compete with the human imagination: "[N]o such combination of scenery exists in nature as the painter of genius may produce. No such paradises are to be found in reality as have glowed on the canvas of Claude.... While the component parts may defy, individually, the highest skill of the artist, the arrangement of these parts will always be susceptible of improvement."[5]

Poe, and his symbolist-surrealist French followers, understood that we project our desires and emotions *onto* landscape. As Poe asks in one of his poems, "Is *all* we see or seem / But a dream within a dream?"[6] We create an imaginary ideal long before we find a correlative *location* on which to project it. Ellison travels for years to find the place he eventually transforms into Arnheim: "A thousand spots with which I was enraptured he rejected without hesitation,"[7] the narrator explains, and, in a very real sense, the realization of Ellison's ideal is irrelevant, for he has already created it in his mind. When we understand this, we also understand why Poe exerted such an influence on the decadent school at the turn of the nineteenth. For Des Esseintes, the neurasthenic hero of Huysmans' *À Rebours*, traveling anywhere is made redundant by his realization that his own imagination is far more powerful than anything beyond it, and that it is consequently the only environment in which he will not be disappointed. ("I must be out of my senses to have tried thus to repudiate my old settled convictions," Des Esseintes exclaims, "to have condemned the obedient figments of my imagination, to have believed like the veriest ninny in the necessity, the interest, the advantage of a trip abroad."[8]) All landscape art is already an abstraction of nature because it enshrines an imaginative ideal. It merely amplifies the emotional state of mind we bring to such scenes (not the other way round, for landscape itself is surely indifferent to the purpose of landscape art). And if natural phenomena were sufficient in themselves, there would be no need for artistic representations of them.

America's answer to Huysmans, Ben Hecht (1894–1964), created vivid interior landscapes in his novel *The Kingdom of Evil,* the once-banned sequel to his *Fantazius Mallare* of 1922. This novel, concerning the dream world of an exhausted onanist, creates an erotic topography, a sexualized, decadent version of Poe's vivid landscape descriptions in "The Domain of Arnheim":

> As the tremendous stalk wilts, toppling into an ever deeper and more sinister arc, its walls blaze with a continual sunset. Phosphorescent seas appear to run down its broken sides. The flames and banners of decay creep out of its roots and spread in slow and ghostly conflagrations toward its summit. Daily the spectacle of its dissolution increases. Alkaline pinks and excremental yellows, purples and lavenders like tumorous shadows; browns that float like colossal postules through seas of lemon; reds that ferment into wavering islands of cerise and salmon, that erupt into ulcerous hills of scarlets and magentas...
>
> But I no longer watch. Like a gigantic lamp the Kingdom sputters and expires. The stone hills move with carnelian shadows. The towers vanish in fanfares of color. The very earth swims in fulgurations. The veins of life burst and pour themselves out in a carnival of death.[9]

Landscape is only significant if it means something, if it expresses a state of mind or an emotion. Erotic obsessions inform the landscape of *The Kingdom of Evil.* For Poe, Arnheim was the paradise that is only realizable in death, in as much as death is our most powerful metaphor of imaginative freedom. Poe's rapturous description of Arnheim at the end of the story is his equivalent of Isolde's Liebestod at the end Wagner's *Tristan und Isolde.* Both evoke the imaginative and emotional freedom we can only really imagine being realized in death.

> There is a gush of entrancing melody; there is an oppressive sense of strange sweet odor,— there is a dream-like intermingling to the eye of tall slender Eastern trees—bosky shrubberies—flocks of golden and crimson birds—lily-fringed lakes—meadows of violets, tulips, poppies, hyacinths and tuberoses—long intertangled lines of silver streamlets—and, upspringing confusedly from amid all, a mass of semi-Gothic, semi-Saracenic architecture, sustaining itself as if by miracle in mid-air; glistening in the red sunlight with a hundred oriels, minarets, and pinnacles.[10]

The tale ends with references to Sylphs, Fairies, Genii, and Gnomes. Such perfection is indeed no place for humanity as we are constituted here on earth. If it *is* possible, it can only be attained in some other state where there are no limits to imaginative and emotional freedom.

"The Domain of Arnheim" also relates Poe to the aims of those nineteenth-century American artists of the Hudson River School who began by exploiting the nationalistic power of landscape and ended up by making landscapes metaphors of a specifically American paradise. Landscape, for them, suggested moral purity and social freedom. Similarly, the novelist James Fenimore Cooper's descriptions of a nature uncorrupted by European civilization, and of natives who dwell in it as therefore morally superior to modern city dwellers, is related to the Transcendentalism of Emerson and Thoreau, as well as inspiring a host of "Arnheim"-style canvases by the likes of Frederic E. Church, Albert Bierstadt and Thomas Cole, who, somewhat ironically, made a fortune out of their peons to "unexploited," un-commercialized nature. Cooper's descriptions of landscape, alongside the works of these painters, inevitably informed the landscape of the Hollywood Western, but if we compare Cooper's prose with European writers, we discover that what he is purveying is not so much a specific *national* landscape as an international Romantic model. Cooper wrote,

> The river was confined between high and cragged rocks, one of which impended above the spot where the canoe rested. As these, again, were surmounted by tall trees, which appeared to totter on the brows of the precipice, it gave to the stream the appearance of running through a deep and narrow dell. All beneath the fantastic limbs and ragged tree-tops, which were, here and there, dimly painted against the starry zenith, lay alike in shadowed obscurity.... It seemed, in truth, to be a spot devoted to seclusion, and the sisters imbibed a soothing impression of security as they gazed upon its romantic, though not unappealing beauties."[11]

That passage from *The Last of the Mohicans* does not differ materially from Walter Scott's description of Scottish savage scenery in *Waverley*:

> Advancing a few yards, and passing under the bridge which he had viewed with so much terror, the path ascended rapidly from the edge of the brook, and the glen widened into a silvan amphitheatre, waving with birch, young oaks, and hazels, with here and there a scattered yew-tree. The rocks now receded, but still shewed their grey and shaggy crests rising among the copse-wood. Still higher, rose eminences and peaks, some bare, others splintered into rocks and crags. At a short turning, the path, which had for some furlongs lost sight of the brook, suddenly placed Waverley in front of a romantic waterfall.[12]

Poe's Arnheim conforms to this model, though is more hallucinatory than either Cooper or Scott. None of these descriptions have much to do with reality, being imaginative terrains and specifically literary landscapes.

We are now familiar with Poe's relation to Wagner, and via Wagner's influence on the British composer Frederick Delius (1862–1934), we may find a musical equivalent of Poe's vision of Arnheim. Deeply informed by the example of Wagner's *Parsifal* (an opera that also includes a landscape of paradise in the Good Friday music of Act III), the most famous excerpt from Delius' opera *A Village Romeo and Juliet* (written in 1901) is "The Walk to the Paradise Garden," which is taken by the two lovers on their way to an inn of that name. In Petr Weigl's 1992 film adaptation of the opera, he chooses to depict the walk in terms of ravishing natural imagery: Shafts of sunlight pierce a glade in which a waterfall (along the lines of Walter Scott's "romantic" example) offers an opportunity for the Adam-and-Eve-style bathing of the two young lovers. Poe resonates even here.

The Duc De L'Omelette

"A golden cage bore the little winged wanderer, enamored, melting, indolent, to the Chaussée D'Antin, from its home in far Peru. From its queenly possessor La Bellissima, to the Duc De L'Omelette, six peers of the empire conveyed the happy bird."[1]

In this apparently comic tale, first published in 1832, the eponymous aristocrat finds himself in Hell and plays cards with the devil to escape; but is it really as flippant as it at first appears? Could this be the reverse of the apparently "serious" tale, which turns out to be a secret satire? It certainly contains an echo of Poe's "serious" imagery elsewhere.

Hell's furnishings include a Poe favorite: an ottoman, as does the bridal chamber in "Ligeia," and the narrator describes hell's decor in voluptuous terms that suggest the extravagant settings of both "Ligeia" and "The Assignation." Compare, for example, the "Duc De L'Omelette's" description of Hell: "Mussulman never dreamed of such when, drugged with opium, he tottered to a bed of poppies,"[2] with "Ligeia's" "I had become a bounden slave in the trammels of opium, and my labors and my orders had taken a coloring from my dreams."[3] In Hell, the Duc experiences "the glorious, the voluptuous, the never-dying melodies which pervaded that hall, as they passed filtered and transmuted through the alchemy of the enchanted window-panes." In fact, these sounds are the "howlings of the hopeless and the damned,"[4] but the description reminds one of "the low, melancholy music, whose origin was not to be discovered"[5] amongst the extravagant decor of "The Assignation." Hell is perfumed with "the ecstatic breath of those innumerable censers"[6]—an obviously ironic purple passage, which perhaps undermines the seemingly straight-faced "perfumes, reeking up from the strange convolute censers"[7] in "The Assignation," itself a possible parody in disguise!

David H. Hirsch argues that behind the comic parody of "The Duc De L'Omelette" lies a serious argument about the nature of the soul. Poe begins with the statement, "Keats fell by a criticism," a reference to Shelley's elegy to Keats, "Adonais," which argued that Keats was destroyed by the devastating review of his poem "Endymion." (The evidence in fact suggests that Keats was not actually that bothered by reviews,[8]) But Poe is no doubt referring here to Shelley's image of Keats' soul living posthumously "like a star," which "[b]eacons from the abode where the Eternal are."[9] Poe then observes that the Duc De L'Omelette "perished of an ortolan." What on earth can this mean? Hirsch argues that Poe is playing with the well-known metaphysical question of the chicken and the egg: "In 'The Duc,' the egg is metamorphosed into De L'Omelette, while the chicken is translated into the ortolan,"[10] which the Duc begins to eat at the beginning of the story, but which causes his death from a paroxysm of disgust, as it has no feathers and is not correctly wrapped. For Poe, therefore, the question is not so much whether the chicken or the egg came first, but what happens after death. The ortolan represents the soul; the Duc represents the body. The Duc cannot endure the idea of being a naked soul, stripped of the sensual self-indulgences of materialism. This is why he cannot endure the sight of the featherless bird. When the Duc finds himself in Hell, a suitable destination for so materialistic and sensual a man, the devil orders him to strip off his fine clothing—a metaphorical command to strip his soul bare. This the Duc refuses to do, and having beaten the devil at cards, he returns to his materialistic world.

Poe, in various cryptic ways, suggests that idea of metempsychosis—the reincarnation of the soul on its way to enlightenment: The ortolan is conveyed to the Duc in a golden cage, by six peers of the empire in far Peru. The peers are the six previous hosts of the soul, the golden cage a symbol of the exterior trappings and vanities of the physical world. The metaphysical complexity of this short caprice should not, therefore, be underestimated. "The Duc De L'Omelette" is a serious "comic" tale, much as "Metzengerstein" was intended as a comic "serious" tale—a parody of the German Gothic model, but simultaneously another example of Poe's fascination with the concept of metempsychosis.

The comic encounter with the devil in Hell may have influenced Bernard Shaw (an unqualified admirer of Poe) when he wrote his play *Man and Superman* (1903). In the famous "Don Juan in Hell" scene, the characters meet in Hell to discuss the advantages of the place (art, beauty, sensualism, enjoyment) over those of Heaven, which Shaw regarded as embodying reason, enlightenment and the evolution of the Life Force. This Life Force is another way of describing reincarnation, for the aim of the Life Force is to stimulate evolution so that a human brain will be able to understand itself. The Devil, conversely, has no interest in anything but having a good time: "It is true that the world cannot get on without me," says Shaw's Devil, "but it never gives me credit for that: in its heart it mistrusts and hates me. Its sympathies are all with misery, with poverty, with starvation of the body and of the heart. I call on it to sympathize with joy, with love, with happiness, with beauty."[11] Certainly, Poe's description of Hell is fully in accord with Shaw's. Poe describes it as being filled with paintings, statues and music. Such an environment should appeal to the Duc, and he acknowledges the fact in his final words: "If I weren't the Duc I would have no objection to being the devil."[12] But he prefers to return to their earthly manifestation, and certainly has no interest in stripping his soul bare to prepare for another incarnation.

Shaw summed up the connection in his laudatory article on Poe:

> America and England are wallowing in the sensuality which their immense increase of riches has placed within their reach. I do not blame them: sensuality is a very necessary and healthy and educative element in life. Unfortunately, it is ill-distributed, and our reading masses are looking on it and thinking about it and longing for it, and having precarious little holiday treats of it, instead of sharing it temperately and continuously, and ceasing to be preoccupied with it. When the distribution is better adjusted and the preoccupation ceases, there will be a noble reaction in favor of the great writers like Poe, who begin just where the world, the flesh, and the devil leave off.[13]

"The Duc De L'Omelette" shares its satiric approach with two other tales which were written alongside it in 1831, and together with "Metzengerstein" (the fourth of the group) they all demonstrate Poe's interest in the destiny of the soul. In "Bon Bon" a restauranteur discusses philosophy with the devil, who reveals that he eats souls as other men eat chef Pierre Bon-Bons' inestimable *fricandeaux* and *omelettes*. The devil's verdict: "Aristophanes—racy: Plato—exquisite."[14] There is something rather vampiric about this habit, and in "Loss of Breath," another story of this group, Poe might even be said to have foreseen the dilemma of the vampire Barnabas Collins in Tim Burton's Gothic comedy *Dark Shadows* (2012). Poe's narrator literally loses his breath, and consequently cannot die. After a series of picaresque experiences, he is condemned to death but survives his own hanging. "My body *was,* but I had no breath *to be,* suspended: and but for the knot under my left ear (which had the feeling of a military stock) I dare say I should have experienced very little inconvenience."[15] Barnabas Collins (played by Johnny Depp) is similarly indestructible, having no soul. When a 1970s descendent, perplexed by his old-fashioned mannerisms, asks, "Are you stoned?" Barnabas replies, "They tried stoning me, my dear. It did not work."

Eleonora

They who dream by day are cognizant of many things which escape those who dream only by night. In their gray visions they obtain glimpses of eternity, and thrill, in waking, to find they have been upon the verge of the great secret.[1]

I have included this short tale from 1842 in my selection because of its descriptions of landscape, which, like the rest of the story, were partly inspired by a reading of Shelley's elegy to the memory of Keats in "Adonais." It also reflects the illness of Poe's "child-bride" Virginia. Like her, Eleonora, the narrator's cousin, is hardly more than a child. The narrator and Eleonora live with Eleonora's mother, just as Poe and Virginia lived with *her* mother, Maria Clemm. In Shelley's poem, Adonais/Keats is similarly a "gentle child."[2] He is called "A Lost Angel of a ruined Paradise,"[3] and Shelley asks, "Why didst thou leave the trodden paths of men / Too soon [...]?"[4] But Adonais is not dead: He has become "a portion of the loveliness / Which once he made more lovely."[5] He has, indeed, become "made one with Nature."[6] Similarly, Poe's narrator (called Pyrros in the original version of the story) lives with Eleonora in the paradise of the Valley of Many-Colored Grass, until she, like Adonais—and like Poe's Virginia—dies. The image of "Many-Colored Grass" is also derived from Shelley, who refers to Life as being "like a dome of many-coloured glass [*sic*]" which "Stains the white radiance of Eternity, / Until Death tramples it into fragments."[7] Poe was also deeply inspired by the pastoral imagery of Shelley's poem, which refers to "faded violets, white, and pied, and blue"[8]; Poe transforms them into the "dark, eye-like violets" which colonize this paradise after Eleonora's death. Poe's valley also has "star-shaped flowers," and these echo Shelley's imagery when he speaks of "flowers of gentle breath; / Like incarnations of the stars, when splendour / Is changed to fragrance."[9]

Like Shelley's image of Keats, undying and forever remembered, Poe's Eleonora asks her lover never to leave the Valley of Many-Colored Grasses when she is dead, and to remain true to her memory. She, like Keats-in-Nature, becomes the spirit of the place. Pyrros, as the narrator was originally called, hears "the sounds of the swinging of the censers of the angels; and streams of holy perfume floated ever and ever about the valley; and at lone hours, when my heart beat heavily, the winds that bathed my brow came unto me laden with soft sighs; and indistinct murmurs filled the night air; and once—oh, but once only! I was awakened from a slumber, like the slumber of death, by the pressing of spiritual lips upon my own."[10]

However, unlike Poe's other revenant female characters Morella and Ligeia, Eleonora does not seek revenge when Pyrros breaks his vow, leaves the valley for the world of men and marries Ermengarde at the end of the story. Instead, rather enigmatically, she absolves him with the words, "in taking to thy passionate heart her who is Ermengarde, thou art absolved, for reasons which shall be made known to thee in Heaven, of vows unto Eleonora."[11] Free-love, in the manner espoused by Shelley himself, therefore seems to be the most important thing here; or, in the words of John Lennon, "All you need is love"— it doesn't so much matter with whom. Poe, however, was dissatisfied with the ending of his story, which no doubt reflects his own lack of conviction in the message. As Kenneth Silverman observes, Poe's true belief was that those we have loved and who become lost to us "can never be forgotten, and that however painful it may be to remember them, it is still more painful to give them up."[12] Indeed, Silverman used the phrase "Mournful and Never-ending Remembrance" from Poe's "The Philosophy of Composition"[13] as the title of his biography, because this was Poe's major theme.

But what makes "Eleonora" most interesting from the point of view of its influence on other media, is the imagery, which anticipates the psychedelia of the 1960s. Like two spaced-out hippies, Eleonora and Pyrros have dropped out from the ordinary world—not that they were ever really a part of it. They know nothing of the world beyond the valley, and love to gaze at "the pearly pebbles" of the "River of Silence," wandering over the carpet of "soft green grass, thick, short, perfectly even, and vanilla-perfumed, but so besprinkled throughout with the yellow buttercup, the white daisy, the purple violet, and the ruby-red asphodel, that its exceeding beauty spoke to our hearts in loud tones, of the love and of the glory of God."[14] This is flower-power 127 years before Woodstock, reminding the twenty-first century reader of the multi-colored world of "Lucy in the Sky with Diamonds" in George Dunning's Beatles film *Yellow Submarine* (1968). It also suggests the kind of hallucinations Aldous Huxley described in his study of mescalin in *The Doors of Perception* (1954), a work whose title lent its name to Jim Morrison's rock group, The Doors. "Mescalin raises all colours to a higher power.... Like mescalin takers, many mystics perceive supernaturally brilliant colours, not only with the inward eye, but even in the objective world around them."[15] In *Heaven and Hell* Huxley compares the "praeternatural colour" induced by mescalin with many images of paradise in mythology and religion: "'The land,' we read in the *Ramayana*, 'is watered by lakes with golden lotuses. There are rivers by thousands, full of leaves of the colour of sapphire and lapis lazuli; and the lakes, resplendent like the morning sun, are adored by golden beds of red lotus. The country all around is covered by jewels and precious stones, with gay beds of blue lotus, golden-petalled. Instead of sand, pearls, gems and gold form the banks of the rivers, which are overhung with trees of fire-bright gold. These trees perpetually bear flowers and fruit, give forth a sweet fragrance and abound with birds.'"[16]

Poe's Valley of Many Colored Grass is awash with "the glories of many millions of fragrant flowers."[17] And, anticipating the lyrics of Manfred Mann's 1966 hit, pretty pink flamingos punctuate this psychedelic paradise. (Byam Shaw's 1909 "Eleonora" illustration feature a great many of them.) This is very much a paradise along the lines of Ellison's Arnheim; and the passion of the lovers for each other makes "Strange, brilliant flowers, star-shaped, burst out upon the trees where no flowers had been known before."[18] The grass grows greener, the ruby-red asphodels take over the daisies, the flamingos grow scarlet plumage, the clouds grow "gorgeous in crimson and gold."[19] Poe describes the effect as one of "delirious bliss."[20] And like the "gentle people" of Scott MacKenzie's seminal hippy anthem "San Francisco (Be Sure to Wear Some Flowers in Your Hair)," Eleonora is "artless and innocent."[21]

This is, so to speak, the "good acid trip," but the bad trip starts when Eleonora becomes ill. The Valley then grows more troubling: "The star-shaped flowers shrank into the stems of the trees, and appeared no more. The tints of the green carpet faded; and one-by-one, the ruby-red asphodels withered away; and there sprang up, in place of them, ten by ten, dark, eye-like violets, that writhed uneasily and were ever encumbered with dew."[22] The flamingos lose their vivid coloring and the murmuring of the stream dies down. The imagery is comparable to the destruction of Klingsor's magic garden at the end of the second act of Wagner's *Parsifal*. (Indeed, the so-called "Cockney Wagner," Josef Holbrooke, responded in an unlikely musical fashion to Poe's story in the 1940s with a Bassoon Quintet, op. 134, entitled *Eleonora*.)

In *The Tomb of Ligeia*, Roger Corman covered the grave of Ligeia with the red-asphodels Poe mentions in the Valley of Many-Colored Grass in "Eleonora." "Terribly sorry to have trampled these lovely asphodels!" Elizabeth Shepherd's Lady Rowena apologizes, having been thrown from her horse and hurled before the tomb. "They're so bright."

"The flowers of death," Vincent Price's Verden Fell explains.

"How very appropriate," Rowena agrees.

Corman also took a cue from the psychedelic imagery of the Valley of Many-Colored Grasses in his swirling oil and ink title sequences for *The Raven* and *Pit and the Pendulum*, while similarly inspired multi-colored filters made Ray Milland's nightmares in *The Premature Burial* vividly unnerving.

Eureka

That God may be all in all, each must become God.[1]

Poe thought his often ignored essay on the nature of the universe was his masterpiece. "I must die," he wrote to his mother-in-law Maria Clemm in 1849, exactly three months before he did indeed die. "I have no desire to live since I have done 'Eureka.' I could accomplish nothing more."[2] He claimed that this essay "solved the secret of the universe,"[3] but though apparently a scientific treatise, he called it a Prose Poem: "I present the composition as an Art-Product alone;—let us say as a Romance; or, if I be not urging too lofty a claim, as a Poem."[4] This is just as well, as much fault has been found with some of his so-called scientific facts. But Poe also made some remarkable predictions in this astonishing treatise. He formulated the idea of the Big Bang and the expanding universe:

> My general proposition, then, is this:—*In the Original Unity of the First Thing lies the Secondary Cause of All Things, with the Germ of their Inevitable Annihilation.*[5]

He also put forward what we now call Chaos theory:

> If I venture to displace, by even the billionth part of an inch, the microscopical speck of dust which lies now upon the point of my finger, what is the character of that act upon which I have adventured? I have done a deed which shakes the Moon in her path, which causes the Sun to be no longer the Sun, and which alters forever the destiny of the multitudinous myriads of stars that roll and glow in the majestic presence of their Creator.[6]

He anticipated Einstein's theory of relativity (*"Space and Duration are one"*[7]) and predicted Einstein's proposition that the finite Universe of Stars is in a continual and ever-increasing state of collapse:

> If the propositions of this Discourse are tenable, the "state of progressive collapse" is *precisely* that state in which alone we are warranted in considering All Things; and, with due humility, let me here confess that, for my part, I am at a loss to conceive how any *other* understanding of the existing condition of affairs, could ever have made its way into the human brain. "The tendency to collapse" and "the attraction of gravitation" are convertible phrases.[8]

The destruction of the Universe is inevitable because "[t]he atoms, now, having been diffused from their normal condition of Unity, seek to return to——what?... To be brief, the condition, Unity, is all that is really sought."[9]

Poe's principal idea was not, however, a new one. The theosophical Wagnerian Edouard Schuré (1841–1929) interpreted the myth of Dionysus, "torn to pieces by the Titans and restored to life by Athene," as "a summary of the entire cosmic evolution, i.e., of the dispersion of the deity throughout the visible world and its return to eternal and infinite harmony by the sufferings of incarnation."[10] Poe's conception of cosmic unity can also be traced back to the ancient wisdom recorded on the so-called Emerald Tablet of Hermes Trimegistus: *quod superius est sicut quod inferius et quod inferius est sicut quod superius ad perpetranda miracula rei unius,* ("That which is above is like that which is below and that which is below is like that which is above, to achieve the wonders of the one thing"[11]). This "one thing" is God. As the Hermetic philosopher Robert Fludd (1574–1637) expressed it: "The One is all things and all things are One. GOD is all there is; from Him all things proceed and to Him all things must return."[12] Fludd's words here correspond closely with Poe's:

> The assumption of absolute Unity in the primordial Particle includes that of infinite divisibility. Let us conceive the Particle, then, to be only not totally exhausted by diffusion into Space. From the one Particle, as a centre, let us suppose to be irradiated spherically—in all directions—to immeasurable but still to definite distances in the previously vacant space—a certain inexpressibly great yet limited number of unimaginably yet not infinitely minute atoms.[13]

For Poe, God was not beyond matter. In "Mesmeric Revelation," he claimed that God "is not spirit, for he exists":

> Nor is He matter, *as you understand it*. But there are *gradations* of matter of which man knows nothing; the grosser impelling the finer, the finer pervading the grosser. The atmosphere, for example, impels the electric principle, while the electric principle permeates the atmosphere. These gradations of matter increase in rarity or fineness, until we arrive at a matter *unparticled* without particles—indivisible—one; and here the law of impulsion and permeation is modified. The ultimate, or unparticled matter, not only permeates all things but impels all things—and this is all things within itself. This matter is God. What men attempt to embody in the word "thought," is this matter in motion.[14]

This metaphysical preoccupation lies at the center of Poe's entire literary oeuvre, and it also informs his correspondence. In a letter to James Russell Lowell he wrote:

> Matter escapes the senses by degrees—a stone—a metal—a liquid—the atmosphere—a gas—the illuminiferous ether. Beyond this there are other modifications more rare. But to all we attach the notion of a constitution of particles—atomic composition. For this reason only, we think spirit different; for spirit, we say is unparticled, and *therefore* is not matter. But it is clear that if we proceed sufficiently far in our ideas of rarefaction, we shall arrive at a point where the particles coalesce; for, although the particles be infinite, the infinity of littleness in the spaces between them, is an absurdity.—The unparticled matter, permeating & impelling, all things, is God. Its activity is the thought of God—which creates. Man, and other thinking beings, are individualizations of the unparticled matter.[15]

But these ideas are really only an elaboration of what the Spirit of the Earth says in the first part of Goethe's *Faust*:

> I surge to and fro,
> Up and down I flow!
> Birth and the grave
> An eternal wave,
> Turning, returning,
> A life ever burning:
> And thus I work at Time's whirring wheel,
> God's living garment I weave and reveal.[16]

For Poe, as for the Hermetic philosophers who preceded him, everything is a part of the first cause—and therefore an expression of God. And this explains why he called *Eureka* a poem, and devoted its early pages to a defense of *intuitive* rather than strictly scientific thinking: As our minds are part of God—part of the symmetry of the universe, along with everything else—we are able to understand the nature of the Universe purely *instinctively*: "We may take it for granted, then, that Man cannot long or widely err, if he suffer himself to be guided by his poetical, which I have maintained to be his truthful, in being his symmetrical, instinct."[17]

In conclusion, Poe triumphantly claims, "[T]he processes we have here ventured to contemplate will be renewed forever, and forever, and forever; a novel Universe swelling into existence, and then subsiding into nothingness, at every throb of the Heart Divine? And now—this Heart Divine—what is it? *It is our own*."[18]

In Peter Ackroyd's 1993 novel *The House of Doctor Dee*, the same idea is expressed by Dee:

> The human form is more powerful than the sun because it contains the sun, more beautiful than the heavens because it contains the heavens, and he who sees it truly is richer than any king, for he has the entire art and understanding of the earth.[19]

But these ideas are really a re-working of a key aspect of the philosophy of G.W.F. Hegel. Hegel argues that we feel alienated from the world until we realize that Mind is no different from matter. Matter is "merely" the expression of Mind. Hegel suggests that all of our minds, ideas and culture, which are a part of the Universal whole, are therefore also an expression of Mind, or, as Hegel terms it, "Geist." If everything is everything else (in quantum terms, my hand, at a sub-atomic level, is no different from the table on which I rest it), our individual minds are "merely" part of the Universal Mind. Hegel's description of the historical process as thesis, antithesis and synthesis is the means by which Mind ultimately grows to understand itself. (This is the entire point of the historical process as defined by Hegel—and it is an idea George Bernard Shaw expressed in his plays *Man and Superman* and *Back to Methuselah*.) This does suggest that the Idea of the entire universe is linked in some way with the concept of God. Ironically, Schopenhauer, who so derided Hegel, surely agrees with him here when he declares at the beginning of his magnum opus *The World as Will and Idea*, "The world is my idea"—or, rather (in Hegel's view), it is an understanding that the world is Geist—the expression of a Universal Idea—or of a Universal Mind.

In this, we might find salvation from alienation in all its forms. Might "the peace of God that passeth all understanding" in fact be "simply" our understanding of the reality of the world—that it is, in Hindu terminology, illusory "Maya." The only reality is Mind, our own minds being, in Byronic terms, "portion of that around me"—i.e., a fragment of the Universal Mind—and, as Hegel concludes his *Philosophy of Mind*, "The activity of the intellect is life—but the intellect is the activity; and activity that is in itself is the intellect's best and eternal life. We say that God is an eternal living thing, the best. So life and unceasing and eternal duration belong to God. For this is what God is."[20]

Via Poe's mystical astro-physics, these Hegelian ideas also went on to inform twentieth-century science fiction. The star-child that brings Stanley Kubrick's *2001—A Space Odyssey* (1968) to an end might usefully be interpreted along Poe's lines as an image of unity with the universe—and hence with God. Kubrick's film is about human evolution, perhaps under the guidance of extra-terrestrial life forms which have become pure energy.

It may be that, as pure energy, these extra-terrestrial intelligences are no longer a "mere" expression of the "unparticled matter" that is God but have indeed *become* God. The star-child is therefore a way of depicting a state of human evolution which has arrived at a similarly unparticled and consequently invisible state. But as this is a film, Kubrick had to find a way of expressing the invisible.

Gerry Anderson tackled the same problem in the "Black Sun" episode of the television science fiction series *Space 1999*. In David Weir's screenplay, Moonbase Alpha is drawn into a Black Hole, and during the process, Commander Koenig (Martin Landau) realizes that "everything is everything else and the whole universe is living thought...

"That is true," says a God-like voice (interestingly voiced by a female actor), who announces itself as "a friend."

"Every star is just a cell in the brain of the universe," Koenig continues.

"That is a lovely way to understand it," the voice agrees.

"Why have I never talked with you before?" asks Professor Bergman (Barry Morse).

"Because of Time," the voice replies. "You think at what you call the speed of light. In eternity, I have no hurry. I think a thought, perhaps, in every thousand years. You are never there to hear it?"

"Are you God?" the professor asks. He receives no answer, only an enigmatic farewell: "It was good to have known you."

As in *2001—A Space Odyssey*, it seems that something is looking after the humans on Moonbase Alpha, who survive the Black Hole against all the odds. Kubrick chose the now famous opening bars from Richard Strauss' tone poem *Also Sprach Zarathustra* to accompany the opening sunrise of the film. This was appropriate, as it was a sunrise that Strauss had intended to portray in his symphonic poem. The piece is also a musical evocation of man's evolution into the Superman, derived from Nietzsche's book of the same name, and is therefore doubly appropriate for Kubrick's evolutionary vision. Written in Biblical style, Nietzsche's book is a prophecy of the new man who lives positively, free of superstition and deadening morality, and unified with nature and his own reality. Though Nietzsche claimed that God was dead, his vision was nonetheless a mystical one. As his translator R.J. Hollingdale observed, the concept of the Superman can usefully be compared with Christian ideals:

> *Superman:* God as creator and "highest being," the "Son of Man," as God, man as the receptacle of divine grace who rejoices at the idea of eternity" the embodiment and actualization of everything regarded as desirable. What the Christian says of God, Nietzsche says in very nearly the same words of the Superman, namely: "Thine is the kingdom, and the power, and the glory, for ever and ever."[21]

In "The Intoxicated Song," the penultimate section of *Zarathustra,* Nietzsche wrote:

> For all joy wants itself, therefore it also wants heart's agony! O happiness! O pain! Oh break, heart! You Higher Men, learn this, learn that joy wants eternity, joy wants the eternity of all things, *wants deep, deep, deep eternity!*[22]

Such sentiments are very close to Poe's concept of unity—the will to unite with God. In Nietzsche's Godless universe, this unity is a more psychological affair—what Jung would later call the process of individuation—the integration of the psyche leading us to become the fullest expression of who we are. Poe would have regarded such an integrative state as a unification with God. In such a state, man becomes God. Indeed, Jung said much the same thing at the end of his life. When asked if he still believed in God, he paused for a moment and then responded, "It's difficult to answer. I know. I don't need to believe: I know,"[23] by which he presumably meant he had attained the individuation he had been offering as the ultimate cure for the ills of modern man.

The founder of anthroposophy, Rudolf Steiner (1861–1925), used this approach to interpret Nietzsche's philosophy. Despite their apparently contradictory worldviews, they had in common the shared understanding that the world of thought is far more significant than the world of mere sensations, no matter how painful they may be. Steiner wrote:

> The truth is entirely overlooked that mere "beholding" is the emptiest thing imaginable, and that it receives content only from thinking... When one who has a rich mental life sees a thousand things which are nothing to the mentally poor, this shows as clearly as sunlight that the content of reality is only the reflection of the content of our minds, and that we receive from outside merely the empty forms. Of course, we must possess the inner power to recognize ourselves as the creator of this content.[24]

This sounds remarkably like Poe's belief that Man "cannot long or widely err, if he suffer himself to be guided by his poetical, which I have maintained to be his truthful, in being his symmetrical, instinct," and it links Poe, via Steiner, to the ideas of Madame Blavatsky's Theosophical Society and their musical expression by the Russian composer Alexander Scriabin (1872–1915). Scriabin's last symphony, *Prometheus—The Poem of Fire,* is a depiction of human evolution in musical terms following Blavatsky's theory of Root Races, of which there are seven. These have gradually transformed humanity from its origins as a kind of invisible jellyfish to his present state (the fourth Root Race), out of which he will evolve into the super-intelligent pure energy envisioned by Kubrick, and the "unparticled matter" of Poe's God.

Scriabin chose the form of a piano concerto to depict the evolutionary struggle of humanity, the microcosm (represented by the piano) to be absorbed into the macrocosm of the universe (the orchestra). Beginning with a musical representation of chaos, he then describes a Big Bang event: The universe is created. Humanity then appears with the entrance of the piano, which becomes increasingly virtuosic as the species develops its intellectual faculties through sexual play and generation. (Scriabin believed that, in thought-form, "ecstasy is the *highest synthesis. In the guise of space, ecstasy is the highest development and destruction.* Generally, ecstasy is the summit, the last moment, which comprehends the whole history of humanity as a series of appearances. Time and space objectify this longing, Deep eternity and unending space are constellations around divine ecstasy illuminating it."[25] Finally, a choir singing vowel sounds suggests that the new man of the final Seventh Root Race (or the Superman of Nietzsche) is released into the universe as pure spirit. The vowel sounds suggest the first attempts at speech of a newborn baby, but this baby is truly like the giant star-child that brings *2001—A Space Odyssey* to a close. The new man is united with the universe and with the essence of the universe, which is God.

Scriabin, borrowing from Theosophical doctrine, formulated this process as follows:

0 Nothingness—Bliss.
1 I wish. I rise out of the Original Chaos, the Primordial Ooze.
2 I differentiate the undifferentiable.
3 I differentiate. I begin to define the elements of time and space, the future of the universe.
4 I reach the summit, and from there recognize that all is one.
0 Bliss—Nothingness.[26]

Though Poe's central idea of "Unity" was derived from much older metaphysical thinking, not to mention Hegelian idealism, he was really the first modern writer to popularize it, long before the occult revival took Europe and America by storm later in the nineteenth century and on into the early years of the twentieth century. Alas, he did not live to see the fruition of these ideas in twentieth-century culture. He had dreamed of an edition of 50,000 copies of *Eureka*, but his publisher brought out only 500, and despite some good reviews, these sold very slowly.

The Facts in the Case of M. Valdemar

"For God's sake!—quick!—quick!—put me to sleep—or, quick!—waken me!—quick!—I say to you that I am dead!"[1]

This 1845 story is interesting not only in its own right but also because it is the root of that branch of the twentieth-century horror genre that specialized in gore. Poe included a considerable amount of gratuitous medical detail here, to heighten not only the apparent truth of the story but also to heighten the horror of what might happen if a man should be mesmerized *in articulo mortis* (Poe's self-consciously erudite Latin translating as "at the moment of death"), and then, some time later, awoken from his trance. This hoax was believed by many as an account of genuine fact—even Elizabeth Barrett Browning, to whom Poe had dedicated his *The Raven and Other Poems* of 1845. (He had also borrowed the meter of "The Raven" from Elizabeth's 1844 poem "Lady Geraldine's Courtship.") She wrote to him expressing "dreadful doubts as to whether it can be true."[2] Considering her husband Robert's dismissal of the spiritualist Daniel Dunglas Home, whom he satirized in his poem "Mr. Sludge, the Medium," he presumably did not share her opinion.

As so often with Poe, death is the subject here, but unlike so many of the tales about premature burial or reanimation, the eponymous Monsieur Valdemar literally disintegrates at the end of the story into a "nearly liquid mass of loathsome—of detestable putrescence."[3] This gruesome finale was really the first example of instantaneous corporeal disintegration in modern fiction. (Dickens included spontaneous combustion in *Bleak House* but that was nine years later.) "The Facts in the Case of M. Valdemar" is hence the ultimate ancestor not only of visceral horror in subsequent fantasy fiction (H. P. Lovecraft was obviously influenced by it), but also of all the disintegration scenes of countless horror movies, from the many deaths of Dracula to the melting and exploding heads in *Raiders of the Lost Ark* (dir. Steven Spielberg, 1981) and *Scanners* (dir. David Cronenberg, 1981).

Poe had read about mesmerism in Chauncey Hare Townshend's *Facts in Mesmerism* (1840), among other writings, and he was particularly interested by Townshend's theory of an elastic fluid, which, as Mesmer's biographer Vincent Buranelli, points out "can be stirred by the human will in such a way as to influence the nervous system of another human being and dominate his ideas, volitions and emotions."[4]

But it was also the element of hoax, which plays such a significant role in Poe's fiction, that was largely responsible for the gore element of the tale. Poe wanted his readers to think the tale was fact, not fiction. Not only Elizabeth Browning, but also many other readers wrote to him, utterly convinced. He achieved this deception by crowding his

Putrefying Price—Vincent Price and Debra Paget in "The Case of M. Valdemar" from *Tales of Terror* (dir. Roger Corman, 1962).

narrative with as much medical detail as possible, describing the condition of M. Valdemar more in terms of a medical text book than a work of fiction:

> The left lung had been for eighteen months in a semi-osseous or cartilaginous state, and was, of course, entirely useless for all purposes of vitality. The right, in its upper portion, was alas, partially, if not thoroughly, ossified, while the lower region was merely a mass of purulent tubercles, running one into another.[5]

Such details add nothing to the narrative, but immensely aid the sense of its verisimilitude.

Poe's other interest here is the power of the will. As we shall see in "Ligeia," willpower fascinated Poe. Quoting Joseph Glanville in that tale, he even suggests that Man "doth not yield himself to the angels, nor unto death utterly, save only through the weakness of his feeble will." Willpower in "The Facts in the Case of M. Valdemar" cannot quite do that, but it can certainly postpone death's triumph. Mesmerism's professed ability to control the wills of others of course has sinister connotations, and these were exploited by Roger Corman's film version of the story in the third section of *Tales of Terror*. Basil Rathbone plays the mesmerist here, but his motives are not merely in the cause of disinterested scientific investigation: He aims to manipulate Valdemar's (Vincent Price) mind and thus inherit not only his estate but also his widow. None of this exists in Poe's story, but Poe was nonetheless fascinated by the ambivalent power of mesmerism, mentioning how the mesmerist performs "the fullest exertion of the will."[6] Corman's elaboration of this in *Tales of Terror* comes via later mesmeric fantasies, notably George du Maurier's *Trilby* (1894), with its sinister mesmeric villain Svengali. Rathbone's mesmerist in *Tales of Terror* triumphantly proclaims of his patient: "His body is dead but his mind lives on controlled by me!"

Poe's mesmerist is not sinister, though what he does is truly unnerving: suspending the spirit of the dead man in a kind of limbo. Du Maurier's great granddaughter Daphne explored a similar theme in her 1966 short story "The Breakthrough," which was dramatized by the BBC in Irene Shubik's paranormal television series *The Mind Beyond* in 1976. In that story, Ken Ryan, a human guinea pig with an incurable disease, allows himself to be experimented upon. At the moment of his death, his personality or "soul" is captured by a complex machine, which is appropriately named after Charon, the ferryman of ancient Greek mythology, who rows souls across the river Styx; but the girl with whom he was in telepathic contact during life keeps saying, "He wants you to let him go."[7]

Corman's adaptation takes a similar approach to du Maurier's later tale, having Valdemar's disembodied spirit (voiced in unnervingly distorted fashion by Price) eerily imploring "Release me! Give me peace!" When the mesmerist threatens his widow with violence, Valdemar awakens from his trance and advances on his tormentor, finally collapsing upon him in a mound of revolting putrescence. Poe's Valdemar does not awaken himself in this manner. Instead, the mesmerist performs the operation, and Valdemar is subsequently terrified at the prospect of being awoken: "For God's sake!" he gasps "—quick!—quick!—put me to sleep—or, quick!—awaken me!—quick!—*I say to you that I am dead!*" Valdemar is obviously confused in his state of utter panic. Part of him realizes that if he is awoken he will disintegrate, but the other part is thinking of the moment when he was mesmerized seven weeks earlier. It is now too late to escape his fate, and his whole body, as the narrator puts it, "absolutely *rotted* away beneath my hands."[8]

Such literary special effects were to have a profound impact on future macabre entertainments. Corman's adaptation is still the most graphic visualization of Poe's gruesome dénouement, but the most interesting effects in that film are Corman's various uses of color: Rathbone's mesmerist employs a lantern with multi-colored glass panels to hypnotize Valdemar. These bathe his face in a psychedelic spectrum, again relating Corman's film to the period in which it was made, and further explaining Poe's appeal to The Beatles.

The Fall of the House of Usher

He was enchained by certain superstitious impressions in regard to the dwelling which he tenanted, and whence, for many years, he had never ventured forth—in regard to an influence whose suppositious force was conveyed in terms too shadowy here to be re-stated—an influence which some peculiarities in the mere form and substance of his family mansion had, by dint of long sufferance, he said, obtained over his spirit.[1]

Of all Poe's tales, this is the one to have attracted the most interest from musicians and filmmakers—not because it is any more overtly "dramatic" than any of the other tales but because of its powerful atmosphere and profound aesthetic and allegorical meaning. A classic Gothic story, it is also a prototype of psychoanalysis in that it exploits the imagery of the house as a metaphor for the mind of Roderick Usher. Poe spells this out at the beginning of the tale, by observing that the peasantry of the district used the term "House of Usher" as an appellation for both the family and the family mansion.

What of the House of Usher itself? Its environs suggest that all is not well. The weather is dark and dull. It is autumn when the narrator approaches it. The landscape is bleak, filled with decaying trees. The mansion walls are white, drained of color, the windows are vacant and "eye-like," and the prospect fills the narrator with "a sickening of the heart." Already the House is a character in the tale—indeed, its leading role. Later, Poe emphasizes the metaphor of the house as a symbol of the mind in the poem Roderick Usher recites. In this "Haunted Palace" the palace is Usher's own head. The monarch—Thought—commands the dominions of the body; the yellow banners on the roof are his hair. The "luminous windows" are his eyes; the pearl and ruby glowing door are his teeth and lips, and through it troop echoes of "surpassing beauty." In other words, the owner of the palace is originally rational, but madness eventually assails him. The eyes become bloodshot (red-litten windows) and maniacal laughter flows out of the unsmiling door. All becomes discordant in this apposite portrait of Roderick's deranged mind. Like his house, his mind is collapsing. The fissure that zigzags down the front of the building, from the roof to "the sullen waters of the tarn" below is, of course, a metaphor of the crack in Roderick's sanity. (Roger Corman greatly emphasizes what Poe describes as a "barely perceptible fissure"[2] in his *House of Usher* film.)

But Roderick is not only mad, he is also an aesthete. Skilled in poetry and music, he composes and plays the lute. The epigraph by de Béranger with which Poe prefaces the story alludes to Roderick's super-sensitive nervous state. His heart is indeed like a suspended lute, which resonates at the slightest touch.

> He suffered much from a morbid acuteness of the senses; the most insipid food was alone endurable; he could wear only garments of certain texture; the odors of all flowers were oppressive; his eyes were tortured by even a faint light; and there were but peculiar sounds, and these from stringed instruments, which did not inspire him with horror.[3]

Such neurasthenic aestheticism appealed immensely to the symbolist and decadent sensibilities of Baudelaire, Debussy and Florent Schmitt, as we shall see. Usher is a prototype of the ivory tower artistic recluse—a type that fully emerged later in the nineteenth century as industrialism and bourgeois vulgarity increasingly prevailed. (As Richard Gilman observed, "Baudelaire spoke of the good bourgeois as "an enemy of art, of perfume, a fanatic of utensils."[4]) Poe himself was a prototype. The nineteenth-century decadent novelist Paul Bourget suggested in his 1881 essay on Baudelaire that Poe "stretched his nervous system to the point of hallucination," and that, like many decadent rhetoricians, he too used a language "laced with the green of decay."[5]

If Usher's artistic temperament was all he had to contend with, all might have been well, but Roderick fears that the continuation of his line will continue the insanity from which he suffers. The implication is that he and his sister Madeline have had an incestuous relationship—a possibility explored in more specific detail in Philip Glass' operatic adaptation and Melville Webber and James Watson's extraordinary avant-garde film of the story, made in 1928, where we see Roderick's kinkily gloved hand run erotically over the supine body of his stricken sister prior to her interment. D.H. Lawrence predictably focused on this aspect of the story: "It is the same old theme of 'each man kills the thing he loves,'"

Expressionist Usher: Melville Webber in *The Fall of the House of Usher* (dir. James Sibley Watson and Melville Webber, 1928).

he wrote in his essay on Poe. "He knew his love had killed her.... The Ushers, brother and sister, betrayed the Holy Ghost in themselves. They would love, love, love, without resistance. They would love, they would merge, they would be as one thing. So they dragged each other down into death. For the Holy Ghost says you must *not* be as one thing with another being. Each must abide by itself, and correspond only within certain limits."[6]

Madeline has been an invalid from some mysterious illness which has "long baffled the skill of her physicians."[7] It may be that Roderick is responsible for this malady. (Indeed, Webber and Watson make this explicit by showing Roderick offer Madeline wine at dinner. This has a noticeable effect upon her, and is followed by the highly surreal superimposition of a coffin, which floats from nowhere and is served up inside a domed serving dish, offered to her by the black gloved hands of a servant, the rest of whose body remains out of frame.) When Madeline apparently dies, Roderick makes haste to bury her. He buries her alive—and he knows it.

Poe is also careful to list some of the esoteric volumes that the narrator and Usher read together. These include Swedenborg's *Heaven and Hell,* along with works by Ludwig Tieck (1773–1853), Robert Fludd and Machiavelli (1469–1527). Together they form a library almost as celebrated as the once very obscure Gothic novels listed by Jane Austen in *Northanger Abbey* (1817). Webber and Watson surreally stack all these up, having them tower precipitously over their protagonist, before his friend—represented at this stage by only his top hat and hands—turns the pages, which are revealed to be blank, suggesting by purely visual means that Roderick is not really listening to his friend's voice, being far more absorbed in the other sounds he can hear.

As Poe's narrator reads aloud from "The Mad Trist" of Sir Launcelot Canning, various noises seem to correspond to incidents mentioned in Canning's text. Roderick grows increasingly agitated until he can bear it no more. The sounds are actually those of Madeline clawing her way out of the coffin. She makes her way to Roderick's chamber and kills him as the house of Usher falls into the waters of the tarn that surround it.

Debussy, like so many of his contemporaries in France, came to the American writer's work through Baudelaire's translations. Robert Orledge, who has reconstructed Debussy's unfinished opera *La Chute de la maison Usher*, explains that the French symbolists found in Poe "an expression of the new sensibility they were themselves seeking, and the emergence of the collective unconscious."[8] Debussy was also fascinated by the symbolist aesthetic of Maurice Maeterlinck, whose *Pelléas et Mélisande* he transformed into his only completed opera. The attraction to both writers is not surprising, as Orledge points out: "Pelléas and Roderick Usher are both indecisive, neurasthenic, hypersensitive and guilty of loving within their own families; Mélisande's fragile charm and mysterious death link her to Poe's Morella or Ligeia, and even to the sickly Madeline Usher."[9] Unfortunately, Debussy took so long over the construction of his libretto for the Usher opera that by the time he began the music in 1916 he was diagnosed with rectal cancer. Even though the music came so slowly (Debussy worked on it between 1908 and 1917), his identification with the story, no doubt a parallel universe to his own medical disintegration, was complete and obsessive. He confessed that "there are moments when I lose contact with the ordinary things around me: if Roderick Usher's sister came into the room, I should not be particularly surprised."[10] In a letter to his friend André Caplet in 1909, he confessed: "I have recently been living in the House of Usher which is not exactly the place where one can look after one's nerves—just the opposite. One develops the curious habit of listening to the stones as if they were in conversation with each other and of expecting houses to crumble to pieces as if this were not only natural but inevitable."[11]

But Debussy faced the same problems in adapting Poe as later filmmakers. The lack of conventional action requires expansion if it is to occupy a dramatization of any considerable length. (This is partly why Webber and Watson's roughly 12-minute film is such a success.) To achieve this aim, Debussy greatly inflated the role of the doctor who attends Madeline, making him a sinister figure who competes with Roderick for Madeline's favors. So evil is this doctor that it is he who buries Madeline alive, unknown to Roderick.

After a troubling, mysterious prelude, which exploits the lonely sound of a solo trumpet and the unnerving interval of a tritone (the "devil in music" which is itself part of the whole tone scales with which Debussy is so often associated), the first scene introduces Lady Madeline, who sings the first stanza of "The Haunted Palace" as she crosses the stage. A flute introduces her drifting, ethereal presence. The doctor next makes his displeasure of the visitor's arrival known; points out that Roderick is a madman; and hints at his own feelings for Madeline. "What does she matter to you?" snaps the doctor.[12] "Many a time he [Roderick] makes her sing music fit to damn angels!" the doctor continues. "It's incomprehensible and dangerous. A woman, after all, is not a lute." And here, Debussy applies the de Béranger epigraph to Madeline rather than to Roderick as in Poe's original.

Roderick enters and sings a long monologue of his "endless, endless torments." "Pierres mauvaises, vos figures blêmes glaçaient mes ombres froides." ("Evil stones, your livid masses froze me chilled shadows.") Debussy described this monologue as being "sad enough to make the stones weep.... The music has an attractive mustiness obtained by mixing the low notes of the oboe with harmonics of the violin. Don't speak of this to anyone for I am rather proud of it."[13]

Roderick eventually recognizes his old friend as Madeline appears once more and sings another stanza of "The Haunted Palace," and this is as far as Debussy got with the music. Sketches for other parts of the opera, many of them written as melodrama (the text unset above a short score sketch), exist, and over the years have been collated by musicologists. The Chilean composer Juan Allende-Blin realized an early performing version of this material in 1976. Another, less successful version was prepared by Caroline Abbate and Robert Kyr from Yale University, but those who had been fascinated by Debussy's mysterious torso had to wait until 2007 for Robert Orledge's full-length reconstruction. This includes a spectacular storm, and music for the exotic scenes Roderick imagines when being read to by his friend. The music builds to a terrifying climax. The last line Debussy composed was Roderick's "Ah! Damné! Tu me l'as volée..." (Ah! Damn you! You stole her from me...), followed by a startling moment for timpani, but Orledge provides a true ending to the work, with Madeline's return and the terrifying confrontation between her and Roderick, as they shriek their mutual destruction. Debussy apparently forgot to let the friend get away, and added his exit "as an afterthought."[14]

Another "reconstruction" from 1976, which none of the Debussy scholars took much notice of at the time, actually proved to be the first recording of Debussy's Usher music, though only extracts were used and adapted to form the second side of the Alan Parsons Project's 1976 prog-rock album *Tales of Mystery and Imagination*. As Debussy always referred to his Usher opera as "Le projet," Parsons and his collaborator Eric Woolfson felt it appropriate to use that word to define their own ensemble. Parsons saw himself not so much as a musician as a record producer, a role he equated with a film director like Alfred Hitchcock. Conceiving the future of rock music as a producer's rather than performer's medium, the Alan Parsons Project began life as a hybrid affair, employing different musicians for each album, which were conceived along the conceptual lines of Pink Floyd's *Dark Side of the Moon,* on which Parsons had been creatively involved as a recording engineer. The longest and most interesting section of *Tales of Mystery and Imagination* is the five-part "Fall of the House of Usher" instrumental track, which was co-written by Parsons, Woolfson and Andrew Powell. In 1972, Debussy's sketches were hardly known about, and so few people realized that they were actually listening to Debussy, who, it should be noted, Parsons did not credit on the original album—an omission that was not rectified on the re-mastered CD of 1987, which also incorporated readings of Poe by Orson Welles. The suite in this final mix begins with Welles reading an obscure passage derived in part from Poe's introduction to his *Poems of 1831*. Parsons and Woolfson undoubtedly chose this because of its connection with music, in which Poe was so interested. Poe's original text, indebted, as we have already seen, to Coleridge, is:

> A poem, in my opinion, is opposed to a work of science by having, for its *immediate* object, pleasure, not truth; to romance, by having, for its object, an *indefinite* instead of a *definite* pleasure ... romance presenting perceptible images with definite, poetry with *in*definite sensations, to which end music is an *essential*, since the comprehension of sweet sound is

our most indefinite conception. Music, when combined with a pleasurable idea, is poetry; music, without the idea, is simply music; the idea, without the music is prose from its very definitiveness.[15]

As intoned by Orson Welles, over a synthesized drone, the latter part of this passage provides a compelling portico to this musical evocation of the Usher domain. The Prelude proper begins subsequent to this, and this is for the most part entirely Debussy's music, drawn from *La Chute de la maison Usher* but compressed by Andrew Powell into a highly effective collage. The second track, "Arrival," segues from this Prelude via the introduction of an electric bass guitar pulse with synthesizer effects and a thunderstorm recorded outside London's Abbey Road Studio Two. (It is intriguing that the location of the thunderstorm is credited here, while Debussy is not mentioned.) An organ takes over and the percussion eventually suggests the hammering of a door knocker, as Usher's friend finally arrives on the scene. In the "Intermezzo," an electric guitar and piano are blended with orchestral strings, which perform some atmospheric effects such as glissandi and playing behind the bridge. Next, "Pavane" suggests one of Roderick's guitar improvisations. (Poe specifies a guitar, despite the reference to a lute in the de Béranger epigraph.) Powell uses a mandolin (played by the well-known English mandolinist, Hugo D'Alton), which is introduced by synthesized wind instruments. The harp adds delicacy, suggestive of Usher's neurotic condition, while the kantele and cimbalom add a suitably alien quality. This track then fades into the "Fall" section, which involves some avant-garde orchestral effects—notably a gigantic orchestral tone cluster in the manner of Krzysztof Penderecki, to suggest the final cataclysm. (Powell had worked for Karlheinz Stockhausen and Pierre Boulez, so was well-versed in such effects.)

One year after the initial release of Alan Parsons' Poe album, in 1973, Peter Hammil of the British prog-rock band Van Der Graaf Generator began his own rock tribute to "The Fall of the House of Usher" with what he described as an opera, setting Chris Judge Smith's libretto, but it is more like a musical. This wasn't released until 1991, with Hammil performing the dual role of Roderick and the House of Usher itself, with Lene Lovich as Madeline, Andy Bell as a character named after Montresor in "The Cask of Amontillado," Herbert Grönemeyer as an equivalent of Poe's doctor, called "The Herbalist," and Sarah Jane Morris as the chorus. It has little of the melodic and orchestral appeal of the Alan Parsons Project.

Another opera on the subject had been composed in 1965 by the Australian composer Larry Sitsky with a libretto by Gwen Harwood. Harwood was aware of the potential (and possibly intentional) absurdity of the text, and in a letter to Sitsky included a satirical rhyme:

> Usher's residence was cracked.
> Usher was a noddy.
> Any sense his sister lacked
> Wasn't found in Roddy.
> Madeline reported sick
> Which she did too often.
> Roddy nailed her double-quick
> In a solid coffin.[16]

But Sitsky's approach to Poe was serious. He described his own musical style as intensely expressionistic, with "improvisatory aspects," "ejaculatory phrases" and "abrupt changes of dynamics with its associate expressiveness."[17] He much admired the work of Ferruccio Busoni (1866–1924), who was himself fascinated by Poe. From an early stage in his career, Sitsky's approach to composition was oriented towards mysticism and its expression in musical terms. Poe very much stimulated this preoccupation. In a revealing footnote to her essay "The *Nuctemeron* of Sitsky," Judith Crispin observes:

> In *Fall of the House of Usher*, Poe describes Usher's study, listing various book titles from his shelves. Many of these titles were imaginary but there were several that were real. Sitsky used Poe's Usher list as a reading guide for private research into the occult. Pieces composed by Sitsky in response to Poe include his *Fall of the House of Usher* (1965) and *In Pace Requiescat* (song cycle after Poe) (1989). In a diary entry from 9 June 1959, Sitsky records a conversation he had had with Petri about Busoni's interest in Poe, and particularly in "Fall of the House of Usher." (Manuscript. Sitsky Archive. Box 27. National Library of Australia.)[18]

The Russian classical guitarist and composer Nikita Koshkin composed an "Usher Waltz" for the guitarist Vladislav Blaha in 1984, and it has since been made famous by the British guitarist John Williams. It might usefully be compared to André Caplet's 1908 *Conte fantastique* for harp and orchestra, which is based on Poe's "The Masque of the Red Death." Caplet's piece is also a waltz, and towards the end it requires the player to rap his knuckles against the sound box of the harp. Similarly, Koskin instructs the guitarist to snap the strings against the fingerboard of his instrument, and also calls for ghostly string harmonics to suggest the increasingly deranged state of Usher's mind.

Philip Glass' opera on the subject followed in 1987. It differed considerably from Debussy's approach in two important ways: First, it was completed, and second, Glass applied his characteristically repetitive minimalist style to the story, which is a singularly appropriate kind of music for a tale so very concerned with obsession. Glass's oscillating and arpeggiated patterns, always folding in upon themselves, gradually varied only to initiate a new repeated pattern provide the perfect stylistic metaphor for Usher, locked in his home and troubled by his *idée fixe* of madness. Glass also scores the piece for a much smaller ensemble than Debussy's grand orchestra, which again reflects the domestic, intimate setting of the story.

Gordon Getty is one of those rare flowers: a billionaire composer, and son of oil tycoon J. Paul Getty. He released his own operatic adaptation of Poe's tale in 2013, called *Usher House*. He describes his musical style as "undoubtedly tonal, though with hints of atonality, such as any composer would likely use to suggest a degree of disorientation."

> I'm strictly tonal in my approach. I represent a viewpoint that stands somewhat apart from the twentieth century, which was in large measure a repudiation of the nineteenth and a sock in the nose to sentimentality. Whatever it was that the great Victorian composers and poets were trying to achieve, that's what I'm trying to achieve.[19]

Getty has said, "[A] good composer doesn't care whether he's original or not. We're after integrity. We're after looking way down inside and what do I want—what do I think the world needs? I don't mind if somebody said the same thing first."[20] Like Debussy, Getty wrote his own libretto, and seems to have been inspired by Debussy's decision to give the doctor a much more important role than in Poe's original. Getty makes his Dr. Primus the source of evil, against which Roderick and Madeline are powerless; and following on from the family portraits Roger Corman included in his *House of Usher* film adaptation, Getty also includes ghostly ancestors in his libretto. "It's always hard to create something new, no matter who you are," says Philip Ens, who sings Dr. Primus on the recording of Getty's opera conducted by Lawrence Foster. "I applaud Mr. Getty for having the integrity to do what he believes in and creating it. It's in the line of [Samuel] Barber and [Benjamin] Britten—in that style, I believe—so, I think, very approachable for the ear,"[21] which indeed it is.

Film adaptations of Poe's tale vary in length. The shortest is surely Webber and Watson's 12-minute Usher film from 1928. Taking an expressionist approach, the film is America's answer to Wiene's *The Cabinet of Dr. Caligari* made only nine years earlier. Herbert Stern plays Roderick as a suitably white-faced aesthete in a dressing gown. Hildegarde Watson plays Madeline first as a kind of Virginia Woolf figure, who ends up looking like Elektra in Richard Strauss' opera of that name. Melville Webber also appears as the "Traveler," but he is eventually reduced to a pair of hands and a top hat, perhaps suggesting the lack of interest Roderick has in him as a person, merely needing him as a distraction from his appalling state of mind.

The film begins with a kaleidoscopic montage of the title page of the story highlighting the de Béranger epigraph and the opening line. The kaleidoscopic technique returns on several occasions later in the film. Webber and Watson were also fond of superimposition, beginning here with a shot of clouds drifting over the text. A shot of the traveler on horseback advancing on the artificial turrets of the House of Usher, is highly reminiscent of comparable shots in such films as Fritz Lang's *Nibelungen* (1924) and F.W. Murnau's *Faust* (1926), thus firmly grounding the film in the tradition of the German expressionist cinema. One of the film's recurring images is of staircases moving up and down, often opposite each other. Given the incestuous subtext of the story, they suggest a Freudian interpretation as sexual symbols. (Freud identified staircase imagery in dreams as indicative of sexual excitement.)[22]

A jagged shape now divides the frame in two, to reveal Madeline sitting in a corner of her room smelling flowers. The dagger shape specifically relates this film to *The Cabinet of Dr. Caligari,* the stylized sets of which feature dagger shapes throughout, indicative of its murderous theme. A similar interpretation lies here, but the jagged intrusion also symbolizes the fissures in the fabric of the house and the even more worrying disintegration of Roderick's mind.

Madeline approaches her brother who is sitting at a table laid for dinner. Lilies decorate the setting very aesthetically, but further dagger shapes inform the background. The Ushers appear to have a servant, but we see only his black-gloved hands pouring wine. The rest of his body is deliberately kept out of frame, suggesting that he is a curiously disembodied presence. The wine appears to be drugged, as Madeline swoons, and a superimposed image of a coffin floats down inside a serving dish. This is then elaborately presented to Madeline by the servant's hands, while Roderick, framed by the V-shape arrangement of lilies, looks on.

We cut to ripples in the tarn surrounding the mansion. The traveler appears at the door, and we are shown kaleidoscopic images of bells ringing, followed by shots of Madeline approaching the door. The traveler wears a top hat, with a very expressionist-style make-up line running down his nose and forehead, suggesting that he too has a split personality. As Madeline faints, the shadow of a hammer raps overhead, followed by more kaleidoscopic shots of moving staircases and floating coffins. Madeline closes her eyes and Roderick runs his hands over her supine body, suggesting very clearly the unhealthy nature of their relationship. The shadow of the hammer falls repeatedly to suggest the nailing down of Madeline's coffin lid. The hammer then falls to the floor with Roderick's gloves, succinctly combining the imagery of death and sex in a single shot.

Madeline's face, shot from contrasting angles, is now presented kaleidoscopically. Roderick walks towards the camera with awkwardly stiff movements, strongly suggesting, once again, the movements of César the somnambulist (Conrad Veidt) in *Caligari*. Roderick's point of view of the house shows it to be distorted and double-exposed, suggesting his state of mind, as does a superimposed shot of Madeline's hands, which reach out to clutch him. Further hammer imagery follows. Roderick is unable to stop miming the action of hammering, even though he no longer holds the hammer, as an image of Madeline's spirit wanders through the house in a brilliant use of shadows, superimposition and double exposure. Webber and Watson also indulge in reverse motion, showing the Traveler's top hat bounce magically up in the air.

Then, again echoing *Caligari*'s use of "magic" letters ("Caligari" is spelled out in the film during the action of Wiene's film), Watson and Webber suggest three words, "BEAT," "CRACK" and "SCREAM," to evoke the action of Madeline fighting her way from her premature burial, but some of the letters are upside down or in the wrong order. Nonetheless, the meaning is made quite clear. Madeline then appears. Two hands push back the double doors, behind which Madeline is seen opening the doors herself. Like a crazed Elektra, eyes heavily blackened, she advances upon her brother. The Traveler escapes, the house collapses, the waters of the tarn boil, and a shot of the moon brings the film to its disturbing end.

Jean Epstein's *La Chute de la maison Usher* dates from the same year and offers an intriguing contrast to the expressionism of Webber and Watson. Epstein takes a more naturalistic approach, though one that is much more poetic than Roger Corman's later sound version with Vincent Price. Eschewing the *Caligari*-style expressionism of that film, Epstein transforms his location shooting into distinctly symbolist images in a much more gallic manner. Usher's friend is called Allan, echoing Poe's middle name. The damp and dreary autumn weather of the story's opening sentence is atmospherically conveyed with real puddles, genuine trees and authentic skies. When Allan inquires about the location of the Usher residence at a wayside inn, the name has the same kind of effect that "Dracula" has when uttered by Renfield to the innkeeper in Universal's *Dracula* (1931).

Usher's house in this film is vast, in contrast to the claustrophobic interiors of Webber and Watson. Indeed, lovers of Gothic interiors had to wait until Roman Polanski's *The Fearless Vampire Killers* (1968) for interiors of comparable spaciousness. Roderick is painting Madeline's portrait. As Roderick dabs paint onto the canvas, Madeline touches her face, as though she can feel the brush touching her skin. Later, in a spectacularly poetic use of cinematic technique, Epstein shows her collapse in slow motion as the portrait reaches its completion, her spirit having been transferred onto the canvas, as in Poe's "Oval Portrait." (Oscar Wilde's *The Picture of Dorian Gray* was similarly indebted to this tale.) Corman, of course, would later follow this approach, incorporating "Hop-Frog" into his version of *The Masque of the Red Death*, and, as we have seen, combining "The Cask of Amontillado" with "The Black Cat" in *Tales of Terror*.

Epstein's exterior of the Usher mansion resembles Arthur Rackham's famous illustration of a stark, white-walled edifice. Inside, however, there are long corridors with billowing curtains. One of the portraits also alludes to "Ligeia Usher"—a rather unexpected allusion to another of Poe's doomed women. The coachman cannot hurry away from this deathly domain quickly enough as Roderick and his friend sit down at an elegantly laid table, the decanters and glassware of which Corman may have had in mind when dressing his sets for Vincent Price in 1960. Allan, the friend, is very hard of hearing, in contrast to the super-sensitivity of Usher himself, and Epstein further emphasizes the difference between Usher's greater perception and sensitivity by later having the doctor's spectacles mist over, suggesting his blindness to the true condition of Madeline.

Roderick strums his guitar and wanders about the hall as mists rise over the surrounding tarn. The music he summons seems to affect the weather. A storm rises, though the friend hears nothing. Wind blows down the corridors and causes an avalanche of books from their precarious position in the cupboards. Roderick then stares into the portrait of his unfortunate sister, and a closeup of his features provides an eloquent expression of his unstable mind. He then observes the preparations for Madeline's funeral from the top of an impressive flight of steps, down which he hurries, such symbolism again prompting a Freudian interpretation, its sexual implications suggesting the incestuous feelings he has for his sister, especially as the coffin is then carried upstairs.

Epstein makes effective use of the funeral cortège through the woods with burning candles superimposed over the images. This is followed by particularly beautiful superimposition of these candles with the river bank of the island on which the mausoleum is situated, while Madeline's shroud billows around the boat. Then, to emphasize what the staircase symbolism only suggested before, two toads are shown copulating.

Now Epstein concentrates on the empty spaces of the mansion, with more billowing drapes suggesting the presence of Madeline's spirit haunting the place. A black cat also makes a brief appearance, echoing Poe's ill-omened feline of another tale, and anticipating Roger Corman's use of that animal to suggest the transmogrified spirit of Ligeia in *The Tomb of Ligeia*. Epstein also references the clock in "The Masque of the Red Death," the slow, inexorable swinging of its pendulum, captured at an oblique angle, obviously suggesting "The Pit and the Pendulum."

Roderick suffers from double vision, which Epstein makes us share with him, and he is terrorized by the mechanism of the clock as it counts the seconds that bring him closer to his doom. The guitar strings snap as the clock chimes and a storm symbolically begins to rumble around the place. As Allan reads the "The Mad Trist," Madeline's coffin tumbles off its plinth and Madeline's shroud billows from the door of the crypt. As the candles gutter, books tumble and a suit of armor falls over, she appears to exact her revenge. The destruction scene is quite spectacular, and Roderick seems to be looking forward to it, death being his deliverance from dread, but also, presumably, a metaphor for imaginative freedom. As Madeline walks towards him, the stairs burst into flames—a Freudian elaboration which needs no further explanation here. Curiously, however, Epstein contrives a relatively happy ending, having Roderick and Madeline escape destruction in the family mansion, embracing in safety at the end.

Roderick Usher (played by Stephen Courtleigh) made his first television appearance in 1949 in an adaptation for NBC's series *Lights Out*. NBC's *Matinee Theater* made another version in 1956, transmitted live in color. The tiny sets were suitably claustrophobic but hardly atmospheric in the manner of Epstein. Everything was carried by the acting, which was competently provided by Eduardo Ciannelli as the doctor and Helen Wallace as an interpolated housekeeper, Della, who somewhat resembles Judith Anderson's Mrs.

Danvers in Hitchcock's *Rebecca* (1940). Tom Tryon as Roderick and Marshall Thompson as his friend David were perhaps less convincing, but the production did manage to make the collapse of the House of Usher at the end look more exciting than the obviously limited means at its disposal suggested. This version also had Roderick discuss his evil and debauched ancestors by name (a detail not to be found in Poe), and Roger Corman would expand upon this in *House of Usher* by having Roderick (played by Vincent Price) give his friend a guided tour of the Usher family portraits. (Could there have been a nod towards Price's other career as an art historian here?)

An unsuccessful British film adaptation was directed by Ivan Barnett in 1949. Lasting just under forty minutes, it stars Gwen Watford as Lady Usher. Watford is suitably wan and wistful, drinking her drugged milk like an obedient girl, but she is given an opportunity to exhibit the rather more menacing abilities which would later flourish in her greatest Gothic performance as the sinister Ayah in Freddie Francis' *The Ghoul*, 26 years later. Kay Tendeter plays Roderick with stagey stiffness, and the House itself is merely an undistinguished example of Victorian suburbia, with prosaic brickwork and sash windows. There's plot but no real poetry here.

Such is not the case with Roger Corman's full-color classic, though the addition of color and the presence of Vincent Price are largely responsible for what poetry there is. The film opens with a spectrum of different colors shot through swirling dry-ice: purple, blue, green, pink, scarlet and magenta. Again, these colors and their subsequent return in the first of Corman's many Poe-inspired dream sequences, express the emergent psychedelia of the time. But these opening colors also contrast effectively with the much bleaker, blasted landscape of the area around the House of Usher in the opening shot. Corman achieves a marvelous image of the House itself, nestling in more swirling dry ice, vast, melancholy and forbidding.

Let me out!—Gwen Watford as Madeline Usher in *The Fall of the House of Usher* (dir. Ivan Barnett, 1949).

In this version, Roderick's friend is called Philip Winthrop (Mark Damon) and he is engaged to marry Madeline. This arrangement allows for much more screen time for the sister (played by Myrna Fahey), not to mention a love interest that, if not entirely lacking in the original story, is less shocking than Poe's implied incestuous relationship, which would surely have been deemed unsuitable for a mainstream horror film made in 1960. The production design of Daniel Haller stresses the inevitable staircase, with

Throne of Usher: Vincent Price in his most celebrated role for Roger Corman's *The House of Usher* (1960).

all its Freudian symbolism, and Corman uses it to full advantage, staging two of its shock sequences on it (the collapse of the chandelier and the banister, both of which nearly kill the young hero). Les Baxter's very mainstream Hollywood score also contains the novel effect of plucking a piano's strings rather than hitting them, which creates the same effect as America's rather more avant-garde composer, Henry Cowell, whose "The Banshee" of 1925 employs the same technique. We first hear Baxter's "Banshee" effect as Winthrop and the Ushers' servant, Bristol (played by Harry Ellerbe), ascend the staircase (Philip having dutifully removed his boots to prevent alarming his hypersensitive host). It will return in a later scene during which Usher entertains his guest with an improvisation on the lute. "Remarkable," Winthrop exclaims, politely inquiring, but surely not meaning, "May we have another?"

Roderick is introduced in a classic shock scene, appearing suddenly from behind the door of his study. The film is utterly dependent upon Price's performance, which provides the poetry lacking elsewhere, for no amount of scarlet drapes, scarlet coats, red candles and red furnishings can compete with the monochrome expressionist invention of Webber and Watson or the similarly black-and-white symbolist sophistication of Epstein. Price, however, elevates the film to a considerable height, complementing the impressive exterior shots of the House itself with its immense fissure, which is so much more impressive than the "hairline fracture" mentioned by Poe. Price speaks his lines so caressingly and holds himself with such delicacy, splaying his fingers when sitting, moving his head like a strange, terrified bird and generally expressing his oddness with great elegance and restraint. As he picks up his lute, Roderick explains that he and Madeline "are like figures of fine glass. The slightest touch and we may shatter," and by this means the screenwriter, Richard Matheson, is able to incorporate the de Béranger epigraph without specific quotation of it. Hammer films never tackled Poe, concentrating instead on variants of their English sources: Mary Shelley and Bram Stoker, for whom Peter Cushing and Christopher Lee proved more than adequate. Price and Corman cornered the market for Poe films, not that American International were at first convinced that Poe would attract the young audiences they needed. They assumed that such audiences, having had to study Poe at high school, would hate him and stay away in droves. (The Larry Grossman-Hal Hackady musical *Snoopy!* (1975) articulated this anxiety in the "Edgar Allan Poe" number, in which the children worry about being asked a question about the writer they cannot answer.) But, as Corman pointed out to his producers, the House was the monster. And Corman lived up to his word, making it creak and shake, shudder and rumble through many effective scenes. When the chandelier nearly crushes Philip, it resembles a malevolent octopus, alive with blood red, tentacle-like candles. Indeed, scarlet is the film's overall color. Roderick pours out wine into scarlet glasses over the subsequent dinner scene, before we return to the scarlet-draped study where the lute performance is given.

More creaking and door-slamming awaken Philip that night and after much searching he discovers Madeline, who takes him down to the crypt. There he is introduced to her dead family before the House throws down a coffin and displaces the skeleton that molders within. Madeline's coffin is also there. "It waits for me," she groans. Philip wants to take her away, but this is not so easy, as Madeline is under the thumb of her mad brother. Roderick then shows Philip the portraits of his evil ancestors, painted for the film by Bert Schoenberg. He points out that the House was brought stone by stone from England and retains the evil of its past—an amusingly concise reflection, on Matheson's part, of the spirit of American independence and its distrust of English oppression. The same idea recurs in Corman's *The Haunted Palace* (1963).

The dream sequence follows in which Philip battles with the evil Usher ancestors to save Madeline from Roderick's clutches. Again, Corman indulges in psychedelic blues, pinks and magentas before Philip is startled awake by a scream. The concluding sequence, featuring the essential storm, fiery climax and Madeline's truly unnerving expression as she strangles her brother, are nicely handled, and the House of Usher sinks like the *Titanic* in the final animated shot on which Poe's concluding sentence is superimposed.

Five years after Corman's film, Ken Russell made his first foray into the House of Usher in his television biopic *The Debussy Film,* with Oliver Reed as Debussy—and looking very like the composer too. Towards the end of the film, Vladek Sheybal's narration explains that "for the last years of his life Debussy locked himself away. There is mention of his daughter but of no one else. His dreaming became a sort of endless, isolated self-communion. Time, place, a pattern of life, none of these had ever mattered much to him. Now they mattered not at all." Reed's Debussy wanders around an immense castle, and confesses, "Roderick is sensitive, and I am sensitive. He hears and feels everything in the world and tried to force these impulses into his work." Sheybal continues, "Debussy became obsessed with Roderick Usher.... Enormous effort, all his impulses were put into this, which was to be his greatest work. For twelve years, this composition drove him to anguish, and all that he had, after those twelve years, were two or three sheets of music." Russell was unable to use this music to accompany his striking images, as none of it had then been recorded, but the imagery makes up for this. Debussy reiterates, "I am Roderick Usher," and we see Madeline ascending a staircase, bathed in diffused light. Debussy paces down an immense white-walled corridor, closing the shutters as he goes. When darkness engulfs the corridor, Russell then cuts to a close-up of Reed's disturbingly brooding features, behind which stretches an seemingly endless expanse of checkerboard floor tiles, as though Debussy were the sole piece left in life's game of chess. Madeline advances towards him and Debussy is revealed to be sitting, as if enthroned, in the middle of the corridor's chessboard. She collapses at his feet and the film swiftly draws to a conclusion. However, Russell's fascination with "The Fall of the House of Usher" continued, and later found expression in his last film, with the punning title of *The Fall of the Louse of Usher* in 2002.

One year after *The Debussy Film*, British Independent Television commissioned David Campton to adapt *Usher* with Denholm Elliott as Roderick, Susannah York as Madeline and David Buck as Richard Beckett, a character who linked all the episodes of the *Mystery and Imagination* series of which this formed a part. Campton expanded the confines of the story somewhat by having earlier scenes in which Madeline visits Richard, having escaped from her brother. He also interpolates another new character: Beckett's wife Lucy (Mary Miller), who takes care of Madeline until she is abducted by Usher's servant, Finn (Oliver McGreevy). The sets for this production were much more lavish than the earlier American TV versions. They were also rather more stylized, the walls of Roderick's study being covered in macabre murals of skeletons, the floor of his magnificent hall decorated with the mosaic of a demon, and various martyrs hanging from nooses painted on the walls of Madeline's chambers. Elliott, replete with a weird white wig, ranks as perhaps the most overtly insane of all the dramatized Rodericks on offer. What he lacks in Vincent Price's elegance, he more than makes up for in goggle-eyed irrationality and fractious facetiousness. Mirroring his own mental collapse, the collapse of the house is, by television standards of the time, quite remarkable.

A rather different approach was taken in 1982 by the Czech filmmaker Jan Svankmajer. His version of *The Fall of the House of Usher* takes Poe's title at its word, and concentrates on the house itself at the expense of human characters. The latter are instead represented by objects: Roderick by his chair and Madeline by her coffin. The house itself becomes a vehicle for the characters' emotions. Madeline's name is even written by inanimate objects such as fallen leaves. The house sprouts her lips and her eyes. The coffin carries itself to the vault. Echoing the approach of Webber and Watson, we see the hammer and nails that sealed the coffin come to life. The key that locks Madeline in the vault also trembles. When she returns in spirit, a white light appears behind the chair that represents Usher. Other chairs (previous Ushers whose spirits inhabit the house) then hurl themselves out of the windows into the tarn, before the house collapses. This is an attempt to express the poetry of Poe's story without recourse to plot, which is singularly lacking in the tale itself. Consequently, it is perhaps the closest a film can get to visualizing Poe's metaphorical vision.

In 1989, Oliver Reed again found himself wandering through Roderick's haunted palace when he played a dangerously controlled Roderick in Alan Birkinshaw's *The Fall of the House of Usher*. Produced by Harry Alan Towers, who was responsible for Christopher Lee's increasingly down-market Fu Manchu films, this version, alas, rips Poe to shreds—quite literally, in the case of the several slasher-style murders that splatter the movie. Parts of it do have some visual interest, however. Lord Lytton's mock Gothic ancestral pile, Knebworth House, near Stevenage in Hertfordshire, stands in for the House of Usher, though the over-dressed and decadent 1980s interiors are plainly studio-bound. The heroine's boudoir is decorated with a mural featuring a figure from one of the Victorian painter Albert Moore's paintings (*Shells* from 1874, to be precise), which reflects the revival of interest in such art at the time, and Ann Stradl, who plays the wife of Norman Coombes' sinister butler. Mr. Derrick, wears threatening shoulder pads, contriving to resemble the British prime minister at the time, the late Baroness Thatcher (though in fact Mrs. Derrick is one of the few benevolent characters here). More significantly, the film somewhat changes Poe's premise. Instead of a sister, Roderick has a brother called Walter (played by Donald Pleasence), who is at first presented as the saner of the two siblings, though the electric drill he has strapped onto his right hand suggests otherwise. Roderick lures Walter's son Ryan (Rufus Swart) to the family mansion, but is really interested in Ryan's fiancée Molly (Romy Windsor). He buries Ryan alive and plans to impregnate Molly to maintain the Usher line (though he could have left Ryan to do that). Walter, however, has other ideas. He wants the line to die out, and anyway is not happy about what Roderick has done to his son.

Aspects that this crazy parallel universe shares with Poe's original tale include Roderick's hypersensitivity (he cannot abide Molly's perfume and brightly colored '80s style ra-ra skirts—but who could?), the house obligingly creaks and shudders, the chandelier sways, there are storms, and a mad doctor who, as in Debussy's opera, fancies his chances with Molly; but Roderick (in an oblique reference to the rats of "The Pit and the Pendulum") arranges to have his sexual equipment nibbled off by a particularly voracious rodent. There are a couple of references to other films on the subject. There is a dream sequence *à la* Corman (not to mention skeletons falling out of coffins), and books tumble off shelves *à la* Epstein. There are also two ghostly children (long-dead Ushers) reminiscent of the two little girls in *The Shining* (dir. Stanley Kubrick, 1980). Other images are indebted to the Italian *giallo* films of Argento and Fulci. (Poor Mrs. Derrick has her head severed and served for dinner with an apple in her mouth like a stuck pig.) The presence of Oliver Reed also reminds one of the operatic excesses of Ken Russell, though without his guiding intelligence; but as an unintentional allegory of the madly materialistic, morally bankrupt period of Thatcher's Britain, the film works rather well.

Russell had his own stab at the story in *The Fall of the Louse of Usher: A Gothic Tale for the 21st Century* (2002). Described by the director as "a bit of a romp," it combines various Poe stories with echoes of *The Cabinet of Dr. Caligari* into a kind of comedy-horror rock musical. Rock star Roddy Usher (James Johnston) is accused of killing his wife in a fit of madness. The rotting corpse of his wife, named after Poe's poem "Annabel Lee," is discovered walled up, an eye hanging from its socket. Even though a dog leaps out of her stomach, the reference is obviously to "The Black Cat." This is not Russell's only reference to other Poe tales. The film opens with Roddy charging around in a yellow jumpsuit reciting lines from "The Tell-Tale Heart." He is also seen singing lines from "The Bells," intercut with shots of a blood-smeared nude being tormented by Playboy devils. "Ligeia" is transformed into a pop video featuring Roddy's Cleo Lane-lookalike sister, Madeline. In it, we see Roddy's wife, Annabel, laid in the back seat of a sports car. The hood is lowered and then pulled back again to reveal Madeline transmogrified as Ligeia. This is a significant modification of Poe's "Ligeia" as Russell eventually reveals that it was Madeline who killed Roddy's Annabel: she simply couldn't cope with her beloved brother having a wife. She accordingly rescued a gorilla from a traveling circus and trained it to be the instrument of her vengeance. By this means, Russell manages to include a reference to "The Murders in the Rue Morgue" as well. Even "The Facts in the Case of M. Valdemar" turns up with the unfortunate Monsieur Valdemar given a white (later green) face with scarlet lips and tongue.

The grotesque comedy of the whole film includes inflatable sex toys making love to each other and an inflatable Godzilla, a knife-edged pendulum which threatens to slice off Roddy's drug-induced erection while his nurse gorges on a large banana, a resurrected mummy, awful puns ("He's raven mad!"), fellatio with a purple foxglove, and an array of dentures echoing the exhumed teeth of "Berenice," one of which comes to life. There is also a kinky nurse, a bouncy castle, a sexy Slinky toy and a false nose in the shape of an erect penis. Even the name of Russell's production company, "Gorsewood," is a joke at the expense of Pinewood. (This movie was filmed in and around his own thatched cottage in the New Forest; the property is surrounded by gorse bushes.) The lunatic asylum in which Roddy is incarcerated is run by the obviously insane Dr. Calahari (played by Russell), which nicely draws a comparison between Wiene's *The Cabinet of Dr. Caligari* and Poe's "The System of Doctor Tarr and Professor Fether." (Russell was a great admirer of the Golden Age of German expressionist cinema.) Made with a camcorder for only £2000, *The Fall of the Louse of Usher* is not perhaps Russell's most polished film but it nonetheless proves that with Poe there really are no limits to the imagination. The film is not only a riposte to a film industry that no longer regarded the director as bankable in 2002, but it might also be said to expose the satire which, as we have already seen, some critics, like G.R. Thompson, regard as the sometimes hidden agenda of Poe's entire output.

Thompson regards the conclusion of "The Fall of the House of Usher," in which the narrator reads from "The Mad Trist" of Sir Launcelot Canning, as "purposefully ludicrous; it reads like a parody, and even the narrator comments on its absurdity. The correspondence of sounds, especially, heightens the ludicrous effect. But the intruded tale of the 'Mad Trist' also has a clear ironic effect; it destroys the Gothic illusion."[23] If Thompson is right, Russell's *The Fall of the Louse of Usher,* far from being a tacky, no-budget self-indulgence, is revealed as perhaps one of the most authentic film adaptations of Poe's general approach to fiction. There's plenty of horror in Russell's sexy romp but, to use one of the words Poe himself used to describe the body of his fiction, it is *grotesque* horror. And "grotesque" embraces both the frightening and the absurd. It requires extravagance, even a certain camp quality. It implies the fantastic, the ugly, the incongruous and the distorted. Like our response to reflections in a fairground mirror, we might simultaneously laugh and shudder at those distortions. In Thompson's words, Russell's approach is also "purposefully ludicrous." (Think of the steaming remains and screaming skull of Russell's dead Monsieur Valdemar, one of whose goggle eyes pops out on cue like a jack-in-the-box.) If Poe really did mean to be ironic, Russell was, of all film directors, the very best one to adapt his story for the screen. Even on its own terms, *The Fall of the Louse of Usher* still demonstrates Russell's particular genius. His biographer Joseph Lanza wrote,

> Russell still proves his gift for composition and his instinct for vibrant colors. An English flower garden never looks more surreal, old gravestones never exude more sinister grandeur, and even one of his trademark slow-zooms onto James Johnston's rotting teeth exposes the undiscovered beauty behind what the consensus finds hideous.[24]

The Gold-Bug

It is of a brilliant gold color—about the size of a large hickory-nut—with two jet black spots near one extremity of the back, and another, somewhat longer, at the other.[1]

This famous treasure-hunting story is noted for the ingenuity of its cipher, but its real attraction lies in the atmospheric writing that conveys the loneliness of Sullivan's Island where the treasure is eventually found. Poe's series of coincidences, which lead to the discovery of the cipher on a piece of parchment, are also masterfully plotted: the discovery of the parchment itself on the beach, the arrival of the narrator in Legrande's hut, the attempt of Legrande to draw on the parchment the remarkable gold-bug he has discovered, the entrance of his dog, which leaps on the narrator, causing him to hold the parchment near the fire, the heat of which causes the invisible ink to be revealed, and so forth. The story also contains some of Poe's most lively and realistic dialogue, as well as a dose of the macabre: to find the treasure, the gold-bug, attached to a plumb-line, must be dropped through the left eye socket of a skull that has been left by Captain Kidd in the branch of a tree. Jules Verne admired this Poe tale more than any other:

> This strange, disturbing story grips us through the use of techniques that no one tried before. It is crammed with observation and infallibly logical deductions; and it alone would suffice to make the writer worthy of his fame. To my mind, it is the most remarkable of all the Tales.[2]

This 1843 story became Poe's most famous tale in his own lifetime, and was read by more people than anything else he wrote. It won him a prize of $100, and Poe reported that 300,000 copies had been circulated in less than a year. As Kenneth Silverman adds, "Eventually 'The Gold-Bug' became, worldwide, one of the most popular stories ever written."[3] But despite all this, and despite the story's ingenuity and atmosphere, its impact on the cinema has been nowhere near as considerable as Robert Louis Stevenson's *Treasure Island* (1883), which it partly inspired. There have been numerous television and film adaptations of *Treasure Island*, but curiously very few of "The Gold-Bug." A less than riveting stage adaptation appeared in Poe's lifetime, but no feature film has ever been made based on the story. It was adapted for American television in 1953, in an episode of the series *Your Favorite Story,* directed by Robert Florey, but the best small-screen adaptation so far was directed in 1979 by Robert Fuest (well-known for his work on *The Avengers* and the two Dr. Phibes films). In this, Poe's adult narrator is recast as a boy (played by Anthony Michael Hall). The Negro, Jupiter (Geoffrey Holder), becomes rather more sinister than Poe's jovial fool—and he is mute as well, which adds to his sinister nature. Edward Pomerantz's teleplay also incorporated a character from Herman Melville's *Moby Dick,* a novel in part inspired by Poe's *The Narrative of Arthur Gordon Pym.* The character referenced from *Moby Dick* is the terrifying Queequeg, who has a tattooed face. In the TV version of "The Gold-Bug" he is called Mr. Tattoo (Philip Bruns), and he helps the boy find the place mentioned in the cipher called Bishop's Hostel. Pomerantz also gave the story a tragic ending by having Roberts Blossom's Legrande murdered by Jupiter, who then unsuccessfully attempts to steal the treasure for himself. His body is found on the beach by the boy but the treasure has mysteriously vanished and we are left wondering about what exactly happened.

The lonely desolation of Sullivan's Island might well have been in David Greene's imagination when he filmed an adaptation of a novel by August Derleth, which was based on an idea by that great admirer of Poe, H.P. Lovecraft. Though filmed in England, *The Shuttered Room* (1967) evokes all the coastal desolation described by Poe in passages like these:

> The island is a very singular one. It consists of little else than the sea sand, and is about three miles long. Its breadth at no point exceeds a quarter of a mile. It is separated from the mainland by a scarcely perceptible creek, oozing its way through a wilderness of reeds and slime, a favorite resort of the marsh-hen.[4]

Eric Woolfson and Alan Parsons named one of the tracks on their album *The Turn of a Friendly Card* (1980) after Poe's story. It begins with a sustained trill on a harpsichord over which a whistling syrinx-like theme floats somewhat desolately, perhaps suggesting the landscape of Sullivan's Island, before the rhythm section enters and we embark on a typical Alan Parsons Project instrumental, with its hypnotic ostinati and, in this case, a swaggering saxophone and backing group. But if this is intended to reflect Poe's story, it is very much left to the imagination of the listener.

The Haunted Palace

And travellers now within that valley,
Through the red-litten windows see
Vast forms that move fantastically
To a discordant melody.[1]

This poem, recited by Roderick Usher in "The Fall of the House of Usher," is an allegory of insanity, the "palace" being the head of the lunatic. As we have seen, the "Banners yellow, glorious, golden" are his hair, the "luminous" (later "red-litten") windows are his once intelligent, now bloodshot eyes, the fair palace door encrusted with pearl and ruby is the mouth, lips and teeth, which eventually gives vent to a "hideous throng" of insane babble. Maniacal laughter streams from it, but the lips smile no more.

The 1963 Roger Corman film called *The Haunted Palace*, starring Vincent Price, takes the title of Poe's poem and combines its imagery with H.P. Lovecraft's novella, "The Case of Charles Dexter Ward." Corman himself recalled, "I made some gestures towards bringing some Poe into it so that it could be sold, I think, as Poe and Lovecraft, but it was really primarily Lovecraft and it was slightly misleading advertising."[2] However, the idea of combining Lovecraft with Poe is a sensible one, as Lovecraft was a great admirer of his famous predecessor in fantastic fiction, In his essay on "Supernatural Horror in Literature," Lovecraft wrote:

> Poe studied the human mind rather than the usages of Gothic fiction, and worked with an analytical knowledge of terror's true sources which doubled the force of his narratives and emancipated him from all the absurdities inherent in merely conventional shudder-coining. This example having been set, later authors were naturally forced to conform to it in order to compete at all; so that in this way a definite change began to affect the main stream of macabre writing. Poe, too, set a fashion in consummate craftsmanship; and although today some of his own work seems slightly melodramatic and unsophisticated, we can constantly trace his influence in such things as the maintenance of a single mood and achievement of a single impression in a tale, and the rigorous paring down of incidents to such as have a direct bearing on the plot and will figure prominently in the climax. Truly, may it be said that Poe invented the short story in its present form.[3]

"The Case of Charles Dexter Ward" concerns the reincarnation of Joseph Curwen, a diabolical warlock, in the body of his eponymous descendant. By means of the grimoire, *The Necronomicon*, Curwen aimed to mate human beings with the elder gods of Lovecraft's infamous mythology. Hideous mutants were the result, and they wander around Arkham like ghouls. The screenwriter for Corman's film, Charles Beaumont, followed Lovecraft's story fairly closely, incorporating into it a massive palace, which Ward inherits from his ancestor. Beaumont also inserted various stanzas from the poem (read by Price) into the film, but these bear little relevance to the plot. When, for instance, Ward arrives in Arkham one hundred years after Curwen's execution, Beaumont brings in the lines "Wanderers in that happy valley, / Through two luminous windows, saw / Spirits moving musically, / To a lute's well-tunèd law"—but the only relevant line here is the one referring to the wanderers. Ward and his wife have arrived in Arkham to take possession of their inheritance—the Curwen mansion. The innkeeper they encounter insists that it isn't a house: "It's a madman's palace."

"A palace?" Ward's wife (played by Debra Paget) inquires. "In America?"
"Brought over stone by stone," the innkeeper explains.
"Brought over?" Ward inquires. "Brought over from where?"
"Europe somewhere. No one knows. No one wants to know, but if you value your lives don't go there."

In time-honored tradition, they ignore this advice, and gradually, under the influence of the evil that resides in the old stones of the palace, the portrait of the ancestor that bears so uncanny a resemblance to Ward, and Curwen's old servant, Simon (played by Lon Chaney, Jr.), Ward begins to transform into his evil ancestor. If this process can be interpreted as creeping insanity, the screenplay does more justice to the poem than merely exploiting its title. The implication of Lovecraft's story, though, is that the transformation really does take place. When Dr. Willet (Frank Maxwell) and the inhabitants of Arkham destroy the palace, Curwen-Ward, having been rescued from the flames, ambivalently says, "I don't know how I can ever repay you for what you've done, Dr. Willet, but I intend to try."

So far, this is the only cinematic adaptation of Poe's poem, unless we include the various versions of "The Fall of the House of Usher," from which it comes. There are, however, two striking musical responses to the poem by Florent Schmitt and Josef Holbrooke.

Schmitt (1870–1958) won the coveted Grand Prix de Rome in 1900 when he was thirty. (Berlioz had failed four times before success on his fifth attempt. Ravel, after five attempts, never won it.) While in Rome, he composed one of his most celebrated works, a setting of *Psalm XLVI,* op. 38, but when he first arrived at the Villa Medici he also sketched out his *Etude* inspired by "The Haunted Palace." It took him four years to complete the work, and it was first performed in 1905, making it perhaps the first piece by a French composer based on Poe. Schmitt had worked from Mallarmé's French translation, but his primary concern was to create a work that obeyed musical rather than literary structure. The *Etude* is in sonata form, with a slow introduction which sets the mood and states the work's first important motif on a bass clarinet. A flute later intones the embryo of what will be the main theme of the following Allegro section that begins the exposition. The ensuing development section introduces a lyrical melody, but this is gradually undermined by music which expresses the advance of the insanity described in the poem. A recapitulation leads to a ruthlessly violent ending to the piece.

Holbrooke's setting of this poem forms the first movement of his Choral Dramatic Symphony, op. 48. In his comments on the work as a whole, George Lowe again reflected the Anglo-Saxon suspicion of Poe's aesthetic by observing that the piece, "in spite of its occasional uncanny quality, is both healthy and sane. Its very boldness saves it from the reproach of being designated as morbid in fancy. Fantastic it may be, but fantasy is a legitimate generator of art."[4] Later, he adds, "Perhaps it is well that he has dealt with the allegorical side of his subject rather than with its inner side, or the result might have been too acutely painful."[5] In the final analysis, however, "[t]he purely orchestral prelude is by far the best portion of the movement, and here we find the composer in one of his most delightful and picturesque moods. This is arranged for separate performance, and, even apart from its programmatic derivation, it has very definite and decided charm. The vocal writing, though interesting, has no great distinction."[6]

Lowe's comments unintentionally express the often disappointing effect of so much of Holbrooke's Poeana, the "lack of distinction" he refers to being the result of the element that Lowe singled out for praise: their avoidance of the "too acutely painful." To ears exposed to the sophisticated *frissons* of Debussy—and even Florent Schmitt—Holbrooke's approach is often rather tame by comparison.

Ligeia

An intensity *in thought, action, or speech was possibly, in her, a result, or at least an index, of that gigantic volition which, during our long intercourse, failed to give*

> *other and more immediate evidence of its existence. Of all the women whom I have ever known, she, the outwardly calm, the ever-placid Ligeia, was the most violently a prey to the tumultuous vultures of stern passion.*[1]

Poe regarded "Ligeia" (1838) as his best story. In it, he commemorates his love for the mother he never really knew, the stepmother who cared for him, the wife whose death left him fully the equal of his unnamed narrator's grief-stricken condition, and his child-bride's own mother, who was perhaps more of a mother to him than anyone else. The action of the tale is slight: Ligeia dies. Her husband remarries and installs his wife in the gloomy English abbey he has purchased to incarcerate his grief. He then poisons his new wife, but in his deranged state he is almost unaware of doing so (the poison he uses seems to drip "as if from some invisible spring in the atmosphere of the room"[2]). Rowena dies but after a suspenseful evening is eventually reanimated by the spirit of the lost Ligeia, who transforms Rowena's physical attributes like a sinister moth emerging from the pupa of an innocent caterpillar. There is no guarantee that any of this occurs beyond his own imagination.

It is, however, Poe's *idée fixe* of a *"Mournful and Never-ending Remembrance"* that is the story's sole *raison d'être*. Throughout, the narrator recalls the memory of a woman—or an ideal of an imaginary woman—who assumes a more-than-human significance. She becomes a demonic deity of unearthly beauty and immense intelligence—an adept of the occult and physical sciences, who writes poetry (specifically, the work Poe called "The Conqueror Worm"). She is also a woman who gives her husband the unconditional, undying love of a mother, but who, in the process, swamps his own identity along with his ability to relate to other women as anything more than substitutes for the one irreplaceable love of his life—Ligeia, "the beloved, the august, the beautiful, the entombed."[3]

Here, then, is the ultimate expression of Freud's Oedipus complex: an erotic, obsessional, psychologically paralyzed peon of passion to an archetype of the mother. No real mother could possibly approach the idealized majesty and intellectual brilliance of such an archetype. Harry Clarke's famous illustration for this tale appropriately shows the Lady Ligeia as a Madonna, her striking features surrounded by a star-spangled aureole, her raven-black hair cascading from her shoulders in an inky pyramid of occult power; her husband, with hooded, sunken eyes and satanic goatee, anticipating the manner of Terence Stamp in his 1960s heyday, kneels at her feet, holding aloft that raven-black hair in one hand, while in the other he supports a cane, suggesting something of the flagellator about him (or his wife—surely a dominatrix of some sort?). The cane is festooned with what might be black rosary beads, complicating the imagery yet further by combining fetishistic imagery with religious symbolism. Clarke unmistakably responded to the devotional, sexual and esoteric imagery of the tale in this superb image.

"Ligeia" is a satanic invocation to a dead mother—an onanist's dream of the perfect, unassailable, sexually sublimated woman. The narrator is not at all interested in *real* women. He has no interest in reality at all. Like so many of Poe's heroes, he locks himself away in an aesthetic ivory tower, filled with curios from antiquity: an Egyptian sarcophagus, an Indian couch, ottomans, golden candelabras, tapestries, an immense sheet of unbroken glass from Venice, and a Saracenic censor suspended from a semi–Gothic, semi–Druidical ceiling. Lady Rowena, who hopelessly finds herself in this domain of fantasy, is a mere physical vessel for the resurrection of Ligeia. The narrator calls her his wife, but she is really his own anima, the female aspect of his own psyche, whom his mother most nearly approximated but whom not even she could embody entirely.

The narrator is unreliable. Not only is he unsure if he has poisoned Rowena or if it was done to some magical event beyond his control, but also, he cannot even remember how he met Ligeia. Which of us, however, can remember our growth in the womb, which is presumably what is also implied here? Ultimately, we cannot be sure that Rowena actually exists beyond his own imagination and, if she does, that her resurrection as Ligeia at the end is real or merely the result of the narrator's opium addiction. Whether real or imaginary, that revivification could never continue in reality. There is no possible sequel to such an event beyond bathos. The effect is purely psychological—the description of an immense effort of will: the will to remember—to resurrect what is past by active *memory*—perhaps to create what never existed by the power of active imagination.

In this sense, "Ligeia" anticipated (in Poe's admirably condensed manner) that vast monument to the revivifying power of memory that is Proust's *À la recherche du temps perdu,* the opening novel of which, with its similarly hallucinatory "Overture," is also an invocation of the author's lost mother, along with a description of his equally dependent relationship with her:

> My sole consolation when I went upstairs for the night was that Mamma would come in and kiss me after I was in bed. But this good night lasted for so short a time, she went down again so soon, that the moment in which I heard her climb the stairs, and then caught the sound of her garden dress of blue muslin, from which hung little tassels of plaited straw, rustling along the double-doored corridor, was for me a moment of the utmost pain; for it heralded the moment which was bound to follow it, when she would have left me and gone downstairs again. So much so that I reached the point of hoping that this good night which I loved so much would come as late as possible, so as to prolong the time of respite during which Mamma would not yet have appeared.[4]

Proust knew and admired Poe's work, particularly *The Narrative of Arthur Gordon Pym,* which remained "in the desolation of my life one of the blessings of memory."[5] Michael Murphy has suggested a "transmigration" of *Pym* into *À la recherche*: "the ships' wooden hulls becoming the slats and headboards of Marcel's various beds at Combray, Balbec, Paris, Venice, and elsewhere. Similarly, Poe's dual authorial voice, divided as the writing of *Pym* is between the fictional Pym and the textual Poe, echoes the blurring of Proust's own narrative between Marcel and the Narrator. We might also consider how Proust, a lifelong sufferer from debilitating asthma attacks, responded to Pym's obsessive fear of being buried alive, a terror that recurs throughout Poe's *oeuvre*."[6]

The Oedipal and memory elements of "Ligeia" are what mark it out from the conventional tales of revenants, which were a staple of so much nineteenth-century supernatural fiction. More than a mere vampire, Ligeia is a psychological archetype very much in the Jungian sense of the term, though conceived of a century before Jung coined the term. "Ligeia" did, however, inform subsequent vampire imagery. Ligeia's dying exclamation "O God! O Divine Father!—shall these things be undeviatingly so?" has all the intensity of Mina Harker's outburst after having been polluted by Dracula's blood: "Unclean, unclean! Even the Almighty shuns my polluted flesh!"[7]—and when we filter Lucy Westenra's resurrection as a vampire woman through the historical influence of the gruesomely real exhumation of Dante Gabriel Rossetti's wife Elizabeth Siddal, we gain another genealogical connection with Poe. Stoker was fully aware of this exhumation, which discovered the corpse of Rossetti's first wife to be remarkably well-preserved, like a vampire indeed; but Rossetti himself was considerably influenced by Poe's theme of mournful and never-ending remembrance, particularly as manifested in "The Raven" and "The Oval Portrait," both of which he illustrated. The infatuated hero of "Ligeia" and the *femme fatale* qualities of Ligeia herself would inevitably have made their mark on Rossetti's similarly obsessional imagination which combined "Ligeia" with the equally idolatrous story of Dante's love for Beatrice. Whereas Stoker (not to mention Gottfried Bürger before him, in his once-famous revenant poem "Lenore") was primarily interested in the gruesome horror of resurrection along with its sexual connotations, Poe's theme of memory is at its most powerful in his most powerful resurrection tale. "Ligeia" is a testament to the power of memory to revive what is gone seemingly forever—to nurture one's remembrance so endlessly that remembrance becomes reality. Again, therefore, we see here a masterly testament of Poe's belief in the transfigurative power of the imagination, which nurtured those symbolist and decadent writers such as Villiers de L'Isle Adam and J.-K. Huysmans, for whom imagination *replaces* reality.

Intriguingly, given the power of the story's theme, relatively few films have been directly inspired by it. Roger Corman's *The Tomb of Ligeia* remains the most faithful cinematic testament to the power of Poe's most deeply felt tale, and of all Corman's Poe series it is the most faithful to the story on which it is based—even to the extent of filming it on location in England at Castle Acre Priory. Of course, more characters than we find in Poe are included in the film to increase its dramatic possibilities: Rowena's father (played by Derek Francis), various servants, a doctor (Richard Vernon) and the hero's friend (played by John Westbrook). Even though Corman allows Rowena to survive in this adaptation, he retains the overall shape of the tale without padding out the action with extraneous material. Inevitably, a dramatization of this supremely psychological narrative is bound to distort certain things. Vincent Price does an excellent job at portraying Verden Fell's descent into obsessive psychosis (this is perhaps his finest portrayal in the Corman Poe series), but we are left in no doubt at the end that Ligeia has indeed returned from the dead, which is not, despite the narrator's insistence that "I can never be mistaken," the case in the tale. Also, Rowena becomes a much more prominent figure in the film. In the story she is a mere vehicle. It is the narrator's viewpoint that carries the narrative weight. But Elizabeth Shepherd's confidently swaggering portrayal is perhaps too definite, and we become involved in her predicament far more than Poe concerns himself with her in his story. She becomes a damsel in distress, whereas she is really of no account in Poe's vision other than as a means to bring Ligeia back to life (even if only in the narrator's own mind).

Drawing on the imagery of Poe's black cat, Corman personifies Ligeia's spirit as a satanic feline which haunts her tomb and prowls the abbey in which her widower has virtually entombed himself. Into this vast Gothic pile of self-pity and reclusive obsession (the narrator of Poe's tale significantly expresses a fascination with Ligeia's "pearly teeth," as does the narrator of "Berenice") comes Lady Rowena, stumbling from her horse onto the "lovely asphodels" that grow around Ligeia's tomb.

Sensibly, Corman never shows us Ligeia as she was when alive, thus emphasizing the tale's theme of mournful and never-ending remembrance. He improvises on that theme in the powerful after-dinner scene in which Fell hypnotizes Rowena, regressing her to her own childhood, the innocent memory of which is startlingly interrupted by the spirit of Ligeia, who eventually speaks through her: "I will always be your wife." Though not drawn from the original story, the insertion of a scene of Mesmeric revelation (as Poe termed it in his story of that name) is fully in accord with Poe's preoccupations. Indeed, "Ligeia" is largely a story about belief in the power of the will, as the opening epigram drawn from Joseph Glanville makes clear: "And the will therein lieth, which dieth not.... Man doth not yield himself to the angels, nor unto death utterly, save only through the weakness of his feeble will." Poe opens his "Mesmeric Revelation" (incidentally, the first of his tales to be translated by that arch-priest of the decadent movement, Baudelaire) with the observation that "man, by mere exercise of the will, can so impress his fellow, as to cast him into an abnormal condition."[8]

Corman also references Poe's "The Bells" by having Ligeia, in black cat form, lure Rowena up to a bell tower for no apparent reason. There a giant bell terrorizes the unfortunate woman, suggesting the lines:

> What a tale of terror, now their turbulency tells!
> In the startled ear of night
> How they scream out their affright![9]

Verden and Rowena marry and honeymoon at Stonehenge (a suitably antique location for a man so obsessed by the past). Corman's evocation of the English countryside here and elsewhere is wholly in keeping with the elegiac mood of the story, and it adds immeasurably to the atmosphere of the film: the rolling green fields and wooded hillsides, the brief but poetic shot of the newlyweds by the sea, etc. On their return there, Rowena is troubled by a nightmare in which her maid appears to be an agent of Ligeia's malevolence. This is Corman's best of several film dream sequences, which became something of a trademark for his Poe adaptations. The maid smiles in a distinctly demonic fashion as she hands Rowena a bouquet of flowers (something that had happened earlier when awake, without the demonic implication). The fox, which Rowena and her father had been chasing at the beginning of the film, and which mysteriously vanishes from a wicker basket, now emerges from the dream-bouquet. Later it will wake Rowena from her slumbers, having been draped on her eiderdown by Verden himself in one of his strange somnambulant seizures. (Corman leaves open the possibility that Ligeia, in the form of the cat, has brought it there to terrorize her successor. By this means, he is able to suggest the unreliability of Poe's narrator.) This cat also prowls through Rowena's nightmare, as it does through the environs of the abbey which, we later learn, actually belongs to Ligeia, not Verden. As there was no record of her death, he is therefore unable to sell the place and move away. Ligeia has trapped him and Rowena, awaiting the moment when she will return to claim what is hers in every sense of the word.

And return she does. Verden has dug up her very well-preserved body and keeps it in a turret room where the fires of hell (or what might very well be presumed to be the fires of hell) flare from a large enclosure in the middle of the chamber. Rowena stumbles across an entrance to this hideaway when a mirror in an anteroom in the tower shatters. Corman seems here to be referencing the scene in Jean Cocteau's *Orphée* (1950), in which Orphée (Jean Marais) and Heurtebise (François Périer) enter the domain of the underworld by walking through a mirror. Their mirror does not shatter, however. Instead, they are allowed access to the other world by means of magic rubber gloves, which open a way through the glass for them. Rowena, however, makes her way to the domain of death through the broken shards, accidentally slashing her wrist as she does so, and this accident, as she shall see, removes the necessity of having Verden actually poison her, as the narrator presumably does in the story.

Rowena now discovers Verden in his strange trance-like state, but it is left to the butler, Kendrick (Oliver Johnston), to explain what has been going on: Ligeia apparently hypnotized Verden as she was dying, making him believe that she could never die. It would therefore appear that Verden has been responsible for the saucer of milk left in Rowena's room, along with the dead fox apparently stolen by his cat at the beginning of the film, and all the other "evidence" of Ligeia's haunting spirit. Verden arranged it all in his strange trance-like episodes. So Rowena decides to reverse the process. She stares into Verden's eyes and pretends to be Ligeia (Elizabeth Shepherd plays both roles anyway, so this is not difficult for Verden to believe). She tells him she is dying and that he will be released from his hypnosis when she is dead. But the severe blood loss from her wound makes her swoon, and Verden, smeared with her blood as she falls to the floor, thinks she really has died. Overcome with remorse at what he has done, he hurls the corpse of Ligeia into the flames and lays the "body" of Rowena on the couch which Ligeia's corpse had previously occupied. But the black cat jumps up and, despite Verden's hurling it away, the spirit of Ligeia would appear to have entered Rowena. She revives and advances towards Verden, revealing from beneath her shroud Ligeia's raven-black hair. They struggle and Verden strangles her. But when he looks down, it appears he has strangled Rowena, not Ligeia. He insists that Rowena be taken away while he deals with the black cat, whom he eventually strangles properly as the room goes up in flames, but not before the cat blinds him, giving Corman a vivid opportunity to emphasize the Oedipal nature of the story by showing Price's eyes dripping with blood as in the gory climax of Sophocles' *Oedipus Rex*. "What should I do with eyes," Oedipus says, "where all is ugliness?"[10] What indeed? Oedipus pays the price for his unlawful love but, though outwardly blinded, he symbolically gains inner vision and wisdom. Can the same be said of Verden, or is he merely mad? Has he imagined the whole thing, which Poe offers as a distinct possibility in his tale? Corman suggests otherwise in the final shot, as we see Verden and Ligeia lying together in the all-consuming flames.

Two other film versions followed Corman's classic, riding the twenty-first century's tidal wave of interest in vampires. *The Tomb* (dir. Michael Staininger, 2009) updated the action and emphasized Ligeia's vampiric nature by having her steal the souls of various people, not just Rowena's. The tag-line, "Eternal Life, Eternal Lust, Eternal Damnation" sums up this rather crude riff on Poe's masterpiece. Alexander Emmert's *Ligeia*, currently being filmed, will star Kirsten DeLuca in the title role. "Ligeia" has also inspired a 1994 opera by the contemporary American composer Augusta Read Thomas. "I try to write a rich, harmonic, serious work," she has explained. "My music is chromatic [but] I wouldn't say that it's dissonant.... I love Poe. I've loved him from my early childhood, from stories my father used to tell us, but the work also incorporates fragments of many of [Poe's] poems, as well as bits from other stories and from his factual life."[11]

One of the other reasons why this story should have appealed to Thomas is the relevance of its feminist subtext. Erin Leigh Helmey has usefully interpreted Ligeia as a representative of "the rising of a new kind of woman in society":

> Although Ligeia is the narrator's first wife, she symbolizes the new woman, perhaps created by the emanation of feminism in the nineteenth century.... Although the narrator cannot forget Ligeia and devote himself to Rowena, he is in control while he is with her as opposed to his time with Ligeia, which accounts for his horror when Ligeia is revived in Rowena's body. His response is to shriek aloud when Ligeia returns because the woman he could not

control returned, which clearly illustrates his position as an antifeminist, for he is fearful of the "new woman," a woman who is independent and powerful.[12]

"Ligeia" has also inspired the name of a Massachusetts-based heavy metal band, whose songs "Heroin Diaries," "I've Been Drinkin,'" and "Thanks for Nothing" might have raised a wry smile of recognition from the famously addictive, alcoholic and abused Poe. It seems likely that Ligeia will continue to be resurrected.

Maelzel's Chess-Player

A figure is seen habited as a Turk, and seated, with its legs crossed, at a large box apparently of maplewood, which serves as a table. The exhibitor will, if requested, roll the machine to any portion of the room, suffer it to remain altogether on any designated spot, or even shift its location repeatedly during the progress of the game.[1]

Here, Poe applies the ratiocinative approach of his fictional detective Auguste Dupin, to solve the riddle of Baron von Kempelen's famous, apparently automotive chess player, later exhibited by the entrepreneur and inventor of the metronome Johann Nepomuk Maelzel (1772–1838). The essay dates from 1836, two years before Maelzel's death. Von Kempelen (1734–1804) was described by Poe as "a nobleman of Presburg, in Hungary, who afterward disposed of it, [the chess-player] together with the secret of its operation to its present possessor. Soon after its completion it was exhibited in Presburg, Paris, Vienna, and other continental cities. In 1783 and 1784 it was taken to London by Mr. Maelzel. Of late years it has visited the principal towns in the United States."[2]

Johann Wolfgang Ritter von Kempelen was a linguist, artist, poet and inventor, whose famous chess-playing Turk was not exposed as a hoax until 1785. Many of his inventions were complex automata, but there was uncertainty as to how a mechanical machine could possibly play chess and actually beat its opponents. (Frederick the Great of Prussia was one of them.)

Poe identified himself with both the hoaxer, von Kempelen, and with the entrepreneur Maelzel. He not only sold his articles and stories in entrepreneurial style, but also specialized in hoaxes of his own. To solve the machine's mystery was the perfect problem for Poe's approach to detection, based on observation and deduction. He was firmly and correctly convinced that human agency was involved.

While the Chess-Player was in possession of Baron Kempelen, it was more than once observed, first, that an Italian in the suite of the Baron was never visible during the playing of a game at chess by the Turk, and, secondly, that the Italian being taken seriously ill, the exhibition was suspended until his recovery. The Italian professed a total ignorance of the game of chess, although all others of the suite played well. Similar observations have been made since the Automaton has been purchased by Maelzel. There is a man, Schlumberger, who attends him wherever he goes, but who has no ostensible occupation other than that of assisting in the packing and unpacking of the Automaton. This man is about the medium size, and has a remarkable stoop in the shoulders.[3]

The implication is obvious: that both the Italian and Schlumberger were somehow hidden within the mechanism of the machine and were the power behind the Turk's mysterious proficiency.

Von Kempelen also appears in Poe's alchemical tale "Von Kempelen and His Discovery" (1849). Whereas Poe's earlier piece about Maelzel had exposed the hoax, this later work was designed as a hoax, suggesting that a relative of von Kempelen had discovered the secret of the philosopher's stone and had turned lead into gold. Poe give him a complicated genealogy to help authenticate the fabrication:

> The Literary World speaks of him, confidently, as a native of Presburg (misled, perhaps, by the account in the Home Journal) but I am pleased in being able to state positively, since I have it from his own lips, that he was born in Utica, in the State of New York, although both his parents, I believe, are of Presburg descent. The family is connected, in some way, with Mäelzel, of automaton-chess-player memory. [If we are not mistaken, the name of the inventor of the chess-player was either Kempelen, Von Kempelen, or something like it—ED.][4]

Though it was nowhere near as successful as his earlier "Balloon Hoax," Poe really thought his Von Kempelen piece would create a similar sensation. It didn't. However, his linkage of these two stories certainly kept the name of von Kempelen and the chess-player in the public mind far more than it would subsequently have done if he had not written these pieces. Though no film has been based specifically on either of them, the hoax Poe exposed has been filmed twice. In 1927, Raymond Bernard directed a silent film version of *Le joueur d'échecs* (*The Chess Player*), starring Charles Dullin as Kempelen. The screenplay was by Henry Dupuis-Mazuel, who based it on his own novel of the same name, which suggested that von Kempelen used the chess-player to help smuggle a Polish nobleman out of Russia. Another version was made in 1938 with Conrad Veidt in the role of von Kempelen and Françoise Rosay as Catherine the Great. (Rosay would later appear in Hammer Films' *The Full Treatment* aka *Stop Me Before I Kill* [dir. Val Guest, 1960], a murder thriller which would definitely have appealed to Poe's love of mystery and somewhat warped imagination.) In the Veidt film, directed by Jean Dréville, the Turk is splendidly realized as a sinister figure, almost alive, which is certainly the case with the various other automata with which von Kempelen entertains the empress, as these are all animated by living actors. A startling scene occurs when von Kempelen sets his army of automated soldiers to surround the story's villain and bayonet him to death. The film thus conflates echoes of E.T.A. Hoffmann's "The Sandman" with history and memories of Poe's two stories featuring the name of von Kempelen.

The Man That Was Used Up

There was something, as it were, remarkable—yes, remarkable, *although this is but a feeble term to express my full meaning—about the entire individuality of the personage in question.*[1]

First published in 1839, "The Man That Was Used Up" is a very early manifestation of what we would now refer to as a "cyborg" fantasy. The man of the title is the very model of a modern brigadier general, who is extraordinarily handsome, six foot tall and broad-shouldered, eloquent, manly, heroic, irresistible. But in fact, he is no more than a mechanical construct. When the narrator visits the brigadier's home, he is amazed by what he finds:

Lee Majors on the cover of a DVD release of *The Six Million Dollar Man*.

It was early when I called, and the General was dressing, but I pleaded urgent business, and was shown at once into his bedroom by an old negro valet, who remained in attendance during my visit. As I entered the chamber, I looked about, of course, for the occupant, but did not immediately perceive him. There was a large and exceedingly odd-looking bundle of something which lay close by my feet on the floor, and, as I was not in the best humor in the world, I gave it a kick out of the way.

"Hem! ahem! rather civil that, I should say!" said the bundle, in one of the smallest, and altogether the funniest little voices, between a squeak and a whistle, that I ever heard in all the days of my existence.²

The negro then proceeds to put the various parts of the brigadier together: legs, arms, shoulders, bosom, teeth, eyes—all are replacement prosthetics. The brigadier, having been "used up" by the occupational hazards of his military career, hardly exists at all, but the impression his artificiality creates ironically makes the military career that reduced him to such a sorry state even more attractive to those who come in contact with him.

The parallel to such a story in popular culture is Martin Caidin's much more straight-faced novel *Cyborg* and the 1970s television series *The Six Million Dollar Man* which was based upon it. *The Six Million Dollar Man* starred Lee Majors as the similarly wrecked and re-constituted semi-cyborg Steve Austin, an astronaut who is severely injured when his experimental aircraft crashes. "Gentlemen, we can rebuild him," the famous introduction intones. "We have the technology. We have the capability to make the world's first bionic man. Steve Austin will be that man. Better than he was before. Better ... stronger ... faster." The really significant word here is "better." The implication is that not only can technology improve humanity but also that somehow humanity needs to be improved. Poe, deeply distrustful of progress and technology as he was, was the arch-enemy of such a view:

> I have no faith in human perfectibility. I think that human exertion will have no appreciable effect upon humanity. Man is now only more active—not more happy—nor more wise, than he was 6000 years ago. The result will never vary—and to suppose that it will, is to suppose that the foregone man has lived in vain—that the foregone time is but the rudiment of the future—that the myriads who have perished have not been upon equal footing with ourselves—nor are we with our posterity.[3]

By ridiculing the brigadier's artificiality, Poe was simultaneously ridiculing technology in general, which, along with its many undeniable benefits, also has the tendency to dehumanize people. The brigadier is, by contrast, a great champion of "progress":

> "There is nothing at all like it," he would say; "we are a wonderful people, and live in a wonderful age. Parachutes and railroads—man-traps and spring-guns! Our steamboats are upon every sea, and the Nassau balloon packet is about to run regular trips (fare either way only twenty pounds sterling) between London and Timbuctoo."[4]

And Poe is also attacking the dangerous allure of masculine militarism here. Like masculinity itself, it is also a kind of illusion, and a very dangerous one at that. The British academic Antony Easthope echoed Poe's tale in his own deconstruction of the masculine myth in his book *What a Man's Gotta Do* (1986):

> In terms of the myth masculinity wants to present itself as an essence—fixed, self-consistent, pure. In fact it has no essence and no central core. Gender is marked in three areas or levels of human experience—that of the body and the biological; that of social roles; and that at which gender is defined internally in the unconscious. The myth aims to bring together all three levels in a perfect unity, the completely masculine individual.
> But it can never work like this because the levels are distinct and never simply overlap.... The masculine myth has always tried to perpetuate its power by feigning invisibility. As soon as masculinity can be seen *as* masculinity, its power is challenged, it is called into question.... The masculine myth is also threatened by the very existence of a book such as this, which attempts to define it.[5]

Poe anticipated such a post–Freudian deconstruction by well over a century.

The Masque of the Red Death

There were much of the beautiful, much of the wanton, much of the bizarre, something of the terrible, and not a little of that which might have excited disgust.[1]

This most decadent of Poe's tales uses the format of a horror story to present what is basically a disquisition about ivory-tower synestheticism. Poe combines all the senses here in a manner that truly foreshadows the approach of Des Esseintes. Prince Prospero, the anti-hero of the tale, summons friends to his palace, locks the door and hopes by this means to avoid the plague outside; but there is no escape and eventually the Red Death penetrates his elegant defenses. He provides his guests with a truly Wagnerian melange of improvisations and spectacle. They dance through a suite of rooms arranged in an enfilade. Each is decorated with a different color, and lit by similarly tinted glass. Poe combines this spectrum with references to music, costume, dance, wine—and ultimately death, for a life devoted entirely to beauty can lead nowhere else. As the German poet August von Platen (1796–1835) suggested, "Whoever has beheld beauty with his eyes, is already dedicated to death."[2]

Like his Shakespearean namesake, Prospero is also a kind of magician, in the Wagnerian sense of being an artist who can achieve miracles. In Prospero's case these are miracles of décor. The rooms are decorated successively in blue, purple, green, orange, white, violet and black, the latter being illuminated by scarlet-tinted windows. The choice of colors here is significant: Blue was the favored hue of the German Romantic poet Novalis (1772–1801), representing the mystical goal sought by the hero of his novel *Heinrich von Ofterdingen*. (Poe was familiar with the writings of Novalis, as the epigram of "The Mystery of Marie Rogêt" demonstrates.) In the first chapter of the novel, Novalis writes, "[T]ake notice particularly of a little blue flower, which you will find above here; pluck it, and commit yourself humbly to heavenly guidance."[3] Purple is the chief color of decadence. Orange was later identified by D.H. Lawrence (himself an expert analyst of Poe) as another decadent color. In the unlikely context of his play *A Collier's Friday Night,* the eponymous collier's son, Ernest, reads Baudelaire to his girlfriend Maggie and compares the "heavy and full and voluptuous" effect of the words to "oranges falling and rolling a little way along a dark-blue carpet."[4] Green became another color associated with decadence, culminating in Oscar Wilde's infamous green carnation. White, the color of the aesthetic lilies so admired by symbolist artists such as Carlos Schwabe (1866–1926), also conforms to this scheme of associations. Violet, much earlier in the nineteenth century, had been identified with the vampire heroine of "Wake Not the Dead," a tale from 1800 attributed to Johann Ludwig Tieck (1773–1853), a writer close to Poe's heart. Tieck describes how the vampire woman, Brunhilda, "began to fix her blood-thirsty lips on Walter's breast, when cast into a profound sleep by the odor of her violet breath."[5] Finally, Poe's black room with its scarlet window no doubt inspired the devil-worshipping element of Roger Corman's film adaptation, an element that is otherwise entirely lacking in the original story.

Prospero's ivory tower is a self-sufficient, hermetically sealed temple to the self, which anticipates all those later ivory towers of *fin-de-siècle* artists and writers—particularly the home of the Belgian symbolist artist Fernand Khnopff (1858–1921), whose motto was "on a que soit"—"one has only oneself." Prospero has, admittedly, a whole host of guests to keep him company, but in effect they are no more than animated set dressings. He does not so much invite them to his hideaway to save them from the Red Death as to enhance his distraction from reality. Indeed, Poe's description of this state of affairs, "The external world could take care of itself,"[6] foreshadows that famous line from Villiers de l'Isle Adam's similarly aloof symbolist drama *Axel:* "As for living—our servants will do that for us."[7]

The Red Death might well be interpreted as the reality that threatens Prospero's magically imaginative kingdom. Poe is keen to emphasize Prospero's Wagnerian self-indulgence with adjectives such as "voluptuous," "magnificent," "eccentric," "bizarre," and "barbaric," and he strings multiple nouns together in a single sentence to create an iridescent effect, such as "glare" and "glitter," and "piquancy" and "phantasm." Overall the impression is one of an "arabesque," the coalescence of "a multitude of dreams."[8]

The dancers move through the variously colored rooms to the music of an orchestra, but the "brazen lungs" of an ebony clock always interrupts them on the hour, when they all listen to the sinister knell of their approaching death. In effect, Poe was aestheticizing the medieval idea of a Dance of Death around the same time that Liszt was writing his *Totentanz* for piano and orchestra. (The latter was originally conceived in 1838 but revised twice in 1853 and 1859.) Liszt's piece combines virtuoso display with the Dies Irae plainchant melody, which Berlioz had been the first composer to demonize in his *Symphonie fantastique* of 1831. Like the poem "The Conquerer Worm," which Ligeia recites prior to her death, Poe uses a theatrical metaphor in "The Masque of the Red Death" to express the transience of life, comparing it into a dance. It is a "gay and magnificent 'revel,'"[9] which Death terminates at the stroke of midnight. In the 1883 illustration of the story, drawn in charcoal and black ink by Odilon Redon (1840–1916), a motley group of masked revelers are represented as they listen to the three-quarter chime before midnight. The fleetness of time is symbolized by a winged minute hand (a feather, rather than the more traditional pointer). The revelers stare out towards the viewer with a mixture of dumbfounded, vacant and anxious expressions, made all the more static as they are meant to be wearing grotesque masks, from behind which their hopeless eyes stare out in bewilderment. They are aware of their fate and yet simultaneously desperate to ignore it. Poe's tale is already an allegory of the human condition, but in Redon's vision, the allegory is made more intimate, their predicament more pathetic. We take pity on each face individually, not merely on a symbolic crowd, as in Roger Corman's more lurid dénouement (see below). Redon's dancers are truly pitiable, lost—even childlike in their helplessness.

A more grotesque, less moving but nonetheless magisterial visual response to Poe's story is Jean Delville's charcoal and pastel drawing from 1890, entitled simply *Death*. The inclusion of a clock in the background emphasizes the association, leading one to interpret the gaunt blood-stained and seemingly disembodied head as that of the Red Death itself. But Delville also includes a reference to his interest in the occult by enclosing the head in an esoteric triangle. As Bruno Fornani has explained, "A few highlights in red pastel suggest the scarlet window-panes and the purple marks of the plague."[10]

Poe's macabre dénouement was also echoed by Ravel's choreographic poem *La Valse* (1919–1920), which combined the idiom of a Viennese waltz with Ravel's sumptuously terrifying style to create the musical image of Europe tottering on the brink and then falling into the abyss of the First World War. Foreshadowing such a catastrophe, Poe wrote: "There were much of the beautiful, much of the wanton, much of the *bizarre,* something of the terrible, and not a little of that which might have excited disgust."[11] He refers to the revelers as "dreams"—the insubstantial dreams of life itself, which come to life only when stimulated by *music*.

When the orchestra pauses to listen to the clock chiming, "the dreams are stiff-frozen"[12] Poe's interest in music is crucial here, for he often refers to it as a life-giving principle: "And now again the music swells, and the dreams live."[13] Similarly, in the quotation used by Alan Parsons to introduce the "House of Usher" track on his *Tales of Mystery and Imagination* album, Poe suggests that "since the comprehension of sweet sound is our most indefinite sensation, music, when combined with a pleasurable idea is poetry. Music without the idea, is simply music. Without music or an intriguing idea, color becomes pallor, man becomes carcass, home becomes catacomb, and the dead are but for a moment motionless." Poe's words here anticipate Schopenhauer's celebrated defense of music as the art most in touch with the Will—the noumen beyond the merely phenomenal world, the Thing in Itself: "For this reason the effect of music is so very much more powerful and penetrating than is that of the other arts, for those speak only of the shadow, but music of the essence."[14]

In Poe's metaphysical use of music in "The Masque of the Red Death" we find another link between his work and the later symbolist generation via Wagner's adherence to the Schopenhauerian view of music, and the subsequent idolatry of Wagnerian art by the symbolists themselves.

That connection was clearly demonstrated by André Caplet's "Conte fantastique" for harp and orchestra (1924), which was directly inspired by "The Masque of the Red Death." Caplet (1878–1925), a protégé and amanuensis of Debussy, combined the idea of a one-movement concertante piece with a highly programmatic response to Poe's tale in 1908. A seductive waltz, which looks back to the Flower Maiden's music in Act Two of Wagner's *Parsifal* (as, indeed, does Debussy's ballet *Jeux*, written for Diaghilev in 1913), Caplet's waltz also anticipates Ravel's *La Valse*, growing wilder and more frenetic as each of the successive sections is interrupted by the chimes of the ebony clock. These are imitated by the harp itself. Finally, the harpist is instructed to rap on the soundboard of the instrument to suggest Death knocking at the door of the abbey, before a flurry of notes brings this most sinister piece to its unnerving conclusion.

A decade earlier in England, Josef Holbrooke had brought out a ballet (Op. 65) on the subject, complete with its own chiming clock effects and waltz rhythms, consisting of a prologue outside the gates of the palace and three numbers inside the ballroom. The first of these, lit in purple, sets the scene. The second is a bacchanal (in blue) and the third is a dance of death in a "scarlet room." Holbrooke not only changed Poe's color scheme but also modified the emphasis of the story in his scenario, having the Red Death unmasked at the end as "Beauty," Prospero's beloved, with whom he has been dancing all along. Poe refers to Beauty as a quality rather than an individual, but Holbrooke decided to personify it. The final revelation is striking but illogical, as we have already seen "a shrouded figure in grey, clinging garment, splotched with scarlet blobs," as Holbrooke puts it, while Prospero has been dancing with "Beauty." George Lowe was also aware of this modification:

> In his desire to give a less gruesome ending to his work, the composer has sacrificed the dramatic completeness that the story possessed, and the eerie character of the Red Death as imagined by Poe loses its symbolical significance, and becomes an uninteresting and unconvincing personage. Holbrooke's music, however, is so realistically vivid and fine that one comes to the conclusion that it was rather Poe's version of the story than this altered version that he had in mind when writing most of it.[15]

Though Holbrooke's modification is unlikely to have influenced Charles Beaumont and R. Wright Campbell's screenplay for Roger Corman's 1964 film adaptation, it is comparable to what Beaumont and Campbell wrote for their own conclusion. In it, Vincent

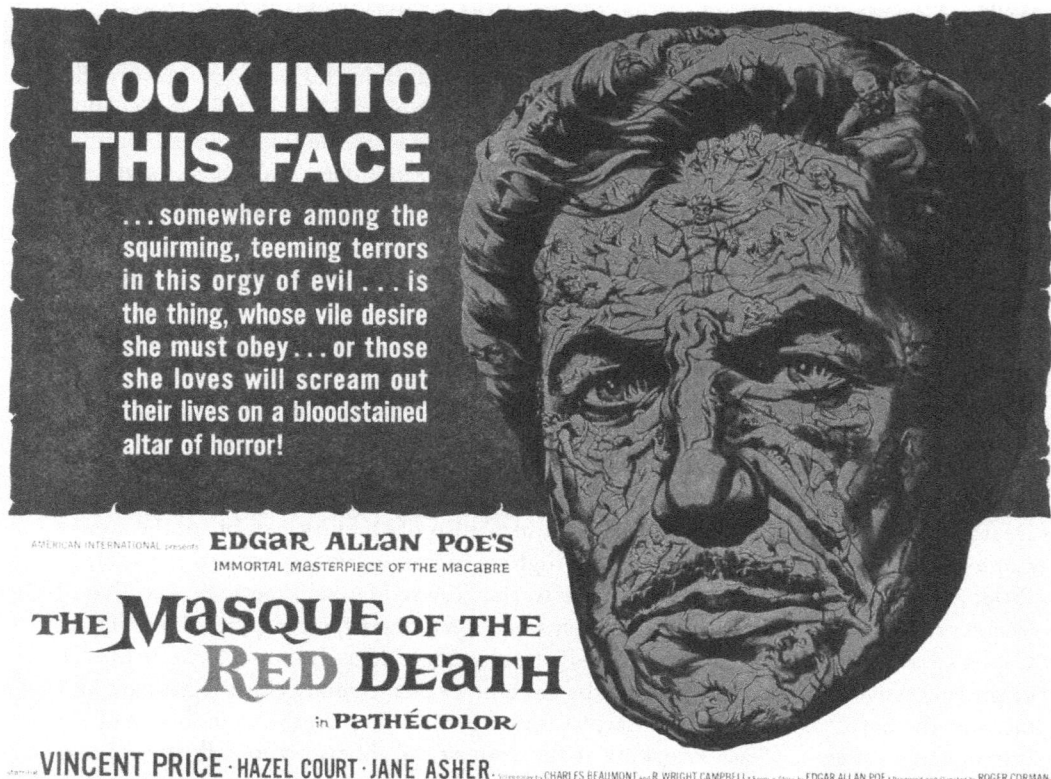

Nose of Evil: the only time Vincent Price's nose became the backside of a nude woman, in this poster for *The Masque of the Red Death* (dir. Roger Corman, 1964).

Price's Prospero has a "Beauty" of his own to dance with in the shape of Jane Asher, who plays an innocent village girl called Francesca; but when Prospero confronts the Red Death at the end of the film, the mysterious red-robed figure is revealed to have Prospero's own face. Death is only ever *personal,* after all: "There is no face of Death until the moment of your own death," he explains. "You are your own heaven and hell." In this, Corman and his screenwriters anticipated the controversial ending to Patrick McGoohan's complex television fantasy series *The Prisoner,* the dénouement of which has McGoohan's character confront the mysterious "No. 1" only to find his own face staring back at him and laughing. (The implication here is that No. 1 is no more or less than our primary personality.)

Corman's film, regarded by some to be the best of the Poe series, is immensely aided by Nicolas Roeg's flamboyant color photography. This not only emphasizes the varied hues of the dancers' costumes and the various attires of Prospero (who at one stage sports Titian-blue head-gear in semi–Saracenic style) but also the blue and green candles which illuminate the castle and its dungeons, not to mention Corman's approximation of Poe's enfilade. (The colors are limited to yellow, purple, white and black.) In addition, Corman references the famous imagery of Death in Ingmar Bergman's *The Seventh Seal* (1957), but unlike Bergman's black-and-white nemesis, Corman's Death (played by John Westbrook) appears in full color, and opens the film in a scene set on a blasted heath in which he instructs an old woman to tell her village, "The day of your deliverance is at hand." As a token of his intention, he passes his hand over a white rose, which promptly turns blood red. Whether Death means that the deliverance of the villagers will come when the Red Death visits Prince Prospero, or that soon they will also die is left deliberately ambiguous. In the event, both eventualities occur. Having found out that the Red Death has preceded him, Prospero orders the destruction of the village. The Red Death's brethren appear at the end of the film in various other colors, emblematic of the effect of their respective diseases.

Price's Prospero is a rather more complex character than Poe's. He has theological preoccupations and, as a devil worshipper, he wants to corrupt (he says "instruct") Francesca's innocence: "I want to save your soul so that you can join me in the glories of hell," as he somewhat absurdly puts it. Countering Francesca's clumsily expressed commitment to Christianity (most of Asher's lines are clumsily written and even more clumsily delivered), he insists, "If a God of love and life ever did exist, he is long since dead. Someone, something rules in his place." The subsequent hefty dose of Satanism that Corman's film injects into Poe's tale continues with Hazel Court's Juliana, who is preparing herself to become betrothed to Satan. Fearing that Prospero has transferred his interest from her to Francesca, she is more than usually keen to demonstrate her commitment to the cause. She performs her own marriage ceremony by plunging a branding iron in the form of an inverted crucifix on her decorously exposed cleavage and promptly experiences a distinctly Freudian dream sequence in Corman's best, highly characteristic manner.

Even with the addition of a Satanic subplot, Beaumont and Campbell realized that there wasn't enough material in Poe's original to fill a feature film, and so incorporated another of Poe's tales, "Hop-Frog" (1849), into the mix. The adaptation follows the basic idea of Poe's story, though the dwarf-jester Hop-Frog is, for some reason, renamed Hop-Toad in the film. One of Prospero's friends (played by Patrick Magee) has insulted the tiny dancer Esmeralda ("Trippetta" in Poe's tale). Hop-Toad, who loves the dancer, plans revenge by appealing to the man's vanity, and suggests that he will make a great impression at the masque ball if he dresses up as an orang-outang. (Poe's interest in man's primitive ancestor was not confined to "The Murders in the Rue Morgue.") The corrupt fellow falls for the trick and, upon his entrance, is hoisted up into the ceiling by the dwarf, where he is promptly set on fire. In Poe's original, seven of the king's ministers along with the corrupt king himself are strung up and immolated, and these "eight chained Orang-Outangs," as the original (but later withdrawn) subtitle calls them, have been interpreted by various critics, including Kenneth Silverman, as substitutes for the friends of a certain Sarah Helen Whitman, whom Poe unsuccessfully courted previous to his writing of the tale. Silverman suggests that the courtiers are based on "a small army of people by whom [Poe] had come to feel abused and misled,"[16] and these included Helen's friends, with Poe himself cast as the gleefully revengeful dwarf. The method by which the courtiers are set on fire involves their orang-outang costumes to be soaked in highly combustible tar, and this suggests an echo of Poe's earlier story about a lunatic asylum, "The System of Doctor Tarr and Professor Fether" (1845), as we shall see later.

Mellonta Tauta

Get ready your spectacles and make up your mind to be annoyed. I mean to write to you every day during this odious voyage.[1]

Futuristic fiction was nothing new when Poe wrote this dystopian satire in 1848. Jane Webb's *The Mummy: A Tale of the Twenty-Second Century* (1827) predicted many inventions that indeed came to pass, such as mobile phones, air-conditioning and coffee machines. The difference with Poe's approach was that he rejected the optimism in the future shared by writers up to that time. Mary Shelley took a darker approach to the future in *The Last Man* (1826), but for most predictive writers, extending their eighteenth-century enlightenment principles, the future was bright. Poe, however, did not believe in progress and for him technology and over-population would bring nothing but disaster. The phrase "Mellonta Tauta" derives from Sophocles' *Antigone* and translates as "These things are in the future." For Poe, the word "future" was a frightening prospect. The writers who followed him, such as H.G. Wells, whose novel *The Shape of Things To Come* (1933) echoes the meaning of Poe's title here, shared his view and further contributed to the predominantly negative frisson of the word "future" in most twentieth-century science fiction.

Poe's story is also a platform to argue that imaginative intuition, rather than the traditional deductive or inductive approaches, is the only way to achieve advances in knowledge. As such, it forms a thematic pendant to his essay *Eureka*, which argues the same point. But "Mellonta Tauta" also takes the form of a series of letters written by the narrator on board the balloon *Skylark* in the year 2848. The name *Skylark* is Poe's ironic reference to the Utopian optimist Shelley, via Shelley's famous lyric "To a Skylark." Poe had no such optimism. In his vision of 2848, the sky is crowded with balloons, as ours are indeed crowded with airplanes. War, accidents and plague are welcomed to keep the population under control. When a man falls overboard on a ship he is not permitted to get on board again: "I rejoice, my dear friend, that we live in an age so enlightened that no such thing as an individual is supposed to exist. It is the mass for which the true Humanity cares."[2] Indeed, when the *Skylark* collapses and falls to the earth, the narrator is not overly concerned. All she says is, "Ah, I see—the balloon has collapsed, and we shall have to tumble into the sea."[3] Such a totalitarian state of affairs indeed foreshadows those dystopian worlds we encounter in the society of Morlocks and Eloi in Wells' *The Time Machine* (1895) and Michael Anderson's 1976 film adaptation of William F. Nolan's novel *Logan's Run*, in which the population of a post-nuclear holocaust society are culled when they reach the age of thirty. Poe also anticipates the imagery of both *Logan's Run* and the famous dénouement of the film adaptation of Pierre Boulle's novel *The Planet of the Apes* (dir. Franklin F. Schaffner, 1968) in his satire regarding the cornerstone of the Monument to the Memory of George Washington, which is discovered and misinterpreted by the archaeologists of the future. The fact that only the cornerstone is discovered leads them to think that "actual monuments had fallen into disuse—as was all very proper—the people contenting themselves, as we do now, with a mere indication of the design to erect a monument at some future time; a cornerstone being cautiously laid by itself 'solitary and alone' ... as a guarantee of the magnanimous intention."[4] When Logan (Michael York) manages to escape his artificial environment, he discovers the ruins of the Washington Capitol building, much as

Charlton Heston realizes that the Planet of the Apes is actually the Earth after a nuclear war, when he stumbles across the remains of the Statue of Liberty.

Metzengerstein

Let it suffice to say, that at the period of which I speak, there existed, in the interior of Hungary, a settled although hidden belief in the doctrines of the Metempsychosis.[1]

"Metzengerstein" may have been designed (but not originally—or, for that matter, posthumously—interpreted) as a satire of the German *Schauerromantik* tradition. This claim is still disputed, and most readers have taken it at face value. Whatever the truth of the matter, the story is undeniably a disquisition on metempsychosis, one of Poe's favorite themes. He wrote no werewolf tales, but here we have a kind of were-horse story involving two rival families who resemble Shakespeare's Montagues and Capulets in their intergenerational enmity. The elderly Berlifitzing is killed trying to save his horses when his stables are vindictively burned to the ground by young Metzengerstein. Soon after, Berlifitzing's spirit animates the tapestry of a gigantic horse in Metzengerstein's palace, and it also seems to inhabit the body of a wild, fiery horse which gallops into Metzengerstein's courtyard. Metzengerstein is obsessed by this mysterious animal, which he rides in all weathers. When the castle is set on fire at the end of the story, Metzengerstein rides his equine nemesis into the flames and a gigantic plume of smoke in the shape of a horse hovers over the charred battlements. (Poe repeated this final effect with the ghostly impression of the black cat—also the result of a catastrophic fire—in his 1843 tale of that name.) Published in 1832, "Metzengerstein" intriguingly anticipated by one year Alexander Pushkin's similarly equine narrative

Jane Fonda as a female Metzengerstein in Roger Vadim's adaptation of Poe's equine metempsychosis story from *Histoires extraordinaires/Spirits of the Dead/Tre passi nel delirio* **(1968).**

poem "The Bronze Horseman," in which Falconet's famous equestrian statue of Peter the Great in St. Petersburg comes to life having been cursed by a peasant.

There is a subtle homoerotic subtext to "Metzengerstein," which Roger Vadim made explicit in what is perhaps the weakest of the three segments of *Tre passi nel delirio* (*Three Steps to Madness*), aka *Spirits of the Dead* aka *Histoires extraordinaires* (1968). By casting Jane Fonda as a female version of the corrupt Metzengerstein, Poe's subdued erotic aspect is made explicit, for this Metzengerstein is patently attracted to Berlifitzing, who is presented (by Fonda's brother Peter) as a young man. There is no erotic attraction between Poe's young male Metzengerstein and elderly male Berlifitzing, but when Berlifitzing appears as a horse with "human-looking eye," Poe is keen to emphasize Metzengerstein's "extraordinary affection" for the beast. At the same time, he "never vaulted into the saddle without an unaccountable and almost imperceptible shudder,"[2] suggesting a certain guilt, or even a revulsion over his infatuation. In Vadim's film much less is left to the imagination. Jane Fonda wears, among other post–Barbarella costumes, a kinky leather bodice, while Peter sports similarly fetching leather trousers like Dirk Bogarde's camp cowboy Anacleto in *The Singer Not the Song* (dir. Roy Ward Baker, 1961); but before they get together we are treated to a variety of orgy scenes at which Poe only hints. In a perhaps unintentional nod to Corman's *The Masque of the Red Death,* Jane Fonda's Fredericke Metzengerstein takes her court to her castle and indulges in a variety of sadistic entertainments. Even the flute and harp music here echoes David Lee's score for Corman's *The Masque of the Red Death*. Passing a gibbet outside the castle, Fredericke confesses "I love this place. It's beautiful." Then, William Tell-style, she shoots her arrows at a terrified serving boy, has him hung from a branch and then shoots the rope in two. Back indoors, she plays with a baby leopard, indulges in lesbian threesomes, bathes with her entourage and spouts such lines as "If I find who did this, I'll have him flogged for two hours and apply the vinegar myself"—all this in French, being a Vadim film.

After this extemporized build-up, including many shots of Fredericke riding her horse by the sea, we cut to the meat of the story. Vadim leaves us in no doubt that Fredericke is smitten by the handsome, leather-clad Berlifitzing, but he rejects her. Unaccustomed to such behavior, she accordingly burns down his stables and Berlifitzing duly re-appears as a horse. Fredericke can't stop herself from riding him. She has the tapestry repaired and is equally fascinated by the image of the horse it depicts. She sings to the other horse and kisses it. (One expects her to take it to bed with her like Caligula, but we are spared that extravagance.) The obligatory thundery dénouement brings the tapestry horse's eyes to red fiery life and Fredericke rides the three-dimensional one into the fire caused by the lightning, like Brünnhilde on her steed, Grane, at the end of *Götterdämmerung*. This is not the only Germanic resonance the tale enjoys, for along with its Gothic mood, Poe introduces the narrative with a quotation from Martin Luther: "Pestis eram vivus—moriens tua mors ero"—"Living, I was your plague ... dying, I shall be your death."

Morella

And then, hour by hour would I linger by her side, and dwell upon the music of her voice—until, at length, its melody was tainted with terror,—and there fell a shadow upon my soul—and I grew pale, and shuddered inwardly at those too unearthly tones.[1]

Like Ligeia, Morella is a student of metaphysical philosophy, in particular "the doctrines of *Identity*, as urged by Schelling"[2] This philosophical element is what distinguishes such a story from the German *Schauerromantik* models with which Poe was acquainted from the pages of *Blackwood's Magazine*. As Kenneth Silverman puts it, it helps "deepen the mood of dire awe, and with such details that lend the improbable events a feeling of reality."[3]

Poe's glittering prose style is the equivalent of a well-dressed film set, such as we find in Roger Corman's cinematic adaptation of the story in *Tales of Terror*. Poe's tales are as much about *mood* as meaning, and his descriptions of furnishings and decor complement the way in which he uses language to create atmosphere, both emotional and sensual. Silverman draws our attention to Poe's use of "the full range of English punctuation, calculating commas, semicolons, dashes for their variety and effect ... an arsenal of sentence structures and attention-getting devices—questions, exclamations, italics, inversions—to keep the prose surface moving and alive."[4]

In "Ligeia," the spirit of the narrator's dead wife returns not only to inhabit the body of his new wife Rowena, but also to transform it physically into a replica. In "Morella" (1835), the same thing happens, but this time it happens to Morella's daughter, to whom the father cannot bring himself to give a name; but at a baptismal ceremony on the child's tenth birthday, he impulsively uttered his wife's name, to catastrophic effect:

> What more than fiend convulsed the features of my child, and overspread them with hues of death, as starting at that scarcely audible sound, she turned her glassy eyes from the earth to heaven, and falling prostrate on the black slabs of our ancestral vault, responded—"I am here."[5]

When the reborn Morella is buried, there is no trace of the original's corpse in the tomb. The narrator is left with nothing but his grief-stricken obsession. "I kept no reckoning of time or place, and the stars of my fate faded from heaven, and therefore the earth grew dark, and its figures passed by me, like flitting shadows, and among them all I beheld only—Morella."[6]

This foreshadowing of the decadent aesthete drew forth one of Harry Clarke's most successful illustrations in which a heavy-browed, goatee-bearded exquisite gazes out of the frame, his tapering fingers be-ringed and bejeweled, while the flowers around him transform into women's faces (presumably representing Morella in her various moods). Morella herself (though we cannot be sure if this is the daughter or the mother) lies—or floats—before him, covered with hallucinogenic flowers. Clarke's model for the narrator here must surely have been informed by the likes of Huysmans' Des Esseintes and the imagery of Aubrey Beardsley, but Poe lies behind all of them. Both the narrator of "Morella" and Egaeus, the cousin of Berenice, are the true models of the decadent, obsessive introvert who could all say, like the narrator of Christina Rossetti's poem "Who Shall Deliver Me?": "I lock my door upon myself, And bar them out; but who shall wall Self from myself, most loathed of all?"[7]

"Morella"'s philosophical basis—the question of identity—is really the whole point of the supernatural events the story details. In a work of fiction, which itself is an experiment with language, Poe seems to be asking if identity can be attained without language—

if it is language itself that generates meaning; for only when the daughter is named does she attain her true identity.

But other anxieties are present here concerning a fear of having one's identity overwhelmed by another person's will. In this kind of psychological vampirism, the will, so central a concept to "Ligeia," becomes a frightening weapon. The narrator of "Morella" is aware of this ability in his wife before she dies, and it causes him to distance himself from her: "[M]y wife's manner oppressed me as a spell. I could no longer bear the touch of her wan fingers, nor the low tone of her musical language, nor the lustre of her melancholy eyes."[8] Like a drug addict, he is terrified of his growing dependence upon and infatuation with her and yet he cannot free himself of the relationship.

In Roger Corman's film adaptation of this story in *Tales of Terror* (1962), the philosophical element inevitably made way for the supernatural and horrific elements. While Vincent Price eloquently conveys the introverted decadence of the grief-stricken husband, gloomily attired in a long purple dressing gown, a major difference is that Morella herself is already dead when the action begins, and her corpse has been left to rot on her bed. Her daughter (played by Maggie Pierce) is now a twenty-six-year-old woman, rather than Poe's ten-year-old child. She also has an incurable disease, and consequently has but a short time to live. Richard Matheson's screenplay calls her Lenora, which reminds us of "the lost Lenore" in "The Raven," but as a whole, the film emphasizes the story's similarities to "Ligeia" rather more than Poe's "Morella," grafting on the scene from "Ligeia" in which Lady Rowena Trevanion of Tremaine repeatedly seems to die and then to come back to life in what the narrator calls a "hideous drama of revivication."[9] Just as Lady Rowena turns into Ligeia, so too does Lenore metamorphose into Morella (played by Leona Gage).

Also like Ligeia, Morella has raven black hair and scarlet lips. The final scene also replays the dénouement of "The Fall of the House of Usher," with Morella strangling her husband (Price) in a fiery climax. Corman's *House of Usher* is also recalled in the opening scenes in which a coach brings Lenore to the family mansion, which is surrounded, like Daniel Haller's moody design for the House of Usher, with swirling mist and petrified trees. Inside the mansion, Corman obliges with a vast set of decayed, bleached splendor, replete with a cobwebby banquet table on which rotting food and wandering spiders remind one of Miss Haversham's wedding breakfast in *Great Expectations*.

Love and loathing are strongly linked in this adaptation. The father originally loathes the daughter for causing Morella's death, and Morella's dying words express her desire to avenge herself on the child that has killed her. Why Morella loathes her husband sufficiently to strangle him at the end can only be explained by the implicitly incestuous subtext. It would seem that Morella is jealous of her daughter's love for the father. Having grown attached to his daughter during the course of the action, he is horrified to discover that Morella has returned through her.

This interchangeability of mother and daughter with its incestuous implications seems to have fascinated Corman, who returned to the story in the role of producer for a second film adaptation called *The Haunting of Morella* (dir. Jim Wynorski, 1990), which confronted this taboo head on.

In *The Haunting of Morella,* Nicole Eggert plays both Morella and her daughter, while David McCallum plays the husband, here called, Biblically, Gideon. "Call me mad if you will, but my wife has returned to take possession of my daughter," he says. This

Morella, however, is depicted as "pure evil," which is certainly not what she is in Poe's tale. Indeed, the film echoes Bram Stoker's *The Jewel of Seven Stars* (1903), which took Poe's idea of identity theft and gave the incest theme an exotic Egyptian treatment. In this novel (Stoker's best after *Dracula*), we learn how an ancient Egyptian queen, called Tera, has planned her reincarnation in the body of Margaret Trelawny, the daughter of an Edwardian archaeologist. (Stoker quietly overlooked the fact that the ancient Egyptians did not believe in reincarnation.) Margaret not only finds her own personality gradually overpowered by Tera, she also physically resembles Tera. And her own mother died giving her life—as is the case with Morella. Just as the narrator of Poe's tale is infatuated with both his wife and daughter, Abel Trelawny is infatuated with Tera and (rather more implicitly) with Margaret. The psychological landscape of Stoker's story is quite similar to Poe's, with the important difference that Tera is a force of evil. Stoker was familiar with Poe's work (he even contemplated dramatizing "The Fall of the House of Usher"[10]) and it is quite possible that "Morella" formed part of his inspiration for the novel. *The Haunting of Morella* might therefore be approached as the product of a union between the original Poe story, Stoker's novel, and the three cinematic adaptations of it, which increasingly emphasized the malevolence of Tera's psychological take-over and the incestuous subtext of the whole. (David McCallum's Gideon does indeed shout to his possessed daughter-wife: "Come on, it's me you want!"). The films in question—*Blood from the Mummy's Tomb* (dir. Seth Holt, 1970), *The Awakening* (dir. Mike Newell, 1980), *Bram Stoker's Legend of the Mummy* (dir. Jeffrey Obrow, 1998), along with the "Morella" episode from *Tales of Terror* and *The Haunting of Morella*—are also relatives of Don Siegel's science fiction–Cold War paranoia classic *Invasion of the Body Snatchers* (1956) (this movie was based on a 1955 novel by Jack Finney that was a 1954 serial in *Collier's* magazine), but their true ancestor is surely Poe.

The Murders in the Rue Morgue

As a strong man exults in his physical ability, delighting in such exercises as call his muscles into action, so glories the analyst in that moral activity which disentangles. *He derives pleasure from even the most trivial occupations bringing his talent into play. He is fond of enigmas, of conundrums, hieroglyphics; exhibiting in his solutions of each a degree of* acumen *which appears to the ordinary apprehension preternatural.*[1]

This famous detective story from 1841 inspired virtually all subsequent writers of detective fiction. It created the genre and, as the above quotation eloquently demonstrates, the character of Poe's gentleman detective Auguste Dupin strongly foreshadows that of Sherlock Holmes. Dupin's almost absurdly complex deductions are fully the measure of Holmes.' The narrator is also fully the equal of Dr. Watson in his amazement at Dupin's powers of observational deduction: "I do not hesitate to say that I am amazed, and can scarcely credit my senses," he exclaims at one point.[2] Also like Holmes and Watson, the two men decide to share the same accommodation, in their case "a time-eaten and grotesque mansion, long deserted through superstitions."[3] There is an element of the mystical about Dupin too, which again influenced the quasi-magus Holmes:

King Kong in waiting: Bela Lugosi as Dr. Mirakle, with friend in *The Murders of the Rue Morgue* (dir. Robert Florey, 1932).

At the first dawn of the morning we closed all the massy shutters of our old building; lighted a couple of tapers which, strong perfumed, threw out only the ghastliest and feeblest of rays. By the aid of these we then busied our souls in dreams—reading, writing, or conversing, until warned by the clock of the advent of the true Darkness. Then we sallied forth into the streets, arm in arm, continuing the topics of the day, or roaming far and wide until a late hour, seeking, amid the wild lights and shadows of the populous city, that infinity of mental excitement which quiet observation can afford."[4]

    The element of the macabre also made itself felt on Conan Doyle's stories. The horrific, extraordinarily violent murders in the Rue Morgue (a macabre street to begin with) take place in a gloomy old house. One of the victims has her head cut off and the other is stuffed up a fireplace. (Hammer Films were to reprise this latter feat in *Dracula Has Risen from the Grave* [dir. Freddie Francis, 1968], in which a female victim of the count is hung upside down in a bell in the opening scenes.) The Rue Morgue murderer is eventually discovered to be an orang-outang, and the owner of this outrageously violent creature is eventually tracked down by Dupin, who has deduced that only such a beast could have had the strength and agility for such a crime. He places an advertisement in a newspaper informing whoever it may concern that the beast has been caught (when in fact it has not). Thus lured to Dupin's chambers, the owner (a sailor) is cornered and forced to tell the tale of what really happened, and the seemingly impossible situation of a murder committed for no motive in a sealed room is fully explained.

Though an immense influence on subsequent literary detectives, "The Murders in the Rue Morgue" has (curiously, given its highly serviceable plot) made less of an impact on the cinema, though its imagery of a rampaging orang-outang no doubt helped to fertilize that modern archetype of the Id that was (and still is) King Kong. The first film version of Poe's tale appeared in 1917 but the first full-length screen adaptation was Robert Florey's *Murders in the Rue Morgue* (1932) starring Bela Lugosi as Dr. Mirakle, a character who doesn't appear in Poe's original. In fact, short of its Parisian setting and an ape bursting into a young woman's bedroom, very little from Poe's story finds its way into this film. The story's most interesting element—the character of the detective Auguste Dupin—is watered down to Leon Ames' Pierre Dupin, who relies on the police to help him, rather than the other way round (which is surely the entire point of the Auguste Dupin character, who, like Sherlock Holmes, is far cleverer than the police).

Mirakle uses his ape, Erik, as a means of abducting young women into whom the doctor injects ape-blood in a doomed attempt to prove Darwin's theories fourteen years before they were published (the film is set in 1845). The similarities with *The Cabinet of Dr. Caligari* are at once apparent (Erik taking over the role of César, the somnambulist). The ape's name also echoes that of Gaston Leroux's Phantom of the Opera, while Mirakle's dungeons are re-dressed sets from James Whale's production of *Frankenstein*, made the previous year. Mirakle tortures his victims in a laboratory above these dungeons and when he has finished with them, presses a lever, Sweeney Todd-style, to release a trap door which dispatches the bodies down below.

Consequently, all the key factors that made Poe's story so inventive have been lost. Foremost among them was that "The Murders in the Rue Morgue" was the world's first locked-room mystery. (Gaston Leroux followed in Poe's footsteps in this respect with his *The Mystery of the Yellow Room* in 1907.) This central element is lost in the film. Poe's Dupin also applies the kind of observational deductive logic to the mystery which would characterize Sherlock Holmes' investigations later in the century, but again, the film jettisons this element. What we are left with, as is so often the case in movie adaptations of Poe, is a film with Poe's title but little of the original story intact.

Undeniably atmospheric, the film marvelously conveys the dark, unnerving streets of nineteenth-century Paris, with moody sets and even more moody photography by Karl Freund. The film also gives Lugosi the opportunity to develop his sinister persona. "What a funny-looking man," observes Sidney Fox's Camille L'Espaneye. "Did you notice his accent?" Pierre asks. "I wonder where he comes from. I never heard an accent like it." Indeed, Hollywood certainly hadn't, which was a part of Lugosi's strength as a heavy.

If Lugosi looked back to *Dracula*, the dungeons to *Frankenstein*, and Erik to *The Phantom of the Opera*, the rooftop finale in which Erik carries off the heroine simultaneously looks back to *Caligari* and forwards to *King Kong* (dir. Merian C. Cooper and Ernest B. Schoedsack), which would appear the following year.

Poe's story also provided a starting point for Gordon Hessler's *Murders in the Rue Morgue* (1971), with a typically revisionist screenplay by Christopher Wicking, which had almost nothing to do with the story itself, and rather more to do with *The Phantom of the*

Opera (it even cast Herbert Lom as the villain, just as Hammer had done in their 1962 version of Gaston Leroux's thriller). Wicking did take several of Poe's obsessions (including premature burial) and concocted a story out of them. Hessler's explanation for this approach was that, as it is a detective story, "once you know the dénouement—it was a monkey who did it—the whole thing is over; so you've got to invent within that, and the challenge is, ... how do you make it better and make it work? That was the creative process.... The idea was to make a play within a play. The play of *Murders in the Rue Morgue* is going on when another drama is taking place on the outside."[5]

Much more faithful to the original plot, though less visually atmospheric than the Lugosi *Rue Morgue*, was Jeannot Szwarc's 1986 TV adaptation with George C. Scott as Dupin. Shot on location in Paris, this version is certainly faithful to Poe's story and has some very atmospheric shots of Paris at night. Indeed, the city becomes one of the characters, but while Dupin's rationative powers are as Poe wrote them, Dupin is made a member of the professional police, undergoing enforced retirement. This rather changes his air of detachment, which was to play so crucial a part in the development of Sherlock Holmes. He is also given a daughter, which helps with the love interest, but damages his aesthetic-decadent credentials.

The story even appears as part of Eric Woolfson's Edgar Allan Poe prog-rock musical from 2003 in which the choir reiterates "Murder, Murder in the Rue Morgue" against a driving rhythm, with recited interjections from onlookers and Poe's famous detective (sung by Steve Balsamo), which includes the clever half-rhyme coupling "Auguste Dupin" with "orang-outang." Even songs by Bob Dylan and the Heavy Metal rock group Iron Maiden mention the Rue Morgue in their lyrics. Poe would have been amazed—and probably delighted.

The Mystery of Marie Rogêt

Experience has shown, and a true philosophy will always show, that a vast, perhaps the larger, portion of truth arises from the seemingly irrelevant.[1]

The second of Poe's three detective stories, "The Mystery of Marie Rogêt" (1842) is generally regarded as the least successful of the trio, but its impact on Sir Arthur Conan Doyle was considerable, for it inspired many of the deductive techniques employed by Sherlock Holmes. The above quotation equates to Holmes' celebrated dictum that "the little things are infinitely the most important."[2] Another similarity with the same Holmes adventure from which that line is drawn is Dr. Watson's remark, "'The cases which come to light in the papers are, as a rule, bald enough, and vulgar enough.'"[3] Poe's Dupin had earlier observed that "in general, it is the object of our newspapers rather to create a sensation—to make a point—than to further the cause of truth."[4]

After lengthy theorizing, Dupin's final suggestion is that a naval officer killed Marie:

> Let us sum up now the meagre yet certain fruits of our long analysis. We have attained the idea either of a fatal accident under the roof of Madame Deluc, or of a murder perpetrated, in the thicket at the Barrière du Roule, by a lover, or at least by an intimate and secret associate of

the deceased. This associate is of swarthy complexion. This complexion, the "hitch" in the bandage, and the "sailor's knot" with which the bonnet-ribbon is tied, point to a seaman.
[...]
Now we are to understand that Marie Rogêt was precipitated from a boat. This would naturally have been the case. The corpse could not have been trusted to the shallow waters of the shore. The peculiar marks on the back and shoulders of the victim tell of the bottom ribs of a boat. That the body was found without weight is also corroborative of the idea. If thrown from the shore, a weight would have been attached. We can only account for its absence by supposing the murderer to have neglected the precaution of supplying himself with it before pushing off.
[...]
Now where is that rudderless boat? Let it be one of our first purposes to discover. With the first glimpse we obtain of it, the dawn of our success shall begin. This boat shall guide us, with a rapidity which will surprise even ourselves, to him who employed it in the midnight of the fatal Sabbath. Corroboration will rise upon corroboration, and the murderer will be traced.[5]

"The Mystery of Marie Rogêt" was based on the genuine American murder case of Mary Rogers, the action, such as it is, being transplanted to Paris to enable Poe's detective, Dupin, to apply his analytical mind to the conundrum. Unlike "The Murders in the Rue Morgue" and "The Purloined Letter," there is no conclusive solution to the problem of who the murderer was, this piece being really an opportunity for Poe to demonstrate the process of deduction, rather than anything else. Though Poe himself visited the various scenes of the episode, his fictional detective does not. Dupin relies entirely on newspaper reports (as Poe largely did himself) and he thus became the model for the sedentary armchair detective, Mycroft Holmes, the brilliant but lethargic elder brother of Sherlock. In fact, Poe's suggested solution was contradicted by the later police evidence of a botched abortion, and he modified his inconclusive conclusion accordingly.

Poe's tale has little of the excitement and atmosphere of "Rue Morgue," nor the intrigue and elegance of "The Purloined Letter," but it nonetheless contains one element, gleaned from newspaper reports of the time, which prefigured the action of what is now regarded as the cinema's first film noir, *Laura* (dir. Otto Preminger, 1944). Dupin, in fact, discounts this explanation, originally published in *The New York Brother Jonathan*, which Poe re-named *L'Etoile*. It suggested "that Marie Rogêt still lived—that the corpse found in the Seine was that of some other unfortunate."[6] In *Laura*, a similar eventuality occurs: Laura is assumed to be dead, returns midway through the film, and the corpse originally assumed to have been hers is identified as that of a model, Diana Redfern. The *Brother Jonathan* theory, for which we have an unnamed journalist to thank rather than Poe, therefore anticipated the psychological complexity of *Laura*: its central conceit of the police detective falling in love with the presence of an apparently dead woman.

Universal's 1942 adaptation *The Mystery of Marie Rogêt* (dir. Phil Rosen) also expanded upon the newspaper article quoted by Poe, thus changing the events significantly. In this adaptation, also known as *The Phantom of Paris*, Marie disappears, and it is assumed that the body found in the Seine is hers; she then reappears and her involvement in a plot to murder her wealthy sister is revealed. She then disappears again, and another body is found mutilated in the Seine. This time it really is Marie's. Her grandmother (played by the marvelous Maria Ouspenskaya) is then put under suspicion of having murdered Marie by means of deliberately setting loose her pet leopard upon her; but the real murderer is eventually unmasked as Marcel, Marie's lover and the fiancé of her sister. The first body is revealed to be Marcel's first English wife.

Rosen's film therefore departs radically from Poe, which is not surprising, given the static action and inconclusiveness of the story. Now one of Universal's more obscure films, it is most fondly remembered for Jack Otterson's characteristically brooding Parisian street sets and Elwood Bredell's atmospheric photography. Though Poe's story has nothing to do with Gothic horror, this film, due to its connection with the Universal Studios horror films, further ensured the popular conception of Poe as a "horror" writer: Ouspenskaya had appeared as the gypsy Maleva in *The Wolf Man* (dir. George Waggner, 1941), Otterson had also been art director on that film. Bredell had photographed *The Mummy's Hand* (dir. Christy Cabanne, 1940) and *Black Friday* (dir. Arthur Lubin, 1940).

The Narrative of Arthur Gordon Pym of Nantucket

At every step we took inland the conviction forced itself upon us that we were in a country differing essentially from any with which we had been formerly conversant. The trees resembled no growth of either the torrid, the temperate, or the northern frigid zones, and were altogether unlike those of the lower southern latitudes we had already traversed. The very rocks were novel in their mass, their color, and their stratification; and the streams themselves, utterly incredible as it may appear, had so little in common with those of other climates, that we were scrupulous of tasting them, and, indeed, had difficulty in bringing ourselves to believe that their qualities were purely those of nature.[1]

This once underrated, even ignored tale of adventure can, and perhaps should, be interpreted as a journey into the unconscious—a place of utter strangeness, as described above. Poe liked to dismiss it, calling it "a very silly story," and it is true that he was laboring under the demands of his publishers, who required from him a full-length novel rather than Poe's preferred short story format. This is, indeed, Poe's only novel. Working under pressure, he incorporated many a plagiarism from previous travel writers. There are also inconsistencies and anomalies in the plot—not to mention a very abrupt and inconclusive ending, which might suggest that he had grown bored with the story.

Perhaps he really was ashamed of a novel that was cobbled together almost against his will to meet the needs of a popular audience he made no bones about despising; but this was not how Baudelaire, Proust, Huysmans, Verne, W.H. Auden, Arthur Rimbaud—even Henry James (no great fan of Poe's other works)—viewed the work. We have already encountered Proust's high opinion of the novel. Baudelaire translated it as *Aventures d'Arthur Gordon Pym* in 1858 (he even tracked down English and American sailors to confirm that he had fully understood Poe's nautical terms[2]); Auden regarded the novel as one of Poe's greatest works and "the finest adventure stories ever written."[3] Rimbaud in his poem "Le bateau ivre" ("The Drunken Boat") suggested an echo of the milky waters which bring the novel to its close in the stanza:

> Et dès lors, je me suis baigné dans le Poème
> De la Mer, infusé d'astres, et lactescent,
> Dévorant les azurs verts; où, flottaison blême
> Et ravie, un noyé pensif parfois descend
>
> (Then I bathed in the Poem of the Sea,
> Infused with stars, the milk-white spume blends,
> Grazing green azures: where ravished, bleached
> Flotsam, a drowned man in dream descends)[4]

Henry James mentioned the story at the beginning of his novel *The Golden Bowl*:

> He remembered to have read, as a boy, a wonderful tale by Allan Poe, his prospective wife's countryman—which was a thing to show, by the way, what imagination Americans *could* have: the story of the shipwrecked Gordon Pym, who, drifting in a small boat further toward the North Pole—or was it the South?—than anyone had ever done, found at a given moment before him a thickness of white air that was like a dazzling curtain of light, concealing as darkness conceals, yet of the colour of milk or of snow.[5]

As we have seen, Huysmans had the hero of *À Rebours* own a copy of *The Adventures of Arthur Gordon Pym* "bound in sea-green morocco ... specially printed for his behoof on pure linen-laid paper, hand-picked, bearing a sea-gull for water mark."[6] Verne, as we shall see, wrote his own sequel to the novel, *Le Sphinx des glas*, in 1897.

Arthur Gordon Pym might be said to be a version of Poe himself. The syllables of the character's name certainly match those of Edgar Allan Poe, Pym and Poe obviously sharing an orthographic similarity. Pym's family also has connections with a place called Edgarton New Bank, and Poe even includes himself as a "character" in the story, distancing himself from the narrator in the guise of being Pym's literary advisor. Pym confesses that his account is uncouth and rough, and in need of being "got up."[7] This might be interpreted as Poe's covert apology for a work of which he was not proud, or it may be a double bluff, pointing out that it was precisely these qualities that the public seemed to appreciate. If the novel is "about" Poe himself, how else might this be so? There are various interpretations that might help us to understand this, but first, the plot needs to be addressed.

Pym is fascinated by the sea. His sole ambition is to explore it. From an early age he loved stories of the sea. An early adventure leads to near-disaster: Pym and his friend Augustus Barnard sail out to sea in a sailboat called *Ariel* (a significant name, as this was also the name of Shelley's boat, which similarly caused that poet's death). The *Ariel* collides with a whaler called the *Penguin* and the boys are very nearly killed. Returned safely to dry land by the crew of the whaler, they keep the adventure a secret from their parents.

This early accident only increases Pym's passion for the sea. He and Augustus stow away on the *Grampus*, where they experience a mutiny, in which some members of the crew are killed by the mutineers. One of these latter, Dirk Peters, later repents of his role in the uprising, and together with Pym and Augustus they set about regaining control of the ship by spreading panic in the shape of an improvised ghost. The other sailors are thrown overboard or killed in the melée. They next encounter a genuine ghost ship—a Dutch vessel, reminding the reader of the legend of the *Flying Dutchman*, made famous five years after Poe's tale was first published, in Wagner's opera of that name. The Dutch ship in Pym's narrative is crewed by rotting corpses. Poe's description of one of the corpses "leaning on the bulwark, and still nodding his head to and fro"[8] may well have inspired

One of Gustave Doré's illustrations for Coleridge's *The Rime of the Ancient Mariner* (1870).

Bram Stoker when describing the dead captain of the *Demeter* who has lashed himself to the ship's wheel in *Dracula* (1897). But Poe's ghost ship (like much else of the imagery of the novel) also looks back to Coleridge's "The Rime of the Ancient Mariner" in which we read:

> The steersman's face by his lamp gleamed white;
> From the sails the dew did drip—
> Till clomb above the eastern bar
> The hornèd Moon, with one bright star
> Within the nether tip.[9]

Without food, Pym and his friends face starvation. In desperation, they turn to cannibalism, drawing straws to decide who must die. Eventually they are rescued by the *Jane Guy*, which takes Pym to his final destination in the South Pole. He and the crew encounter a race of entirely black natives on an island called Tsalal. (Even their teeth are black.) These natives have an abject horror of whiteness. Apparent understanding between the crew and the natives eventually breaks down to reveal a duplicitous attitude on both sides. A massacre follows.

Finally, Pym and Peters (could there be an implied homosexual attraction between them?) drift in a small boat to waters of a milky white color. Fog descends, and pallid white birds shriek the same strange word shouted by the Tsalal when they encountered anything white: "Tekeli-li!" Then a massive white figure appears in the distance. The primal sound of terror suggested by the word "Tekeli-li" might also be usefully compared with H.P. Lovecraft's similarly chilling coinages in stories such as "The Case of Charles Dexter Ward": "Y'AI'NG'NGAH," "YOG-SOTHOTH," "H'EE-L'GEB," "F'AI THRODOG," "UAAAH."

Poe's novel ends abruptly. The introduction, apparently written by Pym himself, along with the first-person narrative of the novel as a whole, suggests that Pym survives this ordeal, but the sequel, Poe explains in his footnote, has been lost, due to Pym's unexpected death. Verne felt that this was an unsatisfactory state of affairs and set about writing a sequel. The result was the Antarctic mystery *Le Sphinx des glaces*, which takes the form of a journal written by a man called Jeorling, who believes that Pym's narrative is "merely" a piece of fiction by Poe. He voyages to Trustan da Cunha on a schooner, *Halbrane,* whose captain, Len Guy, believes that Pym's story is true and that the survivors of the *Jane* are still alive. One of the *Halbrane* crew members turns out to be Dirk Peters, who explains that he gave Poe the information of the *Narrative* which Poe then "wrote up." Later, Verne explains what the strange white figure that brings Poe's novel to a close actually is: a gigantic magnetic Sphinx. With this revelation, the explorers also discover the body of Pym, hanging from the strap of his rifle which was drawn irresistibly to the magnetic force of this curious Sphinx. Such an ending, strange though it is, meets the demands of narrative closure, but in doing so misunderstands the more complex approach of Poe's perhaps deliberate ambiguity.

The much stranger ending of *Pym* could, of course, be accounted for simply by Poe's boredom and frustration with the project. Having run out of steam, he may have made a virtue out of necessity and implied a profounder meaning to his novel by means of ambiguity just to be done with it. This explanation may indeed be partly the case, but other aspects of the story suggest a rather more complex series of interpretations were intended. Critics such as Jean Ricadou have seen the imagery of whiteness at the end of the narrative as a metaphor for "voyage to the end of the page."[10] Poe's description of huge chasms over this white surface, which resemble written characters, suggests that he is actually discussing the process of writing itself. The narrative of Arthur Gordon Pym is really a self-referential metaphor of the narrative written by Edgar Allan Poe. The strange figure at the end might be a symbol of inspiration, the eternal whiteness of the scene suggesting the frightening blank page that confronts all writers—which is particularly unnerving when a deadline stares him in the face. It may also be the case that the novel's ending suggests a connection with the Hollow Earth theory of John Cleves Symmes, Jr. (1779–1829). Poe describes a giant cloud of smoke billowing from the pole, which certainly suggests Symmes' belief that the earth's interior is warmer than the rest of the pole. Possibly, the strange white figure is one of the subterranean inhabitants of that strange world?

Marie Bonaparte's Freudian interpretation suggested that the figure at the end of the narrative is symbolic of a psychological quest for the Mother. The surrounding imagery of warm, milky waters therefore represents an infantile desire for a return to the womb.[11] But, as with all symbolic material, multiple interpretations are possible. We have already seen how Poe's ghost ship foreshadowed Wagner's *The Flying Dutchman,* and Wagner also used sea imagery as a feminine symbol of music.

> The sea divides and connects the continents; thus the art of tone divides and connects the two extreme antitheses of human art, the arts of dancing and of poetry.... Music encircles her sisters in affectionate entwinement; they are the shores by means of which she, the sea, unites two continents.[12]

What is music for Wagner is the imagination in general for Poe. The compulsive urge to engage with the sea experienced by Pym from his earliest youth could be seen as the equally compulsive need of the artist to create, the dangerous, near-fatal accidents Pym experiences having their parallel in the vicissitudes of the writer's uncertain career, his frequent collision with critics and the public.

Pym has also been interpreted in terms of race. Poe, as a Southern gentleman, has often been accused of holding racist opinions himself, but Poe's treatment of the Tsalal in *Pym* suggests, on the contrary, a much more enlightened view. He inverts the then-well-established racism of a white man's horror of black people, by having a race of entirely black people express an equal horror of anything white. Pym's patronizing opinion of the Tsalal, whom he regards as child-like and unsophisticated, exposes him as a representative of the kind of attitude that was held by slave owners in Poe's own time. Pym has no idea that his own intolerance of the Tsalal has its mirror image in the Tsalal's horror of whiteness. When, after a period of apparent trust and cooperation, both sides fight with each other, Poe might be implying that each side is as bad as each other.

Racism has been addressed by popular culture countless times since then, but one film in particular, *The Thing with Two Heads* (dir. Lee Frost, 1972), takes a similar approach to Poe from within a shared fantasy context. In it, a white bigot, played by Ray Milland, has his head grafted onto the body of a black criminal (Rosey Grier). The ensuing comedy in which both men are forced to live literally side by side, constantly bickering with each other, exposes the illusory basis of racism, deconstructing it from within the context of a blaxploitation chase movie, just as Poe had inverted racialist prejudices within the context of a popular maritime adventure story.

But perhaps the most intriguing interpretation of *Pym* is the view that it is a disquisition on the need for meaning and the realization that there can be no ultimate meaning to life and no ultimate Truth. The surrealist, Magritte, was fully aware of this and referenced *Pym* in his painting *La reproduction interdite* from 1937. This shows his English patron, Edward James, looking into a mirror. We observe the back of his head. We expect therefore to see James' face in the mirror, but the mirror—impossibly—shows the same rear view. By this visual pun, Magritte was able to sum up Poe's belief that we can only know ourselves—and only a kind of self-reflection at that. Any other "objective" truth is denied us on our journey through life. To cement the connection with Poe, Magritte includes a green-bound copy of *Pym* on the mantelpiece beneath the mirror, which is reflected according to the expected laws of nature. If the ending of Poe's novel suggests Symmes Jr.'s Hollow Earth theory, perhaps Poe summoned the association as an allegory of his own belief that the mind is ultimately hollow too. After a lifetime of mental exploration in pursuit of the ultimate truth, he discovered only emptiness. Magritte certainly felt the same, and suggests as much in this highly unorthodox portrait of his patron.

Poe was fond of mystification. He devoted an entire tale to this subject, called, appropriately, "Mystification" which concerns a letter written by a Hungarian baron. This sounds convincing but actually means nothing at all: "The language was ingeniously framed so as to present to the ear all the outward signs of intelligibility, and even of profundity, while in fact not a shadow of meaning existed."[13] But the mystification of *Pym* has more meaning behind it. As J. Gerald Kennedy suggests, "Poe's novel delivers an ironic critique of our human compulsion to make sense, literally to manufacture meaning; intelligence abhors a cognitive vacuum and must fill a discernible void with satisfaction."[14] The white figure at the novel's close might well symbolize this problem: "The white figure marks the limit of human knowing and the threshold of the numinous; thus it remains inexplicable, irreducible, and—to modern critics of Pym—relentlessly disconcerting."[15]

The ending reflects the reality that life itself has no narrative resolution, which is perhaps why we all crave a well-structured plot in our fiction, to give us the reassuring illusion that life has a shape, a meaning, a knowable Truth. Similarly, conspiracy theories offer, no matter how sinister they may be, a structure and meaning, which the chaos of reality cannot. An atheist would argue that God is just another conspiracy theory—giving us the false comfort of a belief that we have been born for a reason. Negotiating an unreasonable existence has been a preoccupation of much twentieth-century fiction, but just as Poe identified that murder does not require a motif, he also points out in *Pym* that life has no trajectory towards ultimate revelation.

This will to interpret seems to be deliberately summoned and denied by Poe's abruptly mysterious ending, and further emphasized by his final line with its esoteric, Biblical obscurity: "I have graven it within the hills, and my vengeance upon the dust within the rock."[16] Poe knowingly anticipates the question "What does this mean?" from his readers in a manner that anticipates the modernist hoaxes of Dadism in the twentieth century and the deliberate obscurities of T.S. Eliot's poem *The Wasteland* (1922). While Poe knows that his audience (particularly the popular audience he held at disdainful arm's length) expected resolution, revelation and closure, he was fully aware that life itself offers none of these things. Its only full stop is the abrupt arrival of death, which terminates the plotless journey of life with the same peremptory surprise with which the novel ends.

Though there have been no film adaptations of *Pym*, Poe's theme of the yearning for and impossibility of meaning finds a parallel cinematic expression in Alain Resnais' famously ambiguous film *L'Année dernière à Marienbad* (*Last Year at Marienbad*, 1961). Resnais takes a similarly mystificatory approach in this film with an implied narrative, which in fact doesn't exist at all. The non-action inevitably invites various interpretations, particularly with regard to the relationship between the three unnamed characters, who are referred to merely as A, X and M (played respectively by Delphine Seyrig, Giorgio Albertazzi and Sacha Pitoëff), as they perambulate around the elegant, chaste surroundings of a baroque hotel. Like Poe, Resnais challenges his audience to ask, "What does this mean?" The geometric gardens, the carefully framed shots, the harmonic proportion of the architecture and the formal elegance of the film's overall aesthetic implies a corresponding narrative organization at the same time as utterly denying it. This approach may be the key to understanding Poe's only novel, as well as pointing the way to the influence of its submerged existential themes, if not its narrative substance, on twentieth-century culture.

Never Bet the Devil Your Head

I saw the old gentleman limping off at the top of his speed, having caught and wrapt up in his apron something that fell heavily into it from the darkness of the arch just over the turnstile.[1]

Tre passi nel delirio (*Three Steps to Madness* aka *Spirits of the Dead*) was originally to have included seven Poe adaptations directed by Orson Welles, Ingmar Bergman, Joseph Losey and Jean Renoir. By the time Federico Fellini had been contracted to join the project, Welles had bowed out, Bergman never agreed in the first place, and Renoir had been replaced by Claude Chabrol. Then Chabrol left the project before it got going, and Fellini found himself in the company of Louis Malle and Roger Vadim instead. Originally, he thought of adapting "The Tell-Tale Heart" but his assistant Liliana Betti drew his attention to the obscure Poe story "Never Bet the Devil Your Head."[2] He now set about transforming Poe's story of a gambler from Virginia into one about a self-destructive film star, which

International Poe: a French language poster for *Tre passi nel deliro* (1968), also known as *Spirits of the Dead,* after Poe's poem of that name (though, predictably, having nothing else to do with it).

gave him ample opportunities to satirize the film business in general and indulge in fashionably psychedelic imagery. He sent out a call for the most decadent British actor available, and Terence Stamp fitted the bill, particularly so as Stamp was still reeling from his rejection by Michelangelo Antonioni, who had, until the last minute, intended to cast him in the leading role of *Blow Up* (1966). Stamp now found himself flown to Rome like Toby Dammit, the character he had been hired to play.

Toby is to star in "the first Catholic western" made by a production company run by priests. Under the influence of drugs, he makes his way through the surrealistically golden light of an airport, turning heads and rubbing shoulders with nuns, Muslims, Americans and flowers, all of which mingle in a hallucinogenic vision, as he makes his way out to the waiting limousine, which is to take him to the film studio. The usual Fellini *bric-a-brac* is in evidence even in this early section: the blinding flashbulbs of paparazzi, pouring rain, carcasses of meat in a van, a golden sky, a shop full of chandeliers, a whore, a gypsy fortune teller, a fashion shoot in the middle of road works with a group of nuns in a mini. During the journey, the director who is to make the film explains that it is a critique of the decadence of the capitalist system, stylistically being a cross between the work of Carl Dreyer and Pier Paolo Pasolini, with a touch of John Ford.

Fellini wanted Stamp to resemble Poe himself, though Stamp felt closer to Chuck Berry.[3] The film is really an excuse to explore Toby's drug-induced state of mind and the absurdity of show business, before he drives a sports car over a fallen bridge and has his head severed in the process. Like Poe, Toby is obsessed by death. During a television interview, he confesses that doesn't believe in God but does believe in the Devil, who appears to him in the guise of a little girl bouncing a white ball before her. Just as Fellini would go on to satirize the Roman Catholic church in the ecclesiastical fashion show of *Roma* (1972), he satirizes the whole idea of film awards in "Toby Dammit." Toby finds himself at an awards ceremony, drunk and confused as he recites Shakespeare and receives his award—but for what? The film hasn't even been made yet. Foreshadowing the famous midnight bike ride through the city at the end of *Roma,* Fellini brings "Toby Dammit" to its climax by having Stamp drive his Ferrari sports car through the dark streets and squares of various villages in a very trippy road trip. Eventually, he once more encounters the devil girl with her white ball waiting for him on the opposite end of the unbridged chasm before him. He revs his engine and races forward, but a cable slices off his head. The girl lifts this up (the white ball was an eerie symbol and anticipation) and wanders off into the dark. This aspect of the film is about the only one that relates it to Poe's original tale. In "Never Bet the Devil Your Head," Poe's Toby Dammit has so often bet

Twentieth-Century Poe: Terence Stamp as Toby Dammit in Federico Fellini's adaptation of Poe's "Never Bet the Devil Your Head," in *Histoires extraordinaires/Spirits of the Dead/Tre passi nel delirio* (1968).

the Devil his head that the Devil, in the shape of a black-suited elderly gentleman, takes him at his word. The Devil appears on a covered bridge, the stile at the end of which Toby bets his friend he can leap over. He attempts this, but an iron girder decapitates him and the Devil wraps up the fallen head in his black silk apron before wandering off.

The producers of the film were so impressed by Fellini's "Toby Dammit" that they suggested he should adapt Poe's "A Predicament," in which a tourist traps her head between the hands of a clock, which act like scissors and chop off her head too. Unfortunately, this failed to materialize.

The Oblong Box

The box in question was, as I say, oblong. It was about six feet in length by two and a half in breadth;—I observed it attentively, and like to be precise. Now this shape was peculiar.[1]

Gordon Hessler's turgid 1969 American International film starring Vincent Price and Christopher Lee borrowed the title of this story but served up an overwrought mix

The Wrong Box: AIP's poster for *The Oblong Box* (dir. Gordon Hessler, 1969), which has nothing to do with Poe's story.

of voodoo, premature burial, Jack the Ripper-style murders, grave robbing, medical malpractice, tavern brawls, sibling rivalry, blackmail and disfigurement that is quite different from Poe's story, which is one of the author's more straightforward tales of ratiocination. The oblong box in Poe's story contains the dead body of a woman, the wife of one Cornelius Wyatt, who is bringing the corpse back to New York for interment. To avoid causing panic on a sea voyage, Wyatt's maid poses as his wife; but unfortunately, there is a terrible storm and Wyatt is washed out to sea with the improvised coffin of his wife.

Poe's story, with its maritime setting, anticipates by fifty-three years the oblong boxes of earth which Count Dracula transports by sea from Varna to Whitby in Bram Stoker's novel: Stowaway Dracula also uses one of these boxes in which to rest during the voyage.

The Oval Portrait

It was the portrait of a young girl just ripening into womanhood. I glanced at the painting hurriedly, and then closed my eyes.[1]

"The Oval Portrait" forms part of that large body of Poe's work that is concerned with the death of beautiful women. Like those tales, it is perfectly possible to interpret this one as yet another example of Poe's obsessive, mournful and never-ending remembrances of his dead wife Virginia. (For Poe, the death of a beautiful woman was "unquestionably, the most poetical topic in the world."[2])

Slim though this anecdotal tale is, it went on to influence Oscar Wilde's much better known *The Picture of Dorian Gray* (1890), and it marks the beginning of the whole question of the conflict between life and art, which so fascinated *fin-de-siècle* artists and writers. As we have seen, Wilde was a great admirer of Poe. During his American tour in 1882 he even visited the room in which "The Raven" was written,[3] and *Dorian Gray* must inevitably have been inspired by Poe's idea of a portrait that absorbs the very life-force of its subject.

> "How sad it is!" murmured Dorian Gray, with his eyes still fixed upon his own portrait. "How sad it is! I shall grow old, and horrible and dreadful. But this picture will remain always young. It will never be older than this particular day of June.... If it were only the other way! If it were I who was to be always young, and the picture that was to grow old! For that—for that—I would give everything! Yes, there is nothing in the whole world I would not give! I would give my soul for that!"[4]

And Dorian does indeed give his soul to the picture. Less willingly, perhaps, the lady in Poe's story does the same:

> And when many weeks had passed, and but little remained to do, save one brush upon the mouth and one tint upon the eye, the spirit of the lady again flickered up as the flame within the socket of the lamp. And then the brush was given, and then the tint was placed and, for a moment, the painter stood entranced before the work which he had wrought; but in the next, while he yet gazed, he grew tremulous and very pallid, and aghast, and crying with a loud voice, "This is indeed *Life* itself!" turned suddenly to regard his beloved:—*She was dead!*[5]

According to Barbara Belford, "The Oval Portrait" also influenced Bram Stoker when writing *Dracula*. That Stoker was acquainted with Wilde and even married Wilde's former flame, Florence Balcombe, only helps consolidate the constellation that gathered around Poe's legacy:

> Stoker's affinity with the exchange and depletion of energy—so vital to vampire life—was a version of Edgar Allan Poe's short story "The Oval Portrait." ... Stoker considered an artist character called Francis Aytown, who would complement a specific vampire characteristic: painters cannot make a likeness of a vampire, or as Stoker put it, "however hard the artist tries, the subject always ends up looking like someone else." A fascinating plot twist that did not survive.[6]

As one might expect, "The Oval Portrait" also attracted Arthur Rackham, whose illustration for the tale, however, is ironically one of the weakest of his responses to Poe (an elegant young man in silk breeches raises his brush and palette in astonishment as he completes the painting, his sitter elegantly expired on a well-upholstered chair). A much more intriguing visual response can be found in Jean-Luc Godard's 1962 film, *Vivre sa vie* in which Anna Karina plays Nana, a young woman who leaves her husband to become a film star but ends up becoming a prostitute. She is killed in the crossfire of an argument between two pimps at the end of her brief life, and Godard shows Nana's life in twelve scenes, the last of which includes a reading of extracts from Poe's tale. As the actor Peter Kassovitz reads from a paperback edition of Poe's *Complete Works*, Godard's camera lovingly lingers over Karina's feline features, as if, indeed, Godard wishes to preserve everything about his muse on celluloid, just as the artist in Poe's story does on canvas. Behind Karina, however, is a photograph of Elizabeth Taylor, pinned carefully to the wall. That, of course, is a portrait—but we are so interested in the close-up of Karina that we might fail to realize the smaller image behind her. Are Godard's shots of Karina as Nana portraits too? She could become one as a film still, but here she is a moving image, apparently alive—a character in the real world. The irony is that what seems so alive is nothing more than the illusion of film. Nana seeks eternal life as a movie star like Elizabeth Taylor, but ends up dead, shot by a pimp. Is art, which extracts life's essence and preserves it for all time, therefore greater than life? Or is it merely an illusion which distracts us from living? Multiple layers of meaning pile up here in Godard's philosophical and aesthetic response to Poe's only apparently simple little tale.

Poe was intrigued by the ambivalent qualities of representational imagery. Usher paints reflections of his troubled mind. In "Ligeia," the room in which Lady Rowena dies and is subsequently resurrected as Ligeia is hung with tapestries, whose undulation in the draft causes the narrator to imagine they have come to life. "A hideous and uneasy animation" is Poe's phrase.[7] In "Metzengerstein," the tapestry of a horse indeed *does* come to life. In "The Pit and the Pendulum," grotesque paintings in metal panels glow in the heat of fires behind them, giving them a diabolical animation: "Demon eyes, of a wild and ghastly vivacity, glared upon me in a thousand directions, where none had been visible before, and gleamed with the lurid lustre of a fire that I could not force my imagination to regard as unreal."[8] And, as we shall see, the malevolent doppelgänger of "William Wilson" is a kind of mirror image—a reflection of certain aspects of Wilson's psyche, which he would rather have remained hidden. Poe also pointed out that we can easily be deceived by optical illusions, as in his story "The Sphinx" (1846), in which a convalescent mistakes an insect viewed at close range for a gigantic monster. In "The Spectacles" (1844), short-sightedness causes the embarrassing situation of a man marrying an ugly woman whom he imagined to be a beauty.

"The Oval Portrait" begins as an homage to the Gothic novelist Ann Radcliffe (1764–1823). Like Emily St. Aubert, the heroine of Radcliffe's *The Mysteries of Udolpho* (1794), Poe's unnamed narrator takes refuge in a chateau in the Apennines. (Poe acknowledges the influence in the text.) He spends the night in a room filled with paintings, but one—secreted in a niche—attracts his particular attention. The following morning he is told the legend behind it, and this forms the remainder of the story.

Radcliffe had included a similar fascination with pictures in *Udolpho* with the once much-gossiped-about mystery of a veiled painting, which Emily eventually reveals. She is so horrified by what she sees that she hurries forthwith from the chamber and the reader is left in suspense until the end of the novel for an explanation. Jane Austen's *Northanger Abbey* (1817) commemorates this celebrated cliffhanger in the dialogue between Catherine Morland and her friends:

"I am got [*sic*] to the black veil."
"Are you, indeed? How delightful! Oh! I would not tell you what is behind the black veil for the world! Are you not wild to know?"
"Oh! yes, quite; what can it be?—But do not tell me—I would not be told upon any account. I know it must be a skeleton, I am sure it is Laurentina's skeleton."[9]

In fact, the veil conceals a waxwork model of a corpse.

No doubt linked to the idea of the ghostly double, portraits have a particularly unnerving aspect, along the lines of the cliché that the eyes of Franz Hals' *Laughing Cavalier* follow one around the room. The portrait of the Flying Dutchman, which so mesmerizes Senta, the heroine of Wagner's opera, is another example. The oppressive portraits that adorn the walls of Rosmersholm in Ibsen's 1866 play of that name is another. So too are the family portraits in Benjamin Britten's only television opera, *Owen Wingrave* (1971), and, on a comic level, the paintings that come to life in Gilbert and Sullivan's operetta *Ruddigore* (1887). Robert Wiene used this idea in his film *Genuine* (1920), a vampiric follow-up to his expressionist masterpiece *The Cabinet of Dr. Caligari*.

These magical portraits, along with the tapestry that comes to life in Alexander Tcherepnin's ballet *Le Pavillion d'Armide* (1907), and the portrait that Dana Andrews' detective falls in love with in Otto Preminger's *Laura* (1944), all join Dorian Gray as the multitudinous offspring of Poe's modest but highly influential two-page tale. Indeed, in the case of *Laura*, the detective falls asleep beneath Laura's portrait and then awakens to the real Laura, whom he thought to be dead, standing before him—a portrait truly come to life, and thus, the mirror image of Poe's "Oval Portrait."

Philosophy of Furniture

The corruption of taste is a portion or a pendant of dollar-manufacture.[1]

This piece from 1840 is really an essay rather than a story. It resembles "Landor's Cottage" (1849), "The Domain of Arnheim" and "The Island of the Fay" (1841) in that it solely concerns setting and environment. "Landor's Cottage" sets out giving the impression of being a narrative, which "Philosophy of Furniture" does not, but these stories nonetheless balance each other, "Philosophy of Furniture" being concerned with the aesthetic effect of indoors, "Landor's Cottage" "The Domain of Arnheim" and "The Island of the Fay" with that of outdoors. Poe's interest in interior decor at the expense of narrative foreshadowed the kind of films that Visconti became famous for towards the end of his career, such as *Death in Venice* (1971), in which long scenes almost entirely concerned with the evocation of decor and mood make the plot, temporarily at least, subordinate. Similarly, Michelangelo Antonioni dwells upon decor and architectural imagery in *L'Eclisse* (1962); following the principles laid down by Ellison in "The Domain of Arnheim," he even manipulated nature for his 1966 British-based film *Blow Up*. (For the celebrated scenes in the London park, Antonioni had all the wooden fences smartened up and painted a subtle shade of green, and even had the grass painted to create a surreal uniformity. As Seymour Chatman explains, *à propos* of Antonioni's 1953 film *I vinti*, "[T]he backgrounds achieve a greater degree of autonomy. Here, we see the beginnings of the detached photographic brilliance that proves so startling in Antonioni's later films.... The camera [is] interested more in its own eccentric trajectory and the space evoked than in recording the plot."[2]

Poe's exploration of a "tale" in which nothing happens might be said to have anticipated Samuel Becket's *Waiting for Godot* (1953) were it not that Poe's purpose in so doing was purely aesthetic, which can hardly be said for Beckett's far more rigorously existential purpose. Again, one is more usefully drawn to a comparison with decadent aesthetics at the turn of the nineteenth century. As Oscar Wilde put it in the preface to *The Picture of Dorian Gray*: "The artist is the creator of beautiful things.... The only excuse for making a useless thing is that one admires it intensely. All art is quite useless."[3] Huysmans' *À Rebours*, to which Wilde was so indebted, took Poe's approach to its ultimate literary expression in a book in which truly very little happens but aesthetic reflection. In "Philosophy of Furniture," Poe is not concerned with the commonly held purpose of literature to convey narrative, and in "Landor's Cottage" he makes this explicit at the end of the piece: "It is not the purpose of this work to do more than give, in detail, a picture of Mr. Landor's residence—as I found it."[4]

Poe's other purpose in "Philosophy of Furniture" was to attack what he regarded as nineteenth-century American bad taste. "We have no aristocracy of blood, and having therefore as a natural, and indeed as an inevitable thing, fashioned for ourselves an aristocracy of dollars, the display of wealth has here to take the place and perform the office of the heraldic display in monarchical countries."[5] Alas, such parvenu style fails to impress Poe, who attacks its "flashiness," "glitter" and vulgarity. In 1882, Wilde would do much the same thing in the lectures he gave during his extensive American tour. Lecturing on "The House Beautiful," Wilde similarly attacked "glaring light," "ugly heating stoves" and "artificial flowers,"[6] while in his play *Lady Windermere's Fan,* he applied Poe's attack on tasteless American wealth to Lord Darlington's definition of a cynic: "A man who knows the price of everything and the value of nothing."[7]

Poe ends his piece with a description of the ideal room. Though much simpler than the decadent interiors of Huysmans or D'Annunzio (to say nothing of the furnishing excesses of Poe's own story "The Assignation"), Poe's interest in decor at the expense of everything else anticipated the approach of those writers. A great deal of the "point" of D'Annunzio's novels is the mood summoned by his descriptions of aesthetic objects. For example, in *Il piacere* (*The Child of Pleasure,* 1889), we read, "On the mantlepiece a great white rose in one of the vases was dropping its petals softly, languidly, one by one, giving the impression of something subtly feminine and sensuous. The cup-like petals rested delicately on the marble, like flakes of snow."[8] (It was indeed D'Annunzio's lush decor that made filming his novel *L'Innocente* particularly attractive to Visconti, for whom no expense or trouble was too much when it came to the creation of the ideal settings he envisaged.) But D'Annunzio was not as avant garde as Poe, as he did not dispense with narrative. Poe dared to be modern long before that, though we might compare D'Annunzio's languid rose with Poe's description of "[f]our large and gorgeous Sèvres vases, in which bloom a profusion of sweet and vivid flowers."[9] In "Philosophy of Furniture," Poe is similarly concerned with aesthetic effect: "There is a pianoforte (rosewood, also), without cover and thrown open. An octagonal table, formed altogether of the richest gold-threaded marble, is placed near one of the sofas. This is also without cover—the drapery of the curtains has been thought sufficient."[10] He then describes the aforementioned vases of flowers along with "[a] tall candelabrum, bearing a small antique lamp with highly perfumed oil.... Some light and graceful hanging shelves, with golden eagles and crimson silk cords with golden tassels, sustain two or three hundred magnificently bound books."[11] The Edgar Allan Poe museum in Philadelphia, Pennsylvania, has furnished a room along the principles laid down in "Philosophy of Furniture." There is an octagonal table, a reproduction of a painting by Thomas Sully (1783–1872), a crimson carpet "relieved simply by the appearance of a gold cord,"[12] crimson upholstery and crimson drapes held in place by gold cord, all as Poe recommends.

The Edgar Allan Poe reading room in Philadelphia, realizing Poe's ideal as expressed in "Philosophy of Furniture" (photo by "Midnightdreary").

This obsession with the details of decor was certainly echoed in *À Rebours* where, significantly, Des Esseintes has his edition of Poe's *Narrative of Arthur Gordon Pym* bound "in sea-green morocco ... on pure linen-laid paper, hand-picked, bearing a sea-gull for water mark."[13] Wilde's Dorian Gray, along with his interest in ecclesiastical garments, jewels, embroideries, and perfumes, has "nine large paper copies of the first edition, and had them bound in different colours, so that they might suit his various moods."[14] In "Philosophy of Furniture," therefore, we not only see the origin of late nineteenth-century decadence but also its visual manifestation in film, a medium which is most suited of all to the effect of aesthetic arrangement.

The Pit and the Pendulum

Down—steadily down it crept. I took a frenzied pleasure in contrasting its downward with its lateral velocity. To the right—to the left—far and wide—with the shriek of a damned spirit! to my heart, with the stealthy pace of the tiger![1]

First published in 1842, "The Pit and the Pendulum" is Poe's most famous story. One of his most straightforward tales of terror, it describes the torment of a prisoner of the Inquisition, who is condemned to the pitch blackness of a dungeon in which a pit awaits his destruction. He avoids this, only to be strapped to a bench above which a slowly descending blade swings overhead. He escapes from the path of this avenging pendulum by encouraging rats to gnaw through his confining surcingle, but a final torment awaits him: The walls of the dungeon begin to press together, to drive the unnamed narrator into the pit he originally managed to avoid. He is saved at the last minute by General Lasalle, the French army having entered Toledo; but if this is the Lasalle of Napoleon's army, the anachronism is extreme, as the Inquisition had been dissolved long before Napoleon's Peninsular Wars.

The tale begins with a quatrain in Latin, supposed to have been composed for the gates of a market erected upon the site of the Jacobin Club House at Paris. This is a doubtful provenance, which Baudelaire disputed, and it is likely that Poe came across the quatrain in *The Southern Literary Messenger,* which he edited. In translation it runs "Here an unholy mob of torturers, with an unquenchable thirst for human blood, once fed their long frenzy. Our homeland is safe now, the baneful pit destroyed, and what was once a place of savage death is now a scene of life and health." It is an appropriate enough epigram, but the fact that Poe does not provide a translation himself, and had probably merely lifted it from a newspaper suggests that its purpose is to impress, as his satirical "confession" about such posturing in "How to Write a Blackwood Article," mentioned above, lead one to believe.

Though the events of this story are straightforward, it is written with a sophistication that uses poetic cadences and loosely pentametric rhythms to extrude the gathering tension into one long crescendo. Poe's prose is heightened through these poetic devices. From the very beginning, many phrases suggest the Shakespearean iambic pentameter: "I was sick—sick unto death with that long agony." Indeed, many sentences from the tale can be divided up into a kind of blank verse in which five stresses can be found amid triplet and quintuplet rhythms:

> After that, the sound of the inquisitorial voices
> Seemed merged in one dreamy indeterminate hum.
> It conveyed to my soul the idea of revolution—
> Perhaps from its association in fancy with the burr of a millwheel.[2]

In addition, Poe uses nouns and adjectives to suggest the hissing swish of the pendulum, as in this particularly sibilant sentence:

> The odor of the sharp steel closed itself into my nostrils.... I grew frantically mad, and struggled to force myself upward against the sweep of the fearful scimitar.[3]

Poe again incorporates the synesthetic elements that are so marked a feature of his general approach. Even on the first page of "The Pit and the Pendulum," he compares the "thought of what sweet rest there must be in the grave" to a "rich musical note."[4] He describes the nervous thrill of the narrator, which he compares to touching "the wire of a galvanic battery,"[5] and, later, describes the sensation of swooning in terms close to Baudelaire's heart:

> He who has never swooned, is not he who finds strange palaces and wildly familiar faces in coals that glow; is not he who beholds floating in the mid-air the sad visions that the many may not view; is not he who ponders over the perfume of some novel flower; is not he whose brain grows bewildered with the meaning of some musical cadence which has never before arrested his attention.[6]

This synesthetic element in the story is reflected psychedelically in the main and end titles of Roger Corman's 1961 film adaptation *Pit and the Pendulum* in which multi-colored inks swirl and mix to the equally abstract musical accompaniment of Les Baxter's desolate, high-pitched strings, piano tone clusters and glissandi, foreboding timpani and pizzicato effects.

The compelling resonance of the pit and pendulum themselves can, of course, be illuminated if interpreted along Freudian lines as being symbolic representations of the phallus and vulva. Bram Stoker similarly emphasized the sexual terrors of the pit in his last novel *The Lair of the White Worm* (1911), in which the worm emerges to wreak havoc on the neighborhood. Stoker describes it as a "fathomless pit whose entrance was flooded with spots of fresh blood."[7] and the hero, Adam Salton, slips on "some sticky acrid-smelling mass."[8] It exudes a stench of "chemical waste and the poisonous effluvium of the bilge of a water-logged ship whereon a multitude of rats had been drowned" and reminds Adam of "the drainage of war hospitals" and of slaughterhouses.[9] A more complete description of a (probably) gay man's horror of the female sexual organ would be hard to find.

Poe is not so explicit, but the pit in his story is also terrifyingly devouring. He throws a stone into its depths and listens to its "reverberations as it dashed against the sides of the chasm in its descent."[10] The terror of the pendulum is increased by its slow descent, and there is a sense of sexual anticipation in the way in which Poe describes this process. "Down—certainly, relentlessly down! It vibrated within three inches of my bosom!... I gasped and struggled at each vibration. I shrunk convulsively at its every sweep.... Still I quivered in every nerve to think how slight a sinking of the machinery would precipitate that keen, glistening axe upon my bosom." The equally terrifying imagery of the vampire brides in Stoker's *Dracula* is surely comparable to the subtextual erotic terror of Poe's pendulum:

> Lower and lower went her head as the lips went below the range of my throat. Then she paused, and I could hear the churning sound of her tongue as it licked her teeth and lips, and could feel the hot breath on my neck. Then the skin of my throat began to tingle as one's flesh does when the hand that is to tickle it approaches nearer—nearer. I could feel the soft, shivering touch of the lips on the supersensitive skin of my throat, and the hard dents of two sharp teeth, just touching and pausing there. I closed my eyes in a langourous ecstasy and waited— waited with beating heart.[11]

It was this erotic-horror element that attracted the French composer Olivier Messiaen to equate part of his *Turangalîla Symphony* (1946–1948) with Poe's story. Messiaen fully absorbed the French symbolist aesthetic that had motivated Debussy, which had in turn been fertilized by Poe. Messiaen specifically described the movement called "Turangalîla 2" as a musical response to "The Pit and the Pendulum," and this movement is intended to invoke terror but from within the context of the symphony's overall erotic program. The introduction to the symphony as a whole juxtaposes two complementary and contrasting themes: a "statue theme" and a "flower theme." These are obviously sexual in their symbolism, and have their counterpart in Poe's equally erotic pit and pendulum imagery. Literally translated as "the speed of a horse," the Sanskrit word "turanga" denotes rhythm and time, while "lîla" equates with the idea of cosmic or divine "play"—and here also stands for "love." Hence, "Turangalîla" means "rhythmic games" and "a hymn to love." Messiaen's interest in Indian rhythmic systems informs the rhythmic element, while the exotic electronic timbre of the Ondes martenot, which has a purely decorative function, explores the erotic aspect. In effect, this is Messiaen's version of Wagner's *Tristan und Isolde,* which is similarly concerned with the erotic, transcendence, unity with the cosmic "Welt-Atems" (or "world breath"), and equally infused with oriental, specifically Buddhistic philosophy. This is the erotic context of the *Turangalîla Symphony,* in the middle of which "Turangalîla 2" erupts, graphically expressing the terrors of sex, as earlier and subsequent movements evoke its joys. As Jack Sullan puts it:

> In the most startling of Messiaen's funhouse of special effects, an electronic keyboard slithers downward into Poe's fearful pit, with dissonant brass and percussion shrieking and pounding above. The narrator's "long agony" and "deadly nausea" of spirit are captured with an explicitness that goes beyond the symphonic Gothicism of earlier works such as Berlioz's *Symphonie fantastique* and Liszt's *Todtentanz*. The pendulum's "rushing vibrations" are captured by the Ondes Martinot, an electronic keyboard instrument, in music onomatopoiea.[12]

An American composer named after Poe, Edgar Stillman Kelley (1857–1944), wrote a little-played symphonic poem, *The Pit and the Pendulum,* in 1925. Four years later Josef Holbrooke composed his own symphonic poem on the subject. This is a more melodramatic, late–Romantic affair, indebted to Tchaikovsky's Dante-inspired tone poem *Francesca da Rimini*. Each of its four sections are prefaced with references to Poe's text: "I was sick unto death with that agony," "A noise attracted my attention—I saw rats gnawing," "The vibration of the pendulum. I am free! I am free!" and "A discordant hum of human voices... Loud blasts of trumpets."—"The Fiery walls rushed back." Programatic, energetic and spirited though the piece is, it isn't anywhere near as frightening as it should be, but the same could be said of Les Baxter's music for Roger Corman's film. One can't help thinking that if Hammer Films had made a version of the story, James Bernard would have written something that fully reflected the terror of the text. Neither does Holbrooke pick up on the sexual subtext, however, despite the erotic example of Tchaikovsky's earlier tone-poem.

Such was not the case in the two most famous film adaptations of the tale. The first, directed in 1935 by Louis Friedlander (a.k.a. Lew Landers), starred Boris Karloff and Bela Lugosi and was called *The Raven*, though, as we have seen, it bears only a passing relationship to Poe's poem of that name. Lugosi plays a psychopathic medical man, Dr. Richard Vollin, who is also a Poe fanatic. He suffers from a rather large chip on his shoulder and will only agree to operate on Judge Thatcher's daughter Jean when told that he is the best surgeon around. The news of Jean's condition (caused by a car crash) reaches Vollin during a conversation with the understandably somewhat nervous curator of a museum who has called at the Vollin residence to negotiate the purchase of some Poe ephemera. A threatening shadow of Vollin's rather absurd stuffed raven is cast upon the wall as he declaims lines from Poe's classic, just as Vincent Price would do rather more eloquently in Roger Corman's loosely based tribute to the same poem in 1963. This and an interpolated dance scene is about all the film has in common with Poe's famous poem; the rest of it is really an excuse to exploit Poe's various methods of torture from "The Pit and the Pendulum," though Vollin equates himself with Poe and describes "The Raven" as the story of a genius, like himself, who is driven mad when denied his great love.

Vollin is a thoughtful man, as the small bronze reproduction of Rodin's *Le Penseur* on his desk suggests. Indeed, one of his later houseguests, the bumbling Colonel Bertram Grant (Spencer Charters), calls Vollin "very thoughtful" after being presented with two sleeping powders by the good doctor, who really only wants to be rid of his interruption, as he has far more important things on his mind at the time. But thoughtfulness is not always benevolent. Vollin has thought a great deal about Poe and has gone so far as to reproduce the instruments of torture described by Poe in his extensive cellar. This, as he confesses himself, is more than a mere hobby; it is a compulsion. Death fascinates him. And he justifies himself by arguing that doctors are naturally fascinated by death and pain; but in this he rather more resembles the doctors who were committing the crimes of euthanasia in Nazi Germany at the time the film was made and who would go on to perform sadistic experiments on living victims at Auschwitz during the second world war. Though this might seem a long way from the nineteenth-century Romantic imagination of Poe, Vollin's obsession with death was shared by his idol, and Lugosi's role in *The Raven* provided American audiences with an opportunity to vent their fears of what was happening in Europe at the time, by means of an established American classic. A further ironic comparison between this film and the horrors of Nazi propaganda is the music score of *The Raven*, which was selected from the soundtrack of the earlier Karloff-Lugosi Poe film *The Black Cat*. Both Liszt's B minor Piano Sonata and the opening of his symphonic poem *Les Préludes* are used in the soundtrack, and these works were mercilessly exploited by Nazi propaganda newsreels. Other Romantic classics can be heard in *The Raven*. When we first visit Vollin's private operating theater, we hear the slow movement of Schubert's "Death and the Maiden" string quartet—a singularly appropriate piece given the later predicament of the film's heroine when the action transfers to the torture chamber. The opening of another of Liszt's symphonic poems, *Tasso*, also puts in an appearance as Karloff's ex-con, Edmund Bateman, lies on the operating table to be "transformed" by Vollin's proto-fascist scalpel—and the Italian poet Tasso was himself a mad genius, accused of murder and imprisoned for his crime.

When Bateman comes round from the operation and sees his new, hideous face, we are treated to a scene with which Poe would have been delighted. Like Caliban raging at his own reflection, Bateman shoots to smithereens six mirrors, arranged in an arc all around him and revealed from behind successively drawn curtains. There are consequently no bullets left in his six-shooter to dispatch the maniacally gloating Vollin. The six mirrors vaguely echo the seven differently colored chambers in "The Masque of the Red Death" as well as the mirror in which the sinister doppelgänger of William Wilson appears at the end of Poe's eponymous story. But Poe never wrote a mirror scene quite as spectacular as the one in Friedlander's film.

The Raven was primarily a vehicle for Hollywood's greatest Gothic heavies to do what they did best, but the film also articulates the sexual subtext of "The Pit and the Pendulum" by having Vollin motivated by sexual jealousy. He falls in love with Jean Thatcher (Irene Ware), the woman he saved from death on the operating table; but he is told in no uncertain terms by her no-nonsense, practical man-of-the-world father, Judge Thatcher (Samuel S. Hinds), to back off and leave her to marry her fiancé Jerry Halden (Lester Matthews). This repulsion makes the chip on Vollin's shoulder too heavy to bear. In Judge Thatcher's words, he goes "stark staring mad."

"Extraordinary man," Jean rhapsodizes, as Vollin performs Bach's Toccata and Fugue in D minor for her on his compact but very loud home organ. "You're almost not a man." True, he is much more of a monster—a role that Karloff ostensibly plays here, as an ex-con who has fallen into Vollin's hands after asking him to change his face. Vollin does this but makes him hideous, to encourage his murderous tendencies. Like a good Nazi, he says, "I can use your hate." But Karloff's Bateman has a basic decency entirely lacking in Vollin's character. Hideous he may be, but he saves the day—rescuing the heroine and her lover from Vollin's clutches before being shot by him. Though Karloff received the larger billing, this is really Lugosi's film—and one of his best. He excels as an elegant, very well-dressed but psychopathic aesthete, for whom people are less important than his own perverted imagination. Vollin does not love. He wishes only to possess. Outraged by Judge Thatcher's interposition and Jean's engagement to Dr. Halden, he invites everyone to his creepy but comfortably appointed mansion, during a thunderstorm of course, for a house party; but it isn't long before Bateman is ordered to abduct Judge Thatcher and take him to the torture chamber. There, Thatcher is strapped to the fatal dais below the pendulum. Vollin knows exactly how he feels in his predicament as he has already been in this position during an earlier demonstration of the machine that very nearly went wrong. On that occasion, he had been alone with Bateman, who grasped the opportunity to take his own revenge on the man who has disfigured him. Vollin persuades him to release him from the automatic manacles that have secured him to the slab, by pointing out that only he (Vollin) can restore Bateman's face. And so he escapes. But no such escape seems possible for Judge Thatcher. The pendulum moves down—certainly, relentless down. Judge Thatcher, like Poe's unnamed narrator, gasps and struggles at each vibration, shrinking convulsively at its every sweep. Lugosi then pulls a switch (he can control the window shutters in every room, cut off the telephone lines and operate the secret door in his office from his subterranean console), and Jean's bedroom turns into a giant elevator, which rumbles down to the dungeon for her appointment with Poe's other terrible device from "The Pit and the Pendulum": the room with walls that crush their victims to death. Bateman fortunately comes to the rescue, and Vollin is hoisted by his own petard, crushed, instead of the young lovers, by the walls.

Roger Corman's 1961 film adaptation starring Vincent Price continued to explore

The poster for Roger Corman's adaptation of *The Pit and the Pendulum* (1961).

and expand the sexual subtext of Poe's story. Corman's film displays two swaying circular counterweights to the pendulum (brilliantly visualized by art director Daniel Haller), which dangle like the scrotum of this ghastly phallus. Like Friedlander before him, Corman embroiders the theme of sexual terror around the basic image of Poe's infernal machine, which is really the only part of the story that translates in dramatic terms on the screen. Screenwriter Richard Matheson admitted that *Pit and the Pendulum* "was a lot more of a challenge. Poe's story was just one scene of a guy lashed to a table with a blade that's going to cut him in half. And now most people ascribe what I wrote to Edgar Allan Poe!"[13] Matheson's plot anticipates later Hammer psychological thrillers such as *Taste of Fear* (dir. Seth Holt, 1961) in that the Vincent Price character, Nicholas Medina, is the victim of a plot to drive him insane. There is also the well-worn Gothic device of mysterious music drifting from an apparently empty room, which also features in *Taste of Fear* and many of its successors. The family doctor (played by Tony Carbone) encourages Nicholas in his belief that he buried his wife Elizabeth (Barbara Steele) alive. But Elizabeth is not dead and she and the doctor are in fact conspiring lovers. She eventually emerges from her coffin, vampire-style, in a successful attempt to deprive Nicholas of his reason. The plan backfires, however, when Nicholas takes his revenge. Overwhelmed by the memory of his sadistic father, whose murder in the castle torture chamber of his own unfaithful wife was observed by the young Nicholas, the now virtually possessed, fully grown Nicholas imprisons Elizabeth in an Iron Maiden, hurls the doctor into the terrible pit and then straps Elizabeth's brother (played by John Kerr) to the instrument of torture, deluded, as he is, that the brother is his father's brother—the man who was having an affair with his mother.

Christopher Lee as the curiously named Count Regula in *The Torture Chamber of Dr. Sadism* (dir. Harald Reinl, 1967).

This tangle of marital infidelity and sexual jealousy fully exposes the inherent erotic symbolism of Poe's story. It also draws on several of Poe's other tales, notably "The Fall of the House of Usher." Like the melancholy House of Usher in Corman's previous Poe film, Nicholas Medina's castle (a splendidly Gothic seaside pile) is the real monster of this movie. Its walls are permeated by its malignant history. *Pit and the Pendulum* also features the premature burial of a female family member, comparable to Roderick Usher's decision to inter his own living sister in her tomb. Nicholas describes himself as the spawn of his father's "depraved blood," which mirrors Usher's congenital insanity. Matheson also drew on "The Cask of Amontillado" for the lurid scene in which Nicholas' father walls up his own wife; and when Nicholas pulls down the wall behind which the coffin of Elizabeth has been interred, we are reminded of Poe's description at the end of "The Black Cat." One might also cite Bram Stoker's gruesome tale "The Squaw" in which Stoker's visit to a torture chamber in Nürnberg formed the inspiration for a story about a similarly deadly Iron Maiden: "And then the spikes did their work. Happily the end was quick, for when I wrenched open the door they had pierced so deep that they had locked in the bones of the skull through which they had crushed, and actually tore him—it—out of his iron prison till, bound as he was, he fell at full length with a sickly thud upon the floor, the face turning upward as he fell."[14]

As Nicholas makes his way down to the subterranean torture chamber, he passes two rats (one on the steps, the other perched precariously—and improbably—on a candle sconce built into the wall). The actual pit is not as Poe describes it, being instead a gigantic dry moat surrounding the central podium over which the pendulum swings. The terrifying murals depicting "Demon eyes, of a wild and ghastly vivacity"[15] are faithfully represented, and Matheson amplifies the demonic aspect by providing a list of mythological underworlds for Price's crazed Medina to intone over his hapless victim, whom he believes to be Bartolome, his father's brother, but who is actually Elizabeth's English brother, played by the very American John Kerr:

> You are about to enter Hell, Bartholome, Hell! The nether world, Bartholome, the infernal region, the abode of the damned, the place of torment, Pandemonium, Abaddon, Tophet, Gehenna, Naraka, the pit—and the pendulum. The razor edge of destiny.

Pandemonium was Milton's name for the capital of Hell in *Paradise Lost,* Abaddon is the Hebrew word for destruction, Gehenna and Tophet were names for the sacrificial site near Jerusalem where children were sacrificed to Moloch. Naraka is Sanskrit for the underworld. "The razor edge of destiny" even ironically suggests Somerset Maugham's novel *The Razor's Edge* (1944), with its Hindu-inspired story of a man's quest for transcendence.

Harald Reinl's *Die Schlangengrube und das Pendel* (aka *The Torture Chamber of Dr. Sadism*, 1967) starred Christopher Lee as Graf von Andomai (or Count Frederic Regula in the English version). Reinl's inspired grasp of visual atmospherics here is not matched by the over-dubbed American dialogue or indeed the acting abilities of virtually everyone involved, with the majestic exception of Christopher Lee. Also, Peter Thomas' music is sometimes anachronistic in style. But as a cinematic experience, with its vivid colors and stylish imagery, it has much to offer. Everything builds up to Count Regula's revenge on those who condemned him to death for the murder of twelve virgins. It takes until the finale for Poe's influence to make itself felt. The location work, particularly the shots of Rothenburg ob der Tauber in Bavaria, lend the film something of the quality Poe summoned in his description of the hometown of Ligeia—that "dim decaying city by the Rhine,"[16] far from the Rhine though Rothenburg actually is.

Regula killed the twelve virgins in an attempt to make an elixir of life. He needed thirteen women, however, and was prevented from achieving his goal by the authorities when they found out what he was doing, but before he was executed, he drank some of the potion in concentrate form. Imperfect though it was, it nonetheless enabled him to cheat death (though quite how he survived being drawn and quartered is not discussed). He now has the descendants of those who condemned him in his power. He plans to use the blood of the heroine, Lilian von Brabant (Karin Dor), to complete the elixir, and subjects Lex Barker's Roger von Marienberg, her lover and the son of another of Regula's enemies, to the tortures of the pendulum. As virgin's blood is made all the more efficacious by fear, he forces Liliane to watch. Surrounded by murals inspired by the example of Hieronymus Bosch, the pendulum begins to swing very impressively. Rats, as Poe describes, also appear in the chamber, but Roger does not rely on them to escape his pendulous death. Instead, he dislodges a cobblestone from the floor and uses this to deflect the path of the pendulum. The blade cuts through his restraining ropes and he rolls himself to safety. Meanwhile, the heroine is subjected to the terrors of a snake pit and endures the horrors of a corridor filled with vultures and reptiles before being strapped to Regula's slab.

Roger rushes to the rescue and his crucifix restores order amid this mayhem. "Throw it away!" Regula shouts, just as Lee's Count Dracula would command the following year in *Dracula Has Risen from the Grave*, and his reign of terror comes to an end. He and his servant disintegrate, and the whole castle disappears like Klingsor's magic castle in Wagner's *Parsifal*.

In 1983, the Czech filmmaker Jan Svankmajer combined "The Pit and the Pendulum" with the 1891 story "A Torture of Hope" by the French symbolist Villiers de L'Isle Adam, which in turn had been inspired by Poe's example. Villiers' tale tells a similar story of the Inquisition. A Jewish rabbi finds himself at the hands of his Christian torturers but eventually makes his escape on the eve of an *auto da fé*. He makes his way down dark corridors, observes two monks in cowls going about their ghastly business—indeed looks into the eyes of one of them, who seems to notice him. He observes the bound body of another victim being attended to by other monks, and then starts running. He escapes through an opening in the wall, and emerges into the spring sunshine, but waiting for him is the Grand Inquisitor himself:

> And, while the Rabbi Aser Abarbanel, his eyes convulsed beneath his eyelids, choked with anguish between the arms of the ascetic Dom Arbuez, realising confusedly that all the phases of the fatal evening had been only a calculated torture, that of Hope! the Grand Inquisitor, with a look of distress, an accent of poignant reproach, murmured in his ear, with the burning breath of much fasting:—"What! my child! on the eve, perhaps, of salvation ... you would then leave us?"[17]

Villier's ironic tale complements Poe well, and had contemporary political relevance to Svankmajer at the time he made his film, *The Pendulum, The Pit and Hope*, living, as he was then, in Communist Czechoslovakia. The torture of hope was well-known to every Czech intellectual at that time, and it is this aspect rather than the sexual subtext, that informs Svanmajer's fifteen-minute film. It faithfully visualizes the events of Poe's story, even reproducing Poe's first-person narration by showing us everything that happens from the point of view of the victim, whose hands and feet we also see from his own point of view. With the possible exception of Edward Abraham's strikingly stylized 1962 adaptation for the BBC (with its modish checkerboard floor for the inquisitorial scenes and Gregory Lawson's compelling realization of Poe's various methods of torture—though with no final rescue for Brian Peck's unfortunate prisoner), Svankmajer's film is by far the most faithful visual realization of the events in Poe's narrative filmed so far; we experience the prisoner being taken down to the dungeon, the sound of the inquisitorial voices and the effect they have that reminds the narrator of "the idea of *revolution*—perhaps from its association in fancy with the burr of a mill-wheel."[18] But "revolution" in Svankmajer's film also implies revolution of the political kind. Indeed, Svankmajer includes this passage of text as the film's epigram shortly after the opening images of the decent into the chamber of horror. This later is a faithful representation of Poe's description but with a certain grotesquely comic quality which only increases the horror of the situation, just as Villiers' cold irony inflates the torture of his tale. Living under communism was similarly a grotesquely black comedy. As Nikolaus Martin described in his story of life in Czechoslovakia and Nazi concentration camps during the second world war, the Czechs, in 1951, "were busy preparing a show trial of fourteen of their highest Communist Party functionaries and members of the government of whom eleven would be hanged that same year."[19] After the Prague spring of 1968 and the political backlash, the discussion of politics was forbidden, the country was "normalized" and censorship imposed. Svankmajer's grotesquerie addresses these political implications of Poe's story at the expense of his synesthetic asides and sexual subtext.

Svankmajer's pendulum ghoulishly emerges from the teeth of a skeleton's skull that has been painted on the ceiling, and we are also made aware of the clockwork machinery that operates this fiendish device. We see the pit. We are shown how the narrator encourages the rats to gnaw away the surcingle with which he is confined on the slab by smearing his ration of salty meat over it. We see the pendulum blade cut into the wooden bench after he escapes in the nick of time. Svankmajer reserves his greatest grotesquerie for the walls which force the victim of the Inquisition into the pit. The walls are decorated with devils and demons who impale and decapitate their victims, and Svankmajer animates these two-dimensional horrors in his usual style of stop-motion black comedy, while real flames illuminate their eyes and mouths. Here, however, the Poe tale is interrupted. The prisoner is not saved by General Lasalle. Instead, the infernal walls pull back; the victim is allowed to wander out of the torture chamber and Villiers' story, as described above, takes over.

Stuart Gordon swung Poe's pendulous horror once more in 1991 for yet another adaptation, featuring Oliver Reed, who revisited his involvement in Ken Russell's *The Devils* (1971), this time as a crazy cardinal. As if Poe's instruments of torture weren't horrific enough, Gordon crammed in as many other kinds of violent death and fiendish torture as the running time would allow. Elaborating on Poe's Inquisition setting, this version grafted on a story about the Chief Inquisitor Torquemada (Lance Henriksen), who explains, "Some souls have turned so far from God that pain is the only way to call them back," while Reed's Cardinal holds a perfumed handkerchief against his nose to ward off the physical consequences of this extreme approach to redemption. Innocence is no defense against him: When the heroine, Maria (Rona de Ricci), is described as being like an angel, he replies, "Satan was an angel," and proceeds to torture her as well. Indeed, Torquemada generally reminds one of the sexually repressed atrocities of Ambrosio in Matthew Lewis' Gothic shocker *The Monk* (1796). Sex, decapitation, flogging, religious bigotry, the Iron Maiden, the rack, swordfights, burial alive, burning at the stake, all form part of Gordon's mix here, and, yes, there is a pendulum as Poe describes it, though the pit is enhanced with spikes.

Hollywood returned to Poe's pendulum in James McTeigue's *The Raven* (2012), but before addressing that film, the alphabet dictates that we must examine Poe's preoccupation with decapitation, premature burial and rationation in more detail.

A Predicament

At twenty-five minutes past five in the afternoon, precisely, the huge minute-hand had proceeded sufficiently far on its terrible revolution to sever the small remainder of my neck.[1]

"A Predicament" (1838) is another of Poe's obviously comic tales, which deals with extreme horror in a satirical manner. In the company of her pet poodle and Negro companion, Psyche Zenobia climbs the clock tower of a Gothic cathedral in Edinburgh and gets her head stuck while looking out through a hole in the clock face. The hour and minute hands advance towards her like a pair of scissors. The pressure of them against her neck forces her eyes to pop out and then chops off her head. The companion piece to Poe's article "How to Write a Blackwood Article," this story is the fulfillment of Mr. Blackwood's advice to the same Psyche Zenobia, as reported in that article, to kill herself and write up the result for his journal—for "Sensations are the great things after all."[2]

Poe's comedy violence has certain effects in common with cartoon comedy of the *Tom and Jerry* variety, in which really quite appalling things happen without any serious consequence. After all, Miss Zenobia somehow manages to write up her decapitation:

> I was not sorry to see the head which had occasioned me so much embarrassment at length make a final separation from my body. It first rolled down the side of the steeple, then lodged, for a few seconds, in the gutter, and then made its way, with a plunge into the middle of the street.[3]

Zenobia's sanguine reportage—"The loss of the eye was not so much as the insolent air of independence and contempt with which it regarded me after it was out"[4]—anticipates the kind of stiff-upper-lip irony that characterized the British TV series *The Avengers,* in which similarly scary things happened much to the blithe amusement of Steed and Emma Peel (though it has to be said that they were never in any real danger of mutilation). Blackwood runs off a list of possible demises for Zenobia to write about:

> It is just possible that you may not be able, so soon as convenient, to—to get yourself drowned, or—choked with a chicken-bone, or—or hung,—or—bitten by a—but stay! Now I think me of it, there are a couple of very excellent bull-dogs in the yard—fine fellows, I assure you—savage, and all that—indeed just the thing for your money—they'll have you eaten up, *auriculas* and all, in less than five minutes.[5]

Compare those words with this dialogue from the *Avengers* episode "The Strange Case of the Missing Corpse," in which Emma breezes in and asks,

> "Where is it?"
> "Where's what?" Steed inquires.
> "The Body."
> "The Body?"

"Hmm. The *corpus delecti*. Oh, I'm not particular. It could be stabbed, strangled, riddled with bullets, mutilated beyond recognition."
"You're quite right. Until we find a body..."
"We've nothing to investigate."
"We're defunct."
"Obsolete."
"Out of business."

In a sense, Steed and Emma write up their encounters with death and violence each week during the various seasons of the show, just as Zenobia did for Mr. Blackwood. One might be tempted to add the stylish violence of James Bond to the other descendants of Poe's tale, but *The Avengers* was more archly knowing, more surreal, more bizarre than Bond, and it is those grotesque comic possibilities, first discovered by Poe, which laid the cultural foundations for *The Avengers* and its imitators. Zenobia's obsession with style and fashion is fully the equal of Emma's up-to-the-minute wardrobe. Her poodle (intriguingly named Diana, like one of the actors who played Emma) "had a quantity of hair over her eye, and a blue riband tied fashionably around her neck."[6] Zenobia's appearance "is commanding. On the memorable occasion of which I speak I was habited in a crimson satin dress, with sky-blue Arabian *mantelet*. And the dress had trimmings of green *agrafass,* and seven graceful flounces of the orange-colored *auricula*."[7] We are meant to be as beguiled by this vision as the producers of *The Avengers* wished us to admire Emma's leather jumpsuits and figure-hugging couture. The costumes in either case serve no narrative function; they are purely decorative and entirely to do with style. *The Avengers* certainly had plots, but its primary appeal was visual: the M-appeal of the Emma Peel, the suavity of Steed, the cars, the fashionable settings, the witty dialogue, and the "will-they-won't they?" relationship of the two leads.

Also like Poe, *The Avengers* exposed its own fictional world *as* fiction (something Bond never did), satirizing its own conventions. At the end of the episode "Epic," for example, Emma kicks down the wall of the studio set in which we have been watching her and Steed discuss what film they are going to watch in the evening.

"Why don't we just spend the evening at home?' Steed suggests.
"Why not?" Emma agrees. "Let's get back to my apartment."

As she pushes the wall down with her foot, we see behind it the film studio in which this scene has been shot—the lights, the flats, the microphone boom, etc. The effect in Poe is highly comparable, though obviously *literary,* rather than cinematic: In "How to Write a Blackwood Article," he exposes the illusion of literature in just the same way, revealing the tawdry reality, the tricks, the editing process and the importance of selecting the right style: "Having determined upon your subject, you must next consider the tone, or manner, of your narration. There is the tone didactic, the tone enthusiastic, the tone natural—all commonplace enough. But then there is the tone laconic, or curt, which had lately come much into use. It consists in short sentences. Somehow thus: Can't be too brief. Can't be too snappish. Always a full stop. And never a paragraph"[8]—in fact, the kind of snappy one-liners so often indulged in by Steed and Emma. Poe's approach here foreshadows the inevitable documentaries and commentaries on today's DVDs of movies, which deconstruct the illusion, point out how effects are created, and expose the technical practicalities of the moviemaking process.

But long before such matters became *de rigueur, The Avengers* was sending up itself—

and the very process of filmmaking. That element, along with the series' love of the bizarre, its comedy violence, and its weekly satire of science fiction-spy-romance-crime genres, might all be said to derive from Poe's particular approach in this tale and its very modern companion piece.

The Premature Burial

The boundaries which divide Life and Death are at best shadowy and vague. Who shall say where the one ends, and the other begins?[1]

"The Premature Burial" (1844) combines a newspaper article with a gimmick and an anecdote. It opens with a journalistic account of various sensational examples of catalepsy and premature burial, which prepare us for a description of the narrator's own morbid fear, and his own complex precautions against such a terrible eventuality. These include a specially designed coffin that will spring open at the slightest touch, and a bell to sound the alarm on top of the mausoleum, which constitute the gimmick. Poe ends his piece with the anecdote in which the narrator believes he really has been buried alive while away from home and the securities of his customized tomb. In fact, he has taken refuge for the night, while out hunting, in the confined quarters of a boat's cabin. The boat is carrying a cargo of earth, and this consequently accounts for the impression the narrator has of being six feet under.

While graveyard imagery was hardly anything new when Poe wrote his tale, "The Premature Burial" broke new ground by these means. The effect thus created was originally one of great veracity. Poe also made the idea of premature burial a popular theme. Sheridan Le Fanu (1814–1873) exploited it in his short story "The Room in the Dragon Volant" (1872), in which a traveler finds himself the victim of an elaborate plot, which culminates in his own premature burial. Having been drugged, he describes how he was then "lowered backward, gradually, till I lay my length in [the coffin]. Then the man, whom he called Planard, stretched my arms by my sides, and carefully arranged the frills at my breast, and the folds of the shroud, and after that, taking his stand at the foot of the coffin, made a survey which seemed to satisfy him."[2] To his horror, the young man understands the terrible fate that has been prepared for him: He is to take the place of another man, "to lie in his coffin, with his name on the plate above my breast, and with a ton of clay packed down upon me; to waken from this catalepsy, after I had been for hours in the grave, there to perish by a death the most horrible that imagination can conceive."[3] In Carl Dreyer's adaptation of the collection of stories that make up Le Fanu's *In a Glass Darkly* (1872), of which "The Dragon Volant" is the longest, we experience this terrible predicament from the point of view of the man in the coffin, who is able to look out through a glass panel let into the lid. The staring immobile features of the cataleptic Allan Grey (played by Julian West)—surely one of the cinema's most compelling images—fully capture all the horror that originally inspired Poe. We watch, with him, the coffin lid being drilled, a candle being lit, and the hideous face of the old crone (who derives from the final tale in Le Fanu's collection, the lesbian vampire story, "Carmilla"). The lid having been screwed down, the coffin is carried to the church, and the camera looks up at the ceiling along with

Allan Grey. We emerge into the open air and observe the foreshortened perspectives of trees and the church tower as bells toll. The film is Dreyer's masterpiece *Vampyr* (1932).

Burial alive also forms the climax of Verdi's opera *Aida,* which was first performed in 1871, one year before the first appearance of Le Fanu's story. In a startling anticipation of the cinematic technique of a split-screen, Verdi and his librettist Antonio Ghislanzoni show the audience the priests of the temple going about their business above the gloomy tomb. Rhadames sings

> The fatal stone is closed above me—
> Behold my tomb. The light of day
> I shall see no more. I shall no more see Aida.

Aida responds:

> My heart, prophetic of thy sentence,
> Into this tomb which opened itself for thee
> I furtive made my way.
> And here afar from every human glance
> In thy arms I wished to die.[4]

Perhaps inspired by this ancient Egyptian opera, the makers of *Land of the Pharaohs* (dir. Howard Hawks, 1955) subjected Joan Collins to a similar—though pyramidal—entombment as a punishment for her character's avaricious, indeed murderous scheming.

As a study in neurotic obsession, Poe's "Premature Burial" might well be compared to the obsessive themes of "Ligeia" and "The Fall of the House of Usher." In those two stories, however, death and premature burial form only part of a broader psychological landscape. Here, we have a single *idée fixe,* explored by means of bizarre paraphernalia. While the paraphernalia transfers well to film drama, the anecdote of the story itself is too self-contained to lend much to the possibilities of film action, which is why film adaptations invariably add their own agenda and motivations. An early example starred Erich von Stroheim in the title role of *The Crime of Dr. Crespi* (dir. John H. Auer, 1935). When Dr. Ross (John Bohn) steals his beloved (played by Harriet Russell), he takes his revenge by injecting Bohn with a drug that induces all the effects of death. Echoing Dreyer's approach in *Vampyr,* Auer shows us Crespi from Ross' point of view as he leans over his unfortunate victim and explains what is happening to him:

> Hello, Stephen, my friend, my dear friend—my *dead* friend. No! You're not dead, are you?—despite the fact that I signed your death certificate hours ago. They just *think* you're dead, but we know different, don't we, Stephen? You see, the potency of this, er, drug lasts only for about, er, twenty-four hours. You are just coming out of it [Crespi injects Ross]. Now then, that's better, that'll keep you quiet for another twenty-four hours. Your eyes open and you can see. You can hear everything. Yes—and you can feel, but you can't make the slightest sound and you can't move an eyelash—and here you lie, helpless, paralyzed, unable to shield yourself.

Roger Corman's 1962 film adaptation substitutes Poe's anecdote with a murder plot. Ray Milland's character, Guy Carrell, is married to the apparently devoted and charming Emily (played by Hazel Court) but in fact she is quite the opposite of devotion. She exploits her husband's obsessive fear of premature interment with the aim of bringing his nightmares to life. (Corman cannot resist including another reference to Poe's "Black Cat" by having a similar animal walled up in Carrell's home. It is his scheming wife, we later

Funeral Party. The cast of *The Premature Burial* (dir. Roger Corman, 1962). The only person missing is the star Ray Milland, whose character is in for a nasty shock.

learn, who is responsible for this, hoping it will worry her unfortunate husband to death.) Having terrified him sufficiently to induce a cataleptic seizure and then buried him alive, she is able to inherit his estate—her aim from the beginning. Corman is careful to divert suspicion from Emily to the red herring that is Carrell's sister, Kate (played with tight-lipped furtiveness by Heather Angel), who in fact is quite aware of what is really going on.

The Carrell home is not well-suited to diverting Guy from his obsessions. The grounds are shrouded in permanent swirling dry ice, which is scarcely believable from a naturalistic point of view, but perfectly in keeping with Corman's studio-bound, deliberately stylized approach to his Poe films in general and this film's meditation on death in particular. In keeping with this theme, Carrell becomes so obsessed by death that he virtually takes up residence in his carefully contrived tomb. Like Roderick Usher, he dabbles in painting, and even daubs his disturbing dream visions beside his own coffin, to the extent of ignoring his wife and the outside world. He is thus another forerunner of Huysmans' Des Esseintes and, following Keats' example, is half in love with easeful death, as well as fearing it. He might also be said to echo that nineteenth-century idol of Oscar Wilde, Sarah Bernhardt, who also enjoyed posing in her coffin. So too did those members of the general public in *fin de siècle* Paris who frequented the Cabaret du Néant (Tavern of the Dead), with its coffin tables and skeleton decor. Even such a work as Evelyn Waugh's *The Loved One* (1948) is a descendent of Poe's graveyard reverie here, satirical though Waugh's novel is. Poe's elaborate descriptions of his narrator's tomb, with its coffin "warm and softly padded" with its lid "fashioned upon the principle of the vault door, with the addition of springs so contrived that the feeblest movement of the body would be sufficient to set it at liberty,"[5] is echoed by Waugh in the words of the "Mortuary Hostess" of the Whispering Glades cemetery: "Normal disposal is by inhumement, entombment, inurnment, or immurement, but many people just lately prefer insarcophagusment. That is *very* individual. The casket is placed inside a sealed sarcophagus, marble or bronze, and rests permanently above ground in a niche in the mausoleum, with or without a personal stained-glass window above. That, of course, is for those with whom price is not a primary consideration."[6] Waugh also dwells on sepulture fully as much as the film adaptations of Poe, describing the "host of bronze and Carrara statuary, allegorical, infantile or erotic. Here a bearded magician sought the future in the obscure depths of what seemed to be a plaster football. There a toddler clutched to its stony bosom a marble Mickey Mouse. A turn in the path disclosed Andromeda, naked and fettered in ribbons, gazing down her polished arm at a marble butterfly which had settled there."[7]

Tony Richardson's film adaptation of *The Loved One* (1965) cast Liberace as Mr. Starker, a creepily comic undertaker, played with a poker face. His range of available coffins would have fascinated Poe:

> Now, these are lead-coated steel. Medium price range. The "Silent Night" Special—and very special it is too, if I may say so. Water-proof of course. All our units are water-proof. This offers maximum protection for a unit in the middle price range.
>
> Now here is your handsome "Rest King" in seven gauge steel with a choice of finish in eight color combinations. This unit is guaranteed to give maximum protection. It's moisture-proof, Mr. Barlow.
>
> And here are your bronzes. They are dampness-proof—not merely water-proof, nor moisture-proof, Mr. Barlow, but dampness-proof.
>
> Now then, in addition, your "Emperor" model features not a rayon or a crepe interior but an all-silk interior. Tell me, Mr. Barlow, was your uncle a sensitive person? Rayon chafes, you know. Personally, I find it really quite abrasive.
>
> Now then, Mr. Barlow, have you given any thought to exterior designations? I can give you our eternal flame in either perpetual eternal or standard eternal. With your standard eternal, your flame burns only during visiting hours. It is shut down at night. With your perpetual eternal, your flame is in service twenty-four hours a day. Propane or butane, Mr. Barlow? Propane burns bluer.

Unfortunately for Guy Carrell, the funerary equipment he has ordered is less reliable. In one of Corman's most successful dream sequences, Carrell awakes from his catalepsy to find that his escape mechanisms have failed. The bell designed to summon help from the tomb's roof can no longer be pulled, and the release mechanism to open the door is broken. Finally, Carrell has recourse to his ultimate remedy: the poison he has provided as a last resort. But even this had corrupted into writhing maggots, which disgust him far more than the thought of instant death.

Corman's film is virtually a remake of the previous year's TV adaptation of the story made for the Boris Karloff *Thriller* series. Directed by Douglas Heyes, this black-and-white version is rather more compelling than its full-color rival. It opens in a rainy graveyard where Edward Stapleton is being buried. (Stapleton is played by Sidney Blackmer, who would go on to perform the role of Roman Castevet in Roman Polanski's *Rosemary's Baby* in 1968.) Karloff plays Stapleton's friend Dr. Thorne, who suspects that Stapleton's fiancée is not as devoted as she professes to be, and cannot believe that Stapleton died of natural causes. We then cut to the interior of the tomb to observe the coffin rocking on its shelf and falling to the floor before Stapleton's hand emerges and Stapleton fumbles to release himself from his confinement in one of television's most graphic Gothic images. Bizarrely, Karloff, as himself, then introduces the cast, who are successively revealed lying in coffins as their lids spring open.

Thorne arranges a post mortem, and, recalling his past career as an impersonator of mad scientists (not to mention the scenes in which he was "created" in *Frankenstein*), Karloff intones the line, "I'm going to try the galvanic battery." This has the desired effect— indeed, it exceeds his expectations, as Stapleton leaps from the slab and raises his arms aloft before collapsing again. Later, as he remembers his ordeal in the coffin, he explains, "I have been aware of everything since the moment they pronounced me dead."

Stapleton's revival is very good news for his fiancée Victorine (played by Patricia Medina). She thought she had been cheated from her anticipated inheritance, but now, she is able to marry him and, as in Corman's film, set about finishing him off. Victorine craves not only Stapleton's money, she also lusts after a young, selfish artist called Julian (Scott Marlowe). But unlike Hazel Court's Emily Carrell, Victorine has a conscience and blows hot and cold. Her more complex character contributes to the general inventiveness of this adaptation, making it rather more compelling than Corman's film. At one stage on their honeymoon abroad, she is on the point of renouncing her evil plan and staying with Stapleton, with whom she thinks she really has fallen in love, but his subsequent cataleptic seizure caused by over-exertion settles her mind. She removes the bracelets with their instructions not to bury Stapleton (as he is a cataleptic), and hastens his premature burial in a coffin with a window in the lid, very much in the manner of Dreyer's *Vampyr*. Thorne is immediately suspicious of this foreign burial, as Stapleton has left strict instructions to be buried in the specially prepared tomb.

The dénouement has several things in common with two of Hammer's psychological thrillers: Thorne arranges for a policeman to wear a mask and impersonate Stapleton, wandering in his shroud as though he has escaped from his tomb. (In fact, Stapleton is well and truly dead.) By this means, he is able to extract a confession from Julian which incriminates Victorine. Thus justice is done. (The use of a latex mask and a scheme to "catch the conscience of the king," so to speak, was used in Hammer's *Nightmare* [dir. Freddie Francis, 1964]. A mask also features in *Paranoiac* [dir. Freddie Francis, 1963], but of course, these aspects of the films have nothing to do with Poe.)

Also like Corman, this television version incorporates echoes of another Poe tale, in this instance the guitar playing of Roderick Usher. Stapleton plays an kind of harp-zither, as Victorine reads Walter Scott to him—a pastime that later allows for the inclusion of a classic Gothic cliché: When Victorine hears "ghostly" music, she thinks that her prematurely buried husband has indeed returned from the dead. (Hammer's *Taste of Fear,* directed by Seth Holt in the same year, uses a piano to the same effect.)

"The Premature Burial" also inspired the opening section of Ric White's *Nightmares from the Mind of Poe,* which presents us with a tracking shot of a white hearse being drawn through a cemetery. White, as the Poe-like "Charles," rather nicely balances the real horror of his paranoia here with its grotesquely comic consequences. He awakens from a nightmare in which he has been buried alive. "What is it?" his long-suffering wife asks.

"I had that dream again," he replies.

"The one on the autopsy table?"

"No, the one when I'm in a cemetery, buried alive."

"Other men dream of beautiful women," his wife complains later. "Why must you always dream of rotting ones?"

White then uses the effect Roman Polanski has exploited so unnervingly in *Repulsion* (1965), in which the shape of a pair of hands presses through the wall behind Charles' bed. (Later, a child sitting at her father's grave is disturbed by the sudden appearance of his hands from under the sod.) "What could possibly be worse than being buried alive?" Charles asks his wife.

"To live with someone who is obsessed with it?" she suggests.

In another dream sequence, grave robbers dig up a coffin only to be surprised when Charles jumps out of it. "Trust my luck to get a live one," the grave robber complains. Even the undertaker points out the oddity of Charles' burial instructions. "These requests, they are highly unusual. What will people say?"

"The Premature Burial" also found its way into Jan Svankmajer's 2005 horror film *Lunacy*. In his personal statement at the beginning of the movie, Svankmajer emphasized that it *is* a horror film, rather than "art" ("art is already dead," he insists). He also freely acknowledges the influence of Poe, along with that of the Marquis de Sade, in this exploration of the absurdity and violence of the human condition. "What does nature give us?" asks Jan Tríska's Marquis. "Is she not greedy, destructive, cruel, fickle and utterly callous? Wouldn't you say that what she does best is murder and maim?" But the Marquis' Weltanschaung is not perhaps one of complete nihilism, as he believes that nature is evil: "Don't you see that evil is her natural element?" he continues, "that she uses her creative powers only to fill the world with blood, tears and sorrow?" This is surely a less advanced view than that of Friedrich Nietzsche, who pointed out that in nature, which is "beyond good and evil," there are no laws—only necessities. To worship evil is not quite the same thing as acknowledging the amoral reality of nature, but even so, the marquis wishes to instruct his protégé, Jean Berlot (Pavel Liska) in his philosophy. He hammers nails into a statue of Christ and indulges in blasphemy and sexual perversion. He also takes him to a lunatic asylum, which is indebted to various motives drawn from Poe's story "The System of Doctor Tarr and Professor Fether," in which the asylum is in fact run by the inmates.

Before that, however, the marquis chokes on a banana, while laughing to scorn Jean's moral indignation. The marquis appears to die but, in fact, his accident has triggered catalepsy. The marquis' mute servant Dominic then forces Jean at gunpoint to assist in the burial of his master. The coffin is nailed shut and carried to an underground vault. Dominic then makes preparations for the marquis' possible return from the dead. Fine china and food are laid on and a bell pull suspended from the ceiling. Sure enough, the marquis does return and we are shown the coffin lid smashed through, its now liberated and laughing inhabitant revealing an array of woodworking tools hanging from pockets sewn inside his shroud.

Despite Svankmajer's insistence that this film is a horror film rather than a work of art, it is obviously a work of art about the horror of death. Animated chunks of meat, brains, eyeballs and tongues slither around throughout the film to emphasize the absurdity and horror of our temporary human condition, in which we seem to be nothing more than conscious meat. The marquis' ironical laughter suggests that even the horror of premature burial are ultimately a comic turn. Nothing—not even suffering—is of any significance.

It might be stretching the influence of Poe too far to list other films about being buried alive, such as Nick Hamm's *The Hole* (2001) in which four teenagers find themselves trapped in an underground nuclear bunker, or even Antonio Mercero's cult TV film *The Phone Box* (1972), in which a man also finds himself trapped only to later be transported to a cavernous space filled with similar phone boxes, all occupied by skeletons. However, Poe can certainly be said to have been the first person to popularize the idea in a quasi-documentary fashion, and all subsequent variations on the theme inevitably draw comparisons to Poe's highly influential tale.

The Purloined Letter

At Paris, just after dark one gusty evening in the autumn of 18—, I was enjoying the twofold luxury of meditation and a meerschaum, in company of my friend, C. Auguste Dupin, in his little back library, or book-closet, au troisième, No. 33 Rue Dunôt, Fauberg St. Germain.[1]

The third of Poe's detective stories had perhaps the most influence on Conan Doyle's Sherlock Holmes stories. Poe's detective, Dupin, who was already familiar to his readers from "The Murders in the Rue Morgue" and "The Mystery of Marie Rogêt," does not relate the story himself but has an unnamed Dr. Watson as his Boswell, sharing his living accommodation. Their rooms in Paris are situated in a "time-eaten and grotesque mansion, long deserted through superstitions into which we did not inquire."[2] They furnish it with books and bric-a-brac in a manner of "fantastic gloom" and only venture out at night. True, this is rather different from the more prosaic environment of 221B Baker Street, but even there, Holmes' study is equally eccentric, simultaneously serving as a chemical laboratory, a library, a consulting room and a museum. Holmes' methods also have much in common with those of Dupin, and both men are private individuals who pursue their ratiocinative activities as a pastime rather than a profession.

In "The Purloined Letter" (1844), Dupin discovers that a stolen ministerial document has been hidden in the place least likely to have been suspected: in the very room of the thief, exposed to view for all to see. But it has been disguised by having been re-folded with a new address inscribed on the reverse, and then re-sealed with the thief's own seal.

This story strongly influenced two Sherlock Holmes stories, "The Naval Treaty" (1893) and "The Second Stain" (1904). In the former, a stolen government paper is secreted by the thief in the upholstery of a sofa on which the victim of the crime then languishes for nine months, suffering from a brain fever caused by the anguish of his loss and the damage to his honor as a trusted civil servant. Doyle's arrangement of these circumstances is masterly, as is Holmes' plan to catch the thief, but the idea of the hero actually sitting on the stolen document for nine months derives from the "The Purloined Letter."

In "The Second Stain," the wife of a senior politician finds herself blackmailed. The price asked for the recovery of an incriminating letter is a certain document from her husband's dispatch box—a document that in the wrong hands could cause a European war. Having seen the blackmailer secrete this valuable document in a compartment under the floor of his parlor, she later returns and manages to retrieve it. Holmes discovers the complex chain of events, and realizes that the letter is already back in the politician's home. He therefore requests the letter from the lady before suavely replacing it in the dispatch box where it is discovered, much to the politician's amazement and delight:

> "Thank you! Thank you! What a weight from my heart! But this is inconceivable—impossible! Mr. Holmes, you are a wizard, a sorcerer! How did you know it was there?
> "Because I knew it was nowhere else."[3]

This classic Holmesian dénouement, so superbly dramatized for Granada Television's Sherlock Holmes series starring Jeremy Brett in 1986, has much of Dupin's cool observation that "had the purloined letter been hidden anywhere within the limits of the Prefect's examination—in other words, had the principle of its concealment been comprehended within the principles of the Prefect—its discovery would have been a matter altogether beyond question. The functionary, however, has been thoroughly mystified."[4] Dupin, on the contrary, solves the mystery by applying the appropriate principles to the search.

The celebrated film director Val Guest unfortunately failed to distinguish himself at the helm of an episode from another Sherlock Holmes television series, made in America in 1979. The episode in question was purportedly based on Poe's story but, ironically, given the tale's influence on Conan Doyle, George Fowler's teleplay entirely omits its central point—that the letter is on display for all to see. This stagey, dull and visually flat "The Case of the Purloined Letter" wasted its excellent cast, including Richard Greene as Lord Brompton, Donald Pickering as Dr. Watson, and Patrick Newell, who would appear later in the much superior Granada television adaptation of "The Resident Patient" with Jeremy Brett. Here, Newell plays Inspector Lestrade, with Geoffrey Whitehead as a rather ineffectual Holmes. Instead of following Poe's story, Fowler created one of his own, having Holmes substitute an incriminating stolen letter with a confession from the crook who purloined it. Only Poe's Imp of the Perverse could explain such foolishness.

The Raven

> *Ah, distinctly I remember it was in the bleak December.*
> *And each separate dying ember wrought its ghost upon the floor.*
> *Eagerly I wished the morrow,—vainly I had sought to borrow*
> *From my books surcease of sorrow—sorrow for the lost Lenore—*
> *For the rare and radiant maiden whom the angels name Lenore—*
> *Nameless here for evermore.*[1]

Ironically, the most faithful film adaptation of Poe's most celebrated poem can be found in "Tree-House of Horror 1," a Halloween episode of the animation television series *The Simpsons* (dir. David Silverman, 1990): A truncated version of the poem is recited by

Lisa, with interjections from Homer, who plays the role of Poe. Homer's anarchic son, Bart, turns into the Raven, while Homer's blue-rinsed, towering-permed wife Marge stands in as Lenore, the lost beloved of the tormented narrator. The approach is obviously satirical but also affectionate and respectful of Poe's vision, the recitation continuing regardless of the irreverent interruptions emerging from the framing scenes in which Lisa reads the poem to Bart in their tree-house.

> "Here I opened wide the door," the narrator intones.
> "This better be good," says Bart, as we cut back to the tree-house.
> "Darkness there and nothing more," the narrator continues.
> "Do you know what would have been scarier than nothing?" Bart interjects.
> "What?" Lisa inquires, looking up from the book.
> "*Anything!*"

Even funnier is Bart's interruption at the famous refrain, "Quote the Raven," with his catchphrase, "Eat my shorts."

"Bart, stop it!" Lisa shouts. "He said 'Nevermore!' and that's all he'll ever say." The recital continues, and towards then end, during a chase sequence, Bart-Raven drops various volumes of Poe ("The Tell-Tale Heart," "The Purloined Letter," etc.) on Homer's head.

Back in the treehouse, Bart complains that the poem wasn't very scary, to which Lisa muses, "It was written in 1845. Maybe people were easier to scare back then."

"Oh yeah," Bart realizes, "Like when you look at *Friday 13th Part 1*. It's pretty tame by today's standards."

"The Raven's" immense prestige as an American classic makes it an obvious target for satire. Its central image of a talking bird is already teetering on the precipice of comedy, but this episode of *The Simpsons* is in fact the most detailed dramatic response to the text in any film. True, it inspired a solo dance routine in the Boris Karloff-Bela Lugosi shocker *The Raven* (1935), but the choreography was hardly very specific with regard to the text, despite its being recited while the dance is performed. Lugosi's recital of some famous lines of the poem at the beginning of the film, along with shots of a stuffed raven with a threatening shadow, are about all this nonetheless interesting film has in common with Poe's masterpiece.

"Quoth the Raven—Eat My Shorts"—Bart as the Poe's Raven with Homer as Poe in Matt Groening's *The Simpsons*.

Vincent Price recited choice lines from the poem in Roger Corman's otherwise equally unrelated 1963 film of the same title. By far the most impressive section of the film, these opening moments, accompanied by Corman's characteristic swirling, multi-colored inks, are true cinematic poetry. Later, when the Raven appears in Price's chamber, it is easy to see the derivation of Bart Simpson's "Eat my shorts," for Corman's Raven (voiced by Peter Lorre) responds to one of Price's poetically phrased questions with, "How the hell should I know?"

James McTeighe's 2012 *The Raven* similarly exploited Poe's poem for its title and mood rather than anything else. The plot is entirely different from the poem, involving a murderer who uses the methods of Poe's stories, rather in the manner of the Shakespearean deaths Vincent Price's crazed actor Edward Lionheart arranges for his critics in *Theatre of Blood* (1973). The major difference is that McTeighe takes everything seriously, but he does include a scene set during a performance of *Macbeth*, which might imply an acknowledged debt. We begin with a shot of a raven in a tree above a Baltimore park bench on which Poe (John Cusack) is dying. This is fairly close to the biographical truth, but then we flash back some weeks to a gruesome murder, which bears all the hallmarks of Poe's "The Murders in the Rue Morgue." While that is being investigated by the police, Poe, desperate for a drink, challenges the customers of a bar to complete the line "Quoth the Raven..." No one says "Eat my

Bird in hand: Bela Lugosi in *The Raven* (dir. Lew Landers, 1935).

"How the hell should I know?"—Vincent Price with a well-trained raven in *The Raven* (dir. Roger Corman, 1963).

shorts," but someone does shout "Piss off!" And by this means, Poe's drink problem is addressed.

As this film is about a serial killer who challenges Poe to solve the riddles he sets for him, the logical arena for this to be played out is in the newspaper milieu in which Poe worked for most of his literary life, and the opening scenes are a useful way of showing us Poe the critic and journalist arguing with his long-suffering editor. (Poe was known mostly as a critic during his lifetime.) Cusack doesn't look much like Poe (especially sporting a goatee beard rather than Poe's mustache), but he nevertheless turns in an excellent performance as a tortured genius.

The next murder features one of the best realizations of Poe's infamous pendulum on film. "I hadn't imagined the counterweight to be so large," Poe muses, when he is taken to see it. Having read Poe's tales, the detective in charge of the case naturally suspects Poe of being the murderer, especially when the victim, who has been very graphically sliced in two, turns out to be Poe's literary sparing partner Rufus Griswold.

Meanwhile, Poe embarks on a relationship with a new girlfriend, Emily Hamilton (Alice Eve), a completely fictional character with an equally fictional father who is violently opposed to her having anything to do with Poe. Nonetheless, she visits him in secret and reads his "Annabel Lee" poem to him. Then it is Poe's turn to read lines from "The Raven" to a room full of attentive and beautifully dressed young ladies (Poe was indeed a popular lecturer). But this is only a breather before the next murder occurs, this time based on "The Masque of the Red Death."

A mysterious rider bursts into the Hamiltons' ball, echoing the arrival of the Angel of Death in Hammer's *The Devil Rides Out* (dir. Terence Fisher, 1968). The rider, however, is merely a decoy, for the real murderer has abducted the unfortunate Emily, whom he promptly buries alive, thus notching up yet another reference to the Poe canon. He then issues Poe with an ultimatum: He must write up each atrocity in the newspaper and each new crime will provide him with a clue to discover the whereabouts of his beloved.

The killer's next murders reference "The Facts in the Case of M. Valdemar" and "The Mystery of Marie Rogêt" before the fiend is finally tracked down and revealed to be Poe's humble typesetter at the newspaper office—the ultimate "fan," who had contrived everything as a tribute to his idol. ("If I knew my work would have had such a morbid effect on people I'd have devoted myself to eroticism," Poe had commented earlier in the film.) The murderer now forces Poe to drink poison before he leaves him with a quotation from "The Tell-Tale Heart." Realizing that this is a final clue, Poe accordingly rips up the floorboards to discover a replica of his study, and beneath a second set of floorboards, he discovers his buried but still breathing beloved.

And so we return to the park bench with which he began, and Poe's enigmatic references to "Reynolds" in his final delirium are thus "explained," as Reynolds is the name of the terrible typesetter. (Kenneth Silverman suggests that in fact, "Reynolds" may have been the name of a Baltimore family.[2]) Correctly gasping his well-known last words, "Lord, help my poor soul," Poe then dies. Obvious baloney though all this is, it is much more fun to imagine that Poe was referring to a man who put his fantasies into practice, for, after all, that is what so many Poe movies have attempted to do over the years, and this film succeeds better than many in that department.

Ulli Lommel's appalling, jittery, camcorder-style disaster *The Raven* (2006) has nothing to do with Poe's work, other than the image of the raven and a personal appearance of the writer (absurdly miscast) in the imagination of its Poe-obsessed heroine, Lenore (Jillian Swanson). This is both a ridiculous and unpleasant slasher-rape film about a serial killer (appropriately called Skinner), and as such is about as far removed as possible from what Poe's work is really all about.

Visual artists have responded more respectfully to "The Raven" than film directors. Most celebrated of all is Gustave Doré (1832–1888), whose suite of twenty-six engravings from 1883—the last book he was to illustrate—anticipate the surrealistic imagery of Max Ernst's 1934 collage graphic novel *Un semaine de bonté*. Doré populates the library of the poet with skeletons, angels, specters and even a vision of Lenore's corpse lying on the slab of a tomb which has materialized on the poet's parquet floor. Finally, we are left with a representation of the Sphinx of Death, which, as Joanna Richardson explains, broods "above a promontory, on the mystery which Doré himself had now come to solve."[3] Ernst surrealized Doré's Romantic vision by juxtaposing images of mythological creatures and domestic settings, or ladies in bourgeois clothing with bat-wings growing from their backs, all cut from nineteenth-century illustrations, re-arranged and collaged together.

Édouard Manet (1832–1883) also illustrated "The Raven," as did Alfred Kubin (1877–1959) and Odilon Redon, who included a rather touching Raven image in his Poe portfolio in which the bird of ill omen is portrayed in a much less threatening manner. Another illustration, entitled "Lenore," from 1882, shows the spirit of the poet's lover with the Raven standing at her feet in a woodland setting.

In the realm of music, "The Raven" inspired the first major success of Josef Holbrooke, whose symphonic poem of that name was first performed by August Manns at the Crystal Palace in London in 1900. Like much of Holbrooke's Poeana, the music fails to capture the mood of the poem, despite his liberal quotation from it at salient moments in the score. He does imitate the raven tapping at the poet's chamber door with repeated staccato notes on the strings. The "silken, sad, uncertain rustling of each purple curtain"[4] is suggested by a semi-quaver pattern; a lengthy *agitato* passage, with much fortissimo swirling, suggests a stormy night of a "bleak December," and after the poet has opened his chamber door and found nothing, rising and falling scalic passages suggest the wind "and nothing more." The Raven's entrance is suggested by trills on the strings, while sustained notes in the wind imply its stillness. The Raven's catchphrase "Nevermore" even has a leitmotif of its own, as does "Lenore," and everything ends *pianissimo* in the rather remote key of B major. But there is, alas, none of the emotional power of Debussy's response to Poe in Holbrooke's somewhat stodgy late–Victorian Romanticism. George Lowe disagrees, however, while acknowledging its neglect and the similarity of Holbrooke's approach to what was then "silent" film music:

> The dramatic power and maturity of technique displayed in this work rendered the inauguration of Holbrooke as a serious orchestral writer very conspicuous, and this first "poem" of his never fails to leave a deep impression behind it whenever it is performed (which our conductors do not allow to happen too often!).
>
> Unlike Liszt, Holbrooke calls his works "orchestral poems" and not "symphonic poems," and thereby suggests for them a freedom from all classical form. This freedom, however, renders them rather more reliant upon the derivative poem than is the symphonic form, for, in the former case, the leading events of the subject are reflected in the music with much the same regularity as the leading events of a drama thrown on a cinematograph screen, whilst, in the latter case, only some very general aspects of the subject are defined.[5]

"Nevermore." Illustration by Gustave Doré for Poe's "The Raven," 1883. This was Doré's last published work.

The Lost Lenore: Gustave Doré's illustration for "The Raven" (1882), his only American commission. Doré died the following year.

Lowe identifies "a sinister theme," which "surges up in the orchestra from the lower strings," and a "passage of consecutive chords of the seventh with the minor third and diminished fifth from the wood wind being particularly daring and weird in effect." The whispered word "Lenore!" is represented by the hushed tones of the first violins and cellos following the inflections of the speaking voice, followed "by a wild outburst of fury leading into a ponderous, self-assertive subject descriptive of the lines 'Open here I flung the shutter / Then with many a flirt and flutter, / In there stepped a stately Raven / Of the saintly days of yore.'"[6]

> "Tell me what thy lordly name is!" the student demands, and the phraseology of the music, proceeding from the horns and trumpets, accords with the phraseology of the words, as it also does in the case of the reply, "Nevermore!" heard twice on the horns and once on the oboes.[7]

As the piece concludes, "All is deepest gloom as the clarinets sob out two final 'Nevermores,' followed by a beat of the drum."[8]

Better known as a conductor, Leonard Slatkin composed a musical recitation on "The Raven" in 1971, but perhaps more engaging, depending upon one's taste, is Alan Parsons' 1970s prog-rock response to the poem, in which Leonard Whiting intones lines from the poem using a vocoder—still a relatively new technology in popular music at the time. Whiting, similarly, was still effulgent from his appearances in Zeffirelli's *Romeo and Juliet* (1968) and the Christopher Isherwood-scripted telemovie *Frankenstein—The True Story* (dir. Jack Smight, 1973), and such Romantic-Gothic credentials added another layer of associations to Poe's words. With its up-tempo refrain of "Nevermore, Nevermore, Nevermore," replete with a raunchy electric guitar and bass, the Alan Parsons Project managed to bring Poe's most famous poem up to date (for 1975) while retaining its romance, mystery and unsettling melancholy mood.

Some Words with a Mummy

> *"Had I been, as you say, dead," replied the Count, "it is more than probable that dead I should still be; for I perceive you are yet in the infancy of Galvanism, and cannot accomplish with it what was a common thing among us in the old days. But the fact is, I fell into catalepsy, and it was considered by my best friends that I was either dead or should be; they accordingly embalmed me at once—I presume you are aware of the embalming process?"*[1]

This story about a resurrected mummy, with the punning name of Alemistakeo, is a far cry from the stomping horrors of Universal and Hammer mummy movies. But the story starts out as though it is going to be a Gothic romance. Written in 1845, it may have influenced Bram Stoker's much later ancient Egyptian thriller *The Jewel of Seven Stars* (1903), which similarly begins with a mysterious summons in the night. Compare Poe's "I could not have completed my third snore when there came a furious ringing at the street-door bell, and then an impatient thumping at the knocker, which awakened me at once"[2] with Stoker's "It was evident that the knocking and ringing were at the door of our own house; and it was evident, too, that there was no one awake to answer the call."[3] Even the letter of summons both protagonists receive at the beginning of their respective stories is couched in similar language. Poe: "Come to me, by all means, my dear good friend, as soon as you receive this."[4] Stoker: "Come at once, if you are able to; and forgive me if you can."[5] But Poe's mummy is soon revealed to be a very intelligent, polite but critical fellow, who scathingly satirizes then-contemporary American society on Poe's behalf.

Poe's mix of suspense, satire, science fiction and social criticism here suggests the possibility that we should perhaps exercise caution when interpreting his apparently more straight-faced fictions, for they too could easily have developed into the bathos of this tale, which starts out apparently so seriously (though the narrator's over-indulgence on Welsh-rabbit and Brown Stout does make one suspicious). Poe adds to the apparent authenticity of the events narrated by mentioning the genuine Egyptologist George Robins Gliddon (1809–1857), and he also made sure to include correct Egyptological facts by borrowing relevant passages from the Encyclopedia Britannica. Poe was also familiar with Jane Webb's immense science fiction novel *The Mummy: a Tale of the Twenty-Second Century* (1827), in which a mummy is spectacularly reanimated in a manner that echoed and much amplified the creation of the Creature in Mary Shelley's *Frankenstein* (1816). In "Some Words with a Mummy," Poe uses Frankenstein's method of electrical stimulation, but the result is not one of horror but unexpected farce:

> [T]he Mummy first drew up its right knee so as to bring it nearly in contact with the abdomen, and then, straightening the limb with inconceivable force, bestowed a kick upon Doctor Pommonner, which had the effect of discharging that gentleman, like an arrow from a catapult, through a window into the street below.[6]

Such a scene foreshadows the slapstick humor of *Abbott and Costello Meet the Mummy* (dir. Charles Lamont, 1955), but the story's greatest influence was perhaps on Anne Rice's 1989 novel *The Mummy—or Ramses the Damned*. Poe's conceit of an articulate, intelligent and elegant reanimated ancient Egyptian certainly bares comparison with Rice's hero, to whom she adds an extra element of sexual allure. Ramses takes exactly the same point of view as Alemistakeo in his lack of faith in progress:

> "You're not so difficult to understand," Ramses said. "You've learned to express yourselves too well for anything to remain veiled or mysterious. Your newspapers and books tell everything. Yet you are not so different from your ancient ancestors. You want love, you want comfort; you want justice. That is what the Egyptian farmer wanted when he went out to till his fields. That is what the labourers of London want. And as always the rich are jealous of what they possess. And greed leads to high crimes as it always has.... You haven't found all the answers yet. Electricity, telephones, these are lovely magic. But the poor go unfed. Men kill for what they cannot gain by their own labour. How to share the magic, the riches, the secrets, that is still the problem."[7]

Alemistakeo is more contemptuous of nineteenth-century self-confidence. When asked what he makes of railroads, he opines, "They were rather slight, rather ill-conceived, and clumsily put together. They could not be compared, of course, with the vast, level, direct, iron-grooved causeways, upon which the Egyptians conveyed entire temples and solid obelisks of a hundred and fifty feet in altitude."[8] Poe also facetiously compares the Bowling-Green Fountain in New York ("hideous and distasteful" according to the *Broadway* Journal[9]) with the ruins of Carnac ("an insignificant little building after all"[10]).

Poe concludes his disparaging fantasy with the comment (admittedly uttered by the narrator): "The truth is, I am heartily sick of this life and of the nineteenth century in general. I am convinced that everything is going wrong."[11] Trivializing the enormity of his next thought by prefacing it with the need first to shave and drink a cup of coffee, he decides to have himself embalmed for a couple of hundred years, curious, as he is, to know who will be president in 2045. But Poe had no faith in the future either, as "Mellonta Tauta," his supplement to *Eureka*, demonstrates. "His future," writes Harold Beaver, "is totalitarian and overcrowded. The key is population control. Men as individuals are abandoned; epidemics and wars, welcomed."[12] It was not so far from the truth.

The Sphinx

The very air from the South seemed to us redolent with death. That palsying thought, indeed, took entire possession of my soul. I could neither speak, think, nor dream of any thing else.[1]

First published in 1846, "The Sphinx" is a different kind of hoax, as Poe explains the enigma of the story at the end. In fact, this story is related to his earlier "The Spectacles" (1844), for both are about optical illusions. In the latter, a myopic young man marries an ugly woman believing her to be beautiful. In "The Sphinx," a young man imagines he sees a terrifying monster walking down a hill, but eventually realizes that he has been watching an insect at a very close range. But the context of the tale is important: The narrator has visited his friend to escape a cholera epidemic in New York. He is consequently already obsessed by thoughts of death, as the quotation from the tale above makes clear, and therefore is already prone to macabre thoughts.

Poe's description of the sphinx is truly terrifying:

> The mouth of the animal was situated at the extremity of a proboscia some sixty or seventy feet in length, and about as thick as the body of an ordinary elephant. Near the root of this trunk was an immense quantity of black shaggy hair—more than could have been supplied by the coats of a score of buffaloes; and projecting from this hair downwardly and laterally, sprang two gleaming tusks not unlike those of the wild boar, but of infinitely greater dimension. Extending forward, parallel with the proboscis, and on each side of it, was a gigantic staff, thirty or forty feet in length, formed seemingly of pure crystal, and in shape a perfect prism,—it reflected in the most gorgeous manner the rays of the declining sun. The trunk was fashioned like a wedge with the apex to the earth. From it there were outspread two pairs of wings—each wing nearly one hundred yards in length—one pair being placed above the other, and all thickly covered with metal scales; each scale apparently some ten or twelve feet in diameter.[2]

The poet W. B. Yeats professed to dislike Poe's work, but lines from his poem "The Second Coming" (1919) intriguingly bear comparison not only with the title Poe chose to give his tale, but also the sensation of evil induced by this insect sphinx. "The Second Coming" is Yeats' response to the horrors of the first world war and the disorienting state of postwar European civilization. It ends with the image of a giant stone sphinx, an embodiment of evil, moving towards Bethlehem to be incarnated as the false Messiah:

> The Second Coming! Hardly are those words out
> When a vast image out of Spiritus Mundi
> Troubles my sight: a waste of desert sand;
> A shape with lion body and the head of a man,
> A gaze blank and pitiless as the sun,
> Is moving its slow thighs, while all about it
> Wind shadows of the indignant desert birds.
> The darkness drops again but now I know
> That twenty centuries of stony sleep
> Were vexed to nightmare by a rocking cradle,
> And what rough beast, its hour come round at last,
> Slouches towards Bethlehem to be born?[3]

Poe took a similar approach, his sphinx also being terrifying and apocalyptic:

> While I regarded this terrific animal, and more especially the appearance on its breast [a Death's Head], with a feeling of horror and awe—with a sentiment of forthcoming evil, which I found it impossible to quell by any effort of reason, I perceived the huge jaws at the extremity of the proboscis suddenly expand themselves, and from them there proceeded a sound so loud and so expressive of woe, that it struck upon my nerves like a knell, and as the monster disappeared at the foot of the hill, I fell at once, fainting to the floor."[4]

"The Sphinx" has only inspired one cinematic response, and this is not an adaptation but a dramatized reading, in costume, by Vincent Price in *An Evening of Edgar Allan Poe*. Price enhances the bathetic ending by laughing it off, his previously serious expression converted into an impish grin, which one imagines Poe himself indulging in when writing his elaborate literary jests. Though this is really the only specific cinematic manifestation of the tale, "The Sphinx" nonetheless laid the foundation for all the subsequent films which exploited dramatic re-sizing, now affectionately referred to as Killer-Bug Movies. Admittedly, Jonathan Swift's *Gulliver's Travels* (1726) experimented with re-sizing, but principally from a satirical perspective to expose the evils of human society. Poe's approach in "The Sphinx," despite its rational explanation at the end, was purely for horrific effect. Of the various films that followed in its wake, the one that is most closely related to it is *The Fly* (dir. Kurt Neumann, 1958). Also starring Vincent Price, this film expands a fly's head and places it on a human body—the result of a teleportation experiment gone wrong. Similarly, the fly's body finds itself with a miniaturized human head. There is nothing horrific about a housefly under normal circumstances, but magnification makes it so. David Cronenberg's 1986 remake with Jeff Goldblum extended the influence of Poe's apparently slight conceit. So too did Ernest B. Schoedsack's *Dr. Cyclops* (1940), in which a cast shrunken to twelve inches in height do battle with jungle wildlife, and *The Incredible Shrinking Man* (dir. Jack Arnold, 1957), based on Richard Matheson's 1956 novel. In this adventure, the normally harmless or mundane creatures and objects of everyday life are transformed into life-threatening phenomena because the hero becomes increasingly small, and therefore powerless. The comic possibilities of this situation were exploited in *The Incredible Shrinking Woman* (dir. Joel Schumacher, 1981) starring Lily Tomlin, while Richard Fleischer's *Fantastic Voyage* (1966) expanded the human body from the perspective of miniaturized scientists who are injected into the bloodstream of a full-sized scientist to save his life.

Fueled by the radiation fears of the atomic age, a variety of size-shifting films appeared in the 1950s. *Them!* (dir. Gordon Douglas, 1954) concerned gigantic irradiated ants, a situation played for comic effect in *Honey, I Shrunk the Kids* (dir. Joe Johnston, 1989) in which the shrunken kids of the title befriend a helpful ant they call "Anty." There was a giant tarantula in *Tarantula* (dir. Jack Arnold, 1955), giant wasps in *Monster from Green Hell* (dir. Kenneth G. Crane, 1957), a giant scorpion in *The Black Scorpion* (dir. Edward Ludwig, 1957), giant mollusks in *The Monster That Challenged the World* (dir. Arnold Laven, 1957), giant leeches in *Attack of the Giant Leeches* (dir. Bernard L. Kowalski, 1959) and a giant praying mantis in *The Deadly Mantis* (dir. Nathan Juran, 1957), against which the might of the U.S. military is powerless. More recently, futuristic soldiers took on giant spiders in *Starship Troopers* (dir. Paul Verhoeven, 1997). The many more movies of this type can all claim an ancestor in Poe's "The Sphinx."

The System of Doctor Tarr and Professor Fether

> *The "soothing system," with important modifications, has been resumed at the château; yet I cannot help agreeing with Monsieur Maillard, that his own "treatment" was a very capital one of its kind. As he justly observed, it was "simple—neat—and gave no trouble at all—not the least.*
>
> *I have only to add that, although I have searched every library in Europe for the works of Doctor Tarr and Professor Fether, I have, up to the present day, utterly failed in my endeavors to procure a copy.*[1]

As the title of this 1845 tale suggests, "The System of Doctor Tarr and Professor Fether" is one of Poe's grotesque black comedies, in which the narrator gradually realizes that the lunatic asylum he is inspecting is actually being run by the lunatics themselves, who have overthrown the staff, tarred and feathered them and imprisoned them in the underground cells of the establishment. This story being about madness, it is appropriate that it should begin in the Gothic style of "The Fall of the House of Usher." Whereas "Usher" begins, "During the whole of a dull, dark, and soundless day in the autumn of the year," "Dr. Tarr and Professor Fether" begins, "During the autumn of 18—" and continues with the narrator's description of Monsieur Maillard's asylum as occupying a "fantastic *château*," lying beyond a "dank and gloomy wood."[2] Significantly, this was the scene which Alfred Kubin chose to illustrate the story, showing the two men on horseback approaching the imposing building rising before them on a hill. Monsieur Maillard greets the travelers, just as the equally insane Roderick Usher greets his similarly unnamed guest—for Maillard is indeed mad. The narrator's friend does not realize this, having previously visited when the doctor was in full possession of his faculties, but the situation has changed, and Maillard became one of the inmates. Having incited a revolution and overthrown his warders, he has now resumed control.

Such a state of affairs raises the question of the sanity of authority everywhere, and it is possible to interpret this story as an allegory of society in general, for are not those in control frequently irrational, corrupt, unbalanced—even, as in the case of homicidal personalities such as Nero, Hitler and Idi Amin, insane? The frightening situation of finding oneself in a lunatic asylum in which the lunatics have gained control could well be expanded to the existential dilemma of finding oneself trapped by any other kind of social hierarchy that forces one to accept the horrors of irrational decrees. American youth discovered this during the Vietnam War, as did millions of Jews during the Third Reich; and it was grimly appropriate that the threat of nuclear annihilation during the Cold War was given the acronym M.A.D. (Mutually Assured Destruction). Poe, the practitioner of ratiocination, was well aware that reason is not the guiding force of human history.

He shared this opinion with the Marquis de Sade (1740–1814), who not only spent much of his own life behind the bars of the lunatic asylum at Charenton, but who also devoted much of his literary skill to the analysis of what he regarded as the fundamentally irrational basis of all human behavior. In his novel *Justine* (1791), he demonstrated that the possession of virtue brings about positive misfortune, and in *The 101 Days of Sodom* (1785), he exhaustively catalogued as many forms of sexual perversion as he could imagine. When Jan Svankmejer adapted "Dr. Tarr and Professor Fether" for his film *Silena* (*Lunacy*, 2005), he combined it not only with "The Premature Burial" but also with elements of de Sade's writing, even including de Sade himself (played by Jan Tríska) as one of the main characters. The film begins with two demonic, thuggish warders (in fact lunatics) attempting to strait-jacket a young man called Jean Berlot (Pavel Liska). As we have already seen with regard to the use of "The Premature Burial" in this film, Svankmejer sees the whole of creation as violent and irrational—a truly living nightmare from which the only escape is death—and death, of course, brings its own irrational horrors. De Sade demonstrates that everything that is meant to give life meaning is a fraud. Religion in particular is revealed as just another insane delusion: During a Black Mass, the marquis hammers nails into a statue of Christ crucified, while inmates cut up a chocolate cake in the form of a crucifix. They eat this messily, but ceremoniously (Svankmejer regards the process of eating as grotesquely absurd as sex), while two robed women crawl under the table and fellatio is implied—an interpretation that is backed up by a closeup of another lunatic erotically sucking her thumb. Blood that has been spat into is then painted onto the women's bare buttocks, again in the form of a crucifix, and fragments of holy wafer are sprinkled over her. The women are then raped. The message can only be that sex and violence are our only true reality. All the rest is—even if sublimated into art—no more than an illusion.

The regime of the lunatic asylum in Poe's tale follows what Dr. Maillard calls his "soothing system," which encourages inmates to live out their fantasies and obsessions in freedom. Unfortunately, this has permitted the state of affairs that makes their anarchistic rebellion possible; but the only alternative is control and punishment. Enlarged into the wider world, we see these two extremes as the poles between which all societies fluctuate, never finding a utopian balance. The film's young hero, Jean Berlot, is persuaded to enter a lunatic asylum because he thinks he can rescue a young woman who reveals to him that the director and staff have been imprisoned in the cellars. In the context of the rest of his film, Svankmejer's interpretation of this is made much more explicit than it is in Poe. In Svankmejer's view, the whole world is an asylum run by madmen, with death—the ultimate madman—waiting to embrace us.

Svankmejer is more serious than Poe, jettisoning Poe's grotesque comedy in favor of outraged irony, whereas Poe's lunatics are frighteningly comic creatures: One thinks he is a donkey and eats nothing but thistles; another fancies himself as a teapot—"A Britannia-ware teapot, and was careful to polish himself every morning with buckskin and whiting."[3]

There is a man who thinks he is a Cordova cheese "and went about, with a knife in his hand, soliciting his friends to try a small slice from the middle of his leg."[4] Someone else thinks himself a frog, another a pumpkin who wanted to be made into pies. There's also a man who thinks he has two heads (one of Cicero another of Demosthenes) and a woman who imagines herself to be a chicken-cock. The implication is the same as Svankmejer's, however.

Another element marks Poe's tale out as a work of the Romantic imagination, and suggests that the madmen are better off than the sane. Though very few nineteenth-century creative geniuses were actually clinically insane (Robert Schumann [1810–1856] was one of the exceptions), Romanticism as a whole looked favorably on irrationality. This Romantic view of the irrational mind offered the promise of unveiling mysteries beyond the prosaic world of an increasingly industrial and scientifically ordered society. Like the peasantry, who were supposedly closer to the Earth's natural rhythms and thus closer to a pantheistic conception of God, so the lunatic was able to avoid the "shades of the prison house" cast by the empirical reason and enter into the instinctive, uncontrolled "intimations of immortality" experienced by the child. Insanity, alas, is never so idyllic, but Romanticism exploited it—as it exploited the metaphor of death—as a shorthand for imaginative freedom. As with the addiction to opium (Coleridge) and the use of alcohol (Schumann advocated "getting high" as an aid to inspiration), posing as insane appealed to later writers, such as Strindberg (1849–1912), as a way of accessing the unconscious. Strindberg's *Inferno* (1889) and *Occult Diary* (1896–1908) not only attempt to record a period of mental illness but also a sense of numinous insight into other states of consciousness in ways that anticipated Aldous Huxley's experiments with mescaline in the 1950s and the inspiration he subsequently gave to a generation of flower-powered hippies in the 1960s. Poe made this equation explicit in the opening of "Eleonora" in which he suggested:

> [T]he question is not yet settled, whether madness is or is not the loftiest intelligence— whether much that is glorious—whether all that is profound—does not spring from disease of thought—from *moods* of the mind exalted at the expense of the general intellect.[5]

Linked, but diametrically opposed to this particular preoccupation with lunacy was the terrible fear of asylums shared by nineteenth-century readers in America and Europe. Often run more like prisons, they feature in nineteenth-century sensation novels as convenient places in which to dispose of unwanted relatives who stand in the way of avaricious villains. Laura Fairley, the heroine of Wilkie Collins' *The Woman in White* (1859), is drugged and incarcerated in one, in the guise of her dead illegitimate sister, Anne Catherick, who herself was previously locked away unlawfully. In J. Sheridan Le Fanu's *The Rose and the Key* (1871), the heroine, Maud Vernon, is presented with a parallel situation to that of the narrator in Poe's story. She thinks she is entering the family mansion of Lady Mardykes but this turns out to be the terrifying asylum of the sinister Dr. Michael Antomarchi, who threatens Maud with his regime of shower-baths and emetics—and all because her various enemies hope that by certifying her and thus preventing her forthcoming marriage, they will gain financially:

> In Maud's ears, the monotonous downpour grew louder and louder, as minute after minute passed. The yells became sobs, and the sobs subsided. And still the rush of water thundered on.
> "Oh! my God! She's drowning!" cried Maud.

"You perceive," said the doctor, "when treatment of this kind is necessary, we don't flinch."
"It is cruel; it is horrible; it is frightful cruelty!" cried Maud.
"Cruelty! My dear Miss Vernon, have you no compassion for an honest keeper whom she would have killed, if she could?"[6]

Only gradually does Maud realize she is an inmate of an asylum rather than a guest at a stately home, the truth being introduced to her very gradually, just as Poe teases out the ambiguity of his narrator's situation. By having the narrator's friend introduce him, we cannot quite believe Maillard is as mad as he eventually seems. Also like Poe, Le Fanu makes sure to include some very disturbing behavior among the inmates, whom Maud at first thinks are "guests" like herself. She is nonetheless treated rather as the supposedly mad (but surely merely only sociopathic and eccentric) King Ludwig II of Bavaria (1845–1886), who was similarly placed under house arrest and controlled by the psychiatrist Dr. Bernhard von Gudden. Maud is given an elegant room of her own. She "accordingly tried the handle of the particular door, through which she thinks she had entered, but it will not turn; then another, with the same result."[7] She then hears "other men's voices, now in low and vehement dialogue, as if a determined struggle were going on; once or twice a low laugh was heard; and then came a yell loud and long."[8] All these techniques of ambivalent suspense derive from Poe's earlier tale.

Later horror films reinforced this image of the Victorian lunatic asylum. Freddie Francis' *The Creeping Flesh* (1973) starred Christopher Lee as the ruthless director of the Hildern Institute for the Criminally Insane, an institution run much more like a prison than a hospital, where electro-therapy is commonplace and the inmates are incarcerated in cells. Lee's Dr. James Hildern is also quite capable of shooting his own patients; but closer in spirit to Poe's story is Hammer's last Frankenstein film *Frankenstein and the Monster from Hell* (dir. Terence Fisher, 1974). In this, Peter Cushing's Frankenstein—surely quite mad by now, though as urbane and seemingly lucid as ever—presides over a lunatic asylum despite being officially one of the inmates. Using blackmail, he has managed to usurp the feeble director, killed off Baron Frankenstein in a fake accident and recreated himself as Dr. Victor.

Bram Stoker, too, was indebted to Poe's influential tale, in those scenes in *Dracula* which take us to Dr. Seward's mental asylum, wherein Mr. Renfield fluctuates between complete craziness and apparent lucidity, all the time under the influence of Count Dracula, who infiltrates his way into the establishment. Renfield, a disciple of Dracula, is consequently closer to the truth but the other characters fail to understand this until some time after his death.

Various films have taken Poe's basic theme of lunatics in charge and improvised variations around it. A Grand Guignol play based on the tale informed the first film adaptation by Maurice Tourneur, *Le Systeme du Docteur Goudron et du Professeur Plume* (1913). But Poe's grotesquerie is replaced here with Sweeney Todd-style bloody horror, the cure for insanity being the cutting away of patients' eyes before slitting their throats. Robert Oswald retained the black comedy, however, when he combined "Dr. Tarr" and "The Black Cat" with Robert Louis Stevenson's *The Suicide Club,* for his German expressionist fantasy *Unheimliche Geschichte* (*Uncanny Tales,* 1932), starring Paul Wegener. This was a remake of an earlier silent version from 1919 with the same title and director and featuring Conrad Veidt in the leading role.

The two most intriguing adaptations, Juan Moctezuma's *Las Mansiones de la Locura*

(*Mansions of Madness,* 1973) and S.F. Brownrigg's *The Forgotten* (aka *Don't Look in the Basement,* 1973), are very different in style from each other. Moctezuma's Mexican film is a surrealistic period fantasy, whereas the Texan Brownrigg plays the story as a low-budget horror soap opera in modern dress. In *The Forgotten,* the insane asylum director, ironically called Dr. Masters, is played by a woman (Anne MacAdams), and her ambiguous role is skillfully handled by both actor and director. After one of the inmates fells the real director, Dr. Stevens, with an axe, "Dr. Masters" appears in a white coat, seems shocked by what has happened and takes control of the situation. She is completely convincing. A nurse who has just resigned, being unable to cope with the freedom granted to the lunatics, is then killed by another female patient who is distraught at having her baby doll taken away from her. This conveniently leaves Dr. Masters in sole control without giving the game away to the audience.

But then another character arrives, Nurse Beale, a genuine psychiatric nurse previously hired by Dr. Stevens, and various sinister things begin occur: The phone is cut, and an old lady called Mrs. Cunningham urges Nurse Beale to leave. Then, a hapless telephone repairman is attacked by the institution's resident nymphomaniac who subsequently threatens Nurse Beale with a large carving knife. Ultimately everyone dies with the exception of Nurse Beale, who witnesses the brutal murder of Dr. Masters by all the patients she has dominated.

Moctezuma's film has a great deal more visual flair and incorporates other references. He quotes the famous dictum of Aleister Crowley (1875–1947), "Do as thou wilt shall be the whole of the law," as the basis of the asylum director's "system." And during a hallucinatory dream sequence, we hear lines from Coleridge's *The Rime of the Ancient Mariner.* The asylum itself resembles a derelict factory—a very serviceable architectural metaphor for the shattered minds it accommodates, following in the tradition of Poe's poem "The Haunted Palace." We are also treated to a Javanese-style exotic dance which culminates in an attempt to sacrifice the man who visits the asylum.

In the dungeons, Moctezuma indulges in the image of a crucified Dante, along with Dante's famous motto for the Gate of Hell "Abandon all hope ye who enter here." There is a naked woman covered in grapes, and the insane director presides over his mad entourage like Mr. Kurz in Joseph Conrad's *Heart of Darkness* (1899)—particularly in the climax in which the real asylum director is paraded in humiliating captivity before his distraught daughter. The film also features striking dream-like imagery, such as the celebrated image of a naked woman on horseback riding through a wrecked hall of museum display cases. This bears no relationship to the plot but immeasurably aids the film's mood of troubling irrationality.

"The System of Doctor Tarr and Professor Fether" has also inspired musical adaptations, notably by the Italian composer Vieri Tosotti in his opera *Il sistema della dolcezzi* (1948). This begins with an overture written in the lively *giocoso* style of *opera buffa,* which is highly appropriate for the black comedy of Poe's original. It culminates with a cacophonous finale, representing the insane banquet at the end of the tale:

> And then, again, the frog-man croaked away as if the salvation of his soul depended upon every note that he uttered. And, in the midst of all this, the continuous braying of a donkey arose over all. As for my old friend, Madame Joyeuse, I really could have wept for the poor lady, she appeared so terribly perplexed. All she did, however, was to stand up in a corner, by the fireplace, and sing out incessantly at the top of her voice, "Cock-a-doodle-do-dooooooh!"[9]

The Alan Parsons Project Poe album also features a song very loosely based on the story. Taking the Romantic approach to an extreme, the lyrics advocate the Crowleyian hedonism incorporated into Moctezuma's *Las Mansions de la Locura.* Eat, drink and be merry seems to be the message here, which is presumably meant ironically.

A Tale of the Ragged Mountains

On every hand was a wilderness of balconies, of verandas, of minarets, of shrines, and fantastically carved oriels. Bazaars abounded; and there were displayed rich wares in infinite variety and profusion—silks, muslins, the most dazzling cutlery, the most magnificent jewels and gems. Besides these things, were seen, on all sides, banners and palanquins, litters with stately dames close-veiled, elephants gorgeously caparisoned, idols grotesquely hewn, drums, banners, and gongs, spears, silver and gilded maces.[1]

Dreams and reality become confused in this 1844 tale of mesmeric telepathy and implied occult metempsychosis. Augustus Bedloe, a morphine addict who starts each morning with a large dose of the drug, followed by a cup of strong coffee, is in the process of being treated by Dr. Templeton, who uses hypnosis as part of the cure. A psychic rapport is established between them. While walking through a remote part of the Ragged Mountains near Charlottesville, Virginia, Bedloe experiences a vivid hallucination of an insurrection in the Indian city of Benares. The explanation of this phenomenon is later given by Templeton: Bedloe reminds Templeton of a friend of his, a Mr. Oldeb, who was killed in the Indian uprising of 1780. It was for this reason that he decided to take him on as his patient.

When Bedloe was out on his walk, Templeton was in his study writing an account of the uprising as a memorial for his dead friend. By means of the telepathic rapport between them, Templeton's thoughts were transmitted to Bedloe, and consequently changed his perception of reality. Even more curiously, when Bedloe dies at the end of the story, a newspaper obituary prints his name as "Bedlo" without the final "e." As the narrator points out, "[T]ruth is stranger than any fiction—for Bedlo, without the *e,* what is it but Oldeb conversed!"[2] It would therefore appear that in death, Bedloe actually becomes Oldeb. Not merely has the story demonstrated the existence of telepathy, but also suggests the possibility of metempsychosis (a subject we have also seen Poe also address in "Metzengerstein").

Hypnosis has been explored in many films. In *The Tomb of Ligeia,* Roger Corman very effectively interpolates the subject into the middle of his adaptation when Vernon Fell mesmerizes Lady Rowena, regressing her to her childhood and unwittingly releasing the spirit of Ligeia. One film in particular seems to me to be an equivalent of what happens in "A Tale of the Ragged Mountains": Michael Reeves' *The Sorcerers* (1967), in which Boris Karloff plays an elderly hypnotist who invents a machine that not only hypnotizes whoever he subjects to it, but also enables him to experience exactly what the subject is doing and feeling. In fact, the influence is a two-way process—for the controllers of the subject can implant suggestions, even issue commands. "From now on," Karloff's Professor

Montserrat explains to willing victim Mike Roscoe (Ian Ogilvy), "we are going to control your mind, and from time to time we will put thoughts into your head, and you will obey those thoughts." Eventually, Montserrat foresees the dangers of this new development in his researches and decides to go no further, but his wife Estelle (Catherine Lacey), having experienced the thrill of what it is like to inhabit a young, virile body again, grows addicted to the process, reveling in the acts of speed, sex, violence and ultimately murder that she makes Mike perform. Her emotions, as he punches and kicks his adversaries, are positively orgasmic. As she puts it, she can enjoy "ecstasy with no consequence." Unfortunately, there *are* consequences, for both Montserrat and Estelle are destroyed when Mike's car crashes and bursts into flames—an aspect of the two-way telepathic process they had not anticipated.

Though telling a superficially different story, *The Sorcerers* clearly follows a similar agenda to Poe's story. Its psychedelic imagery (so typical of its 1960s origin) also has parallels with Poe's incorporation of mind-altering drugs in his tale. The flashing, multicolored lights of Montserrat's hypnosis machine convincingly suggest a bad LSD trip, and Bedloe has all the signs of being a drug addict, which he shares with so many of Poe's other characters: "His eyes were abnormally large, and round like those of a cat. The pupils too, upon any accession or diminution of light, underwent contraction or dilation, just such as is observed in the feline tribe. In moments of excitement the orbs grew bright to a degree

Grey Eminences: Boris Karloff and Catherine Lacey in *The Sorcerers* (dir. Michael Reeves, 1967).

almost inconceivable; seeming to emit luminous rays, not of a reflected but of an intrinsic lustre, as does a candle or the sun; yet their ordinary condition was so totally vapid, filmy, and dull, as to convey the idea of the eyes of a long-interred corpse."[3]

The vision Bedloe has of Benares, coming apparently from nowhere, also has the effect of a drug-induced hallucination in its surreal and frighteningly irrational verisimilitude:

> There came a wild rattling or jingling sound, as if a bunch of large keys, and upon the instant a dusky-visaged and half-naked man rushed past me with a shriek. He came so close to my person that I felt his hot breath upon my face. He bore in one hand an instrument composed of an assemblage of steel rings, and shook them vigorously as he ran. Scarcely had he disappeared in the mist, before, panting after him, with open mouth and glaring eyes, there darted a huge beast. I could not be mistaken in its character. It was a hyena.[4]

One is reminded here of a Salvador Dalí painting, or the frightening dream sequence in Corman's *The Masque of the Red Death,* or the disturbing appearance of an Australian witch doctor in Jerzy Skolimowsky's *The Shout* (1978). Poe's anticipation of surrealism, the drug culture and the occult revival of the 1960s and '70s—not to mention his distinctly cinematic imagery—is particularly notable in this curious tale.

The Tell-Tale Heart

I then took up three planks from the flooring of the chamber, and deposited all between the scantlings. I then replaced the boards so cleverly, so cunningly, that no human eye—nor even his—could have detected any thing wrong. There was nothing to wash out—no stain of any kind—no blood-spot whatever. I had been too wary for that. A tub had caught all—ha! ha![1]

Poe's famous 1843 monologue about a murderer who kills an old man because he cannot abide his eye, is tailor-made for dramatic recital, written, as it is, in the first person. Vincent Price, exploiting his long association with Poe, fully exploited its dramatic potential in *An Evening of Edgar Allan Poe* (dir. Kenneth Johnson, 1970) in which, before a live audience, he performs four tales, of which "The Tell-Tale Heart" is the first. (The other three are "The Sphinx," "The Cask of Amontillado" and "The Pit and the Pendulum.") Very different in style but no less gripping is Steven Berkoff's very physical, non-illusionistic recital from 1991, in which he not only provides his own vocal sound effects but also a range of brilliant mimes, such as the representation of walking up and down a spiral staircase, and sawing the body of his victim into pieces. He even includes elements of comedy by mouthing (but not vocalizing) "Fuck off!" when the police knock at the door. Indeed, the whole performance is characterized by Berkoff's immediately recognizable brand of black humor.

One of the first film adaptations was by D.W. Griffith in 1914, prior to making his most famous film, *Birth of a Nation* (1915): *The Avenging Conscience* blends "The Tell-Tale Heart" with Poe's poem "Annabel Lee" and even a reference to "The Bells." An element of biography also forms part of the mixture, for the protagonist (played compellingly by Henry B. Walthall) is an orphan, just like Poe himself. He is brought up by his odd uncle, and the relationship becomes difficult, perhaps reflecting Poe's troubled relationship with his own foster father John Allan. The uncle (played by the marvelously named Spottiswoode Aitken) wears an eye-patch, and is indeed half-blind to the heartache he causes his nephew when forbidding him to see the girl (Blanche Sweet) he thinks of as his very own "Annabel Lee." In the poem, Annabel's "high-born kinsmen came / And bore her away from me," but in the film, it is the uncle who is the villain. Like John Allan, he accuses his nephew of ingratitude, and the love affair is terminated.

Uncle and nephew work together in the same room, but the nephew manages to find an opportunity to read "The Tell-Tale Heart," the opening sentences of which Griffith obligingly puts up on screen:

> TRUE!—nervous—very, very dreadfully nervous I had been and am; but why will you say that I am mad? The disease had sharpened my senses—not destroyed—not dulled them. Above all was the sense of hearing acute. I heard all things in the heaven and in the earth. I heard many things in hell. How, then, am I mad? Hearken! and observe how healthily—how calmly I can tell you the whole story.

However, Griffith completely changes Poe's meaning, first by stripping the nephew of any madness implied by the narrator of the tale, and second by providing him with a motive for his crime. As we have seen in the case of "The Black Cat," Poe, fascinated by what he called "The Imp of the Perverse," was concerned to demonstrate that crime is sometimes committed purely for its own sake—that it is part of that "motiveless malignancy" which Coleridge identified in Shakespeare's Iago.[2] In contrast, the nephew's motive for murder is that the uncle stands in the way of sexual fulfillment. Throughout the ensuing love scenes, Griffith intercuts extracts from "Annabel Lee" to emphasize the influence Poe is obviously having on the young man; but the uncle accuses the girl of being no better than a common whore and clenches his fists tyrannically.

Walking home from his last tryst, the young man observes a spider devouring a fly and observes, "Nature is one long system of murder." What applies to the spider and fly is soon applied to the nephew and uncle, whom the former eventually strangles to death. Like the orang-outang in "The Murders in the Rue Morgue," the nephew then thrusts the corpse up the fireplace before bricking it up in the manner of the respective narrators of "The Cask of Amontillado" and "The Black Cat."

Before long, the uncle's ghost begins to haunt the troubled conscience of his murderer, who is further harassed by a blackmailing Italian who happened to be passing when the murder took place. The nephew takes himself off to a sanatorium and returns only to suffer from bitter remorse at what he has done. Christ on the cross appears to him in a vision along with a tablet of the sixth commandment: "Thou shalt not kill."

A policeman now questions the murderer and forces a confession out of him by tapping the end of his pencil against a table. He then taps his foot, as the ticking clock and a screech owl further suggest the beating of the old man's heart, which we read about in the original story. ("It was *a low, dull, quick sound—much such a sound as a watch makes when enveloped in cotton.*"[3]) As Carlos Clarens points out, "rarely has the silent screen so expertly evoked sound as in the confession scene."[4] The nephew's conscience now imagines avenging skeletons and various monsters as his uncle's ghost appears in creepy double-exposure for the final time. Griffith now draws on lines from "The Bells": "They are neither man nor woman; They are neither brute nor human; They are ghouls."

A shootout between murderer and lynch mob brings the film to its climax when the desperate nephew decides to hang himself. Living up to Annabel Lee's dwelling place in a "kingdom by the sea," the nephew's lover then hurls herself off the cliffs into the ocean. But the final scenes reveal the whole thing to have been a dream, caused by the young man's perusal of Poe. Nephew and uncle are reunited, and a final arcadian idyll illustrates lines from the young man's successfully published (and presumably Poe-inspired) book: "In your voice I hear Pan playing in the woods and all the world gives heed." Griffith's imagery here is not far short of absurdity, featuring, as it does, Pan himself, playing his pipes, a host of toddlers dressed as fairy-folk and assorted furry animals. In Max Reinhardt 1935 film *A Midsummer Night's Dream*, such imagery would be compelling, but here it is clumsily handled and distinctly out of place.

Jules Dassin's short 1941 adaptation for MGM stars Joseph Schildkraut as the murderer. An excellent music score by Sol Kaplan emphasizes the murderer's obsessive nature with numerous ostinati. (Towards the end, a piano very effectively suggests the eerie heartbeat which only the murderer can hear.) Lending Biblical weight to Poe's moral, it opens with a quotation from Romans, chapter 2, verse 15: "The law is written in their hearts, their conscience also bearing witness." However, the screenplay unwisely tampers with the story by giving the murderer a reasonable motive for killing the old man, who in this version is his brutal, physically violent employer. He calls his employee a weakling, who has been dependent upon him since he was fourteen years old, and ominously (for him) insists, "You'll be dependent upon me as long as I live," which, as it turns out, is not for very much longer. Though such an alteration made the story more acceptable to public opinion at the time, it does not serve Poe well, again stripping away the motiveless malignancy. However, by turning the old man into an oppressive, paternal figure, Dassin again suggests Poe's unsympathetic foster father; and this is a view upheld by the much later adaptation in Ric White's *Nightmares from the Mind of Poe*.

White's version doesn't impose Dassin's interpretation overtly onto the character of the old man: It is his filmy blue eye, rather than his behavior, that is the cause of the outrage. But the linking segment which introduces that section of the film does clearly point out a connection with John Allan and suggests that the story was a sublimation of Poe's possible patricidal impulses.

Ernest Morris' 1961 adaptation for the Danziger brothers brought together Laurence Payne and Adrienne Corri. Set in Paris, appropriately in the Rue Morgue, it also echoes certain details from Dessin's film by having Payne, as the murderer (here called Edgar Poe), tormented by the dripping of a faucet and the ticking of a clock. Both of these he silences, but he cannot stop hearing the heartbeat of his conscience. His conscience also manifests itself in the weird movement of inanimate objects. Most disturbing of all, the carpet under his grand piano begins to undulate as though someone is breathing beneath it. The screenplay for this intriguing low-budget British thriller was in part written by Brian Clemens, the creator of the British television series *The Avengers*. He blends Poe's basic theme with a love triangle drama echoing Ibsen's *Hedda Gabler* (1891), in which Payne's Poe resembles the headstrong Hedda's feeble husband Jørgen Tesman. Tesman is a dry-as-dust academic, Edgar, a lonely librarian. Early on we learn all we need to know about his character: He rejects a prostitute in a bar, returns home where he brushes his hand lovingly over a large portrait of his mother on the stairs, and then secretively produces a portfolio of porn. All this, needless to say, has absolutely nothing to do with Poe's story, interesting though this particular adaptation is. When Corri's character moves in nearby, Edgar falls in love with her. Like Norman Bates in Hitchcock's *Psycho* (1960), he voyeuristically watches her undress. (Her room is opposite his own, and she seems to have foresworn drapes.) He finds out that she works for a florist.

"What do you have in mind?" she asks, thinking he has come for flowers. Of course, Edgar can't tell her. Like Hedda, Edgar's young woman isn't really interested in him, but she takes pity on him and consequently finds herself trapped by his clumsily clinging enthusiasm for her. When Edgar introduces her to his handsome friend Carl (Dermot Walsh), the inevitable happens. Unfortunately for them, Edgar observes their assignation and murders his competition. This is performed quite brutally with a fire iron, and Edgar promptly sets about returning to his namesake's original text by hiding the body under the floorboards.

"The Tell-Tale Heart" also inspired the world's first X-rated animated film: James Mason narrated a 1953 UPA cartoon directed by Ted Parmalee. Here, the old man's eye turns into the moon and the white, glazed surface of a jug, which promptly smashes on the floor. Parmalee also dares to maintain an entirely black screen for over thirty seconds, effectively relying entirely on Mason's narration. The yellow and black checkered bedspread with which the murderer smothers his victim is exploited as a visual metaphor for his descent into madness, the checkerboard being distorted in a manner that anticipated the style of pop artist Bridget Riley. Parmalee also puts the beginning of the story at the end, when there is no doubt that the narrator has ended up in a lunatic asylum.

Loosely based on Poe was *Tell-Tale* (dir. Michael Cuesta, 2009), which is perhaps more indebted to *The Hands of Orlac* (dir. Robert Wiene, 1924) than "The Tell-Tale Heart." In *Orlac,* a pianist has a murderer's hands grafted onto his body after losing his own hands in a terrible accident. In *Tell-Tale,* Josh Lucas, as Terry Bernard, has the heart of the murder victim transplanted to replace his own failing organ. After experiencing flashbacks of his donor's final moments, he eventually locates the murderer and exacts revenge, in a manner reminiscent of Hammer's *Frankenstein Created Woman* (dir. Terence Fisher, 1967). A transplanted brain exacts revenge in this one.

Poe's story also has much in common with Dostoyevsky's novel *Crime and Punishment* (1866). There are major differences, however: Raskolnikoff, the anti-hero of *Crime and Punishment,* is not mad. He also has a motive for murdering the old woman, Alyona Ivanovna: He wants her money. As we have seen, Poe, with his interest in irrationality and "the imp of the perverse" was always keen to point out that human actions are often inexplicable according to the everyday expediency of "logic." ("Object there was none. Passion there was none. I loved the old man. He had never wronged me."[5]) Having said that, the opening of chapter seven in the first book of Dostoyevsky's novel echoes the way in which the narrator of "The Tell-Tale Heart" enters the old man's room at night, opening the door "little by little" until he sees the hideous eye "wide, wide open."[6] Raskolnikoff's entrance into the old woman's room is certainly comparable: "The door, as before, was opened a little, and again the two eyes, with mistrustful glance, peeped out of the dark."[7] Though Raskolnikoff commits his crime with an axe, he does not chop up the body and conceal it; but like Poe's narrator, he soon wishes to unburden himself of his guilt. Zametoff, a police official, encounters Raskolnikoff reading a newspaper, and Raskolnikoff is immediately on the defensive:

"You ask me what I am reading, what I am looking for; then I am looking through a number of papers. Suspicious, isn't it? Well, I will explain to you, or rather confess—no, not that exactly. I will give testimony, and you shall take it down—that's it. So then, I swear that I was reading and came here on purpose"—Raskolnikoff blinked his eyes and paused—"to read an account of the murder of the old woman." He finished almost in a whisper, eagerly watching Zametoff's face. The latter returned his glances without flinching. And it appeared to Zametoff that a full minute seemed to pass as they kept fixedly staring at each other in this manner.

"Oh, so that's what you have been reading?" Zametoff at last cried impatiently. "What is there in that?"

"She is the same woman," continued Raskolnikoff, still in a whisper, and taking no notice of Zametoff's remark, "the very same woman you were talking about when I swooned in your office. You recollect—you surely recollect."

"Recollect what?" said Zametoff, almost alarmed.

The serious expression on Raskolnikoff's face altered in an instant, and he again commenced his nervous laugh, and laughed as if he were quite unable to contain himself. There had recurred to his mind, with fearful clearness, the moment when he stood at the door with the hatchet in his hand. There he was, holding the bolt, and they were tugging and thumping away at the door."[8]

Such an example of guilt causing the criminal to protest too much was fully understood by Poe, whose madman, like Raskolnikoff, destroys his very real chance of getting away with the perfect crime. When the police call in "The Tell-Tale Heart," the madman bids them to search the house *well*:

I led them at length to *his* chamber. I showed them his treasures, secure, undisturbed. In the enthusiasm of my confidence, I brought chairs into the room, and desired them *here* to rest from their fatigues, while I myself, in the wild audacity of my perfect triumph, placed my own seat upon the very spot beneath which reposed the corpse of the victim.[9]

Similarly, in "The Black Cat" the narrator actually calls the police back, after they are satisfied that no crime has been committed:

"I delight to have allayed your suspicions. I wish you all health and a little more courtesy. By the bye, gentlemen, this—this is a very well-constructed house," (in the rapid desire to say something easily, I scarcely knew what I uttered at all),—"I may say an *excellently* well-constructed house. These walls—are you going gentleman?—these walls are solidly put together"; and here, through the mere frenzy of bravado, I rapped heavily with a cane which I held in my hand, upon that very portion of the brickwork behind which stood the corpse of the wife of my bosom.[10]

We could therefore include the various film and television adaptations of *Crime and Punishment* as further lateral responses to "The Tell-Tale Heart." Robert Wiene's *Raskolnikow* (1923) exploited to great effect the expressionist sets of the architect Andrei Andriev to exteriorize the nightmare going on inside the student's mind by means of distorted staircases, peopled with ghosts. As Lotte H. Eisner explains, the sets and characters "act upon each other through a sort of reciprocal hallucination."[11] Peter Lorre's Raskolnikoff in Josef von Sternberg's 1935 film of that name has all of the arrogance of Poe's madman, who boasts, "You should have seen how wisely I proceeded—with what caution—with what foresight—with what dissimulation I went to work!"[12] Dostoyevsky's Raskolnikoff similarly compares himself to Napoleon, but is far more tormented by his conscience than the rather more controlled Lorre. Neither should one forget John Hurt's outstanding performance as a highly strung Raskolnikoff in a 1979 BBC television adaptation by Jack Pulman which combines arrogance with anxiety in equal measure, in a manner which would certainly not have been out of place in a version of Poe's tale.

Musical responses to "The Tell-Tale Heart" range from Alan Parsons' *Tales of Mystery and Imagination* (the old man's heartbeat giving an excellent opportunity for musical realization in a track that sounds rather like an Alice Cooper number), to a short operatic adaptation by Stewart Copeland, ex-drummer of The Police, from 2011, in which the narrated text is delivered in *Sprechstimme* with choral interjections from fellow asylum inmates.

But perhaps the simplest and most eloquent visual response to the story is the 1883 charcoal drawing by Odilon Redon, which reduces "The Tell-Tale Heart" to its visual essence: a single eye peering through the aperture between the door and the doorjamb. The eye represents both that of the murderer and the loathed eye of the victim, and by this means, Redon was able to suggest in purely visual terms the murderer's ultimate confusion of his own heartbeat with that of the dead man he has buried.

Redon's many disembodied eyes—some floating like balloons, others gazing aspirationally up at the heavens—are all symbols of the self and its quest for self-knowledge. Here, Redon uses a single eye to represent both the murderer's conscience (the eye that looks inwards) and the organ that allows him to look out upon the world. The killer is compelled by his irrational compulsion. Like sexual excitement, his obsession with the old man's eye is utterly beyond his own control. The impulse to murder is as unstoppable as an orgasm. Indeed, Poe describes the preliminaries the murderer makes before actually doing the deed as an almost pornographically detailed foreplay:

> I turned the latch of his door and opened it—oh, so gently! And then, when I had made an opening sufficient for my head, I put in a dark lantern, all closed, closed, so that no light shone out, and then I thrust in my head. Oh, you would have laughed to see how cunningly I thrust it in! I moved it slowly—very, very slowly, so that I might not disturb the old man's sleep. It took me an hour to place my whole head within the opening so far that I could see him as he lay upon his bed.[13]

But the narrator also absolves himself by confessing his crime. The effect of the dénouement is ultimately cathartic, like the breaking of a storm after days of oppressive heat, and the final outburst: "dissemble no more! I admit the deed!—tear up the planks!—here, here—it is the beating of his hideous heart"[14] is, after the immense crescendo of what precedes it, a kind of literary ejaculation. The end of Dassin's 1941 film emphasizes this aspect, when Schildkraut is virtually transfigured by the rapture of his confession.

"Thou Art the Man"

Toward the end of the blood-chilling recital, the words of the guilty wretch faltered and grew hollow. When the record was finally exhausted, he arose, staggered backward from the table, and fell—dead.[1]

Poe not only invented the detective story but also invented that particular branch of it that eventually turned into the psychological thriller. "'Thou Art the Man'" (1844) is often regarded as less successful than "The Murders in the Rue Morgue," but such an opinion ignores its novel element. The point here is not "whodunnit" but rather the ingenuity of the plan to expose the murderer. The murdered man's nephew is the prime suspect, but the culprit is, in fact, the victim's friend, the ironically named Charles Goodfellow. When the narrator of the story discovers this, he sets about exposing him. He sends Goodfellow a crate of his favorite wine, under the pretense that it was bequeathed to him by the murdered man. When it is opened at a party thrown by Goodfellow to celebrate his acquisition, the murdered man's body is discovered inside:

> [T]here sprang up into a sitting position, directly facing the host, the bruised, bloody, and nearly putrid corpse of the murdered Mr. Shuttleworthy himself. It gazed for a few moments, fixedly and sorrowfully, with its decaying and lack-lustre eyes, full into the countenance of Mr. Goodfellow: uttered slowly, but clearly and impressively, the words—"Thou are the man!" and then, falling over the side of the chest as if thoroughly satisfied, stretched out its limbs quiveringly upon the table.[2]

The shock forces a public confession from the murderer, and the innocent nephew is exonerated. Finally, the narrator explains how he arranged the exposure: He discovered where the corpse had been abandoned and sets about preparing it for its spectacular reappearance:

> I procured a stiff piece of whalebone, thrust it down the throat of the corpse, and deposited the latter in an old wine box—taking care so to double the body up as to double the whalebone with it. In this manner I had to press forcibly upon the lid to keep it down while I secured it with nails; and I anticipated, of course, that as soon as these latter were removed, the top would fly *off* and the body *up*.[3]

The narrator's skill in ventriloquism accounts for the ghostly voice of the corpse.

The whole point of this story is the ingenuity of the plan to expose the murderer. This approach, along with the rational explanation of its apparently supernatural agency, foreshadowed a host of subsequent psychological thrillers, principally Henri-Georges Clouzot's *Les diaboliques* (1955), which was based on the novel *Celle qui n'était plus* (*She Who Was No More*) by Pierre Boileau and Thomas Narcejac. In this film, the audience knows who the murderers are from the very beginning. We watch them commit the crime, indeed. The fascination of the film lies in the unexpected ways in which they are exposed. True, the plot is more complex than Poe's story, but despite its reversals and twists, it leads up to a dénouement that is very similar to the accusing corpse of "'Thou Art the Man.'"

The frail Christina (Véra Clouzot) murders her tyrannical schoolmaster husband Michel (Paul Meurisse), with the help of Michel's mistress Nicole (Simone Signoret). But the two women then grow increasingly disturbed by the disappearance of Michel's body, which they have submerged in the school swimming pool to give the impression that he has drowned himself. After further events which suggest that he has come back to life, Clouzot brings us to the literally heart-stopping moment (for Christina) when Michel's body rises from an overflowing bath. His white, iris-less eyes stare out with horrific effect, his arms raised accusingly towards her. Christina collapses and dies. In all but actually vocalizing the words, the corpse is saying, "Thou art the woman!" But then, in the famous twist, Michel removes contact lenses from his eyes and Nicole appears. Their plot is exposed: Michel only pretended to die and the whole thing was designed to do away with Christina so that the lovers may inherit her money and go away together. But their plot has been discovered by a police detective, who apprehends them before they can escape. A further double twist at the end of the film suggests that Christina also faked her heart attack.

Clouzot's blend of detective thriller and horror story certainly has more twists and shocks in it than Poe's story, but its lineage is clear. When Hammer Films' Jimmy Sangster went on to script (and in some cases direct) a series of psychological thrillers, beginning with *The Snorkel* (dir. Guy Green, 1958), the influence of *Les diaboliques* was pervasive. This was particularly the case with *Taste of Fear* in which the corpse of the heroine's father is used by his murderers to terrorize her into insanity. In *Nightmare*, Poe's method of exposing the villains of the piece is adapted in a rather more subtle way. Having contrived events to induce a young heiress to commit a murder and thus be incarcerated in a lunatic asylum, her school mistress, housekeeper and chauffeur use the same methods to terrorize the guilty lovers, causing the woman to suspect her accomplice of trying to drive her insane as well. She kills him, and only then is the plot against her exposed.

Though "'Thou Art the Man'" has never been officially adapted for the screen, it undoubtedly was the blueprint of the cinema's many psychological detective thrillers, including those of Hitchcock (a great admirer of Poe). In *Rope* (1948), for example, the murder is over and done with in the film's opening moments. We know exactly who is responsible, and the rest of the film is constructed around the building tension of whether they will get away with their crime or not. The morality of the time ensured that they did not, though Hitchcock's original intention was to let them succeed.

Three Sundays in a Week

Captain Pratt, ... when he had sailed a thousand miles west of this position, was an hour, and when he had sailed twenty-four thousand miles west, was twenty-four hours, or one day, behind the time at London.[1]

This short anecdotal tale inspired a crucial aspect of Jules Verne's much longer novel *Around the World in Eighty Days* (1873). Consequently, its impact on popular culture is far greater than might at first seem apparent. Not only has Verne's novel inspired two feature films (one of them starring David Niven and forty-eight other stars in cameo roles), but also a Spanish television animation series, a British television travelogue featuring ex–Monty Python comedian Michael Palin, several more real-life attempts to follow in Phileas Fogg's footsteps, and even a board game. None of this might have happened without Poe's conceit that it is quite possible to have three Sundays in a week.

Poe structures this story along the lines of the fairy tale trope of an apparently impossible task such as we meet in "Rumpelstilskin," in which a miller's daughter must spin a room full of straw into gold. Whereas the miller's daughter is helped by Rumpelstilskin to achieve this goal, the hero of Poe's tale uses geography. He wants to marry a girl whom his father doesn't approve of. The father triumphantly informs his son that he may get married only *when three Sundays come together in a week*.

This seemingly impossible eventuality is proved to be quite possible, with the help of a naval acquaintance, who explains:

Now, suppose that I sail from this position a thousand miles east. Of course I anticipate the rising of the sun here at London by just one hour. I see the sun rise one hour before you do. Proceeding, in the same direction, yet another thousand miles, I anticipate the rising by two hours—another thousand, and I anticipate it by three hours, and so on, until I go entirely round the globe, and back to this spot, when, having gone no less than twenty-four thousand miles east, I anticipate the rising of the London sun by no less than twenty-four hours; that is to say, I am a day *in advance* of your time.[2]

Similarly, Phileas Fogg is able to win his bet that he will travel around the world in eighty days, even though the members of the Reform Club in London believe he is late. So too did Fogg, until he realized that "without suspecting it, [he] gained one day on his journey, and this merely because he had travelled constantly *eastward*; he would, on the contrary, have lost a day, had he gone the opposite direction, that is, *westward*."

In journeying eastward he had gone towards the sun, and the days therefore diminished for him as many times four minutes as he crossed degrees in this direction. There are three hundred and sixty degrees on the circumference of the earth; and these three hundred and sixty degrees, multiplied by four minutes, gives precisely twenty-four hours—that is, the day unconsciously gained.[3]

Once again, Poe laid the foundation stone not only for a famous novel and its various spin-offs, but also looked forward to the idea of the package tour, and the cliché of the American tourist who visits as many cities as days spent in traveling to them.

The Unparalleled Adventure of One Hans Pfaall

By late accounts from Rotterdam, that city seems to be in a high state of philosophical excitement. Indeed, phenomena have there occurred of a nature so completely unexpected—so entirely novel—so utterly at variance with preconceived opinions—as to leave no doubt on my mind that long ere this all Europe is in an uproar, all physics in a ferment, all reason and astronomy together by the ears.[1]

Here is another balloon hoax, though not as convincing as the earlier one because Poe's ironic tone is present throughout. Even Pfaall's name has an echo of "phallus" in it, like the bawdy humor of a *commedia dell'arte* play. Also, as Harold Beaver perceptively points out, "Invert 'Phaal,' that other variant of his name! What sound do you hear but *'laugh?'*"[2] There are other comedy names too: Superbus von Underduk, Rubadub and even mention of a "Sauerkraut alley." Hans Pfaall's profession also gives the game away. He is a bellows mender, and Poe's tale is similarly full of hot air. He inflates this story of a voyage to the moon with the hydrogen of fantasy. We have already seen the possible connection between the blank page, which confronts all writers, with the whiteness of the snowy wastes at the end of *The Narrative of Arthur Gordon Pym*. Similarly, one might also see "Hans Pfaall" as a satire on the writing profession itself: Pfaall's balloon is in the shape of "a fool's-cap turned upside down," and foolscap is a size of paper, named after its original watermark of a fool's cap. The hot air that inflates this foolscap balloon is Poe's eloquent persiflage.

Pfaall, like Poe himself, is desperate to escape from his creditors—and what better place to be out of their reach than the moon? But to escape from one's creditors is also to escape from reality, to retreat into an ideal world of the imagination—a situation which Poe shared with his longer-lived contemporary, Richard Wagner.

Poe also includes a great deal of obfuscatory technical information, with the aim of trying to convince us that such a voyage might actually have been possible. This mixture of science, hoax and satire annoyed Jules Verne, who, while admiring Poe's genius, felt that his approach would have been more convincing "had he respected a few elementary laws of physics."[3] According to Verne's grandson Jean, "Verne saw what could be done by mixing fantasy and reason."

> Yet in Poe science plays a secondary role: it is merely a pretext, a frame for Poe's own anguish. His stories are personal fantasies: he cultivates the bizarre for its own sake. He is interested in moral deviation; but the mainspring of his inspiration remains his crushing scorn for the idea of progress and American society.
>
> Verne's approach to fantasy is quite the opposite. He is essentially a realist. His essential belief is that men can achieve consciousness and fulfillment by working on their environment, which is both real and hostile, and not by subscribing to the escapist cult of Truth, Beauty and even Progress, which for him are entities that are emanations of reality and not transcendentals.[4]

Having said that, Verne's response to "Hans Pfaall" in *De la terre à la lune* (*From the Earth to the Moon*, 1865) is also a satire, but one which Verne felt had more science behind it. Verne, a committed pacifist, was horrified by the way in which technology was creating ever more destructive weaponry. He accordingly begins his story with an account of an American Gun Club during "the War of the Rebellion":

> One day, however—sad and melancholy day!—peace was signed between the survivors of the war; the thunder of the guns gradually ceased, the mortars were silent, the howitzers were muzzled for an indefinite period, the cannon, with muzzles depressed, were returned into the arsenal, the shots were replied, all bloody reminiscences were effaced....
>
> "This is horrible!" said Tom Hunter one evening, while rapidly carbonizing his wooden legs in the fireplace of the smoking-room; "nothing to do! nothing to look forward to! what a loathsome existence! When again shall the guns arouse us in the morning with their delightful reports?"[5]

Verne therefore suggested a more peaceful use for guns by using them to propel travelers to the moon. In this respect, Verne's phallic imagery of a gigantic space gun might be said to have chosen a means of transportation that was more suitable to Pfaall's name than a fools-cap balloon; but Verne was much more interested in checking the ballistic facts than Poe was. According to Jean Jules-Verne, Verne asked his cousin Henri Garcet to double-check his own calculations.

> The cosmographer and mathematician established the correct trajectories for the shot at the moon; but many problems remained to be solved: excessive initial velocity, overheating due to friction in the atmosphere, and so on.... Verne does not ignore the problems. He admits that they existed but were overcome thanks to (unspecified) scientific ingenuity. As for the rest, his accuracy is remarkable: the parameters followed by his space vessel are correct; the vessel is made of the right kind of metal, aluminum; its height and weight are correct in relation to the proposed trajectories; and there is even a system of air regeneration on board.[6]

Verne makes specific reference to Poe's "Hans Pfaall" in *From the Earth to the Moon*:

> I will only add that a certain Hans Pfaal [*sic*], of Rotterdam, launching himself in a balloon filled with a gas extracted from nitrogen, thirty-seven times lighter than hydrogen, reached the moon after a passage of nineteen hours. This journey, like all previous ones, was purely imaginary; still, it was the work of a popular American author—I mean Edgar Poe![7]

Despite the initial satire of the arms trade, Verne's fantasy, with the emphasis placed on scientific principles, is much more literal and far less anarchic than Poe's, but the connection between the two is there for all to see. Consequently, though no film has ever been made based specifically on "Hans Pfaall," Georges Méliès' *Le voyage dans la lune* (*A Trip to the Moon*, 1902) is a response to Poe at one remove, inspired as it was by both Verne's novel and H.G. Wells' *The First Men in the Moon* (1901). Méliès' vision is, however, closer in spirit to Poe than either Wells or Verne. Science does not interest Méliès, who was motivated by fantasy, and fantasy of a distinctly whimsical kind.

We begin in a Gothic hall with a group of magician-astronomers wearing traditional star-spangled cloaks and conical hats. The only demonstration of ballistics we are given is a simple chalk drawing on a blackboard showing the intended trajectory of the missile. Having agreed upon their course of action, a group of these magicians change into nineteenth-century garb and set off for their adventure. Tiller girls, who might well have been drawn from the Moulin Rouge, accompany the preparations for the voyage, standing around like cheerleaders and exposing a daring amount of leg for the time. They wave a flag and blow trumpets as the fuse is lit, and we are then shown the film's most famous image of the Man in the Moon being hit in the face by the missile, not unlike a clown receiving a custard pie. Later, stars in the formation of Ursus Major appear in the sky, and from their centers emerge the pretty faces of Méliès' chorus line. Two ladies hold aloft another star, not unlike the famous Columbia Pictures logo. Another girl sits on a suspended crescent, and Saturn himself, replete with graybeard, emerges above the rings of his planet.

Wells' novel now takes over, as the intrepid voyagers encounter the Selenite people, but not before the leader of the expedition plants his umbrella in the ground whereupon it promptly turns into an expanding mushroom. The Selenites fight with the humans, who eventually escape and fall back to Earth. The appearance of mushrooms and dream-like lunar landscape is reminiscent of the almost opium-induced imagery of the extra-terrestrial environment imagined by Hans Pfaall on his voyage:

> Fancy revelled in the wild and dreamy regions of the moon. Imagination, feeling herself for once unshackled, roamed at will among the ever-changing wonders of a shadowy and unstable land. Now there were hoary and time-honored forests, and craggy precipicies, and waterfalls tumbling with a loud noise into abysses without bottom. Then I came suddenly into still noonday solitudes, where no wind of heaven ever intruded, and where vast meadows of poppies, and slender, lily-looking flowers spread themselves out a weary distance, all silent and motionless for ever.[8]

So, though ostensibly based on Verne and Wells, both much more "literal" practitioners of science fiction than Poe, Méliès' film reveals the surreal impossibility and whimsical fantasy of "Hans Pfaall" far more.

Director Byron Haskin's 1958 remake of Méliès' film, starring George Sanders and Joseph Cotten, shamelessly incorporated elements of the electronic soundtrack created by Louis and Bebe Barron for *Forbidden Planet* (dir. Fred M. Wilcox) two years before. A Cold War subtext was also in evidence: Cotten's Impey Barbicane invents a powerful explosive of immense force, which eventually becomes the basis for propelling his projectile. After a demonstration, with a ball of fire that seems deliberately to resemble the mushroom cloud of Hiroshima, Sanders, as Barbicane's opponent Stuyvesant Nicholl, exclaims "May God forgive you! What have you wrought?" (words that might even be said to echo Robert Oppenheimer's quotation from the *Bhagavad Gita* after the first detonation of an atom bomb: "I am become Death, the destroyer of worlds"). Poe, in all this, was left a long way behind.

However, Poe's visionary imagination was astonishingly premonitory. Harold Beaver usefully compares some of Poe's descriptions of the lunar surface with reports of it from the Apollo 11 space mission. Where Poe wrote of "volcanic mountains, conical in shape,"[9] the message from Apollo 11 mentions "a very conical inside wall."[10] Poe wrote, "The view of the earth, at this period of my ascension, was beautiful indeed. To the westward, the northward, and the southward, as far as I could see, lay a boundless sheet of apparently unruffled ocean, which every moment gained a deeper and deeper tint of blue."[11] Michael Collins on Apollo 11 said much the same thing:

> It's really a fantastic sight through that sextant. A minute ago, during that automaneuver, the reticle swept across the Mediterranean. You could see all of North Africa absolutely clear, all of Portugal, Spain, southern France, all of Italy absolutely clear. Just a beautiful sight.[12]

But Hans Pfaall got there first. Again, Poe, the technophobe, would have been more than aware of the irony of this, and would no doubt have agreed with his later champion W. H. Auden, whose 1969 poem "Moon Landing" took a similarly dismissive view of the phallic hubris of the Apollo mission, which stripped the moon of all its ancient poetry. Irreverence, Auden suggests, is a much greater crime than superstition.

William Wilson

I fled in vain. My evil destiny pursued me as if in exultation, and proved, indeed, that the exercise of its mysterious dominion had as yet only begun. Scarcely had I set foot in Paris, ere I had fresh evidence of the detestable interest taken by this Wilson in my concerns. Years flew, while I experienced no relief.[1]

Published in 1839, "William Wilson" is Poe's compelling tale of a doppelgänger. From the outset, in an epigram attributed to the seventeenth-century author William Chamberlayne, Poe makes clear that he is going to treat the idea of a ghostly double in psychological terms, along the lines of "The Tell-Tale Heart." The epigraph reads, "What say of it? what say CONSCIENCE grim, / That spectre in my path?" The fact that this quotation does not appear anywhere in Chamberlayne's 1659 *Pharronida* in no way disqualifies its usefulness, for it points the way to a correct interpretation of the tale. Poe often made up his sources—he was a writer of fiction, after all, and probably rather enjoyed hoodwinking his readers by quoting obscure sources which very few people would have bothered to check up on. Wilson's ghostly double is therefore a projection of his conscience, and accordingly, it exposes all his misdemeanors. When Wilson finally defeats his double in a duel, the alter ego explains that "in my death, see by this image, which is thine own, how utterly thou hast murdered thyself."[2]

The doppelgänger had been a staple of earlier Romantic writers. Goethe's Faust had famously referred to the two souls that dwelt within his heart ("Zwei Seelen wohnen, ach! in meiner Brust"). E.T.A. Hoffmann wrote his story "Die Doppelgänger" in 1821, having already explored the theme in his 1815 novel *Die Elixiere des Teufels (The Devil's Elixir)*. This was soon followed by, and probably influenced, James Hogg's *The Private Memoirs and Confessions of a Justified Sinner* (1824), in which the argument that one person can comprise more than one personality. (Hogg's antihero, Robert Wringhim, believing himself to be one of the Chosen Elect, commits various crimes, aided and abetted by a man called Gil-Martin. Like Wilson's double, Gil-Martin has the "chameleon art"[3] of changing his appearance. Sometimes he resembles Wringhim, sometimes not. He may be the Devil himself, or "merely" an exteriorization of the underside of Wringhim's own personality.) Poe was familiar with Hogg's work, and refers to him at some length in *Eureka*, so it seems highly likely that *Confessions of a Justified Sinner* formed a significant part of the literary background to "William Wilson."

Hogg's narrator, like Poe's, meets his diabolical doppelgänger during his time at school, where his schoolmaster is, tellingly, called Mr. Wilson. Hogg's account of their first encounter as boys is a masterly description of psychological recognition—a kind of schizophrenic seizure, which, while objectifying the two aspects of his personality or soul, simultaneously describes their unavoidable connection and unity:

> As I thus wended my way, I beheld a young man of a mysterious appearance coming towards me. I tried to shun him, being bent on my own contemplations; but he cast himself in my way, so that I could not well avoid him; and more than that, I felt a sort of invisible power that drew me towards him, something like the force of an enchantment, which I could not resist. As we approached each other, our eyes met, and I can never describe the strange sensations that thrilled through my whole frame at that impressive moment; a moment fraught with the most tremendous consequences; the beginning of a series of adventures which has puzzled myself, and will puzzle the world when I am no more in it.[4]

Poe's Wilson similarly feels an attraction to his namesake, but "I secretly felt that I feared him, and could not help thinking the equality which he maintained so easily with myself, as proof of his true superiority."[5]

In Heinrich Heine's poem "Die Doppelgänger," which was set to music by Schubert in 1828, the poet observes a version of himself, a ghost of his former self, standing on the spot where he formerly wooed his beloved. Heine calls this vision a "pale comrade," and this description admirably suits William Wilson's nemesis. But perhaps more significant than any of these influences was a short story by Edward Bulwer (later Lord Lytton) called "Monos and Diamonos," which forms part of his *The Student: A Series of Papers*. First appearing in 1830, the story concerns a misanthropic loner, Monos, who leaves England to live in Africa. Eventually deciding to return home, he is involved in a shipwreck. One of Monos' shipboard companions is described as "an idle and curious being, full of the frivolities, and egotisms, and importance of those to whom towns are homes, and talk has become a mental ailment. He was one pervading, irritating, offensive tissue of little and low thoughts. The only meanness he had not was fear. It was impossible to awe, to silence, or to shun him."[6] This sinister individual (Diamonos) does indeed resemble William

Wilson's persistent, critical double, and like him also, he refuses to leave Monos alone. Even after the shipwreck, when Monos finds himself washed up on a desert island, the companion continues to torment him. Monos, who longs for solitude, attempts various solutions to the presence of his persistent tormentor. He even rolls a rock over the entrance of the cave they share, hoping to bury him alive, but Diamonos escapes through a hidden passageway. Monos attempts to bargain with his nemesis and offers him separate territory on the island, but even this plan fails. In desperation he murders him, but even this does not release him from the spirit of this seeming demon. Diamonos (literally "the double of Monos") is revealed as the avenging conscience of the narrator. Finally, the undying Diamonos delivers the moral: "SOLITUDE IS ONLY FOR THE GUILTLESS—EVIL THOUGHTS ARE COMPANIONS FOR A TIME—EVIL DEEDS ARE COMPANIONS THROUGH ETERNITY—THY HATRED MADE ME BREAK UPON THY LONELINESS—THY CRIME DESTROYS LONELINESS FOR EVER."[7]

The idea of making this sinister double the narrator's *conscience* would have resonated with Poe's psychological approach to supernatural fiction, and given Poe's admiration for Bulwer's works, it is more than likely that "Monos and Diamonos" lies behind "William Wilson" more than any other comparable influence. Bulwer's Edwardian biographer T.H.S. Escott was convinced of this, arguing that the story had given Poe "the idea of his *William Wilson*. Poe took the opportunity of repaying this obligation by a noticeable criticism of [Bulwer's play] the *Lady of Lyons* on its appearance in New York."[8] Incidentally, the pseudo–Biblical tone of Bulwer's story, along with its African setting of rocks and wild beasts, also informed Poe's prose poem "Silence," not to mention the title, at least, of his "Conversation of Monos and Una." Bulwer's shipwreck would also no doubt have resonated with Poe's maritime imagination. It would therefore be unfair to claim that Poe alone popularized the doppelgänger theme that was to make such an impact in Robert Louis Stevenson's *Dr. Jekyll and Mr. Hyde* (1886), Anthony Hope's *The Prisoner of Zenda* (1894) and Alexandre Dumas' *The Corsican Brothers* (1844), to name but three variations on this theme; but it is undeniable that Poe was just as influential as Hogg, Bulwer and Hoffmann.

Poe chose England as the setting of only two of his tales. In "Ligeia," the locale changes from an unspecified German town to an abbey in "one of the least frequented portions of fair England."[9] The English setting of "William Wilson" is, conversely, exchanged for continental locations in the second half of the story. Poe's choice of England to start off "William Wilson" here is both autobiographical and symbolic. Biographically speaking, Poe based Wilson's childhood schooling on his own experience as a pupil at Manor House School in Stoke Newington. It was therefore appropriate that the BBC should have chosen to televise the story as a Christmas chiller in 1976 as part of the *Centre Play* series, dramatized by Hugh Whitemore. Norman Eshley played Wilson and Stephen Murray his headmaster. Anthony Daniels, later to become famous as the robot C-3PO in *Star Wars* (dir. George Lucas, 1977), and Robert Tayman, already incarnated as the vampire Count Mitterhaus in Hammer's *Vampire Circus* (dir. Robert Young, 1972), also put in appearances.

Symbolically speaking, England is a useful "double" for America—the old country as opposed to the new; and Poe, foreshadowing Henry James (not to mention Hollywood horror films of the 1930s and '40s), usually regarded Europe and England as decadent or corrupt—the landscape of the unconscious—the empire of the "other." Strange things can happen in America too (think of Poe's mesmeric "A Tale of the Ragged Mountains") but for Poe, England and Europe (often conflated in the American imagination) are the most likely places to encounter the nightmare alter ego of the American dream. Even Wilson's name carries connotations of duplication: Will is Will's son and vice versa.

Wilson's double develops during the course of the story. In the beginning, the double doesn't look like Wilson, but gradually grows to resemble him until the likeness is exact. Wilson disdains his double, who originally has coarse manners; but the double proves to be far more morally upright. As Wilson grows more debauched and starts to cheat at cards, the double makes sure that his misdemeanors are exposed.

It is this particular incident which forms the basis of Louis Malle's adaptation of the story for the film *Tre passi nel deirio*. Alain Delon stars as Wilson, while Brigitte Bardot plays an old flame, now extinguished, who challenges Wilson to a game of cards. The scene is extended far beyond its relevance to Poe, presumably to exploit the pulling power of Bardot, but in the end, Wilson's methods are exposed, and he is humiliated. Confronted by his double, they fight. Having killed his alter ego in the ensuing duel, Wilson climbs to the top of a bell tower and hurls himself from the parapet in a sequence we see right at the beginning of the episode, presented as a premonition. Malle accompanies this disorienting prologue, which is reminiscent of the urban landscapes of Giorgio de Chirico, with a dreamlike cacophony of clanging bells, as Wilson rushes to a church to confess his crime before passing sentence upon himself.

Earlier in the film, in the scenes concerning his school days, Wilson creates a picture with red ink, folding the page over to create a double of the image, which resembles a butterfly. Thus does Malle introduce the idea of duplication and opposition. Then, in revenge for having snitched on him in class, Wilson pushes the double's head into a barrel of rats. But there is no way to silence his conscience forever. Fascinated by his alter ego, Wilson is nonetheless horrified by what the double does in his name. The double is more than just his conscience: He also enacts Wilson's deepest desires. He even kills a girl, putting into practice what Wilson had not the courage to execute himself.

The three film versions of *The Student of Prague* are rather more atmospheric adaptations of Poe's theme. They obviously have a different setting and also conflate Poe with other sources, but they are by far the most compelling cinematic responses to the story. The first was directed in 1913 by Stellan Rye, with Paul Wegener as the student Balduin, the counterpart of Wilson. For this film, screenwriter Hanns Heinz Ewers combined Poe' story with the Faust legend and Alfred de Musset's poem "The December Night" (1835–1837). Ewers quotes from de Musset's poem in his inter-titles:

> Whene'er in sleep I closed my eye,
> Whenever I wished but to die,
> Whichever way my steps did turn,
> There always came across my track
> A mournful being clothed in black,
> As like me as my brother born.

Balduin is tempted to make a bargain with the Devil, who appears as a little old man in a top hat called Scapinelli (John Gottowt). The Devil offers him riches if Balduin will agree to his taking anything from the room for his own use in return. Balduin agrees, and the Devil accordingly summons Balduin's reflection to step out of the mirror. Balduin is now rich but without a soul. Like Wilson, Balduin gambles at cards, but is not quite man enough to play cards with his own soul. He is also challenged to a duel, but is persuaded not to proceed with it by the distraught father of his opponent. This, however, has no effect on Balduin's double, who breaks the promise. Just as Wilson is persecuted by his double across Europe, Balduin also encounters his forlorn yet threatening doppelgänger everywhere he goes. The double even interrupts a love tryst, causing Balduin's aristocratic girlfriend to faint. In the end, Balduin shoots his tormentor and, again like Wilson, finds, too late, that he has only killed himself.

Often regarded as the first horror film, Rye's *The Student of Prague* certainly contains many of the themes and imagery of later Gothic fantasy films: the use of double exposure to create the ghostly, transparent image of the double, the split screen to present two images of Wegener's Balduin simultaneously, the lack of a reflection when Balduin stands before a mirror (which foreshadows many a vampire movie), coach rides through frightening forests, and dramatic flights of steps with their evocation of descending into the hell of the unconscious mind.

A 1926 remake was directed by Henrik Galeen, who added to Rye's catalogue of Gothic effects not only a magical use of shadows (such a typical effect of German films from this period), but also the gloomy Romantic imagery of Caspar David Friedrich, and the more stylized expressionist acting style of Conrad Veidt (as Balduin) and Werner Krauss, whose Scapinelli always carries a sinister, somewhat phallic umbrella.

Anton Walbrook took over as Balduin in the second remake, directed by Arthur Robinson in 1935. Walbrook's astonishingly histrionic approach to the role certainly heightened the melodrama, but visually, this was a decline in comparison to what had gone before. Scapinelli became Dr. Crespi (Theodor Loos), whose names resembles Crespel, a character in Offenbach's *Tales of Hoffmann*. In fact, Crespi rather more resembles Crespel's nemesis, Dr. Miracle, in that opera. Miracle want to possess Crespel's daughter Antonia, and to prevent her falling into the hero Hoffmann's loving arms, he encourages her to sing herself to death. A similar situation occurs in Robinson's *The Student of Prague*. The singer in question doesn't sing herself to death, but Crespi is equally obsessed by her and does indeed claim that she is his creation. Balduin resembles Offenbach's Schlémil in the third act; Schlémil has given the courtesan Guiletta his shadow and later challenges the fictional Hoffmann to a duel. These operatic elements, in turn derived from the German Romantic fantasies of E.T.A. Hoffmann, add complexities to the story. One major change is that Walbrook's Balduin is the only person who can see his double, a detail that emphasizes the concept of the divided self. The double itself is brilliantly performed by Walbrook, who wanders around somnambulistically in a manner that eerily suggests Adolf Hitler's remark "I follow my course with the precision and security of a sleepwalker."[10] Film historian Siegfried Kracauer regarded Rye and Galeen's versions as Balduin's "fight with his other self."

> The film was a big success in Germany; it seemed to make the Germans realize their own duality, which during the stabilized period [of the Weimar republic] was deepened by the latent conflict between republican institutions and paralyzed authoritarian dispositions. Galeen's picture, which was full of E.T.A. Hoffmann reminiscences, sensitized these dispositions and all the impulses and longings connected with them. It may have been the story's inherent material that caused the Nazis to release another *Student of Prague* [in 1935].[11]

Indeed, the melancholy and menace of Robinson's film eloquently reflected the irrational, schizophrenic nature and Romantic yearnings of Nazi Germany at the time it was made.

Epilogue

Before long, my tribute to Poe will be even more incomplete than it is now. New interpretations and adaptations will always appear. These are the ultimate tribute to Poe, who, far ahead of his time, looked forward to the developments of his own century and even further into the twentieth century's most significant cultural inventions of film, television and sound recording. Only gradually are we catching up with him. His synesthetic appeal to all the senses inspired the symbolists; his appeal to the unconscious inspired the surrealists, his sensationalism appealed to the movies, his logic created the new genre of detective fiction. His distrust and dislike of progress and technology inspired stories that foreshadowed science fiction, and his emphasis on style and technique reach to our own twenty-first century obsessions. But Poe used all these elements merely as vehicles to arrive at his true destination. One paragraph from his theoretical writings has always seemed to me to sum up his quest:

> The truth is that the just distinction between the fancy and the imagination (and which is still but a distinction of degree) is involved in the consideration of the mystic. We give this as an idea of our own, altogether. We have no authority for our opinion—but do not the less firmly hold it. The term mystic is here employed in the sense of Augustus William Schlegel, and of most other German critics. It is applied by them to that class of composition in which there lies beneath the transparent upper current of meaning, an under or suggestive one. What we vaguely term the moral of any sentiment is its mystic or secondary expression. It has the vast force of an accompaniment in music. This vivifies the air; that spiritualizes the fanciful conception, and lifts it into the ideal.[1]

This sentiment lies behind all of Poe's writing, and all the best cinematic responses to his writing. Everyday reality interested Poe only so far as it illuminated the workings of the soul. In this, he also prefigured the expressionist aesthetic, as described by one of its most eloquent practitioners, Emil Nolde:

> The Latin takes his forms from the object as it exists in nature. The German creates his form in fantasy, from an inner vision peculiar to himself. The forms of visible nature serve him as symbols only ... and he seeks beauty not in appearance but in something beyond.[2]

And even if all Poe's tales were satires, as G.R. Thompson would have us believe, they were not satires of social comedy, of politics, or of human relationships, but of style and taste and the public's gullibility.

Poe transmuted the lead of his own experience into the symbolic gold of the imagination, and in so doing he opened up a landscape of the psyche: Stoke Newington school, an underpaid life in journalism, the failure of his military career, memories of his dead mother, the death of his child bride, his fear of premature burial and of his own death, his desperate need for love, his resentment of John Allan and his critics—all informed his fantasies. Poe's writing demonstrated more than any other writer that fiction is a form of alchemy.

He introduced comedy into serious subjects, like those of "Mellonta Tauta" and *Eureka*, to forestall his critics with a facetiousness that disguised profound conviction. Intuition mattered more to him than empiricism, but he lived in a time when the empirical fact reigned supreme over the poetic truth. This was why he claimed *Eureka* as a poem not a scientific essay, for all the scientific jargon it employs.

He introduced the serious into the comic, such as his distaste and contempt for progress in "Some Words with a Mummy," disguising his despair at the state of things with laughing gas. Such a contempt for progress was part of his general dissatisfaction with reality as a whole, a dissatisfaction which is shared by all Idealists—as opposed to Utopians. Poe never believed in Utopia, but was entirely motivated by the Idea.

"As for living? our servants will do that for us,"[3] says the hero of Villiers de L'Isle Adam's play *Axël*. Living was, indeed, for the lower orders, intellectually speaking. Dying to that world of "reality" and entering the world of the mind, of the imagination and its mysteries was always Poe's idea. And beyond the imagination? Perhaps, ultimately, there is nothing beyond the imagination. Poe's dying reference to "Reynolds" might even have been an allusion to this belief, which Poe articulated by means of John Cleaves Symmes, Jr.'s Hollow Earth theory. For Poe, the mental quest into the mind revealed nothing but resonant hollowness. Some years before Poe's death, the journalist and explorer Jeremiah Reynolds was giving lectures on Symmes Jr.'s Hollow Earth theory entitled *Address, on the Subject of a Surveying and Exploring Expedition to the Pacific Ocean and South Seas*. Poe attended the lecture and reviewed it. He even included extracts from it in chapter 16 of *The Narrative of Arthur Gordon Pym*. Perhaps Poe's dying reference to "Reynolds" was a cryptic paraphrase of Macbeth's belief that life is "full of sound and fury, signifying nothing." That is only speculation, but there is no doubt that we are still following Poe on his journey into very distant places deep inside the mind.

Notes

Preface

1. Edgar Allan Poe, *The Portable Poe*, selected, edited and with an introduction by Philip van Doren Stern (Harmondsworth: Penguin, 1977), p. 574, note 6 ("The Poetic Principle").
2. Ibid.
3. John Huntley, *British Film Music* (London: Skelton Robinson, 1947), p. 179 ("Film Music" by Ralph Vaughan Williams).

Introduction

1. Edgar Allan Poe, *The Complete Illustrated Stories and Poems of Edgar Allan Poe* (London: Chancellor Press, 1988), p.167 ("Ligeia").
2. Ibid., p. 168.
3. Kenneth Silverman, *Edgar Allan Poe—Mournful and Never-ending Remembrance* (London: Weidenfeld & Nicolson, 1992), p. 113.
4. Poe, *The Complete Illustrated Stories and Poems of Edgar Allan Poe*, p. 179, note 1 ("Ligeia").
5. D. H. Lawrence, *The Portable D. H. Lawrence*, edited by Diana Trilling (Harmondsworth: Penguin, 1980), p. 677 ("Edgar Allan Poe").
6. Poe, *The Portable Poe*, p. 23 (letter to James Russell Lowell, July 2, 1844).
7. Hallam Tennyson, *Alfred Lord Tennyson—A Memoir by His Son*, vol. 2 (London: Macmillan, 1897), pp. 292–293.
8. Edward Lockspeiser, *Debussy—His Life and Mind*, vol. 2 (London: Cassell, 1965), p. 151.
9. David H. Hirsch, *American Literature* 45, no. 3, p. 459.
10. G. R. Thompson, *Poe's Fiction: Romantic Irony in the Gothic Tales* (Madison: University of Wisconsin Press, 1973), p. 6.
11. Silverman, *Edgar A. Poe—Mournful and Never-ending Remembrance*, p. 467, note 3.
12. Ibid., p. 58.
13. James Russell Lowell, *The Poetical Works of James R. Lowell*, vol. 2 (Boston: Ticknor and Fields, 1863), p. 71 ("A Fable for Critics").
14. Poe, *The Portable Poe*, p. 655, note 6 ("How to Write a Blackwood Article").
15. Poe, *The Complete Illustrated Stories and Poems of Edgar Allan Poe*, p. 619, note 1 ("Diddling").
16. Lawrence, *The Portable D. H. Lawrence*, pp. 676–677, note 5. ("Edgar Allan Poe").
17. Ibid., p. 687 ("Edgar Allan Poe").
18. Thomas Mann, *Essays of Three Decades*, translated by H. T. Lowe-Porter (London: Secker & Warburg, 1947), p.320 ("Sufferings and Greatness of Richard Wagner").
19. Ibid., p. 316: "Wagner's art *is* dilettantism, monumentalized and lifted into the sphere of genius by his intelligence and enormous will-power. There is something dilettante in the very idea of a union of the arts: it could never have got beyond the dilettante had they not one and all been ruthlessly subordinated to his vast genius for expression."
20. Poe, *The Portable Poe*, p. xxxviii, note 6 (introduction).
21. Mann, *Essays of Three Decades*, p. 350, note 10 ("Sufferings and Greatness of Richard Wagner"), p. 350.
22. Poe, *The Portable Poe*, p. 547, note 6 ("The Poetic Principle").
23. George Moore, *Avowals* (London: Heinemann, 1924), p. 88: "Is Poe's English equal to Baudelaire's French? [...] Ma fiancée et ma compagne d'étude et enfin l'épouse de mon cœur seems commonplace and trite when compared with: My friend and my betrothed, who became the partner of my studies and finally the wife of my bosom."
24. Jean Cassou, *The Concise Encyclopedia of Symbolism* (London: Omega, 1984), p. 64.
25. Salvador Dalí, *The Secret Life of Salvador Dalí* (New York: Dover, 1993), p. 435 ("Conquest of the Irrational").
26. Charles Baudelaire, *Baudelaire: Selected Writings on Art and Artists*, translated by P. E. Charvet (Cambridge: Cambridge University Press, 1981), p. 190.
27. Charles Baudelaire, *The Mirror of Art—Critical Studies by Charles Baudelaire*, translated and edited by Jonathan Mayne (New York: Doubleday, 1956), p. 123 ("On Schools and Journeymen").
28. Richard Gilman, *Decadence—The Strange Life of an Epithet* (New York: Farrar, Straus and Giroux, 1979), p. 103.

29. Baudelaire, *Baudelaire: Selected Writings on Art and Artists*, p. 198.
30. Lawrence, *The Portable Lawrence*, p. 672 ("Edgar Allan Poe").
31. Robert Greer Cohn, *Toward the Poetry of Mallarmé* (Berkeley: University of California Press, 1965), p. 153.
32. Edmund Wilson, *Axel's Castle—A Study in the Imaginative Literature of 1870–1930* (London: Collier/Macmillan, 1991), p. 17.
33. Henri Dorra, ed., *Symbolist Art Theories—A Critical Anthology* (Berkeley: University of California Press, 1994), p. 141 (Jules Huret, "Interview with Stéphane Mallarmé").
34. Wilson, *Axel's Castle*, p. 13, note 26 (Poe quoted).
35. Edward Lockspeiser, *Debussy: His Life and Mind*, vol. 2 (London: Cassell, 1965), p. 196, note 8 (Jules Huret, "Enquête sur l'Evolution Littéraire," 1892).
36. Poe, *The Complete Illustrated Stories and Poems of Edgar Allan Poe*, p. 23, note 1 ("The Pit and the Pendulum").
37. See Maurice Maeterlinck, *Pelleas and Melisanda, and The Sightless—Two Plays by Maurice Maeterlinck*, translated by Laurence Alma-Tadema (London: Walter Scott, n.d.
38. Lockspeiser, *Debussy: His Life and Mind*, vol. 2, p. 196, note 8.
39. Poe, *The Complete Illustrated Stories and Poems of Edgar Allan Poe*, p. 55, note 1 ("The Fall of the House of Usher").
40. Maeterlinck, *Pelleas and Melisanda, and The Sightless—Two Plays by Maurice Maeterlinck*, p. 58.
41. Ibid.
42. Ibid., p. 164.
43. Villiers de L'Isle Adam, *Axël*, translated by M. Gaddis Rose (London: Soho, 1986), pp. 149–150.
44. Maurice Maeterlinck, *Sister Beatrice and Ardiane & Barbe Bleue*, translated by Bernard Miall (London: George Allen, 1908), pp. 111–112.
45. Poe, *The Complete Illustrated Stories and Poems of Edgar Allan Poe*, p. 173, note 1 ("Ligeia").
46. Ibid., p. 281 ("The Assignation").
47. Ibid., pp. 113–114 ("The Domain of Arnheim").
48. Ibid., p. 761 ("The Masque of the Red Death").
49. Walter de la Mare, *Ghost Stories* (London: Folio Society, 1964), p. 111 ("The Revenant").
50. Arthur Machen, introduction to Frederick Carter's *The Dragon of the Alchemists* (London: Elkin Matthews, 1926).
51. Theresa Whistler, *The Life of Walter de la Mare* (London: Duckbacks, 2003), pp. 75–76.
52. Thornton Wilder, *Theophilus North* (London: Allen Lane, 1974), p. 141.
53. Ibid., p. 142.
54. Ibid., p. 148.
55. Ibid., p. 146.
56. Ibid., p. 160.
57. Andrew Sinclair, *The Facts in the Case of E. A. Poe* (London: Weidenfeld & Nicolson, 1979), p. 121.
58. Ibid., p. 177.
59. Poe, *The Complete Illustrated Stories and Poems of Edgar Allan Poe*, p. 188 ("Berenice").
60. Ibid., p. 303 ("The Oval Portrait").
61. Ibid., p. 22 ("The Pit and the Pendulum").

The Angel of the Odd

1. Poe, *The Complete Illustrated Stories and Poems of Edgar Allan Poe*, p. 612 ("The Angel of the Odd").
2. Ibid., p. 607 ("The Angel of the Odd").
3. Ibid., p. 608 ("The Angel of the Odd").
4. Ibid., p. 613 ("The Angel of the Odd").
5. http://www.musee-orsay.fr/index.php?id=649&L=1&tx_ttnews%5Btt_news%5D=35134&no_cache=1.
6. http://www.telegraph.co.uk/news/obituaries/culture-obituaries/film-obituaries/10354303/Anthony-Hinds.html.
7. Poe, *The Complete Illustrated Stories and Poems of Edgar Allan Poe*, p. 441, note 1 ("The Imp of the Perverse").
8. Ibid.
9. Ibid., p. 237 ("The Black Cat").
10. Geoffrey Gorer, *The Life and Ideas of the Marquis de Sade* (London: Peter Owen, 1962), p. 188.
11. Oscar Wilde, *Complete Works of Oscar Wilde* (London: Collins, 1977), p. 130 ("The Picture of Dorian Gray").
12. Ibid., p. 915 ("De Profundis").
13. Friedrich Nietzsche, *Twilight of the Idols and The Anti-Christ*, translated by R. J. Hollingdale (Harmondsworth: Penguin, 1981), p. 168 ("The Anti-Christ").
14. Sigmund Freud, *Beyond the Pleasure Principle*, edited by C. J. M. Hubback (London: INTL Psycho-Analytical, 1922), chapter 6, paragraph 19.

Annabel Lee

1. Poe, *The Complete Illustrated Stories and Poems of Edgar Allan Poe*, p. 920.
2. Silverman, *Edgar Allan Poe—Mournful and Never-ending Remembrance*, p. 402.
3. Poe, *The Portable Poe, op. cit.*, p. 557 ("The Philosophy of Composition").
4. Poe, *The Complete Illustrated Stories and Poems of Edgar Allan Poe*, p. 921, note 1.
5. George Lowe, *Josef Holbrooke and His Work* (London: Kegan Paul, Trench and Trubner, 1920), pp. 129–129.
6. Ibid., pp. 81–82.

The Assignation

1. Poe, *The Complete Illustrated Stories and Poems of Edgar Allan Poe*, p. 275. ("The Assignation").
2. Ibid., p. 281 ("The Assignation").
3. Anthony Rhodes, *The Poet as Superman—D'Annunzio—A Life* (London: Weidenfeld & Nicolson, 1959), p. 238.
4. Poe, *The Complete Illustrated Stories and Poems of Edgar Allan Poe*, p. 281, note 1 ("The Assignation").
5. F. J. W. Hemmings, *Baudelaire the Damned* (London: Hamish Hamilton, 1982), p. 110.

6. Poe, *The Complete Illustrated Stories and Poems of Edgar Allan Poe*, p. 283, note 1 ("The Assignation").
7. See Richard Benton, "Is Poe's 'The Assignation' a Hoax?" in *Nineteenth-Century Fiction* 28, pp.193–197, and Thompson, *Poe's Fiction*, pp. 125–130.
8. Byron, *The Letters of Lord Byron,* edited by Mathilde Blind (London: Walter Scott, n.d.), pp. 164–165 (Letter to John Murray, November 8, 1819).
9. Poe, *The Complete Illustrated Stories and Poems of Edgar Allan Poe*, p. 285, note 1 ("The Assignation").
10. Ibid.
11. Poe, *The Complete Illustrated Stories and Poems of Edgar Allan Poe*, p. 279, note 1 ("The Assignation").
12. Ibid., p. 276 ("The Assignation").
13. Ibid., p. 279 ("The Assignation").
14. Ibid., p. 282 ("The Assignation").
15. Ibid.
16. Robert Muller, *Supernatural* (London: Collins/Fonata, 1977), p. 175.
17. Thomas Mann, *Stories of Three Decades* (London: Martin Secker & Warburg, 1946), p. 392. ("Death in Venice").
18. Gabrielle D'Annunzio, *The Flame*, translated by Susan Bassnett (London: Quartet, 1991), p. 152.
19. Ann Radcliffe, *The Mysteries of Udolpho* (London: Oxford University Press, 1966), p. 176.
20. Poe, *The Complete Illustrated Stories and Poems of Edgar Allan Poe*, p. 275, note 1 ("The Assignation").

The Balloon Hoax

1. Poe, *The Complete Illustrated Stories and Poems of Edgar Allan Poe*, p. 423 ("The Balloon Hoax").
2. Ibid., p. 415 ("The Balloon Hoax").
3. *The Extra Sun*, April 13, 1844, p. 1.
4. Poe, *The Portable Poe*, pp. 676–677 (D. H. Lawrence's "Edgar Allan Poe").
5. Poe, *The Complete Illustrated Stories and Poems of Edgar Allan Poe*, p. 418, note 1 ("The Balloon Hoax").
6. Ibid., p. 421 ("The Balloon Hoax").
7. Ibid., p. 422 ("The Balloon Hoax").
8. http://www.eapoe.org.
9. Jean Jules-Verne, *Jules Verne—A Biography*, translated by Roger Greaves (London: Macdonald and Jane's, 1976), p. 31.
10. Ibid., p. 61.
11. Ibid., p. 62.
12. Ibid., p. 63.
13. Ibid., p. 62.
14. Ibid., p. 31.

The Bells

1. Poe, *The Complete Illustrated Stories and Poems of Edgar Allan Poe*, p. 923 ("The Bells").
2. Geoffrey Norris, *Rakhmaninoff* (London: Dent, 1978), p. 30.
3. Lowe, *Josef Holbrooke and His Work*, p. 160.
4. Ibid., pp. 155–156.
5. Josef Holbrooke, *The Bells* (Leipzig: Breitkopf & Härtel, 1906).
6. Ibid., (Ernest Newman's notes).

Berenice

1. Poe, *The Complete Illustrated Stories and Poems of Edgar Allan Poe*, p. 186 ("Berenice").
2. Ibid.
3. Ibid.
4. Ibid.
5. Ibid., p. 187.
6. Joris-Karl Huysmans, *À Rebours* (London: Fortune Press, 1946), p. 30.
7. Ibid., p. 173.
8. Oscar Wilde, *Complete Works of Oscar Wilde* (London: Collins, 1977), p. 106 ("The Picture of Dorian Gray").
9. Ibid., p. 110 ("The Picture of Dorian Gray").
10. Ibid., p. 102 ("The Picture of Dorian Gray").
11. Huysmans, *À Rebours*, pp. 66–67, note 3.
12. Ibid., p. 67.
13. Poe, *The Complete Illustrated Stories and Poems of Edgar Allan Poe*, p. 188, note 1 ("Berenice").
14. Ibid., p. 190 ("Berenice").
15. Ibid., p. 191 ("Berenice").

The Black Cat

1. Poe, *The Complete Illustrated Stories and Poems of Edgar Allan Poe*, p. 237 ("The Black Cat").
2. Ibid., pp. 236–237 ("The Black Cat").
3. Ibid., p. 237 ("The Black Cat").
4. Ibid.
5. Andrew Sinclair, *The Facts in the Case of E. A. Poe,* (London: Weidenfeld & Nicolson, 1979), p. 65.
6. Nicolas Remy, *Demonolatry*, translated by E. A. Ashwin (London: Frederick Muller, 1970), p. 108.
7. Algernon Blackwood, *Ancient Sorceries and Other Weird Stories* (London: Penguin, 2002), p. 128 ("Ancient Sorceries").
8. Ibid., p. 97 ("Ancient Sorceries").
9. Ibid., p. 105 ("Ancient Sorceries").
10. Ibid., p. 118 ("Ancient Sorceries").
11. Poe, *The Complete Illustrated Stories and Poems of Edgar Allan Poe*, p. 236 ("The Black Cat").

The Cask of Amontillado

1. Poe, *The Complete Illustrated Stories and Poems of Edgar Allan Poe*, p. 117 ("The Cask of Amontillado").
2. Silverman, *Edgar Allan Poe—Mournful and Never-ending Remembrance*, p. 315.
3. Ibid., p. 316.
4. Poe, *The Complete Illustrated Stories and Poems of Edgar Allan Poe*, p. 115, note 1 ("The Cask of Amontillado").
5. http://www.eapoe.org/works/criticsm/slm36b01.htm (Poe's review of *Rienzi* by Edward Bulwer-Lytton, *Southern Literary Messenger* II, no. 2 (February 1836): 198).
6. Edward Bulwer-Lytton, *The Last Days of Pompeii* (London: Routledge, 1876), pp. 386–388 (book 4, chapter 13).
7. Douglas W. Druick, ed., *Odilon Redon—1840–1916* (London: Royal Academy of Arts, 1995), p. 185

(Fred Leeman, "Odilon Redon—The Image and the Text").
8. Poe, *The Complete Illustrated Stories and Poems of Edgar Allan Poe*, pp. 117–118, note 1 ("The Cask of Amontillado").
9. Ibid., p. 118 ("The Cask of Amontillado").
10. Thomas Wright, *Oscar's Books—A Journey Around the Library of Oscar Wilde* (London: Vintage, 2009), p. 140.
11. Ibid., p. 318.

The City in the Sea

1. Poe, *The Complete Illustrated Stories and Poems of Edgar Allan Poe*, p. 937 ("The City in the Sea").
2. Ibid., p. 921 ("Annabel Lee").
3. Ibid., pp. 939–940 ("Dream-land").
4. Ibid., p. 967 ("To F -").
5. Ibid., p. 958 ("Eulalie").
6. Ibid., p. 944.
7. Poe, *The Portable Poe*, p. 602 "The Lake: To —").
8. Silverman, *Edgar Allan Poe—Mournful and Never-ending Remembrance*, p. 70.
9. Samuel Taylor Coleridge, *Poetical Works*, edited by Ernest Hartley Coleridge (London: Oxford University Press, 1974), p. 297 ("Kubla Khan").
10. Poe, *The Complete Illustrated Stories and Poems of Edgar Allan Poe*, p. 937, note 1 ("The City in the Sea").
11. Ibid.
12. Samuel Taylor Coleridge, *Poetical Works*, edited by Ernest Hartley Coleridge, p. 298, note 9 ("Kubla Khan").
13. Poe, *The Complete Illustrated Stories and Poems of Edgar Allan Poe*, p. 937, note 1 ("The City in the Sea").
14. Ibid., p. 230 ("Silence—A Fable").
15. Ibid., pp. 934–935 ("The City in the Sea").
16. Edmund Spencer, *The Faerie Queene*, book 2, canto 9, http://spenserians.cath.vt.edu/TextRecord.php?textsid=85.
17. Poe, *The Complete Illustrated Stories and Poems of Edgar Allan Poe*, p. 937, note 1 ("The City in the Sea").
18. Barbara Tuchman, *The Proud Tower* (London: Papermac/Macmillan, 1997), p. 463.
19. Lowe, *Josef Holbrooke and His Work*, p. 173.
20. Ibid., pp. 179–180.
21. http://www.metal-archives.com/reviews/The_Ocean/Aeolian/96643/ (review of The Ocean: *Aeolian*).

The Colloquy of Monos and Una and The Conversation of Eiros and Charmion

1. Poe, *The Complete Illustrated Stories and Poems of Edgar Allan Poe*, p. 253 ("The Colloquy of Monos and Una").
2. Silverman, *Edgar Allan Poe—Mournful and Never-ending Remembrance*, p. 171.
3. Ibid.
4. Cosima Wagner, *Diaries*, vol. 1, translated by Geoffrey Skelton (London: Collins, 1978), p. 313 (entry for Dec. 28, 1870).
5. Poe, *The Complete Illustrated Stories and Poems of Edgar Allan Poe*, p. 251, note 1 ("The Colloquy of Monos and Una").
6. Ibid.
7. Ibid.
8. Ibid., p. 252.
9. Ibid., p. 262 ("The Conversation of Eiros and Charmion").
10. Tove Jansson, *Comet in Moominland*, translated by Elizabeth Portch (Harmondsworth: Penguin, 1970), p. 153.
11. Poe, *The Complete Illustrated Stories and Poems of Edgar Allan Poe*, p. 263, note 1 ("The Conversation of Eiros and Charmion").

A Descent into the Maelström

1. Poe, *The Complete Illustrated Stories and Poems of Edgar Allan Poe*, p. 306 ("A Descent into the Maelström").
2. Dawn B. Sova, *Critical Companion to Edgar Allan Poe: A Literary Reference to His Life and Work* (New York: Facts on File, 2007), p. 51.
3. Jill Purce, *The Mystic Spiral* (London: Thames and Hudson, 1975), p. 26.
4. Poe, *The Complete Illustrated Stories and Poems of Edgar Allan Poe*, p. 311, note 1 ("A Descent into the Maelström").
5. Ibid., p. 312 ("A Descent into the Maelström").
6. Richard Ellmann, *Yeats: The Man and the Masks* (London: Penguin, 1987), pp. 231–232.

The Devil in the Belfry

1. Poe, *The Complete Illustrated Stories and Poems of Edgar Allan Poe*, pp. 584–585 ("The Devil in the Belfry").
2. Ibid., p. 582 ("The Devil in the Belfry").
3. Ibid., pp. 582–583.
4. Lockspeiser, *Debussy—His Life and Mind*, vol. 2, pp. 151–152.
5. Ibid., p. 151.
6. Ibid., p. 144.
7. Robert Orledge, *Debussy and the theatre* (Cambridge: Cambridge University Press, 1985), p. 108.
8. Ibid., pp. 108–109.
9. Ibid., p. 107.
10. See Robin Holloway, *Debussy and Wagner* (London: Eulenberg, 1979).
11. Søren Kierkegaard, *The Sickness Unto Death*, http://www.religion-online.org/showchapter.asp?title=2067&C=1865 (chapter three).
12. Ibid. (chapter three).
13. W. Stephen Gilbert, *Fight & Kick & Bite—The Life and Work of Dennis Potter* (London: Hodder & Stoughton, 1995), p. 217.
14. Ibid., p. 221.
15. Johann Wolfgang von Goethe, *Faust Part One*,

translated by David Luke (Oxford: Oxford University Press, 1987), p. 42.
16. Orledge, *Debussy and the Theatre*, p. 106, note 7 (Debussy's letter to André Messager, July 9, 1902).

The Domain of Arnheim, or The Landscape Garden

1. Poe, *The Complete Illustrated Stories and Poems of Edgar Allan Poe*, p. 106 ("The Domain of Arnheim").
2. Silverman, *Edgar Allan Poe—Mournful and Never-ending Remembrance*, p. 323.
3. Poe, *The Complete Illustrated Stories and Poems of Edgar Allan Poe*, p. 109, note 1 ("The Domain of Arnheim").
4. Ibid., p. 111 ("The Domain of Arnheim").
5. Ibid., p. 106 ("The Domain of Arnheim").
6. Ibid., p. 954 ("A Dream Within a Dream").
7. Ibid., p. 110 ("The Domain of Arnheim").
8. Joris-Karl Huysmans, *À Rebours* (London: Fortune Press, 1946), pp. 129–130.
9. Ben Hecht, *The Kingdom of the Wicked* (New York: Harcourt, Brace Jovanovich, 1978), p. 198.
10. Poe, *The Complete Illustrated Stories and Poems of Edgar Allan Poe*, pp. 113–114, note 1.
11. James Fenimore Cooper, *The Last of the Mohicans* (London: Oxford University Press, 1994), p. 57.
12. Sir Walter Scott, *Waverley* (Edinburgh: Adam and Charles Black, 1860), p. 164.

The Duc De L'Omelette

1. Poe, *The Complete Illustrated Stories and Poems of Edgar Allan Poe*, p. 351 ("The Duc De L'Omelette").
2. Ibid., p. 352 ("The Duc De L'Omelette").
3. Ibid., p. 173 ("Ligeia").
4. Ibid., p. 353 ("The Duc De L'Omelette").
5. Ibid., p. 281 ("The Assignation").
6. Ibid., p. 352 ("The Duc De L'Omelette").
7. Ibid., p. 281 ("The Assignation").
8. John Keats, *Letters of John Keats to His Family and Friends*, edited by Sidney Colvin (London: Macmillan, 1925), pp. 302–303 (Letter to George Keats, Sept. 17-27 1819: "The Edinburgh Reviewers are afraid to touch upon my poem. They do not know what to make of it; they do not like to condemn it, and they will not praise it for fear. They are as shy of it as I should be of wearing a Quaker's hat. The fact is, they have no real taste. They dare not compromise their judgments on so puzzling a question. If on my next publication they should praise me, and so lug in Endymion, I will address them in a manner they will not at all relish. The cowardliness of the Edinburgh is more than the abuse of the Quarterly").
9. Percy Bysshe Shelley, *The Complete Poetical Works of Percy Bysshe Shelley*, edited by Thomas Hutchinson (London: Oxford University Press, 1956), p. 444 ("Adonais").
10. David H. Hirsch, "'The Duc De L'Omelette' as Anti-Visionary Tale," http://eapoe.org/pstudies/ps1970/p1977202.htm.

11. George Bernard Shaw, *The Complete Plays of George Bernard Shaw* (London: Odhams, 1934), p. 372 ("Man and Superman").
12. Poe, *The Complete Illustrated Stories and Poems of Edgar Allan Poe*, p. 353, note 1 ("The Duc De L'Omelette").
13. George Bernard Shaw, "Edgar Allan Poe," *Nation*, January 16, 1909.
14. Poe, *The Complete Illustrated Stories and Poems of Edgar Allan Poe*, p. 741, note 1 ("Bon-Bon").
15. Ibid., p. 568 ("Loss of Breath").

Eleonora

1. Poe, *The Complete Illustrated Stories and Poems of Edgar Allan Poe*, p. 181 ("Eleonora").
2. Shelley, *The Complete Poetical Works of Percy Bysshe Shelley*, p. 437 ("Adonais," XXVII).
3. Ibid., p. 434 ("Adonais," X).
4. Ibid., p. 4 ("Adonais," XXVIII).
5. Ibid., p. 441 ("Adonais," XLIII).
6. Ibid., p. 441 ("Adonais," XLII).
7. Ibid., p. 443 ("Adonais," LII).
8. Ibid., p. 439 ("Adonais," XXXIII).
9. Ibid., p. 436 ("Adonais," XX).
10. Poe, *The Complete Illustrated Stories and Poems of Edgar Allan Poe*, p. 184, note 1 ("Eleonora").
11. Ibid., p. 185 ("Eleonora").
12. Silverman, *Edgar Allan Poe—Mournful and Never-ending Remembrance*, p. 241.
13. Poe, *The Portable Poe*, p. 564 ("The Philosophy of Composition").
14. Poe, *The Complete Illustrated Stories and Poems of Edgar Allan Poe*, p. 182, note 1 ("Eleonora").
15. Aldous Huxley, *The Doors of Perception and Heaven and Hell* (Harmondsworth: Penguin, 1961), p. 25 ("The Doors of Perception").
16. Ibid., p. 83 ("Heaven and Hell").
17. Poe, *The Complete Illustrated Stories and Poems of Edgar Allan Poe*, p. 181, note 1 ("Eleonora")
18. Ibid., p. 182 ("Eleonora").
19. Ibid., p. 183 ("Eleonora").
20. Ibid., p. 182 ("Eleonora").
21. Ibid., p. 183 ("Eleonora").
22. Ibid., p. 184 ("Eleonora").

Eureka

1. Edgar Allan Poe, *The Science Fiction of Edgar Allan Poe*, edited by Harold Beaver (Harmondsworth: Penguin, 1982), p. 309 ("Eureka").
2. Poe, *The Portable Poe*, p. 48 (Letter to Maria Clemm, July 7, 1849).
3. Poe, *The Science Fiction of Edgar Allan Poe*, p. 394, note 1 ("Eureka").
4. Ibid., p. 209 ("Eureka").
5. Ibid., p. 211 ("Eureka").
6. Ibid., p. 236 ("Eureka").
7. Ibid., p. 291 ("Eureka").
8. Ibid., p. 299 ("Eureka").
9. Ibid., p. 249 ("Eureka").
10. Edouard Schuré, *The Genesis of Tragedy*, trans-

lated by Fred Rothwell (London: Rudolf Steiner, 1936), pp. 24–25.
11. Richard Cavendish, *The Black Arts* (New York: Perigree, 1983), p. 12.
12. Jocelyn Godwin, *Robert Fludd—Hermetic Philosopher and Surveyor of Two Worlds* (London: Thames and Hudson, 1979), p. 52,
13. Poe, *The Science Fiction of Edgar Allan Poe*, p. 228, note 1 ("Eureka").
14. Poe, *The Complete Illustrated Stories and Poems of Edgar Allan Poe*, p. 589 ("Mesmeric Revelation").
15. Poe, *The Science Fiction of Edgar Allan Poe*, p. 375, note 1 ("Eureka").
16. Johann Wolfgang von Goethe, *Faust Part One*, translated by David Luke (Oxford: Oxford University Press, 1987), p. 19.
17. Poe, *The Science Fiction of Edgar Allan Poe*, p. 300, note 1 ("Eureka").
18. Ibid., p. 307 ("Eureka").
19. Peter Ackroyd, *The House of Doctor Dee* (London: Penguin, 1994), p. 68.
20. G. W. F. Hegel, *Philosophy of Mind*, translated by W. Wallace and A.V. Miller, revised by Michael Inwood (Oxford: Oxford University Press, 2007), p. 277.
21. Friedrich Nietzsche, *Thus Spoke Zarathustra*, translated by R. J. Hollingdale (Harmondsworth: Penguin, 1980), p. 29 (Hollingdale's introduction).
22. Ibid., p. 332.
23. Carl Gustav Jung interviewed by John Freeman in 1959, two years before his death, for the BBC television program *Face to Face*, presenter John Freeman.
24. Colin Wilson, *Rudolf Steiner: The Man and His Vision* (Wellingborough: Aquarian Press, 1985), p. 89.
25. Faubion Bowers, *The New Scriabin—Enigma and Answers* (London: David and Charles, 1974), p. 118.
26. Ibid., pp. 122–123.

The Facts in the Case of M. Valdemar

1. Poe, *The Complete Illustrated Stories and Poems of Edgar Allan Poe*, p. 207 ("The Facts in the Case of M. Valdemar").
2. Poe, *The Science Fiction of Edgar Allan Poe*, p. 394, note 1.
3. Poe, *The Complete Illustrated Stories and Poems of Edgar Allan Poe*, p. 208, note 1 ("The Facts in the Case of M. Valdemar").
4. Vincent Buranelli, *The Wizard from Vienna* (London: Peter Owen/Scientific Book Club, 1977), p. 221.
5. Poe, *The Complete Illustrated Stories and Poems of Edgar Allan Poe*, p. 203, note 1 ("The Facts in the Case of M. Valdemar").
6. Ibid., p. 204 ("The Facts in the Case of M. Valdemar").
7. Irene Shubik, ed., *The Mind Beyond* (Harmondsworth: Penguin, 1976), p. 49 (Daphne du Maurier, "The Breakthrough").
8. Poe, *The Complete Illustrated Stories and Poems of Edgar Allan Poe*, p. 207, note 1 ("The Facts in the Case of M. Valdemar").

The Fall of the House of Usher

1. Poe, *The Complete Illustrated Stories and Poems of Edgar Allan Poe*, p. 52 ("The Fall of the House of Usher").
2. Ibid., p. 53 ("The Fall of the House of Usher").
3. Ibid., pp. 54–55.
4. Richard Gilman, *Decadence—The Strange Life of an Epithet* (New York: Farrar, Straus and Giroux, 1979), p. 82.
5. Henri Dorra, ed., *Symbolist Art Theories—A Critical Anthology* (Berkeley: University of California Press, 1994), p. 131 (Paul Bourget, "Baudelaire and the Decadent Movement").
6. Lawrence, *The Portable D. H. Lawrence*, pp. 688–689, note 5 ("Edgar Allan Poe").
7. Poe, *The Complete Illustrated Stories and Poems of Edgar Allan Poe*, p. 55, note 1 ("The Fall of the House of Usher").
8. Orledge, *Debussy and the Theatre*, p. 103.
9. Ibid.
10. Ibid., p. 110.
11. Lockspeiser, *Debussy—His Life and Mind*, vol. 2, p. 143.
12. All the quotations from Debussy's libretto are drawn from Elisabeth Buzzard's translation for George Prêtre's recording of Debussy's *The Fall of the House of Usher*, EMI, 1984.
13. Lockspeiser, *Debussy—His Life and Mind*, vol. 2, p. 143, note 11.
14. Orledge, *Debussy and the Theatre*, p. 114, note 8.
15. Poe, *The Portable Poe*, p. 586 (editor's preface to the poems).
16. Gwen Harwood, *A Steady Storm of Correspondence: Selected Letters of Gwen Harwood, 1943–1995* (St. Lucia: University of Queensland Press, 2001), p. 196 (Letter to Sitski, November 14, 1964)
17. Larry Sitsky, "Sitsky on Sitsky," *Music Now*, April 1971, p. 7.
18. Judith Crispin, "*The Nuctemeron of Sitsky*," *Current Issues in Music 2 (2008)*, "In Search of New Worlds: A Festschrift for Larry Sitsky," Linda Kouvaras, Ruth Lee Martin, Graham Hair, eds. (Amaroo: Southern Voices, 2008) Find online at http://www.n-ism.org/Papers/graham_CIIM_2008.pdf.
19. http://www.gordongetty.com/biography.
20. http://www.youtube.com/watch?v=KBgeNPFHcI0.
21. Ibid.
22. Freud, *The Interpretation of Dreams*, p. 472.
23. Thompson, *Poe's Fiction: Romantic Irony in the Gothic Tales*, p. 95.
24. Joseph Lanza, Phallic Frenzy, *Ken Russell and His Films* (London: Aurum, 2008), p. 318.

The Gold-Bug

1. Poe, *The Complete Illustrated Stories and Poems of Edgar Allan Poe*, p. 135 ("The Goldbug").
2. Verne, *Jules Verne*, p. 61.
3. Silverman, *Edgar Allan Poe—Mournful and Never-ending Remembrance*, p. 209.

4. Poe, *The Complete Illustrated Stories and Poems of Edgar Allan Poe*, p. 134, note 1.

The Haunted Palace

1. Poe, *The Complete Illustrated Stories and Poems of Edgar Allan Poe*, p. 938 ("The Haunted Palace").
2. Alan Frank, *The Films of Roger Corman* (London: Batsford, 1998), p. 129.
3. H. P. Lovecraft, *The Fiction* (New York: Barnes & Noble, 2008), p. 1066 ("Supernatural Horror in Literature").
4. Lowe, *Josef Holbrooke and His Work*, p. 173.
5. Ibid., p. 176.
6. Ibid., p. 178.

Ligeia

1. Poe, *The Complete Illustrated Stories and Poems of Edgar Allan Poe*, pp. 169–170 ("Ligeia").
2. Ibid., p. 178 ("Ligeia").
3. Ibid., p. 174.
4. Marcel Proust, *Remembrance of Things Past*, vol. 1, translated by C. K. Scott Moncrieff and Terence Kilmartin (London: Chatto & Windus, 1981), pp. 13–14.
5. Michael Murphy, *Proust in America* (Liverpool: Liverpool University Press, 2007), pp. 160–161.
6. Ibid.
7. Bram Stoker, *Dracula* (London: Constable, 1904), p. 305.
8. Poe, *The Complete Illustrated Stories and Poems of Edgar Allan Poe*, p. 586, note 1 ("Mesmeric Revelation").
9. Ibid., p. 922 ("The Bells").
10. Sophocles, *The Theban Plays*, translated by E. F. Watling (Harmondsworth: Penguin, 1979), p. 63 ("Oedipus the King").
11. Steve McKerrow, "Poe's writings inspire opera called 'Ligeia,'" *The Baltimore Sun*, Jan. 21, 1994 http://articles.baltimoresun.com/1994-01-21/features/1994021150_1_poe-edgar-allan-opera.
12. Erin Leigh Helmey, *"Ligeia": A Triumph Over Patriarchy*, http://www.llp.armstrong.edu/watermarks2/elh.html.

Maelzel's Chess-Player

1. Poe, *The Complete Illustrated Stories and Poems of Edgar Allan Poe*, pp. 688–689 ("Maelzel's Chess-Player").
2. Ibid., p. 688 ("Maelzel's Chess-Player").
3. Ibid., p. 701 ("Maelzel's Chess-Player").
4. Ibid., p. 644 ("Maelzel's Chess-Player").

The Man That Was Used Up

1. Poe, *The Complete Illustrated Stories and Poems of Edgar Allan Poe*, p. 465 ("The Man That Was Used Up").
2. Ibid., p. 470 ("The Man That Was Used Up").
3. Poe, *The Portable Poe*, p. 21 (letter to James Russell Lowell, July 2, 1844).

4. Poe, *The Complete Illustrated Stories and Poems of Edgar Allan Poe*, p. 467, note 1 ("The Man That Was Used Up").
5. Antony Easthope, *What a Man's Gotta Do* (London: Paladin, 1986), pp. 166–168.

The Masque of the Red Death

1. Poe, *The Complete Illustrated Stories and Poems of Edgar Allan Poe*, p. 761 ("The Masque of the Red Death").
2. August von Platen, "Tristan" ("Wie die Schönheit angeschaut mit Augen,/Ist dem Tode schon anheimgegeben"), http://www.deutsche-liebeslyrik.de/platen.htm.
3. Novalis, *Henry of Ofterdingen,* http://www.gutenberg.org/files/31873/31873-h/31873-h.htm, chapter 1.
4. D. H. Lawrence, *The Plays* (Harmondsworth: Penguin 1981), p. 39 ("A Collier's Friday Night").
5. Christopher Frayling, ed., *Vampyres* (London: Faber and Faber, 1991), p. 180 ("Wake Not the Dead").
6. Poe, *The Complete Illustrated Stories and Poems of Edgar Allan Poe*, p. 757, note 1 ("The Masque of the Red Death").
7. Villiers de L'Isle Adam, *Axël,* translated by M. Gaddis Rose (London: Soho, 1986), p. 170.
8. Poe, *The Complete Illustrated Stories and Poems of Edgar Allan Poe*, p. 761, note 1 ("The Masque of the Red Death").
9. Ibid., p. 758 ("The Masque of the Red Death").
10. MaryAnne Stevens and Robert Hoozee, eds., *Impressionism to Symbolism—The Belgian Avant-Garde 1880–1900* (London: Royal Academy of Arts, 1994), p. 940 (Bruno Fornani's essay on Jean Delville's "Death").
11. Poe, *The Complete Illustrated Stories and Poems of Edgar Allan Poe*, p. 761, note 1 ("The Masque of the Red Death").
12. Ibid.
13. Ibid.
14. Arthur Schopenhauer, *The World as Will and Representation*, vol. 1, translated by E. F. J. Payne (New York: Dover, 1966), p. 257.
15. Lowe, *Josef Holbrooke and His Work*, p. 227.
16. Silverman, *Edgar Allan Poe—Mournful and Never-ending Remembrance*, p. 407.

Mellonta Tauta

1. Poe, *The Complete Illustrated Stories and Poems of Edgar Allan Poe*, p. 404 ("Mellonta Tauta").
2. Ibid., p. 405 ("Mellonta Tauta").
3. Ibid., p. 413 ("Mellonta Tauta").
4. Ibid.

Metzengerstein

1. Poe, *The Complete Illustrated Stories and Poems of Edgar Allan Poe*, p. 334 ("Metzengerstein").
2. Ibid., p. 339.

Morella

1. Poe, *The Complete Illustrated Stories and Poems of Edgar Allan Poe*, p. 194 ("Morella").
2. Ibid., p. 196 ("Morella").
3. Silverman, *Edgar Allan Poe—Mournful and Never-ending Remembrance*, p. 113.
4. Ibid., p. 113.
5. Poe, *The Complete Illustrated Stories and Poems of Edgar Allan Poe*, p. 198, note 1 ("Morella").
6. Ibid., p. 198 ("Morella").
7. Christina Rossetti, *The Works of Christina Rossetti* (Ware: Wordsworth, 1995), p. 263 ("Who Shall Deliver Me?").
8. Poe, *The Complete Illustrated Stories and Poems of Edgar Allan Poe*, p. 196, note 1 ("Morella").
9. Ibid., p. 179 ("Ligeia").
10. Paul Murray, *From the Shadow of Dracula—A Life of Bram Stoker* (London: Jonathan Cape, 2004), p. 184.

The Murders in the Rue Morgue

1. Poe, *The Complete Illustrated Stories and Poems of Edgar Allan Poe*, p. 76 ("The Murders in the Rue Morgue").
2. Ibid., p. 79.
3. Ibid., pp. 77–78.
4. Ibid., p. 78.
5. Gordon Hessler, interview for the DVD release of *Murders in the Rue Morgue*.

The Mystery of Marie Rogêt

1. Poe, *The Complete Illustrated Stories and Poems of Edgar Allan Poe*, p. 506 ("The Mystery of Marie Rogêt").
2. Sir Arthur Conan Doyle, *The Adventures of Sherlock Holmes* (London: Leopard, 1996), p. 74 ("A Case of Identity").
3. Ibid., p. 68 ("A Case of Identity").
4. Poe, *The Complete Illustrated Stories and Poems of Edgar Allan Poe*, p. 496, note 1 ("The Mystery of Marie Rogêt").
5. Ibid., pp. 519–521 ("The Mystery of Marie Rogêt").
6. Ibid., p. 491 ("The Mystery of Marie Rogêt").

The Narrative of Arthur Gordon Pym of Nantucket

1. Poe, *The Complete Illustrated Stories and Poems of Edgar Allan Poe*, p. 877 ("The Narrative of Arthur Gordon Pym").
2. F.W.J. Hemmings, *Baudelaire the Damned—A Biography* (London: Hamish Hamilton, 1982), p. 115.
3. Edgar Allan Poe, *Edgar Allan Poe: Selected Prose, Poetry, and Eureka*, edited by W. H. Auden (San Francisco: Rinehart, 1950), vii (Auden's introduction).
4. Arthur Rimbaud, "Le bateau ivre," http://www.poetryintranslation.com/PITBR/French/Rimbaud1.htm#_Toc196916310.
5. Henry James, *The Golden Bowl*, http://www.gutenberg.org/files/4264/4264-h/4264-h.htm, Book First: The Prince, part first.
6. Joris Karl Huysmans, *À Rebours* (London: Fortune Press, 1946), p. 30.
7. Poe, *The Complete Illustrated Stories and Poems of Edgar Allan Poe*, p. 769, note 1 ("The Narrative of Arthur Gordon Pym").
8. Ibid., p. 832 ("The Narrative of Arthur Gordon Pym").
9. Coleridge, *Poetical Works*, p. 195 ("The Rime of the Ancient Mariner").
10. J. Gerald Kennedy, *The Narrative of Arthur Gordon Pym and the Abyss of Interpretation* (New York: Twayne, 1995), p. 17.
11. Ibid., p. 15.
12. Oliver Strunk, ed., *Source Readings in Music History, Vol. 5, The Romantic Era* (London: Faber & Faber, 1981), pp. 143–144 (Richard Wagner, "From *Das Kunstwerk der Zukunft*").
13. Poe, *The Complete Illustrated Stories and Poems of Edgar Allan Poe*, p. 579, note 1 ("Mystification").
14. Kennedy, *The Narrative of Arthur Gordon Pym and the Abyss of Interpretation*, p. 72, note 10.
15. Ibid., p. 74.
16. Poe, *The Complete Illustrated Stories and Poems of Edgar Allan Poe*, p. 909, note 1 ("The Narrative of Arthur Gordon Pym").

Never Bet the Devil Your Head

1. Poe, *The Complete Illustrated Stories and Poems of Edgar Allan Poe*, p. 730 ("Never Bet the Devil Your Head").
2. John Baxter, *Fellini* (London: Fourth Estate, 1993), p. 230.
3. Ibid., p. 232.

The Oblong Box

1. Poe, *The Complete Illustrated Stories and Poems of Edgar Allan Poe*, p. 266 ("The Oblong Box").

The Oval Portrait

1. Poe, *The Complete Illustrated Stories and Poems of Edgar Allan Poe*, p. 299 ("The Oval Portrait").
2. Poe, *The Portable Poe*, p. 557 ("The Philosophy of Composition").
3. Thomas Wright, *Oscar's Books* (London: Vintage, 2009), p. 4.
4. Wilde, *Complete Works of Oscar Wilde*, p. 34 ("The Picture of Dorian Gray").
5. Poe, *The Complete Illustrated Stories and Poems of Edgar Allan Poe*, p. 303, note 1 ("The Oval Portrait").
6. Barbara Belford, *Bram Stoker—A Biography of the Author of Dracula* (London: Weidenfeld and Nicolson, 1996), pp. 261–262.

7. Poe, *The Complete Illustrated Stories and Poems of Edgar Allan Poe*, p. 174, note 1 ("Ligeia").
8. Poe, *The Complete Illustrated Stories and Poems of Edgar Allan Poe*, p. 30, note 1 ("The Pit and the Pendulum").
9. Jane Austen, *Northanger Abbey* (Ware: Wordsworth, 1995), p. 24.

Philosophy of Furniture

1. Poe, *The Complete Illustrated Stories and Poems of Edgar Allan Poe*, p. 718 ("Philosophy of Furniture").
2. Seymour Chatman, *Antonioni or, The Surface of the World* (Berkeley: University of California Press, 1985), p. 24.
3. Wilde, *Complete Works of Oscar Wilde*, p. 17, note 1 ("The Picture of Dorian Gray").
4. Poe, *The Complete Illustrated Stories and Poems of Edgar Allan Poe*, p. 133, note 1 ("Landor's Cottage").
5. Ibid., p. 715 ("Philosophy of Furniture").
6. Richard Ellmann, *Oscar Wilde* (London: Hamish Hamilton, 1988), p. 184.
7. Oscar Wilde, *Complete Works of Oscar Wilde* (London: Collins, 1977), p. 418 ("Lady Windermere's Fan").
8. Gabrielle D'Annunzio, *A Child of Pleasure*, translated by Georgina Harding (Sawtry: Dedalus, 1991), p. 206.
9. Poe, *The Complete Illustrated Stories and Poems of Edgar Allan Poe*, p. 719, note 1 ("Philosophy of Furniture").
10. Ibid.
11. Ibid.
12. Poe, *The Complete Illustrated Stories and Poems of Edgar Allan Poe*, p. 719, note 1 ("Philosophy of Furniture").
13. Joris-Karl Huysmans, *À Rebours* (London: Fortune Press, 1946), p. 30.
14. Wilde, *Complete Works of Oscar Wilde*, p. 34, note 4 ("The Picture of Dorian Gray").

The Pit and the Pendulum

1. Poe, *The Complete Illustrated Stories and Poems of Edgar Allan Poe*, p. 28 ("The Pit and the Pendulum").
2. Ibid., p. 21 ("The Pit and the Pendulum").
3. Ibid., p. 27 ("The Pit and the Pendulum").
4. Ibid., p. 22 ("The Pit and the Pendulum").
5. Ibid., p. 21 ("The Pit and the Pendulum").
6. Ibid., p. 22 ("The Pit and the Pendulum").
7. Bram Stoker, *The Lair of the White Worm* (London: Arrow, 1975), p. 118.
8. Ibid., p. 119.
9. Ibid., p. 117.
10. Poe, *The Complete Illustrated Stories and Poems of Edgar Allan Poe*, p 28, note 1 ("The Pit and the Pendulum").
11. Stoker, *Dracula*, p. 39.
12. Jack Sullan, *New World Symphonies: How American Culture Changed the World* (New Haven: Yale University Press, 1999), p. 92.
13. Alan Frank, *The Films of Roger Corman* (London: Batsford, 1998), p. 92.
14. Bram Stoker, *Dracula's Guest* (London: Arrow, 1975), p. 65 ("The Squaw").
15. Poe, *The Complete Illustrated Stories and Poems of Edgar Allan Poe*, p. 30, note 1 ("The Pit and the Pendulum").
16. Poe, *The Complete Illustrated Stories and Poems of Edgar Allan Poe*, p. 167, note 1 ("Ligeia").
17. Villiers de L'Isle Adam, "A Torture of Hope," http://gaslight.mtroyal.ca/villier5.htm.
18. Poe, *The Complete Illustrated Stories and Poems of Edgar Allan Poe*, p. 21, note 1 ("The Pit and the Pendulum").
19. Nikolaus Martin, *Prague Winter* (London: Peter Halban, 1990), p. 267.

A Predicament

1. Poe, *The Complete Illustrated Stories and Poems of Edgar Allan Poe*, p. 483 ("A Predicament").
2. Ibid., p. 652 ("How to Write a Blackwood Article").
3. Ibid., p. 485 ("A Predicament").
4. Ibid.
5. Ibid., p. 657 ("How to Write a Blackwood Article").
6. Ibid., p. 478 ("A Predicament").
7. Ibid., p. 479 ("A Predicament").
8. Ibid., p. 654 ("How to Write a Blackwood Article").

The Premature Burial

1. Poe, *The Complete Illustrated Stories and Poems of Edgar Allan Poe*, p. 354 ("The Premature Burial").
2. Sheridan Le Fanu, *In a Glass Darkly* (London: John Lehman, 1947), p. 213 ("The Room in the Dragon Volant").
3. Ibid., p. 214 ("The Room in the Dragon Volant").
4. *The Opera Libretto Library* (New York: Avenel Books, 1980), p. 251 ("Aida").
5. Poe, *The Complete Illustrated Stories and Poems of Edgar Allan Poe*, p. 361, note 1 ("The Premature Burial").
6. Evelyn Waugh, *The Loved One* (Harmondsworth: Penguin, 1977), p. 37.
7. Ibid., p. 65.

The Purloined Letter

1. Poe, *The Complete Illustrated Stories and Poems of Edgar Allan Poe*, p. 317 ("The Purloined Letter").
2. Ibid., pp. 77–78 ("The Murders in the Rue Morgue").
3. Conan Doyle, *The Return of Sherlock Holmes* (London: Jonathan Cape, 1974), p. 344 ("The Second Stain").
4. Poe, *The Complete Illustrated Stories and Poems of Edgar Allan Poe*, p. 327–328, note 1 ("The Purloined Letter").

The Raven

1. Poe, *The Complete Illustrated Stories and Poems of Edgar Allan Poe*, p. 915 ("The Raven").
2. Silverman, *Edgar Allan Poe—Mournful and Never-ending Remembrance*, p. 435.
3. Joanna Richardson, *Gustave Doré—A Biography* (London: Cassell, 1980), p. 152.
4. Poe, *The Complete Illustrated Stories and Poems of Edgar Allan Poe*, p. 915, note 1 ("The Raven").
5. Lowe, *Josef Holbrooke and His Work*, pp. 126–127.
6. Ibid., p. 132.
7. Ibid., p. 133.
8. Ibid., p. 135.

Some Words with a Mummy

1. Poe, *The Complete Illustrated Stories and Poems of Edgar Allan Poe*, p. 529 ("Some Words with a Mummy").
2. Ibid., p. 523 ("Some Words with a Mummy").
3. Bram Stoker, *The Jewel of Seven Stars* (Far Thrupp: Alan Sutton, 1996), p. 2.
4. Poe, *The Complete Illustrated Stories and Poems of Edgar Allan Poe*, p. 523, note 1 ("Some Words with a Mummy").
5. Stoker, *The Jewel of Seven Stars*, p. 3, note 3.
6. Poe, *The Complete Illustrated Stories and Poems of Edgar Allan Poe*, p. 526, note 1 ("Some Words with a Mummy").
7. Anne Rice, *The Mummy—or Ramses the Damned* (London: Penguin, 1990), pp. 210–211.
8. Poe, *The Complete Illustrated Stories and Poems of Edgar Allan Poe*, p. 533, note 1 ("Some Words with a Mummy").
9. Poe, *The Science Fiction of Edgar Allan Poe*, p. 386 ("Some Words with a Mummy").
10. Poe, *The Complete Illustrated Stories and Poems of Edgar Allan Poe*, p. 533, note 1 ("Some Words with a Mummy").
11. Ibid., p. 535 ("Some Words with a Mummy").
12. Poe, *The Science Fiction of Edgar Allan Poe*, p. 417, note 9 (Commentary).

The Sphinx

1. Poe, *The Complete Illustrated Stories and Poems of Edgar Allan Poe*, p. 720 ("The Sphinx").
2. Ibid., p. 721 ("The Sphinx").
3. W. B. Yeats, *Collected Poems of W. B. Yeats* (London: Macmillan, 1950), p. 211 ("The Second Coming").
4. Poe, *The Complete Illustrated Stories and Poems of Edgar Allan Poe*, pp. 721–722, note 1 ("The Sphinx").

The System of Doctor Tarr and Professor Fether

1. Poe, *The Complete Illustrated Stories and Poems of Edgar Allan Poe*, p. 562 ("The System of Doctor Tarr and Professor Fether").
2. Ibid., p. 547 ("The System of Doctor Tarr and Professor Fether").
3. Ibid., p. 554 ("The System of Doctor Tarr and Professor Fether").
4. Ibid., p. 555 ("The System of Doctor Tarr and Professor Fether").
5. Ibid., p. 181 ("Eleonora").
6. Sheridan Le Fanu, *The Rose and the Key* (New York: Dover, 1982), p. 357.
7. Ibid., p. 297.
8. Ibid., p. 303.
9. Poe, *The Complete Illustrated Stories and Poems of Edgar Allan Poe*, p. 561, note 1 ("The System of Doctor Tarr and Professor Fether").

A Tale of the Ragged Mountains

1. Poe, *The Complete Illustrated Stories and Poems of Edgar Allan Poe*, p. 70 ("A Tale of the Ragged Mountains").
2. Ibid., p. 74.
3. Ibid., p. 67.
4. Ibid., pp. 69–70.

The Tell-Tale Heart

1. Poe, *The Complete Illustrated Stories and Poems of Edgar Allan Poe*, p. 246 ("The Tell-Tale Heart").
2. The quotation derives from Coleridge's marginalia in his own copy of Shakespeare, when preparing lecture notes during the winter of 1818–1819.
3. Poe, *The Complete Illustrated Stories and Poems of Edgar Allan Poe*, p. 249, note 1 ("The Tell-Tale Heart").
4. Carlos Clarens, *Horror Movies—An Illustrated Survey* (London: Secker & Warburg, 1968), p. 61.
5. Poe, *The Complete Illustrated Stories and Poems of Edgar Allan Poe*, p. 244, note 1 ("The Tell-Tale Heart").
6. Ibid., p. 245 ("The Tell-Tale Heart").
7. Fyodor M. Dostoyevsky, *Crime and Punishment* (London: Heron, n.d.), p. 60.
8. Ibid., p. 118.
9. Poe, *The Complete Illustrated Stories and Poems of Edgar Allan Poe*, p. 249, note 1 ("The Tell-Tale Heart").
10. Ibid., p. 243 ("The Black Cat").
11. Lotte H. Eisner, *The Haunted Screen* (London: Secker and Warburg, 1983), p. 27.
12. Poe, *The Complete Illustrated Stories and Poems of Edgar Allan Poe*, p. 244, note 1 ("The Tell-Tale Heart").
13. Ibid., p. 224 ("The Tell-Tale Heart").
14. Ibid., p. 249 ("The Tell-Tale Heart).

"Thou Art the Man"

1. Poe, *The Complete Illustrated Stories and Poems of Edgar Allan Poe*, p. 545 ("'Thou Art the Man'").
2. Ibid.
3. Ibid., p. 546 ("'Thou Art the Man'").

Three Sundays in a Week

1. Poe, *The Complete Illustrated Stories and Poems of Edgar Allan Poe*, p. 606 ("Three Sundays in a Week").
2. Ibid., p. 606 ("Three Sundays in a Week").
3. Jules Verne, *Around the World in Eighty Days* (London: Dean & Son, n.d.), p. 181–182.

The Unparalleled Adventure of One Hans Pfaall

1. Poe, *The Complete Illustrated Stories and Poems of Edgar Allan Poe*, p. 367 ("The Unparalleled Adventure of One Hans Pfaall").
2. Poe, *The Science Fiction of Edgar Allan Poe*, p. 339.
3. Verne, *Jules Verne* (London: Macdonald and Jane's, 1976), p. 31.
4. Ibid., p. 35.
5. Jules Verne, *From the Earth to the Moon; and, Round the Moon,* http://www.gutenberg.org/catalog/world/readfile?fk_files=3273441&pageno=4.
6. Verne, *Jules Verne,* pp. 70–71, note 3.
7. Verne, *From the Earth to the Moon; and, Round the Moon,* http://www.gutenberg.org/catalog/world/readfile?fk_files=3273441&pageno=10.
8. Poe, *The Complete Illustrated Stories and Poems of Edgar Allan Poe*, pp. 337–338, note 1 ("The Unparalleled Adventure of One Hans Pfaall").
9. Ibid., p. 396 ("The Unparalleled Adventure of One Hans Pfaall").
10. Poe, *The Science Fiction of Edgar Allan Poe*, p. 349, note 2.
11. Poe, *The Complete Illustrated Stories and Poems of Edgar Allan Poe*, pp. 383–384, note 1 ("The Unparalleled Adventure of One Hans Pfaall").
12. Poe, *The Science Fiction of Edgar Allan Poe*, p. 348, note 2.

William Wilson

1. Poe, *The Complete Illustrated Stories and Poems of Edgar Allan Poe*, p. 46 ("William Wilson").
2. Ibid., p. 48 ("William Wilson").
3. James Hogg, *The Private Memoirs and Confessions of a Justified Sinner* (London: Penguin, 2006), p. 103.
4. Ibid., p. 96.
5. Poe, *The Complete Illustrated Stories and Poems of Edgar Allan Poe*, p. 37, note 1 ("William Wilson").
6. Edward Bulwer (Lord Lytton), *The Student—A Series of Papers* (London: Saunders and Otley, 1836), p. 35 ("Monos and Diamonos").
7. Ibid., pp. 47–48 ("Monos and Diamonos").
8. T. H. S. Escott, *Edward Bulwer First Baron Lytton of Knebworth—A Social, Personal, and Political Monograph* (London: Routledge, 1910), p. 247.
9. Poe, *The Complete Illustrated Stories and Poems of Edgar Allan Poe*, p. 173, note 1 ("Ligeia").
10. Adolf Hitler, from a speech given in Munich, March 1936.
11. Siegfried Kracauer, *From Caligari to Hitler—a Psychological History of the German Film* (Princeton: Princeton University Press, 1947), p. 153.

Epilogue

1. Poe, *The Portable Poe*, p. 648 ("Fancy and Imagination").
2. Modris Eksteins, *Rites of Spring—The Great War and the Birth of the Modern Age* (London: Papermac, 2000), p. 82 (Emil Nolde quoted).
3. Villiers de L'Isle Adam, *Axël*, p. 170.

Bibliography

Ackroyd, Peter. *The House of Doctor Dee*. London: Penguin, 1994.

Austen, Jane. *Northanger Abbey*. Ware: Wordsworth, 1995.

Baudelaire, Charles. *Baudelaire: Selected Writings on Art and Artists*. Trans. P. E. Charvet. Cambridge: Cambridge University Press, 1981.

_____. *The Mirror of Art—Critical Studies by Charles Baudelaire*. Trans. and ed. Jonathan Mayne. New York: Doubleday, 1956.

Belford, Barbara. *Bram Stoker—A Biography of the Author of Dracula*. London: Weidenfeld and Nicolson, 1996.

Blackwood, Algernon. *Ancient Sorceries and Other Weird Stories*. London: Penguin, 2002.

Bowers, Faubion. *The New Scriabin—Enigma and Answers*. London: David and Charles, 1974.

Bulwer-Lytton, Edward. *The Last Days of Pompeii*. London: Routledge, 1876.

Buranelli, Vincent. *The Wizard from Vienna*. London: Peter Owen/Scientific Book Club, 1977.

Byron. *The Letters of Lord Byron*. Ed. Mathilde Blind. London: Walter Scott, n.d.

Carter, Frederick. *The Dragon of the Alchemists*. London: Elkin Matthews, 1926.

Cassou, Jean. *The Concise Encyclopedia of Symbolism*. London: Omega, 1984.

Cavendish, Richard. *The Black Arts*. New York: Perigree, 1983.

Chatman, Seymour. *Antonioni or, The Surface of the World*. Berkeley: University of California Press, 1985.

Clarens, Carlos. *Horror Movies—An Illustrated Survey*. London: Secker & Warburg, 1968.

Cohn, Robert Greer. *Toward the Poetry of Mallarmé*. Berkley: University of California Press, 1965.

Coleridge, Samuel Taylor. *Poetical Works*. Ed. Ernest Hartley Coleridge. London: Oxford University Press, 1974.

Conan Doyle, Sir Arthur. *The Adventures of Sherlock Holmes*. London: Leopard, 1996.

_____. *The Return of Sherlock Holmes*. London: Jonathan Cape, 1974.

Cooper, James Fenimore. *The Last of the Mohicans*. London: Oxford University Press, 1994.

Dalí, Salvador. *The Secret Life of Salvador Dalí*. New York: Dover, 1993.

D'Annunzio, Gabrielle. *A Child of Pleasure*. Trans. Georgina Harding. Sawtry: Dedalus, 1991.

_____. *The Flame*. Trans. Susan Bassnett. London: Quartet, 1991.

de la Mare, Walter. *Ghost Stories*. London: Folio Society, 1964.

Dorra, Henri, ed. *Symbolist Art Theories—A Critical Anthology*. Berkeley: University of California Press, 1994.

Dostoyevsky, Fyodor, M. *Crime and Punishment*. London: Heron, n.d.

Druick, Douglas W., ed. *Odilon Redon—1840–1916*. London: Royal Academy of Arts, 1995.

Easthope, Antony. *What a Man's Gotta Do*. London: Paladin, 1986.

Eisner, Lotte H. *The Haunted Screen*. London: Secker and Warburg, 1983.

Ellmann, Richard, *Yeats: The Man and the Masks*. London: Penguin, 1987.

Frank, Alan. *The Films of Roger Corman*. London: Batsford, 1998.

Frayling, Christopher, ed. *Vampyres*. London: Faber and Faber, 1991.

Freud, Sigmund. *Beyond the Pleasure Principle*. Ed. C.J.M. Hubback. London: INTL Psycho-Analytical, 1922.

Freud, Sigmund. *The Interpretation of Dreams*. Trans. James Strachey. Harmondsworth: Penguin, 1983.

Gilbert, W. Stephen. *Fight & Kick & Bite—The Life and Work of Dennis Potter*. London: Hodder & Stoughton, 1995.

Gilman, Richard. *Decadence—The Strange Life of an Epithet.* New York: Farrar, Straus and Giroux, 1979.

Goethe, Johann Wolfgang von. *Faust Part One.* Trans. David Luke. Oxford: Oxford University Press, 1987.

Godwin, Jocelyn. *Robert Fludd—Hermetic Philosopher and Surveyor of Two Worlds.* London: Thames and Hudson, 1979.

Gorer, Geoffrey. *The Life and Ideas of the Marquis de Sade.* London: Peter Owen, 1962.

Harwood, Dwen. *A Steady Storm of Correspondence: Selected Letters of Gwen Harwood, 1943–1995.* St. Lucia: University of Queensland Press, 2001.

Hecht, Ben. *The Kingdom of the Wicked.* New York: Harcourt, Brace Jovanovich, 1978.

Hegel, G. W. F. *Philosophy of Mind.* Trans. W. Wallace and A. V. Miller, rev. Michael Inwood. Oxford: Oxford University Press, 2007.

Hemmings, F. J. W. *Baudelaire the Damned.* London: Hamish Hamilton, 1982.

Hogg, James. *The Private Memoirs and Confessions of a Justified Sinner.* London: Penguin, 2006.

Holloway, Robin. *Debussy and Wagner.* London: Eulenberg, 1979.

Huntley, John. *British Film Music.* London: Skelton Robinson, 1947.

Huxley, Aldous. *The Doors of Perception and Heaven and Hell.* Harmondsworth: Penguin, 1961.

Huysmans, Joris-Karl. *À Rebours.* London: Fortune Press, 1946.

Jansson, Tove. *Comet in Moominland.* Trans. Elizabeth Portch. Harmondsworth: Penguin, 1970.

Keats, John. *Letters of John Keats to His Family and Friends.* Ed. Sidney Colvin. London: Macmillan, 1925.

Kennedy, J. Gerald. *The Narrative of Arthur Gordon Pym and the Abyss of Interpretation.* New York: Twayne, 1995.

Kracauer, Siegfried. *From Caligari to Hitler—a Psychological History of the German Film.* Princeton: Princeton University Press, 1947.

Lanza, Joseph. *Phallic Frenzy—Ken Russell and his Films.* London: Aurum, 2008.

Lawrence, D. H. *The Plays.* Harmondsworth: Penguin 1981.

_____. *The Portable D. H. Lawrence.* Ed. Diana Trilling. Harmondsworth: Penguin, 1980.

Le Fanu, Sheridan. *In a Glass Darkly.* London: John Lehman, 1947.

_____. *The Rose and Key.* New York: Dover, 1982.

Lockspeiser, Edward. *Debussy—His Life and Mind.* 2 vols. London: Cassell, 1965.

Lovecraft, H. P. *The Fiction.* New York: Barnes & Noble, 2008.

Lowe, George. *Josef Holbrooke and His Work.* London: Kegan Paul, Trench and Trubner, 1920.

Lowell, James Russell. *The Poetical Works of James R. Lowell.* 2 vols. Boston: Ticknor and Fields, 1863.

Mann, Thomas. *Essays of Three Decades.* Trans. H. T. Lowe-Porter. London: Secker & Warburg, 1947.

Martin, Nikolaus. *Prague Winter.* London: Peter Halban, 1990.

Maeterlinck, Maurice. *Pelleas and Melisanda, and The Sightless—Two Plays by Maurice Maeterlinck.* Trans. Laurence Alma-Tadema. London: Walter Scott, n.d.

_____. *Sister Beatrice and Ardiane & Barbe Bleue.* Trans. Bernard Miall. London: George Allen, 1908.

Moore, George. *Avowals.* London: Heinemann, 1924.

Muller, Robert. *Supernatural.* London: Collins/Fonata, 1977.

Murphy, Michael. *Proust in America.* Liverpool: Liverpool University Press, 2007.

Murray, Paul. *From the Shadow of Dracula—A Life of Bram Stoker.* London: Jonathan Cape, 2004.

Nietzsche, Friedrich. *Thus Spoke Zarathustra.* Trans. R. J. Hollingdale. Harmondsworth: Penguin, 1980.

_____. *Twilight of the Idols and the Anti-Christ.* Trans. R. J. Hollingdale. Harmondsworth: Penguin, 1981.

Norris, Geoffrey. *Rakhmaninoff.* London: Dent, 1978.

The Opera Libretto Library. New York: Avenel Books, 1980.

Orledge, Robert. *Debussy and the Theatre.* Cambridge: Cambridge University Press, 1985.

Poe, Edgar Allan. *The Complete Illustrated Stories and Poems of Edgar Allan Poe.* London: Chancellor Press, 1988.

_____. *The Portable Poe.* Ed. Philip van Doren Stern. Harmondsworth: Penguin, 1977.

_____. *The Science Fiction of Edgar Allan Poe.* Ed. Harold Beaver. Harmondsworth: Penguin, 1982.

Proust, Marcel. *Remembrance of Things Past*, vol. 1. Trans. C. K. Scott Moncrieff and Terence Kilmartin. London: Chatto & Windus, 1981.

Purce, Jill. *The Mystic Spiral.* London: Thames and Hudson, 1975.

Radcliffe, Ann. *The Mysteries of Udolpho.* London: Oxford University Press, 1966.

Remy, Nicolas. *Demonolatry.* Trans. E. A. Ashwin. London: Frederick Muller, 1970.

Rhodes, Anthony. *The Poet as Superman—D'Annunzio—A Life.* London: Weidenfeld & Nicolson, 1959.

Rice, Anne. *The Mummy—or Ramses the Damned*. London: Penguin, 1990.

Richardson, Joanna. *Gustave Doré—A Biography*. London: Cassell, 1980.

Schopenhauer, Arthur. *The World as Will and Representation*. 2 vols. Trans. E. F. J. Payne. New York: Dover, 1966.

Schuré, Edouard. *The Genesis of Tragedy*. Trans. Fred Rothwell. London: Rudolf Steiner, 1936.

Scott, Sir Walter. *Waverley*. Edinburgh: Adam and Charles Black, 1860.

Shaw, George Bernard. *The Complete Plays of George Bernard Shaw*. London: Odhams, 1934.

Shelley, Percy Bysshe. *The Complete Poetical Works of Percy Bysshe Shelley*. Ed. Thomas Hutchinson. London: Oxford University Press, 1956.

Shubik, Irene, ed. *The Mind Beyond*. Harmondsworth: Penguin, 1976.

Silverman, Kenneth. *Edgar Allan Poe—Mournful and Never-ending Remembrance*. London: Weidenfeld & Nicolson, 1992.

Sinclair, Andrew. *The Facts in the Case of E. A. Poe*. London: Weidenfeld & Nicolson, 1979.

Sophocles. *The Theban Plays*. Trans. E. F. Watling. Harmondsworth: Penguin, 1979.

Sova, Dawn B. *Critical Companion to Edgar Allan Poe: A Literary Reference to His Life and Work*. New York: Facts on File Inc., 2007.

Stevens, MaryAnne, and Robert Hoozee, eds. *Impressionism to Symbolism—The Belgian Avant-Garde 1880–1900*. London: Royal Academy of Arts, 1994.

Stoker, Bram. *Dracula*. London: Constable, 1904.

———. *Dracula's Guest*. London: Arrow, 1975.

———. *The Jewel of Seven Stars*. Far Thrupp: Alan Sutton, 1996.

Strunk, Oliver, ed. *Source Readings in Music History, Vol. 5, The Romantic Era*. London: Faber & Faber, 1981.

Sullan, Jack. *New World Symphonies: How American Culture Changed the World*. New Haven: Yale University Press, 1999.

Tennyson, Hallam. *Alfred Lord Tennyson—A Memoir by His Son*, vol. 2. London: Macmillan, 1897.

Thompson, G. R. *Poe's Fiction: Romantic Irony in the Gothic Tales*. Madison: University of Wisconsin Press, 1973.

Tuchman, Barbara. *The Proud Tower*. London: Papermac/Macmillan, 1997.

Verne, Jules. *Jules Verne—A Biography*. Trans. Roger Greaves. London: Macdonald and Jane's, 1976.

Villiers de L'Isle Adam. *Axël*. Trans. M. Gaddis Rose. London: Soho, 1986.

Wagner, Cosima. *Diaries*, vol. 1. Trans. Geoffrey Skelton. London: Collins, 1978.

Waugh, Evelyn. *The Loved One*. Harmondsworth: Penguin, 1977.

Whistler, Theresa. *The Life of Walter de la Mare*. London: Duckbacks, 2003.

Wilde, Oscar. *Complete Works of Oscar Wilde*. London: Collins, 1977.

Wilder, Thornton. *Theophilus North*. London: Allen Lane, 1974.

Wilson, Colin. *Rudolf Steiner: The Man and his Vision*. Wellingborough: Aquarian Press, 1985.

Wilson, Edmund. *Axel's Castle—A Study in the Imaginative Literature of 1870–1930*. London: Collier/Macmillan, 1991.

Wright, Thomas. *Oscar's Books—A Journey Around the Library of Oscar Wilde*. London: Vintage, 2009.

Yeats, W. B. *Collected Poems of W. B. Yeats*. London: Macmillan, 1950.

Index

Numbers in ***bold italics*** indicate pages with photographs.

À la recherche du temps perdu (Proust) 97
À Rebours (Huysmans) 36–37, 62, 132, 134
Abbate, Caroline 80
Abbott and Costello Meet the Mummy (dir. Charles Lamont, 1955) 161
Abraham, Edward 142
Ackroyd, Peter 71
Address, on the Subject of a Surveying and Exploring Expedition to the Pacific Ocean and South Seas (Reynolds) 188
"Adonais" (Shelley) 65, 67
The Adventures of Sherlock Holmes (television series) 153
Aida (Verdi) 147
Ainsworth, William Harrison 30
Aitken, Spottiswoode 172
Alan Parsons Project 34, 47, 80–81, 93, 160, 169, 176
Allan, John 47, 172, 173, 188
Allen, Irwin 32, 33, ***56***
Allende-Blin, Juan 80
Also Sprach Zarathustra (Strauss) 72
Ames, Leon 117
Amin, Idi 164
Amontillado, Op. 123 (Holbrooke) 47
"Ancient Sorceries" (Blackwood) 43
Anderson, Gerry 72
Anderson, Judith 85
Anderson, Michael 110, 178
Andriev, Andrei 175
Angel, Heather 148
"The Angel of the Odd" (Poe) 7, 17–21
"Annabel Lee" (Poe) 21–23, 48, 91, 156, 171–172, 173
Antigone (Sophocles) 110
Antonioni, Michelangelo 127, 132

Argento, Dario 38, 42, 90
Arianne et Barbe Bleu (Maeterlinck) 13
Armageddon (dir. Michael Bay, 1998) 54
Armytage, J.C. ***29***
Arnold, Jack 163, 164
Around the World in Eighty Days (dir. Michael Anderson, 1956) 178
Around the World in Eighty Days (Verne) 178
Asher, Jane 108, 109
"The Assignation" (Poe) 6, 7, 13, 22–29, 61, 65, 132
Attack of the Giant Leeches (dir. Bernard L. Kowalski, 1959) 164
Auden, W.H. 182
Auer, John H. 147
d'Aurévilly, Barbey 20
Austen, Jane 78
The Avengers (television series) 144–145, 173
The Avenging Conscience (dir. D.W. Griffith, 1914) 23, 171–173
Les Aveugles (Maeterlinck) 12
The Awakening (dir. Mike Newell, 1980) 115
Axël (Villiers de L'Isle Adam) 13, 105, 188

Bach, Johann Sebastian 138
Back to Methuselah (Shaw) 71
Baez, Joan 23
Baker, Roy Ward 112
Balcombe, Florence 130
Balfe, Michael William 23, 33–34
"The Ballad of Reading Goal" (Wilde) 20
"The Balloon Hoax" (Poe) 29, 102

Balmont Konstantin 34
Balsamo, Steve 118
"The Banshee" (Cowell) 87
Bantock, Sir Granville 22
Barber, Samuel 83
Bardot, Brigitte 185
Barker, Les 142
Barnett, Ivan 86, ***86***
Barron, Bebe 182
Barron, Louis 182
Baudelaire, Charles 2, 9–10, 12, 24, 36, 53, 59, 77, 79, 99, 105, 134, 135
Baxter, Les 87, 135, 136
Beardsley, Aubrey 3, 113
The Beatles 6, 76
Beaumont, Charles 94, 107, 109
Beaver, Harold 162, 179, 182
Beckett, Samuel 12, 132
Beckford, William 61
Beecham, Sir Thomas 22
Belford, Barbara 129–130
Bell, Andy 81
The Bells (Holbrooke) 35–36
"The Bells" (Poe) 33–36, 52, 91, 99, 171, 172
The Bells (Rachmaninoff) 6, 34–35
Bennett, Charles 51
Béranger, Pierre-Jean de 77, 79, 81, 83, 88
Berenice (dir. Geoffrey Ciani, 2004) 38
"Berenice" (Poe) 7, 15–16, 36–38, 42, 47, 91, 98
Bergman, Ingmar 108–109
Berkoff, Steven 171
Berlioz, Hector 106, 136
Bernard, James 14, 136
Bernard, Raymond 102
Bernhardt, Sarah 148
Berry, Chuck 127
Betti, Liliana 126
Bhagavad Gita 182

Index

Bierstadt, Albert 63
Birkinshaw, Alan 90
Birth of a Nation (dir. D.W. Griffith, 1915) 171
The Black Cat (dir. Edgar G. Ulmer, 1934) 4, 40, 44, 137
"The Black Cat" (Poe) 20, 38–44, 84, 85, 91, 111, 141, 147, 167, 172, 175
Black Friday (dir. Arthur Lubin, 1940) 120
The Black Scorpion (dir. Edward Ludwig, 1957) 164
Blackmer, Sidney 150
Blackwood, Algernon 43
Blackwood's Magazine 113
Blaha, Vladislav 82
Blake, Anton 47
Blavatsky, Helena Petrovna 73
Bleak House (Dickens) 74
Blood from the Mummy's Tomb (dir. Seth Holt, 1970) 115
Blossom, Robert 93
Blow Up (dir. Michelangelo Antonioni, 1966) 127, 132
Bogarde, Dirk 112
Bohn, John 147
Boileau, Pierre 177
"Bon-Bon" (Poe) 7, 66
Bosch, Hieronymous 142
Boulez, Pierre 81
Boulle, Pierre 110
Bourget, Paul 77
Brahms, Johannes 34
Bram Stoker's Legend of the Mummy (dir. Jeffrey Obrow, 1998) 115
Braun, Daniel von *18*, 19
"The Breakthrough" (Daphne du Maurier) 76
Bredell, Elwood 120
Brett, Jeremy 153
Brimstone and Treacle (Potter) 60–61
Britten, Benjamin 6, 83, 131
Broadway Journal 161
"The Bronze Horseman" (Pushkin) 112
Browning, Elizabeth Barrett 74
Browning, Robert 74
Browning, Tod 44
Brownrigg, S.F. 168
Bruns, Philip 93
Buck, David 89
Bulwer-Lytton, Edward (Lord Lytton) 16, 45, 90, 183, 184
Buranelli, Vincent 74
Bürger, Gottfried 98
Burton, Richard 27
Burton, Tim 66
Busoni, Ferruccio 82
Buttons, Red 33

Byron, George Gordon, Lord 7, 24–25, 26, 27, 29

Cabanne, Christy 120
Cabaret du Néant 149
The Cabinet of Dr. Caligari (dir. Robert Wiene, 1919) 42, 83, 84, 91, 117, 131
Caiano, Mario 26
Caidin, Martin 103
Caminito, Augusto 26, 27
Campbell, R. Wright 107, 109
Campton, David 89
Canning, Sir Launcelot 79, 91
Canova, Antonio 25
Caplet, André 6, 79, 82, 107
Carbone, Tony 140
Carpenter, Horace B. 40
"The Case of Charles Dexter Ward" (Lovecraft) 94–95
"The Case of the Purloined Letter" (dir. Val Guest, 1979) 153
The Cask of Amontillado (dir. Mario Cavalli, 2009) 47
"The Cask of Amontillado" (Poe) 8, 41, 44–48, 81, 84, 141, 171, 172
Cat People (dir. Jacques Tourneur, 1942) 43–44
Cavalli, Mario 47
Celle qui n'etait plus (aka *She Who Was No More*, Boileau & Narcejac) 177
Centre Play (television series) 184
Chabrol, Claude 126
Chamberlayne, William 182
Chaney, Lon, Jr. 94
Chapman, George 25
Chapman, Seymour 132
Charters, Spencer 137
Chéreau, Patrice 53
Childe Harold's Pilgrimage (Byron) 7, 27, 29
Chirico, Giorgio de 185
Choral Dramatic Symphony—Homage to E. A. Poe (Holbrooke) 49, 95
Christensen, Benjamin 40
A Christmas Carol (Dickens) 19
Church, Frederic E. 63
La Chute de la maison Usher (Debussy) 6, 12, 58, 59, 79–81, 90
La Chute de la maison Usher (dir. Jean Epstein, 1928) 84
Ciani, Geoffrey 38
Ciannelli, Eduardo 85
Cinq Semaines en ballon (Verne) 33
City in the Sea (aka *War-Gods of the Deep*, dir. Jacques Tourneur, 1965) *50*, 51–52

"The City in the Sea" (Poe) 6, 48–52
Clarens, Carlos 172
Clarke, Harry 3, 37, 55, 96, 113
Claude (Lorrain) 62
Clemens, Brian 173
Clemm, Maria ("Muddy") 67, 69
Clemm, Virginia 21, 67, 129
Clouzot, Henri-Georges 177, 178
Clouzot, Véra 177
Cocteau, Jean 99
Cohen, Robert Greer 11
Colbert, Robert **55**
Cole, Thomas 63
Coleridge, Samuel Taylor 48–49, 80, *122*, 122, 123, 166, 168, 172
A Collier's Friday Night (Lawrence) 105
Collier's Magazine 115
Collins, Joan 147
Collins, Michael 182
Collins, Wilkie 19, 166
"Colloquy of Monos and Una" (Poe) 10, 52–55
Comet in Moominland (Jansson) 53–54
Conan Doyle, Sir Arthur 116, 118, 152
Connor, Kevin 51
"The Conqueror Worm" (Poe) 5, 96, 106
Conrad, Joseph 168
Conte fantastique (Caplet) 82, 107
Les Contes d'Hoffmann (Offenbach) 27
"The Conversation of Eiros and Charmion" (Poe) 7, 52–55, 184
Conway, Tom 44
Coombes, Norman 90
Cooper, Alice 176
Cooper, Gladys 40
Cooper, James Fenimore 63–64
Copeland, Stewart 176
Cops (dir. Edward F. Cline & Buster Keaton, 1922) 17
Corman, Roger 3, 4, 41, 47, 58, 68, 69, *75*, 75, 76, 77, 82, 84, 85, 86–89, **87**, 90, 94, 98, 99, 100, 105, 106–109, *108*, 112, 113, 114, 135, 136, 137, 138–141, **139**, 147–148, **148**, 150, 154, 155, **155**, 169, 171
Corri, Adrienne 173, 174
The Corsican Brothers (Dumas) 184
Cotten, Joseph 181–182
Court, Hazel 109, 147, 150
Courtleigh, Stephen 85
Cowell, Henry 87
Crane, Kenneth G. 164

Crawford, Broderick 40
The Creeping Flesh (dir. Freddie Francis, 1973) 166
Crime and Punishment (dir. Michael Darlow, 1979) 176
Crime and Punishment (Dostoyevsky) 174–175
The Crime of Dr. Crespi (dir. John H. Auer, 1935) 147
Crispin, Judith 82
Cronenberg, David 74, 163
Crowley, Aleister 168, 169
Cruikshank, Andrew 27
Cuesta, Michael 174
Cushing, Peter 14, 88, 167
Cussak, John 155–156
Cyborg (Caidin) 103

Dahl, Dr. Nikolay 35
Dalí, Salvador 10, 171
Dallopiccola, Luigi 6
D'Alton, Hugo 81
Damon, Mark 86
Daniels, Anthony 184
D'Annunzio, Gabrielle 23, 27, 132–133
Dante 98, 136, 168
Danziger brothers 173
The Dark Side of the Moon (Pink Floyd) 34, 80
Darren, James **55**
Darwin, Charles 117
Dassin, Jules 173, 176
The Day of the Triffids (Wyndham) 53
De la terre à la lune (aka *From the Earth to the Moon,* Verne) 180–181
De Profundis (Wilde) 20–21
The Deadly Mantis (dir. Nathan Juran, 1957) 164
Death (Delville) 106
"Death and the Maiden" string quartet (Schubert) 137
"Death in Venice" (Mann) 21, 26
Death in Venice (dir. Luchino Visconti, 1971) 132
Debussy, Claude 6, 12, 22, 24, 29, 58–59, 77, 79–80, 82, 90, 95, 107, 136, 157
The Debussy Film (dir. Ken Russell, 1965) 89
"The December Night" (de Musset) 185
Deep Impact (dir. Mimi Leder, 1998) 54
Degouves de Nuncques, William 10
De la Mare, Walter 14
Delius, Frederick 64
Delon, Alain 185
Delville, Jean 106

Demonalatry (Remy) 43
Depp, Johnny 66
Derleth, August 93
"A Descent into the Maelström" (Poe) 55–57
"The Devil in the Belfry" (Poe) 7, 57–61
The Devil Rides Out (dir. Terence Fisher, 1968) 156
The Devils (dir. Ken Russell, 1971) 143
The Devil's Elixir (aka *Die Elixiere des Teufels,* Hoffmann) 183
Le Diable dans le belfroi (Debussy) 58–59, 61
Les Diaboliques (dir. Henri-Georges Cluzot, 1955) 177–178
Diaghilev, Sergei 107
Dickens, Charles 19, 36, 74
"Diddling—Considered as One of the Exact Sciences" (Poe) 9
Diller, Phyllis 40
Dr. Cyclops (dir. Ernest B. Schoedsack, 1940) 163
Dr. Jekyll and Mr. Hyde (Stevenson) 184
Dr. Phibes Rises Again (dir. Robert Fuest, 1972) 19
Dr. Who (television series) 55
The Domain of Arnheim (Magritte) 62
"The Domain of Arnheim" (Poe) 4, 10, 13, 61–64, 131, 132
The Doors 68
The Doors of Perception (Huxley) 68
"Die Doppelgänger" (Heine) 183
"Die Doppelgänger" (Hoffmann) 183
Dor, Karin 142
Doré, Gustave 157, **158**, **159**
Dostoyevsky, Fyodor 174, 175
Douglas, Gordon 163
Dracula (dir. Tod Browning, 1931) 44, 84, 117
Dracula (Stoker) 97, 115, 129, 135–136, 167
Dracula Has Risen from the Grave (dir. Freddie Francis, 1968) 116, 142
"A Dream Within a Dream" (Poe) 22
"Dreamland" (Poe) 48
Dreßler, Georg-Sebastian **18**, 19
Dréville, Jean 102
Dreyer, Carl 127, 146, 150
"The Duc de L'Omelette" (Poe) 7, 64–66
Duchen, Jessica 29
Dullin, Charles 102
Du Maurier, Daphne 76
Du Maurier, George 75–76

Dumas, Alexandre 184
Dunning, George 68
Dunst, Kirsten **54**
Dupois-Mazuel, Henry 102
Dylan, Bob 118

Easthope, Antony 104
L'Eclisse (dir. Michelangelo Antonioni, 1962) 132
Eggert, Nicole 114
Einstein, Albert 52, 69
Eisner, Lotte H. 175
"Eldorado" (Poe) 23
Elektra (Strauss) 83
"Eleonora" (Poe) 66–69, 166
Eleonora Bassoon Quintet (Holbrooke) 68
Elgar, Sir Edward 35
Eliot, T.S. 8
Die Elixiere des Teufels (aka *The Devil's Elixirs,* Hoffmann) 183
Ellerbe, Harry 88
Elliott, Denholm 60, 89
Ellmann, RIchard 57
Emerson, Ralph Waldo 63
Emmert, Alexander 100
"Endymion" (Keats) 65
English, Thomas Dunn 45
Ens, Philip 83
Epstein, Jean 84–85, 88, 90
Ernst, Max 20, 157
Escott, T.H.S. 184
Eshley, Norman 184
Esper, Dwain 39
Etude pour le palais hanté (Schmitt) 95
"Eulalie" (Poe) 48
Eureka (Poe) 10, 31, 52, 69–74, 162, 183, 188
Eve, Alice 156
An Evening of Edgar Allan Poe (dir. Kenneth Johnson, 1970) 163, 171
Ewers, Hanns Heinz 185
Exequy (King) 25, 61

Fabian 33
Fact in Mesmerism (Townsend) 74
The Facts in the Case of E. A. Poe (Sinclair) 15, 42
"The Facts in the Case of M. Valdemar" (Poe) 4, 8, 35, 42, 74–76, 91, 156
The Faery Queen (Spenser) 49
Fahey, Myrna 86
Faithfull, Marianne 23
The Fall of the House of Usher (dir. Alan Birkinshaw, 1989) 90
The Fall of the House of Usher (dir. Ivan Barnett, 1949) 86, **86**
The Fall of the House of Usher

(dir. Jan Svankmajer, 1982) 89–90
The Fall of the House of Usher (dir. Melville Webber & James Sibley Watson, 1928) 77, *78*, 79, 83–84
The Fall of the House of Usher (Glass) 82
"The Fall of the House of Usher" (Poe) 7, 8, 10, 11, 12, 14, 58, 76–92, 93, 95, 114, 115, 140, 147, 164
Fall of the House of Usher (Sitsky) 81–82
The Fall of the House of Usher (Van Der Graaf Generator) 81
The Fall of the Louse of Usher: A Gothic Tale for the 21st Century (dir. Ken Russell, 2002) 23, 89, 90–92
Fantastic Voyage (dir. Richard Fleischer, 1966) 163
Fantazius Mallare (Hecht) 63
Farmer, Mimsy 42
Faust (dir. F. W. Murnau, 1928) 83
Faust (Goethe) 61, 70, 183
Fear and Trembling (Kierkegaarde) 60
The Fearless Vampire Killers (dir. Roman Polanski, 1968) 84
Fellini, Federico 126–7, *127*, 128
Ffrangcon-Davies, Gwen 43
Finney, Jack 115
The First Men in the Moon (H.G. Wells) 181
Fisher, Terence 156, 167, 174
Five Weeks in a Balloon (dir. Irwin Allen, 1962) *32*, 33
The Flame (D'Annunzio) 27
Fleischer, Richard 163
Florey, Robert 93, *116*, 117
Fludd, Robert 70, 78
The Fly (dir. David Cronenberg, 1986) 163
The Fly (dir. Kurt Neumann, 1958) 163
Fonda, Jane *111*, 112
Fonda, Peter 112
Foote, Arthur 33
Forbidden Planet (dir. Fred M. Wilcox, 1956) 182
Ford, John 127
The Forgotten (dir. S.F. Brownrigg, 1973) 168
Fornani, Bruno 106
Foster, Lawrence 83
"Four Beasts in One" (Poe) 7
Fowler, George 153
Fox, Sidney 117
Francesca da Rimini (Tchaikovsky) 136
Francis, Derek 98

Francis, Freddie 14, 86, 116, 150, 166
Frankel, Cyril 43
Frankenstein (dir. James Whale, 1931) 117, 150
Frankenstein (Shelley) 26, 161
Frankenstein and the Monster from Hell (dir. Terence Fisher, 1974) 167
Frankenstein Created Woman (dir. Terence Fisher, 1967) 174
Frankenstein—The True Story (dir. Jack Smight, 1973) 160
Frederick the Great 101
Freud, Sigmund 21, 38, 83, 85, 96, 104, 109, 135
Freund, Karl 117
Friedlander, Louis (aka Lew Landers) 14, 137, 138, 140, *155*
Friedrich, Caspar David 186
From the Earth to the Moon (aka *De la terre à la lune*, Verne) 180–181
From the Earth to the Moon (dir. Byron Haskin, 1957) 181
Fuest, Robert 19, 93
Fulco, Lucio 41–42, 43, 90
The Full Treatment (aka *Stop Me Before I Kill*, dir. Val Guest, 1960) 102
Fuseli, Henry 20

Gage, Leona 114
Galás, Diamanda 44
Galeen, Henrik 186
Garcet, Henri 180
Gatto Nero (dir. Lucio Fulco, 1981) 41–42
Geniune (dir. Robert Wiene, 1920) 131
Getty, Gordon 82–83
Ghislanzoni, Antonio 147
"Ghost of Venice" (*Supernatural* episode, dir. Claude Whatham, 1977) 26
The Ghoul (dir. Freddie Francis, 1975) 86
"The Giaour" (Byron) 26
Gifford, Denis 3
Gilbert, W. Stephen 60
Gilchrist, William Wallace 33
Gilman, Richard 10, 77
Gilmore, Lowell 38
Gilmore, Peter 55
Glanville, Joseph 55, 57, 75, 99
Glass, Philip 55, 56, 77, 82
Gliddon, George Robins 161
Godard, Jean-Luc 130
Goethe, Johann Wolfgang von 61, 70, 183
"The Gold-Bug" (Poe) 92–93
Goldblum, Jeff 163

Gordon, Stuart 142
Gorer, Geoffrey 20
Götterdämmerung (Wagner) 27, 112
Gottowt, John 185
Goya, Francisco 20
Great Expectations (Dickens) 114
Green, Charles 30, 31, 33
Green, Guy 178
Greene, David 93
Greene, Richard 153
Griffith, D.W. 23, 171–173
Griswold, Rufus 156
Groening, Matt *154*
Grönemeyer, Herbert 81
Grossmann, Larry 88
Gudden, Dr. Bernhard von 167
Guest, Val 153
Guiccioli, Count Alessandro 24
Guiccioli, Countess Teresa Gamba 24–25
Gulliver's Travels (Swift) 163
Gwynne, Anne 40

Hackady, Hal 88
Hall, Anthony Michael 93
Haller, Daniel 86, 114, 140
Hamm, Nick 152
Hammil, Peter 81
The Hands of Orlac (dir. Robert Wiene, 1924) 174
Hardwicke, Sir Cedric 33
Hardy, Robert 26
Harry, Debbie 52
Hart, Susan 51
Harwood, Gwen 81
Haskin, Byron 181
Hatfield, Hurd 38
The Haunted Palace (dir. Roger Corman, 1963) 88, 94
"The Haunted Palace" (Poe) 49, 77, 79, 80, 93–95, 168
The Haunting of Morella (dir. Jim Wynorski, 1990) 114–115
Hawks, Howard 147
Haydn, Richard 33
Hayles, Brian 51
Heart of Darkness (Conrad) 168
Heaven and Hell (Huxley) 68
Heaven and Hell (Swedenborg) 78
Hecht, Ben 62
Hedda Gabler 173
Hegel, G.W.F. 63, 71, 74
Heine, Heinrich 22, 183
Heinrich von Ofterdingen (Novalis) 105
Helmey, Erin Leigh 100
Henriksen, Lance 143
Henson, William Samuel 30
Herbert, Hugh 40
Hermes Trimegistus 70

Herrmann, Bernard 30
Hessler, Gordon 117–118, *128*
Heston, Charlton 110
Heyes, Douglas 149
Heyward, Louis M. 51
Hinds, Anthony 20
Hinds, Samuel S. 138
Hirsch, David H. 65
Histoires extraordinaires/Spirits of the Dead/Tre passi nel delirio (dir. Roger Vadim, Louis Malle, Federico Fellini, 1968) *111*, 112, *127*, 185
Hitchcock, Alfred 55, 60, 80, 86, 174, 178
Hitler, Adolf 30, 164, 186
Hoffman, Harold 41
Hoffmann, E.T.A. 27, 53, 102, 183, 184, 186
Hog Wild (dir. James Parrott, 1930) 17
Hogg, James 183, 184
Holbrooke, Josef 6, 22, 35, 47, 49–50, 55, 68, 95, 107, 136, 157
Holder, Geoffrey 93
The Hole (dir. Nick Hamm, 2001) 152
Hollingdale, R. J. 72
Hollins, John 30
Hollond, Robert 30, 33
Holt, Seth 115, 140, 150
Home, Daniel Dunglas 74
Honey, I Shrunk the Kids (dir. Joe Johnston, 1989) 164
"Hop-Frog" (Poe) 8, 84, 109
Hope, Anthony 184
Hopkins, Anthony 37
The House of Doctor Dee (Ackroyd) 71
House of Usher (dir. Roger Corman, 1960) 4, 77, 82, 84, 85, 86–89, *87*, 114
Housman, A.E. 23
"How to Write a Blackwood Article" (Poe) 7, 8, 134, 144
Hudson River School artists 63
Hunter, Tab 51
Hurt, John 176
Huxley, Aldous 68, 166
Huysmans, Joris-Karl 36, 62, 63, 98, 113, 132, 148
"Hymn" (Poe) 49

Ibsen, Henrik 131, 173
"The Imp of the Perverse" (Poe) 20, 21, 38, 39, 172
In a Glass Darkly (Le Fanu) 146
In Pace Requiescat (Sitsky) 82
The Incredible Shrinking Man (Jack Arnold, 1957) 163
The Incredible Shrinking Woman (dir. Joel Schumacher, 1981) 163
Inferno (Strindberg) 166
L'Innocente (D'Annunzio) 133
Invasion of the Body Snatchers (dir. Don Siegel, 1956) 115
Iron Maiden 118
Isherwood, Christopher 160
"The Island of the Fay" (Poe) 131, 132
"Israfel" (Poe) 23

James, Henry 6, 8, 120, 121, 184
James, William Milbourne 30
Jansson, Tove 53
Jazz Passengers 52
Jeux (Debussy) 107
The Jewel of Seven Stars (Stoker) 115, 160–161
Johnson, Kenneth 171
Johnston, James 91, 92
Johnston, Joe 164
Johnston, Oliver 100
Le Joueur d'échecs (dir. Raymond Bernard, 1927) 102
Julian, Rupert 117
Jung, Carl Gustav 72–73, 97
Juran, Nathan 164
Justine (de Sade) 165

Kant, Immanuel 62
Kaplan, Sol 173
Karina, Anna 130
Karloff, Boris 4, 40, 51, 137, 138, 149–150, 154, 169, *170*
Kassovitz, Peter 130
Keaton, Buster 17
Keats, John 65, 67, 148
Kelley, Edgar Stillman 136
Kempelen, Johann Wolfgang Ritter von 101, 102
Kerr, John 140, 141
Khnopff, Fernand 105
Kierkegaard, Søren 59–60, 61
Kietel, Harvey 42
King, Henry, Bishop of Chichester 25, 61
King Kong (dir. Merian C. Cooper & Ernest B. Schoedsack, 1933) 117
"King Pest" (Poe) 7
The Kingdom of Evil (Hecht) 63
Kinski, Klaus 26
Kitchen, Michael 60
Kjerulf, Halfdan 33
Korngold, Erich Wolfgang 29
Koshkin, Nikita 82
Kowalski, Bernard L. 164
Kracauer, Siegfried 186
Krämer, Felix 20
Krauss, Werner 186

Kubin, Alfred 3, 157, 164
"Kubla Khan" (Coleridge) 48–49
Kubrick, Stanley 71, 72, 73, 90
Kyr, Robert 80

Lacey, Catherine 170, *170*
Lady of Lyons (Bulwer-Lytton) 184
Lady Windermere's Fan (Wilde) 132
Lahee, Henry C. 33–34
Laine, Frankie 23
The Lair of the White Worm (Stoker) 135
"The Lake. To —" (Poe) 48
Lamont, Charles 161
Land of the Pharaohs (dir. Howard Hawks, 1955) 147
Landau, Martin 72
Landers, Lew (aka Louis Friedlander) 14, 137, 138, 140, *155*
"Landor's Cottage" (Poe) 4, 131, 132
Lang, Fritz 83
Lanza, Joseph 92
The Last Days of Pompeii (Bulwer-Lytton) 45–46
The Last Man (Shelley) 110
The Last of the Mohicans (Cooper) 64
Laura (dir. Otto Preminger, 1944) 119, 131
Laurel and Hardy 17, 19
Laven, Arnold 164
Lawrence, D.H. 5, 9, 11, 30, 77–78, 105
Lawrence, Patricia 60
Lawson, Gregory 142
Lee, Christopher 4, 88, 90, 128, *140*, 141, 142, 166
Lee, David 112
Leeman, Fred 46
Le Fanu, J. Sheridan 146, 166–167
Le Mesurier, John 52
Lennon, John 67
"Lenore" (Bürger) 98
Leroux, Gaston 117, 118
Lewin, Alfred 38
Lewis, Matthew Gregory 143
Lewton, Val 43
Liberace 149
"Ligeia" (Poe) 3, 4, 7, 8, 10, 13, 23, 41, 55, 65, 75, 91, 95–101, 113, 114, 130, 141, 147, 184
Lights Out (television series) 85
"Lionising" (Poe) 7
Liska, Pavel 151, 165
Liszt, Franz 16, 44, 106, 136, 137, 157
Lloyd, Harold 17
Lockspeiser, Edward 6, 12

Loftus, Cecilia 40
Logan's Run (dir. Michael Anderson, 1976) 110
Logan's Run (Nolan) 110
Lom, Herbert 118
Lommel, Ulli 156
Loncraine, Richard 60
Loos, Theodor 186
Lorre, Peter 33, 41, 47, 155, 175, 176
"Loss of Breath" (Poe) 7, 66
"The Lost Reflection" (Hoffmann) 27
Lovecraft, H.P. 74, 93, 94–95
The Loved One (dir. Tony Richardson, 1965) 149
The Loved One (Waugh) 149
Lovich, Lene 81
Lowe, George 22, 35, 49, 95, 107, 157, 160
Lowell, James Russell 5, 8, 70
Lubin, Arthur 120
Lucas, George 184
Lucas, Josh 174
"Lucy in the Sky with Diamonds" (The Beatles) 68
Ludwig, Edward 164
Ludwig II of Bavaria 167
Lugosi, Bela 14, 40, *116*, 117, 118, 137, 154, *155*
Lunacy (aka *Silena,* dir. Jan Svankmajer, 2005) 151–152, 165
Luther, Martin 112

MacAdams, Anne 168
Macbeth (Shakespeare) 155
MacDowell, Edward 34
Machen, Arthur 14
Machiavelli, Niccolò 78
MacKenzie, Scott 68
Maelzel, Johann Nepomuk 101, 102
"Maelzel's Chess-Player" (Poe) 101–102
Maeterlinck, Maurice 6, 12–13, 22, 79
Magee, Patrick 42, 109
The Magic Mountain (Mann) 21
Magritte, René 10, 62
Mahler, Gustav 26
Majors, Lee *103*, 104
Mallarmé, Stéphane 11, 95
Malle, Louis 126, 185
Man and Superman (Shaw) 65–66, 71
"The Man Who Was Used Up" (Poe) 7, 8, 102–104
Manet, Edouard 3, 157
Manfred Mann 68
Maniac (dir. Dwain Esper, 1934) 39–40
Mann, Thomas 9, 21, 26
Manns, August 157
Mansions de la Locura (aka *Mansions of Madness,* dir Juan Moctezuma, 1973) 167–168, 169
Marais, Jean 99
Marlow, Scott 150
Martin, Nikolaus 143
Martini, Alberto 3
Mason, James 174
Mason, Thomas Monck 30, 33
The Masque of the Red Death (dir. Roger Corman, 1964) 4, 8, 84, 107–109, *108*, 112, 171
The Masque of the Red Death (Holbrooke) 107
"The Masque of the Red Death" (Poe) 13, 14, 82, 85, 104–109, 138, 156
The Master (de la Mare) 14
Mathers, Samuel MacGregor 57
Matheson, Richard 88, 114, 140, 141, 163
Matinee Theater (television series) 85
Matthews, Lester 138
Maugham, W. Somerset 141
Maurier, Daphne du 76
Maurier, George du 75–76
Maxwell, Frank 95
McCallum, David 114, 115
McClure, Doug 55
McGoohan, Patrick 108
McGreevy, Oliver 89
McTeigue, James 23, 143, 155
Medina, Patricia 150
Die Meistersinger von Nürnberg (Wagner) 59
Melancholia (dir. Lars von Trier, 2011) *54,* 54–55
Méliès, Georges 181
"Mellonta Tauta" (Poe) 110–111, 162, 188
Melville, Herman 93
Mercero Antonio 152
Mesmer, Franz Anton 74
"Mesmeric Revelation" (Poe) 70, 98–99
Messager, André 61
Messiaen, Olivier 136
"Metzengerstein" (Poe) 7, 65, 66, 111–112, 130, 169
Meurisse, Paul 177
Michelangelo 25
A Midsummer Night's Dream (dir. Max Reinhardt, 1935) 173
The Midwich Cuckoos (Wyndham) 53
Miles, John 48
Milland, Ray 69, 147, *148*
Miller, Mary 89
Miller, William 53
Milton, John 141
The Mind Beyond (television series) 76
Mitchell, Bill 4
Moby Dick (Melville) 93
Moctezuma, Juan 167–168, 169
Monckton, Patrick 47
The Monk (Lewis) 143
"Monos and Diamonos" (Bulwer-Lytton) 183–184
Monster from Green Hell (dir. Kenneth G. Crane, 1957) 164
Monster That Challenged the World (dir. Arnold Laven, 1957) 164
"Moon Landing" (Auden) 182
Moore, Albert 90
Moore, George 10
Moreau, Gustave 37
"Morella" (Poe) 4, 7, 41, 112–115
Mörike, Eduard 22
Morris, Ernest 173
Morris, Sarah Jane 81
Morrison, Jim 68
Morse, Barry 72
"MS. Found in a Bottle" (Poe) 7
Müller, Hans 29
Muller, Robert 26
The Mummy: A Tale of the Twenty-Second Century (Webb) 110, 161
The Mummy—or Ramses the Damned (Rice) 161
The Mummy's Hand (dir. Christy Cabanne, 1940) 120
Murders in the Rue Morgue (dir. Robert Florey, 1932) 117, 118
Murders in the Rue Morgue (dir. Gordon Hessler, 1971) 117–118
The Murders in the Rue Morgue (dir. Jeannot Szwarc, 1986) 118
"The Murders in the Rue Morgue" (Poe) 15, 40–41, 91, 109, 115–118, *116*, 119, 152, 155, 172, 177
Murnau, F.W. 83
Murphy, Michael 97
Murray, John 25
Musset, Alfred de 185
Myaskovsky, Nikolai 6
The Mysteries of Udolpho (Radcliffe) 131
Mystery and Imagination (television series) 89
The Mystery of Marie Rogêt (aka *The Phantom of Paris,* dir. Phil Rosen, 1942) 119–120
"The Mystery of Marie Rogêt" (Poe) 105, 118–120, 152, 156

The Mystery of the Yellow Room (Leroux) 117
"Mystification" (Poe) 7

Nadar (Gaspard-Félix Tournachon) 33
Napoleon 134, 175
Narcejac, Thomas 177
The Narrative of Arthur Gordon Pym (Poe) 36, 42, 48, 93, 97, 134, 179, 188
"The Naval Treaty" (Conan Doyle) 152
Nero 164
Neumann, Kurt 163
"Never Bet the Devil Your Head" (Poe) 7, 126–128
Newell, Mike 115
Newell, Patrick 153
Newman, Ernest 35
Die Nibelungen (dir. Fritz Lang, 1924) 83
Nietzsche, Friedrich 21, 72, 73, 151
Night and Morning (Bulwer-Lytton) 16
Nightmare (dir. Freddie Francis, 1964) 150, 178
Nightmares from the Mind of Poe (dir. Ric White, 2006) 47, 150–151, 173
Niven, David 178
Nolan, William F. 110
Nolde, Emil 187
Norris, Geoffrey 35
Northanger Abbey (Austen) 78, 131
Novalis 105

The Oblong Box (dir. Gordon Hessler, 1969) **128**, 128–129
"The Oblong Box" (Poe) 128–129
Obrow, Jeffrey 115
Occult Diary (Strindberg) 166
The Ocean 52
Ochs, Phil 34
Oedipus Rex (Sophocles) 100
Offenbach, Jacques 27, 186
Ogilvy, Ian 170
The 101 Days of Sodom (de Sade) 165
Oppenheimer, Robert 182
Orledge, Robert 58, 79, 80
Orphée (dir. Jean Cocteau, 1950) 99
Oswald, Robert 167
Otterson, Jack 120
Ouspenskaya, Maria 119–120
"The Oval Portrait" (Poe) 16, 84, 98, 129–131
Owen Wingrave (Britten) 131

Paget, Debra **75**
Palin, Michael 178
Palladio, Andrea 4
Pallance, Jack 14
Palmer, Tony 27
Paradise Lost (Milton) 141
Paranoiac (dir. Freddie Francis, 1963) 150
Parmalee, Ted 174
Parsifal (Wagner) 68, 107, 142
Parsons, Alan 19, 34, 48, 80, 81, 93, 107, 160, 175
Pasolini, Pier Paolo 127
Pavillion d'Armide (Tcherepnin) 131
Payne, Laurence 173
Peck, Brian 143
Pélleas et Mélisande (Debussy) 6, 12–13
Pélleas et Mélisande (Maeterlinck) 79
The Pendulum, the Pit and Hope (dir. Jan Svankmajer, 1983) 142–143
Penerecki, Krzysztof 81
Le Penseur (Rodin) 137
Périer, François 99
The Phantom of Paris (aka *The Mystery of Marie Rogêt*, dir. Phil Rosen, 1942) 119–120
The Phantom of the Opera (dir. Rupert Julian, 1925) 117
The Phantom of the Opera (dir. Terence Fisher, 1962) 118
Pharronida (Chamberlayne) 182
"The Philosophy of Composition" (Poe) 11, 67
"Philosophy of Furniture" (Poe) 131–134, **133**
Philosophy of Mind (Hegel) 71
The Phone Box (dir. Antonio Mercero, 1972) 152
Il piacere (D'Annunzio) 132–133
Piano Sonata in B minor (Liszt) 137
Pickering, Donald 153
The Picture of Dorian Gray (dir. Alfred Lewin) 38
The Picture of Dorian Gray (Wilde) 20, 36–37, 46, 84, 129, 132, 134
Pierce, Maggie 114
Pink Floyd 34, 80
The Pit (dir. Edward Abraham, 1962) 142
Pit and the Pendulum (dir. Roger Corman, 1961) 4, 69, 135, 136, 138–141, **139**
The Pit and the Pendulum (dir. Stuart Gordon, 1991) 143
The Pit and the Pendulum (Holbrooke) 136

The Pit and the Pendulum (Kelley) 136
"The Pit and the Pendulum" (Poe) 12, 14, 16, 85, 90, 130, 133–144, 171
The Planet of the Apes (Boulle) 110
The Planet of the Apes (dir. Franklin F. Schaffner, 1968) 110, 111
Platen, August von 105
Pleasence, Donald 90
Plowright, Joan 60
Plummer, Christopher 27
Plumpton, Alfred 34
Poems of 1831 (Poe) 80
"The Poetic Principle" (Poe) 9
Polanski, Roman 84, 150, 151
The Police 176
Pomerantz, Edward 93
Potter, Dennis 60
Powell, Andrew 80, 81
Powell, Michael 27
"A Predicament" (Poe) 7, 128, 144–146
Les Préludes (Liszt) 137
The Premature Burial (dir. Roger Corman, 1962) 147–148, **148**, 150
"The Premature Burial" (Poe) 8, 15, 146–152, 165
Preminger, Otto 119, 131
Pressburger, Emeric 27
Price, Vincent 4, 19, 41, 47, 51, 68, **75**, 75, 84, 85, 86, **87**, 89, 94, 98, 100, 107–109, **108**, 114, 128, 137, 140, 154–155, **155**, 163, 171
Prideaux, William 30
The Prisoner (television series) 108
The Prisoner of Zenda (Hope) 184
The Private Memoirs and Confessions of a Justified Sinner (Hogg) 183
Prometheus—The Poem of Fire (Scriabin) 73
The Proud Tower (Tuchman) 49
Proust, Marcel 97
Psycho (dir. Alfred Hitchcock, 1960) 60, 174
Pulman, Jack 176
Purce, Jill 56–57
"The Purloined Letter" (Poe) 119, 152–153, 154
Pushkin, Alexander 111

Rachmaninoff, Sergei 6, 34–35
Rackham, Arthur 3, 55, 84, 130
Radcliffe, Ann 27, 131
Raiders of the Lost Ark (dir. Steven Spielberg, 1981) 74

Ramayana 68
Randolph, Jane 44
Raskolnikoff (dir. Josef von Sternberg, 1935) 175
Raskolnikow (dir. Robert Wiene, 1923) 175
Rathbone, Basil 40, 51, 75–76
Ravel, Maurice 106, 107
The Raven (dir. James McTeigue, 2012) 23, 144, 155–156
The Raven (dir. Lew Landers, 1935) 14, 137–138, 154, **155**
The Raven (dir. Roger Corman, 1963) 4, 58, 69, 137, 154–155, **155**
The Raven (dir. Ulli Lommel, 2006) 156–157
The Raven (Holbrooke) 157
"The Raven" (Poe) 21, 41, 98, 114, 129, 153–160, *158*, *159*
The Raven (Slatkin) 160
The Raven and Other Poems (Poe) 74
The Razor's Edge (Maugham) 141
Rebecca (dir. Alfred Hitchcock, 1940) 86
Redon, Odilon 3, 10, 37, 46, 106, 157, 176
Reed, Oliver 89, 90, 143
Reeves, Jim 23
Reeves, Michael 169, **170**
Reinhardt, Max 173
Reinl, Harald **140**, 141
Remy, Nicolas 43
Renoir, Jean 126
Repulsion (dir. Roman Polanski, 1965) 151
"The Resident Patient" (Conan Doyle) 153
The Return of Sherlock Holmes (television series) 153
"The Revanant" (de la Mare) 14
Reynold, Jeremiah 188
Das Rheingold (Wagner) 53
Rhodes, Anthony 23
Ricci, Rona de 143
Rice, Anne 26, 161
Richardson, Joanna 157
Richardson, Tony 149
Rienzi (Bulwer-Lytton) 45
Riley, Bridget 174
The Rime of the Ancient Mariner (Coleridge) *122*, 122, 168
Der Ring des Nibelungen (Wagner) 39, 52, 53
Roberton, Sir Hugh S. 34
Roberton, Kenneth 34
Rodin, Auguste 137
Roeg, Nicolas 108
Roemheld, Heinz 44
Roma (dir. Federico Fellini, 1972) 127

Romeo and Juliet (dir. Franco Zeffirelli, 1968) 160
Romero, George A. 42
Rope (dir. Alfred Hitchcock, 1948) 178
Rosay, François 102
The Rose and the Key (Le Fanu) 166–167
Rosemary's Baby (dir. Roman Polanski, 1968) 150
Rosen, Phil 119, 120
Rosmersholm (Ibsen) 131
Rossetti, Christina 113
Rossetti, Dante Gabriel 23, 97, 98
Ruddigore (Gilbert & Sullivan) 131
Russell, Elizabeth 44
Russell, Harriet 147
Russell, Ken 89, 90, 91, 92, 143
Ryan, Ken 76
Rye, Stellan 185–186

Sade, Marquis de 151, 164
Safety Last (dir. Fred C. Nemeyer & Sam Taylor, 1923) 17
"San Francisco" (MacKenzie) 68
Sanders, George 181–182
"The Sandman" (Hoffmann) 102
Sangster, Jimmy 178
Sätty, Wilfried 3, 55
Scanners (dir. David Cronenberg, 1981) 74
Schelling, Friedrich Wilhelm Joseph 113
Schildkraut, Joseph 173, 176
Die Schlangengrube und das Pendel (aka *The Torture Chamber of Dr. Sadism*, dir. Harald Reinl, 1967) **140**, 141–142
Schlegel, Augustus William 187
Schmitt, Florent 6, 29, 77, 95
Schoedsack, Ernest B. 163
Schoenberg, Bert 88
Schopenhauer, Arthur 71, 107
Schubert, Franz Peter 137, 183
Schumacher, Joel 163
Schumann, Robert 22, 166
Schuré, Edouard 69
Schwabe, Carlos 20, 105
Scott, George, C. 118
Scott, Sir Walter 64, 150
Scriabin, Alexander 73
"The Second Coming" (Yeats) 162–163
"The Second Stain" (Conan Doyle) 152–153
Un Semaine de bonté (Ernst) 157
The Seventh Seal (dir. Ingmar Bergman, 1957) 108
"Shadow" (Poe) 7

Shakespeare, William 19, 105, 111, 127, 134, 155, 172
The Shape of Things to Come (Wells) 110
Shaw, Byam 68
Shaw, George Bernard 2, 65–66, 71
She Who Was No More (aka *Celle qui n'etait plus*, Boileau & Narcejac) 177
Shelley, Mary 26, 88, 110, 161
Shelley, Percy Bysshe 65, 67, 110
Shepherd, Elizabeth 68, 98, 100
Sheridan, Francis 4
Sheybal, Vladek 89
The Shining (dir. Stanley Kubrick, 1980) 90
The Shout (dir. Jerzy Skolimowsky, 1978) 171
Shubik, Irene 76
The Shuttered Room (dir. David Greene, 1967) 93
The Sickness Unto Death (Kierkegaarde) 59–60
Siddal, Elizabeth 97
Siegel, Don 115
Signoret, Simone 177
Silena (aka *Lunacy*, dir. Jan Svankmejer, 2005) 151–152, 165
Silence (Myaskovsky) 6
"Silence" (Poe) 48
"Silence—A Fable" (Poe) 49, 184
The Silence of the Lambs (dir. Jonathan Demme, 1991) 37–38
Silent Running (dir. Douglas Trumbull, 1972) 53
Silverman, David 153
Silverman, Kenneth 3, 8, 21, 45, 48, 52, 67, 92, 109, 113, 156
Simon, Simone 43
The Simpsons 153–154, **154**
Sinclair, Andrew 15, 42
The Singer Not the Song (dir. Roy Ward Baker, 1961) 112
Il sistema della dolcezzi (Tosotti) 168
Sitsky, Larry 81–82
The Six Million Dollar Man (television series) *103*, 103–104
Skolimowski, Jerzy 171
Slatkin, Leonard 160
Smight, Jack 160
Smith, Chris Judge 81
Smith, Kent 44
Snoopy! (Grossman/Hackady) 88
The Snorkel (dir. Guy Green, 1958) 178
"Some Words with a Mummy" (Poe) 7, 8, 160–162, 188
Somervell, Sir Arthur 23
Sophocles 100, 110

The Sorcerers (dir. Michael Reeves, 1967) 169–170, **170**
Sousa, John Philip 23
The Southern Literary Messenger 134
Southey, Robert 47
Space 1999 (television series) 72
"The Spectacles" (Poe) 130, 162
Spenser, Edmund 49
"The Sphinx" (Poe) 130, 162–164, 171
"Spirits of the Dead" (Poe) 126
Spirits of the Dead (aka *Tre passi nel delirio/Histoires extraordinaires,* dir. Roger Vadim, Louis Malle, Federico Fellini, 1968) **111**, 112, **127**, 185
"The Squaw" (Stoker) 141
Staininger, Michael 100
Stamp, Terence 96, 127, **127**
Star Wars (dir. George Lucas, 1977) 184
Starship Troopers (dir. Paul Verhoeven, 1997) 164
Steele, Barbara 140
Steiner, Rudolf 73
Stern, Herbert 83
Sternberg, Josef von 175
Stevenson, Robert Louis 92, 167, 184
Sting 60
Stockhausen, Karlheinz 81
Stoker, Bram 88, 97, 98, 115, 129, 130, 135, 141, 160–161, 167
Stop Me Before I Kill (aka *The Full Treatment,* dir. Val Guest, 1960) 102
Stradl, Ann 90
StrAngel (dir. Georg-Sebastian Dreßler, Daniel von Braun, 2013) **18**, 19
Strauss, Richard 50, 72, 83
Strindberg, August 166
Stroeheim, Erich von 147
Strong, George Templeton 23
The Student: A Series of Papers (Bulwer-Lytton) 183
The Student of Prague (dir. Arthur Robinson, 1935) 186
The Student of Prague (dir. Henrik Galeen, 1926) 186
The Student of Prague (dir. Stellan Rye, 1913) 185–186
The Suicide Club (Stevenson) 167
Sullan, Jack 136
Sully, Thomas 133
"Supernatural Horror in Literature" (Lovecraft) 94
Svankmajer, Jan 89, 142–143, 151, 165, 166
Swanson, Jillian 157
Swart, Rufus 90

Swedenborg, Emanuel 78
Sweet, Blanche 172
Swift, Jonathan 163
Sylvester, Terry 48
Symmes, John Cleaves, Jr. 124, 125, 88
Symphonie fantastique (Berlioz) 106, 136
"The System of Doctor Tarr and Professor Fether" (Poe) 91, 109, 151, 164–169
Le Système du Docteur Goudron et du Professeur Plume (dir. Maurice Tourneur, 1913) 167
Szwarc, Jeannot 118

"A Tale of Jerusalem" (Poe) 7
"A Tale of the Ragged Mountains" (Poe) 8, 169–171, 184
Tales of Hoffmann (dir. Michael Powell and Emeric Pressburger, 1951)
Tales of Hoffmann (Offenbach) 186
Tales of Mystery and Imagination (Alan Parsons Project) 34, 47, 80–81, 107, 160, 176
Tales of Terror (dir. Roger Corman, 1962) 4, 41, 47, 58, **75**, 75, 84, 113, 114, 115
Tarantula (dir. Jack Arnold, 1955) 164
Tasso (Liszt) 137
Taste of Fear (dir. Seth Holt, 1961) 140, 150, 178
Taylor, Elizabeth 130
Tayman, Robert 184
Tchaikovsky, Pyotr 34, 44, 136
Tcherepnin, Alexander 131
Tchérina, Ludmilla 27
Tell-Tale (dir. Michael Cuesta, 2009) 174
The Tell-Tale Heart (dir. Ernest Morris, 1961) 173–174
The Tell-Tale Heart (dir. Jules Dassin, 1941) 173, 176
The Tell-Tale Heart (dir. Ted Parmalee, 1953) 174
"The Tell-Tale Heart" (Poe) 6, 16, 39, 91, 126, 154, 156, 171–176, 182
Tendeter, Kay 86
Tennyson, Alfred, Lord 5, 23
"The Terribly Strange Bed" (Collins) 19
Thatcher, Baroness Margaret 90
Theatre of Blood (dir. Douglas Hickox, 1973) 155
Them! (dir. Gordon Douglas, 1954) 163
Theophilus North (Wilder) 14–15

Thomas, Augusta Read 100
Thomas, Peter 141
Thompson, G.R. 7, 91, 92, 187
Thompson, Marshall 86
Thoreau, Henry David 63
"Thou Art the Man" (Poe) 8, 176–178
"Three Sundays in a Week" (Poe) 178–179
Thriller (television series) 149–150
Tieck, Ludwig 78, 105
The Time Machine (Wells) 110
The Time Tunnel (television series) 55, **56**
Timperley, Rosemary 26
Titian 29
"To F—" (Poe) 48
"To One in Paradise" (Poe) 23
Toccata and Fugue in D minor (Bach) 138
Tom and Jerry cartoons 144
The Tomb (dir. Michael Staininger, 2009) 100
The Tomb of Ligeia (dir. Roger Corman, 1964) 3, 68–69, 85, 98, 169
Tomlin, Lily 163
Tomlinson, David 51
Torture Chamber of Dr. Sadism (aka *Die Schlangengrube und das Pendel,* dir. Harald Reinl, 1967) **140**, 141–142
Torture Garden (dir. Freddie Francis, 1967) 14, 15, 22
"A Torture of Hope" (Villiers de L'Isle Adam) 142
Tosotti, Vieri 168
Totentanz (Liszt) 106, 136
Tourneur, Jacques 43, **50**, 51
Tourneur, Maurice 167
Towers, Harry Alan 90
Townsend, Chauncey Hare 74
Tre passi nel delirio (aka *Histoires extraordinaires/Spirits of the Dead,* dir. Roger Vadim, Louis Malle, Federico Fellini, 1968) **111**, 112, **127**, 185
Treasure Island (Stevenson) 92
"Tree-House of Horror 1" (*The Simpsons,* dir. David Silverman, 1990) 153–154, **154**
Trier, Lars von **54**, 54
Trilby (du Maurier) 75–76
A Trip to the Moon (dir. Georges Méliès, 1902) 181
Tríska, Jan 151, 165
Tristan und Isolde (Wagner) 26, 54, 59, 63, 136
Trumbull, Douglas 53
Tryon, Tom 86
Tuchman, Barbara 49

Turangalîla Symphony (Messiaen) 136
The Turn of a Friendly Card (Alan Parsons Project) 93
Turner, J.M.W. *29*
Two Evil Eyes (dir. Dario Argento & George A. Romero, 1990) 38, 42
2001—A Space Odyssey (dir. Stanley Kubrick, 1968) 71, 72, 73

"Ulalume" (Poe) 15
Ulmer, Edgar, G. 4, 44
Unheimliche Geschichte (aka *Uncanny Tales*, dir. Robert Oswald, 1932) 167
"The Unparalleled Adventure of One Hans Pfaall" (Poe) 7, 179–182
Usher House (Getty) 82–83

Vadim, Roger *111*, 112, 126
"The Valley of Unrest" (Poe) 49
La Valse (Ravel) 106, 107
The Vampire Armand (Rice) 26
Vampire Circus (dir. Robert Young, 1977) 184
Vampires in Venice (dir. Augusto Caminito & Mario Caiano, 1988) 26, 27
Vampyr (dir. Carl Dreyer, 1932) 147, 150
Van Der Graaf Generator 81
Van Doren Stern, Philip 9
Vaughan Williams, Ralph 1
Veidt, Conrad 84, 102, 167, 186
Verdi, Giuseppe 147
Verhoeven, Paul 164
Verne, Jules 7, 31, 33, 51, 92, 178, 180–181
Vernon, Richard 98
Vertigo (dir. Alfred Hitchcock, 1958) 55
A Village Romeo and Juliet (Delius) 64
Village Romeo and Juliet (dir. Petr Weigle, 1992) 64
Villiers de L'Isle Adam, Auguste 6, 13, 98, 105, 142, 143, 188
I vinti (dir. Michelangelo Antonioni, 1953) 132
Violanta (Korngold) 29

Visconti, Luchino 26, 132, 133
Vivre sa vie (dir. Jean-Luc Goddard, 1962) 130
"Von Kempelen and His Discovery" (Poe) 102
Le Voyage dans la lune (dir. Georges Méliès, 1902) 181

Waggner, George 120
Wagner, Cosima 53
Wagner, Richard 1, 9, 16, 26–27, 34, 39, 52–53, 59, 63, 64, 68, 105, 106, 107, 136, 142, 180
Waiting for Godot (Beckett) 12, 132
"Wake Not the Dead" (Tieck) 105
Walbrook, Anton 186
Wallace, Helen 85
Walsh, Dermot 174
Walthall, Henry B. 171
War-Gods of the Deep (aka *City in the Sea*, dir. Jacques Tourneur, 1965) *50*, 51–52
The War of the Worlds (Wells) 30
Warbeck, David 42
Ware, Irene 138
Warlords of Atlantis (dir. Kevin Connor, 1978) 51, 55
Washington, George 110
Watford, Gwen *86*, 86
Watson, Hildegarde 83
Watson, James 77, *78*, 78, 79, 83, 84, 88, 90
Waugh, Evelyn 149
Waverley (Scott) 64
Webb, Jane 110, 161
Webber, Melville 77, *78*, 78, 79, 83, 84, 88, 90
Wegener, Paul 167, 185, 186
Weigl, Petr 64
Weir, David 72
Welles, Orson 4, 30, 80
Wells, H.G. 30, 110, 181
West, Julian 146
Westbrook, John 98, 109
Whale, James 117
What a Man's Gotta Do (Easthope) 104
White, Ric 47, 150, 173
Whitehead, Geoffrey 153

Whitemore, Hugh 184
Whiting, Leonard 160
Whitman, Sarah Helen 109
"Who Shall Deliver Me?" (Christina Rossetti) 113
"Why the Little Frenchman Wears His Hand in a Sling" (Poe) 8
Wicking, Christopher 117–118
Wiene, Robert 42, 83, 84, 91, 131, 174, 175
Wilcox, Fred M. 182
Wilde, Oscar 20–21, 36–37, 46, 47, 84, 105, 129, 132, 134, 148
Wilder, Thornton 14
"William Wilson" (Poe) 7, 130, 138, 182–186
Williams, John 82
Willis, Bruce 54
Wilner, Hal 23
Wilson, Edmund 11, 58
Wilson, William 34, 39
Windsor, Romy 90
Witchcraft Through the Ages (dir. Benjamin Christensen, 1922) 40
The Witches (dir. Cyril Frankel, 1966) 43
Wolf, Hugo 22
The Wolfman (dir. George Waggner, 1941) 120
The Woman in White (Collins) 166
Woods, William 40
Woolf, Virginia 83
Woolfson, Eric 19, 23, 34, 48, 80, 93, 118
The World as Will and Idea (Schopenhauer) 71
Wyndham, John 53

Yeats, W.B. 57, 162
Yellow Submarine (dir. George Dunning, 1968) 68
York, Michael 110
York, Susannah 89
Young, Robert 184
Your Favorite Story (television series) 93

Zeffirelli, Franco 160

www.ingramcontent.com/pod-product-compliance
Ingram Content Group UK Ltd.
Pitfield, Milton Keynes, MK11 3LW, UK
UKHW050528150426
5217IPUK00026B/1841